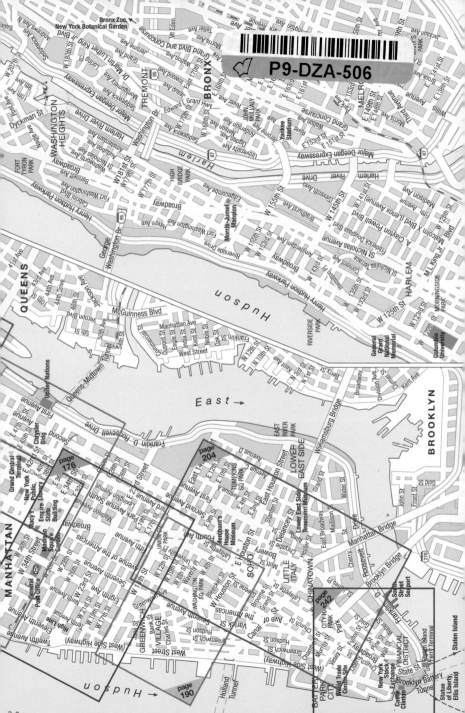

INSIGHT GUIDES

NEW YORK

APA PUBLICATIONS

Part of the Langenscheidt Publishing Group

✳ INSIGHT GUIDE

NEW YORK

Series Editor
Rachel Lawrence
Project Editor
Tom Stainer
Picture Editor
Steven Lawrence
Art Director
Ian Spick
Cartography Editor
Zoë Goodwin
Series Publishing Manager
Rachel Fox

Distribution

United States
Langenscheidt Publishers, Inc.
36–36 33rd Street 4th Floor
Long Island City, NY 11106
orders@langenscheidt.com

UK & Ireland
GeoCenter International Ltd
Meridian House, Churchill Way West,
Basingstoke, Hampshire, RG21 6YR
Tel: +44 (0) 1256 817987
sales@geocenter.co.uk

Australia
Universal Publishers
1 Waterloo Road
Macquarie Park, NSW 2113
sales@universalpublishers.com.au

New Zealand
Hema Maps New Zealand Ltd (HNZ)
Unit 2, 10 Cryers Road
East Tamaki, Auckland 2013
sales.hema@clear.net.nz

Worldwide
Apa Publications GmbH & Co.
Verlag KG (Singapore branch)
7030 Ang Mo Kio Ave 5
08-65 Northstar @ AMK
Singapore 569880
Tel: (65) 570 1051
apasin@signet.com.sg

Printing

CTPS-China

©2010 Apa Publications GmbH & Co.
Verlag KG (Singapore branch)
All Rights Reserved

First Edition 1991
Seventh Edition 2010

No part of this book may be
reproduced, stored in a retrieval system or transmitted in any form or
means electronic, mechanical, photo-
copying, recording or otherwise,
without prior written permission of
Apa Publications. Brief text quota-
tions with use of photographs are
exempted for book review purposes
only. Information has been obtained
from sources believed to be reliable,
but its accuracy and completeness,
and the opinions based thereon, are
not guaranteed.

www.insightguides.com

ABOUT THIS BOOK

What makes an Insight Guide different? Since our first book pioneered the use of full-color photography used creatively in travel guides in 1970, we have aimed to provide not only reliable information but also the key to a real understanding of a destination and its people.

Now, when the internet can supply inexhaustible (but not always reliable) facts, our books marry text and pictures to provide that more elusive quality: knowledge. To achieve this, they rely on the authority of locally based writers and photographers.

This book turns the spotlight on the city that not only never sleeps, but can never be beaten. A fresh optimism has swept over the city since the mourning period for the World Trade Center victims ended, with a seemingly endless array of new skyscrapers, new restaurants and new hip and hap-pening hotspots like the High Line, the Meatpacking District and Alphabet City. *Insight Guide: New York* covers all this, and more, with an edge and an atti-tude worthy of the city itself.

CONTACTING THE EDITORS

We would appreciate it if readers would alert us to errors or outdated information by writing to:

Insight Guides, PO Box 7910,
London SE1 1WE, England.
Fax: (44) 20 7403-0290.
insight@apaguide.co.uk

THE CONTRIBUTORS TO THIS BOOK

This fully updated edition of *Insight Guide: New York* was commissioned by **Rachel Lawrence**, Series Editor for City Guides in Insight's London editorial office, and edited by **Tom Stainer**.

Writer and editor **Sherri Eisenberg** comprehensively updated the guide, cov-ering all the latest hotspots. Although she keeps a suitcase packed at all times and travels frequently to report on far-off des-tinations, she is always happy to return home to her beloved Big Apple, where she has lived for 13 years.

As well as painstakingly amending the text, Eisenberg wrote the new Food on the Move essay and the High Line and Having a Ball features, documenting the city's newest park and stadiums. She also over-hauled the Shopping essay and boosted the coverage of the Meatpacking District, one of the city's most happening areas.

This seventh edition builds on an ear-lier edition, edited by **Martha Ellen Zenfell**, and designed by **Klaus Geisler**. Past contributors whose work is still evi-dent here include **John Gattuso**, who wrote the history section, **Kathy Novak**, **Mimi Tompkins**, **Tom Cavalieri**, **Joanna Potts**, **Divya Symmers**, **Nick Rider**, **David Whelan**, **A. Peter Bailey**, **Michele Abruzzi**, **John Wilcock**, and **John Strausbaugh**.

The principal photographers were **Abe Nowitz** and **Britta Jaschinski**, both regu-lar contributors to Insight Guides. Special thanks also to **Ed Yourdon**. **Tom Smyth** undertook the picture research for the book and cartographic production was by **James Macdonald** and **Mike Adams**.

The book was proofread by **Neil Tit-man** and the index was compiled by **Helen Peters**.

PHOTO FEATURES

Photo features offer visual coverage of major sights or unusual attractions. The map shows where it is, while vital statistics convey practical information: address, contact details, website, opening times, and if there's a charge.

RESTAURANT LISTINGS

Restaurant listings feature the best establishments within each area, giving the address, phone number, opening times and price category followed by a useful review. The grid reference refers to the atlas at the back of the book.

Quality Meats

57 W. 58th St (at 5th and 6th aves) 212-371 7777 D daily $$$ [p334, B4] The name of the place really means something here, at a tiptop, high-style New American steakhouse

TRAVEL TIPS

a MetroCard, which you charge up with a minimum amount and swipe through the entry gates each time you use the subway, or in machines on city buses. If you charge it with over $10, you get a discount on each journey. Unlimited-ride cards are also available, valid for seven or 30 days, or a one-day "Fun Pass." MetroCards and passes can be bought at subway

Advice-packed Travel Tips provide all the practical knowledge you'll need before and during your trip: how to get there, getting around, where to stay and what to do. The A–Z section is a handy summary of practical information, arranged alphabetically.

Contents

Best of New York

Top Sights   **8**

American Museum of
  Natural History **154**
Central Park **82**
Chrysler Building **92**
Empire State Building **71**
Greenwich Village **189**
Lincoln Center **158**
Metropolitan Museum of Art . **138**
Museum of Modern Art **120**
Statue of Liberty **262**
Times Square **118**

Editor's Choice   **10**

Introduction

Guide at a Glance...................... **4**
New York, New Yorkers **19**

History

The Making of New York **27**
Decisive Dates........................ **40**

Features

Culture and the City **47**
Diners, Delis, and Hip Delights.. **55**

Insights

Mini Features:

A Day in the Life **32**
Regards to Broadway............. **108**
Aiming for the Top.................. **144**
The High Line........................ **198**
City of Immigrants **220**
Tall Towers........................... **246**
Having a Ball......................... **288**

Photo Features:

Hollywood on the Hudson......... **52**
Food on the Move................... **58**
Shopping............................... **60**
Central Park........................... **82**
Times Square Then and Now .. **118**
Museum of Modern Art.......... **120**
Museum Mile........................ **136**
The Metropolitan Museum **138**
The American Museum of
  Natural History **154**
Lincoln Center....................... **158**
Ellis Island........................... **260**
The Statue of Liberty **262**

Places

Orientation **67**
- Fifth Avenue **71**
- Midtown East................... **87**
- Midtown West **103**
- Upper East Side.............. **125**
- Upper West Side **143**
- Around Harlem................ **163**
- Gramercy Park to
  Chelsea **175**
- Greenwich Village........... **189**
- The East Village to
  Chinatown **203**
- Soho and Tribeca **227**
- Lower Manhattan **241**
- The Outer Boroughs **267**

Restaurants & Bars

Fifth Avenue............................ **80**
Midtown East........................ **100**
Midtown West **116**
Upper East Side **134**
Upper West Side **152**
Around Harlem...................... **171**
Gramercy Park to Chelsea **185**
Greenwich Village.................. **200**
The East Village to
  Chinatown **224**
Soho and Tribeca **238**
Lower Manhattan **259**
The Outer Boroughs **291**

Travel Tips

TRANSPORTATION
Getting There **294**
Getting Around **295**
Public Transportation **295**
Private Transportation **296**

ACCOMMODATIONS
Choosing a Hotel **297**
Midtown **297**
Upper East and West Side **301**
Murray Hill/Gramercy Park/
  Chelsea **302**
Greenwich Village/East Village/
  Soho and Tribeca/Lower
  Manhattan **304**

SHOPPING
What to Buy and Where **306**
Clothes Chart **309**

ACTIVITIES
Theater and Dance **310**
Concert Halls and Music **311**
Art Galleries **311**
Nightlife **312**
  Jazz **312**
  Rock, Dance, Blues **313**
  Comedy and Cabaret **314**
  Movies **314**
Events **315**
Sports **316**
Tours **317**

A–Z of PRACTICAL INFORMATION
318

Maps

New York **front flap** and **68–9**

Orientation map **66**

Map Legend **325**

Street Atlas **326**

Restaurants and
Accommodations Atlas **334**

Fifth Avenue **72**
Central Park **83**
Midtown East and West **88**
Upper East and
  West Side **126**
Around Harlem **164**
Gramercy Park to
  Chelsea **176**
Greenwich Village **190**
The East Village to Chinatown,
  Soho and Tribeca **204**
Lower Manhattan **242**
The Outer Boroughs **268**

NY Subway **back flap**

THE BEST OF NEW YORK: TOP SIGHTS

At a glance, everything you can't afford to miss when you visit the Big Apple, from high-energy Times Square and tall, iconic monuments to world-class museums and performance spaces

△ The **Museum of Modern Art (MoMA)** has a remarkable collection of 20th-century art. All the greats are here, displayed in a beautiful new gallery. The sculpture garden sets Rodin, Picasso, and others amid trees and reflecting pools. *See pages 120–3.*

▽ **Lincoln Center** is the cultural and intellectual hub of the city. Located on the Upper West Side, it's home to many giants of the performing arts, including the New York City Opera, the New York City Ballet, the American Ballet Theater *(below)*, and the Metropolitan Opera. *See pages 158–61.*

▷ The **Chrysler Building** was erected in 1930. Its distinctive spire was designed in secret and lifted into place as one solid piece. *See page 92.*

◁ If you have time for only one museum, visit the **Metropolitan Museum of Art**, which has a collection of over 2 million pieces, from Native Americans to 21st-century couturiers. *See pages 138–41.*

▷ The **Empire State Building** was the tallest structure in the world when it was completed in 1931. Zoom up to the 102nd-floor observation deck for unsurpassed views of New York City. *See pages 71–4.*

▷ The **Statue of Liberty**, which was unveiled in 1886, was a gift to the US from France, a symbol of freedom and democracy after successful revolutions in both countries. *See pages 262–3.*

▽ The Hayden Planetarium is just one attraction at the **American Museum of Natural History**. *See pages 154–7.* Others include the world's tallest dinosaur, a 34-ton (31,000kg) meteorite, and an Imax theater. Don't even think about doing it all in one visit.

△ The artists have long been priced out, but **Greenwich Village** still has great allure; there's a neighborhood feel to the area with its old brownstones, one-off stores, Italian bakeries, and small theaters. This is where many Manhattanites would live if they could. *See pages 189–201.*

▽ In the 1850s, **Central Park** was created to provide workers with a taste of nature. Today it is the green lung of the city. *See pages 82–5.*

▽ If there's a classic image, then it's surely the bright lights and billboards of **Times Square**, the heart of Broadway's theater district. *See pages 118–19.*

THE BEST OF NEW YORK: EDITOR'S CHOICE

Riverside walks by movie-classic views, bargains in the Big Apple and tours galore. The best hotels, walks, unique sites, family attractions, and money-saving tips personally selected by our editor

BEST HOTELS

- **The Algonquin**
An all-time favorite, the literary Algonquin retains an atmosphere of oak-paneled, low-key elegance and charm. *See page 297.*
- **The Carlyle**
On the Upper East Side, the Carlyle is one of the city's most acclaimed luxury hotels. Woody Allen plays at the Café Carlyle when he's in town. *See page 301.*
- **The Chelsea Hotel**
A landmark to urban decadence and the former home of beatnik poets, Warhol drag queens, and punk Sid Vicious. An affordable place for a taste of bohemia. *See page 303.*
- **Hotel Gansevoort**
The first luxury hotel in the Meatpacking District, with a rooftop bar and breathtaking views of the Downtown skyline. *See page 304.*
- **The Mercer Hotel**
In the heart of Soho, the Mercer attracts a stylish clientele, as does its fashionable restaurant, the Mercer Kitchen. *See page 304.*

CLASSIC NEW YORK

Where to follow in the footsteps of Sinatra, Bacall, Dylan Thomas, and Dorothy Parker.

- **21**
This former speakeasy is still a haunt of the powerful and the beautiful. *See page 80.*
- **The Oak Bar**
The Plaza Hotel may have gone part-condo, but the Oak Bar lives on. *See page 81.*
- **P.J. Clarke's**
Sinatra preferred the back room, along with Louis Armstrong. Johnny Depp comes now. *See page 101.*
- **White Horse Tavern**
Dylan Thomas drank here. And then he died. *See page 195.*

BELOW: lobby of the Hotel Gansevoort, Meatpacking District.

BEST BOOKS TO READ

If you read nothing else before or while you are in New York, make sure it's one from this list of classics:

The Age of Innocence by Edith Wharton. (Oxford World's Classics, 2006)
Another Country by James Baldwin. (Penguin Modern Classics, 2001)
A Tree Grows in Brooklyn by Betty Smith. (Harper Perennial Modern Classics, 2006)
The Bonfire of the Vanities by Tom Wolfe. (Dial Press Trade, 2001)
Washington Square by Henry James. (Signet Classics, 2004)

ONLY IN NEW YORK

● **Stroll and Spend**
While away the afternoon in NoLita. Have an instant massage in a Korean treatment room, eat Italian food and shop in the one-off boutiques: think cute polka dots. *See page 216.*

● **Eat and Drink**
Sip a $10,000 Martini at the Algonquin, or try the new "haute barnyard" cuisine Downtown at Peasant. *See pages 116 and 225.*

● **Be Merry**
Join sports stars, superstars, and jovial shoppers for the annual lighting of the Christmas tree at Rockefeller Center. *See page 75.*

● **Sail the Statue of Liberty**
Climb aboard a Circle Line tour or have brunch on a sleek 1929 sailboat. *See pages 111 and 258.*

● **Moon over Manhattan**
Take a late elevator to the top of the Empire State Building and watch the moon light up Gotham. *See page 72.*

● **Cultivate Irony**
Mingle with models and banter with butchers in the trend-setting Meatpacking District. *See page 197.*

● **Shop and Skate**
Take in the galleries, market and small treasures of Chelsea, then don ice-skates for a spin around the Sky Rink at Chelsea Piers. *See page 180.*

● **Dine with Diplomats**
in the dining room of the United Nations building. *See page 94.*

● **Muse over Music**
Visit the home of a jazz legend and find out why some called him "Dippermouth." *See page 279.*

● **Get Sporty**
Cheer on the New York Knicks and the Harlem Globetrotters at Madison Square Garden. *See page 105.*

● **Get Artsy**
Take the elevator to the top floor of the Guggenheim and make your way down

the spiral ramp, taking in highlights of 20th-century art along the way. *See page 128.*

● **Be Bemused and Confused by History**
Study a lock of George Washington's hair – and his tooth – at Fraunces Tavern Museum. *See page 250.*

BELOW: celebrating the Christmas season at Rockefeller Center began in 1933. The most popular attraction is the Christmas tree, which is spectacularly illuminated from just after Thanksgiving until 12th Night, January 6th.

NEW YORK FOR FAMILIES

These attractions are popular with children, though not all will suit every age group.

● **Children's Museum of Manhattan**
A kiddy kingdom with inventive interactive exhibits; let them touch everything. *See page 150.*

● **Carrousels**
The entire family can ride on New York's carrousels. The one in Central Park has 58 hand-carved horses and operates all year round, while the carrousels in Bryant and Prospect parks are seasonal.

● **Central Park**
From rowing in the lake to a children's area, the park is fun for everyone. *See page 82.*

● **Sony Wonder Technology Lab**
Wondering how to entertain those bored pre-teens? Look no more. *See page 99.*

● **South Street Seaport**
Sailing ships and all things nautical, in an outdoor atmosphere where kids can let off steam without embarrassing their parents. *See page 255.*

● **Circle Line Tour**
View the Statue of Liberty, watch all of Manhattan cruise by, and let the kids go wild. *See page 111.*

● **Fabulous Food**
Inexpensive snacks don't come any easier. Try two NY specialties: Nathan's Famous hot dogs on Coney Island *(see page 277)* and bagels, bagels, bagels.

● **Children's Museum of the Arts**
Based in Soho, this is a successful cross between a museum and a very lively crèche. *See page 231.*

● **Brooklyn Children's Museum.** The oldest kids' museum in the US. *See page 277.*

● **Bronx Zoo**
The largest urban zoo in America. What's stopping you? *See page 286.*

CLOCKWISE: Hans Christian Andersen, Central Park; Circle Line tours for the entire family; St Patrick's Cathedral.

NEW YORK FOR FREE

● **Culture in the Park**
The Metropolitan Opera, the New York Philharmonic, and the Public Theater give free performances in Central Park during the summer months.

● **Native American Art**
is free to see at the George Gustav Heye Center of the National Museum of the American Indian in the US Custom House in Lower Manhattan. *See page 249.*

● **Free Fashion**
The Fashion Institute of Technology (Seventh Avenue at 27th St) shows off legendary costumes, textiles, and the work of well-known photographers in its fashion museum.

● **Free Travel**
Statue of Liberty views are still absolutely free on the Staten Island Ferry *(see page 257),* while Lower Manhattan has a free bus service *(see page 255).*

● **Free Flowers**
The Brooklyn Botanic Garden *(see page 274)* is free to the public on Tuesdays and until noon on Saturdays, also weekdays in the wintertime; while the Queens *(see page 278)* and Staten Island *(see page 283)* gardens are free all the year round.

● **St Patrick's Cathedral**
Visit one of the most spectacular Catholic churches in the United States. *See page 78.*

BEST TOURS

The best tours of New York's buildings are:
- Radio City Music Hall *See page 113.*
- Grand Central Terminal *See page 90.*
- Rockefeller Center *See page 75.*
- Lincoln Center *See page 158.*
- Carnegie Hall *See page 115.*
- NBC Studios *See page 76.*
- Gracie Mansion *See page 133.*
- Madison Square Garden *See page 105.*

BEST WALKS

- Fifth Avenue *See pages 71 and 125.*
- Madison Avenue, especially from 42nd to 75th streets. *See pages 90 and 130.*
- Central Park *See page 82.*
- Times Square *See page 118.*
- Battery Park Esplanade *See page 245.*
- Brooklyn Heights Promenade *See page 270.*

BELOW: The Christmas Spectacular at Radio City Music Hall starring the Rockettes is corny but cozy *(see page 113).*

ABOVE: Tribeca Film Festival, established in 2002 by Robert de Niro, is held every spring *(see page 49).*

BEST FESTIVALS AND EVENTS

For a more complete list of festivals, see page 315.

- **Tribeca Film Festival** Mingle with the stars and see first-run films on the banks of the Hudson River. Every spring. *See page 49.*
- **Ninth Avenue International Food Festival** A street fair in May when Ninth Avenue, from 37th Street to 57th Street, is lined with food stalls. *See page 110.*
- **Feast of San Gennaro** A cheesy but boisterous 10-day festival in September where Little Italy shows off, and the air is heavy with garlic. *See page 218.*

- **New Wave Festival** Some of the most innovative sounds around can be heard at the Brooklyn Academy of Music (BAM) from October to December. This is definitely a hot ticket. *See page 272.*
- **St Patrick's Day** Watch the wearing o' the green on Fifth Avenue every March. *See page 315.*
- **Thanksgiving Day Parade** Started in the 1920s, this is the longest-running show on Broadway, brought to you by Macy's. *See page 104.*

MONEY-SAVING TIPS

Theater Tickets The **TKTS Booth**, at Broadway and 47th Street by Times Square, has discounted seats (25–50 percent off) for that night's performances. It's open Monday through Saturday 3pm to 8pm for evening performances, Saturday and Wednesday 10am to 2pm for matinees, and Sunday 11am to 7.30pm for both shows. Near South Street Seaport in Lower Manhattan, another booth at 186 Front Street sells discounted tickets for the following night's shows. *See page 50.*

Special Passes A way to save on New York's buses and subways is to buy a **MetroCard** (for instance, you get 11 rides for the price of 10). Available for 30 days, 7 days or one day. Go to www.mta.nyc.ny.us

CityPass saves if you plan to visit attractions. Buy the pass at the first destination; then you have several days in which to visit five others. You also avoid most ticket lines. Savings of almost 50 percent; plus discounts on meals. Go to www.citypass.com. The **New York Pass** is a similar scheme. Go to www.newyorkpass.com

Shopping All visitors can find great bargains at New York's **sample sales**, where designers sell off end-of-season clothes, or smaller sizes. Check *Time Out New York* for dates. **Woodbury Common**, an outlet mall about an hour from the city by bus, offers big discounts on many items. *See page 307.*

NEW YORK, NEW YORKERS

New Yorkers come in all colors and cultures. The
town that gave us the phrase "the melting pot"
reinvigorates itself regularly with each wave
of energetic, optimistic newcomers

The first thing that strikes a visitor about
New Yorkers is the talk. They talk a mile
a minute, all the time. They could talk for
their country – their country, of course, being
New York. Locals have always been proud of
their status as New Yorkers, and 9/11 only
served to cement that honor.

Stock market and sculpture

In such a fast-moving, densely packed metropolis, there's a loud background to speak over,
but more surprising is the range and depth of
discourse. Intellectual voracity can be seen on
the street at café tables with chessboards, and
on the subway in the range of literature being
read. You can literally feel the New Yorkers'
lust for fact, knowledge, debate and opinion;
you can barely heft it in the sheer weight of the
Sunday *New York Times*.

The life of the mind and cultural life here
have their rituals, temples, and haunts, like
museum and gallery openings. It is not a

minority thing hidden away in exclusive
speakeasies, where entrance is gained by mur-
muring, "Kierkegaard sent me" at a sliding
door panel; it is the stock market and sculpture, poetry and particle physics – a polyglot
landscape of lectures, plays, concerts, libraries,
films, and, of course, dinner parties. It is the
casual association of great minds: Tom Wolfe
stalking Brooklyn streets, Sonny Rollins prac-
ticing his sax on the Williamsburg Bridge.

Culture and intellect transform the individual, but they also give identity to the mass, to
the city as a whole. In his book *The Art of the
City: Views and Versions of New York*, Peter
Conrad writes, "Every city requires its own

*Although New Yorkers are known for their fast
pace, a 2007 survey of urban walking speeds
put them in only eighth place. Singapore
came top, followed by Copenhagen.*

PREVIOUS PAGES: pedestrians crossing Fifth Avenue;
relaxing in Brooklyn Bridge Park.
LEFT: a rainy Times Square.
RIGHT: old boys enjoying a game of chess on the
Upper West Side.

myth to justify its presumption of centrality," and he cites annotators of New York from songwriter George M. Cohan to painter Saul Steinberg, whose famous cover for the *New Yorker* was of a world shrinking to the far horizon, away from a great, spreading Manhattan.

> Andy Warhol said: "When reporters asked the Pope what he liked best about New York, he replied 'Tutti buoni' – everything is good. That's my philosophy exactly."

Alexander Alland, Jr, former chair of anthropology at Columbia University, said, "The intellectual life is why I am a New Yorker. It's why I stay here. I spend my summers in Europe, and when they ask me if I'm an American, I say, 'No, I'm a New Yorker.' I don't know about everyone else, but for me that's a positive statement."

New York's rise to intellectual prominence did not begin until the 1850s. Through the Colonial era and the early 19th century, New York was at best the third city in the US,

behind Boston and Philadelphia, until the publishing industry decamped to here. New York had a larger population, and publishers were seeking more customers. As seagulls follow great ships, writers, editors and illustrators came in the publishers' wake.

Meanwhile, at the top of the New York economic scale, captains of commerce and industry began to endow museums and to support individual artists. At the bottom of the scale, each wave of immigrants enriched and diversified the intellectual community. City College, established in 1849, acted as the great pedagogue for those without wealth, and came to be known as "the poor man's Harvard."

Immigrants

The German influx of 1848, the Irish flight from famine, migrations of Jews, Italians, Greeks, Chinese, Koreans, and Vietnamese – all brought knowledge and culture to New York, making this American city cosmopolitan. In 1933, the New School for Social Research encouraged that rich resource by founding the University in Exile (now the Graduate Faculty of Political and Social Science) as a graduate school staffed by European scholars who

escaped the Nazi regime. The international dynamic continues with the Soviet Jews in Brighton Beach and the West Indians in Queens joined by the Southeast Asians of Queens' Elmhurst district. In the 2000 census, 18 percent of the Brooklyn population spoke Spanish at home, 6 percent Russian, 4 percent French or a French Creole, 4 percent Chinese, 3 percent Yiddish, 2 percent Italian, and 1 percent Polish, Hebrew, or Arabic. Cantonese, Urdu, Bengali, Greek, Korean, and Albanian were all spoken by more than 5,000 people. There are more Greeks in New York than in any city but Athens, and more Dominicans than in any city but Santo Domingo.

Public schools offer bilingual instruction. Traffic signs, advertisements, and subway signs announce in two or three languages in some neighborhoods, most often in Spanish or Chinese, the city's unofficial second and third languages. There are at least a dozen non-English newspapers published in the city itself and countless others imported. Driving tests can be taken and banking business done in other languages. Automatic cash machines offer transactions in Spanish, Chinese, and French.

The minority majority

Never in the American mainstream, New York is one of the few minority-majority cities, where the majority are from an ethnic minority. The promise for immigrants in New York is a place of opportunity. Some variation of the American dream still lives on these streets, and immigrants come eager to share in it. Once a

migrant group gets into a line of work, others follow in the same trade. In recent years Koreans have dominated the grocery business, Chinese have manned the garment industry, and Indians or Pakistanis run newsstands. Greek coffee shops and Latino bodegas have joined the New York landscape, and every nationality turns the wheel of a yellow cab.

The New York mix is defined by immigration, and also by artists. New York's bards date back to at least 1855, when Walt Whitman

Although there are other US cities with a high percentage of foreign-born residents, none can match the range or diversity of the ethnic communities of New York City.

LEFT: according to a government body, New Yorkers use one quarter of the amount of electricity consumed by the people of Dallas. **ABOVE:** writer Tom Wolfe said "culture seems to be in the air, like part of the weather."

published *Leaves of Grass*. Singer Lou Reed, photographer Robert Mapplethorpe, novelist Jay McInerney and filmmakers Woody Allen and Martin Scorsese have all taken New York as their muse. Their work, in turn, has crafted the world's image of the city.

Greenwich Village became an urban version of the artists' colony, a home to creators of all stripes, the place that gave Eugene O'Neill one of his early stages in the 1920s (at the Provincetown Playhouse) and Bob Dylan a bandstand in the 1960s (at Folk City). Miles Uptown, Harlem was home to a black intelligentsia that included the writers Langston Hughes *(see page 167)*, James Weldon Johnson, and James Baldwin, plus the political theorist W.E.B. Du Bois and the photographer James Van Der Zee, whose record of his era appeared decades later in the album *Harlem on My Mind*.

Urban pioneers

When creative people discovered Soho in the 1970s, it was hard to get a cab to go there. Their presence led to the neighborhood's rebirth, and when it became too expensive for them, they moved to Alphabet City (avenues A, B, C and D) on the Lower East Side of Manhattan, or across the East River to Greenpoint and Williamsburg, or to a part of Brooklyn called DUMBO, for Down Under Manhattan Bridge Overpass. Trendy stores, bars, and restaurants followed, rents soared, and the artists scoped out new territories like Brooklyn's Red Hook.

URBAN WOODLAND

When Henry Hudson sailed up the river that bears his name, his first mate, Robert Juett, wrote: "We found a land full of great tall oaks, with grass and flowers, as pleasant as ever has been seen." New York still has over 28,000 acres (11,300 hectares) of parks, of which 10,000 acres (4,000 hectares) are in more or less their natural state. Peregrine falcons nest on Midtown skyscraper ledges, and coyotes prowl from Westchester County down into the Bronx.

Frederick Law Olmsted, the architect who laid out Central Park, wrote that "the contemplation of natural scenes… is favorable to the health and vigor of men."

Pop culture and high culture are often indistinguishable. Tom Stoppard and Stephen Sondheim have regular Broadway hits, while a gospel version of *Oedipus at Colonus* sold out at the Brooklyn Academy of Music. Religion is a matter both of passion and of intellectual rigor. There are almost a dozen Roman Catholic colleges in New York City, an Islamic Seminary on Queens Boulevard and *shtibels* – houses of study – where Hasidim pursue theology.

News nexus

The intellectual force of New York sends ripples far beyond the city. The principal network news in the United States originates not from the nation's capital but from New York. Two major news magazines, *Time* and *Newsweek*, and two national newspapers, the *New York Times* and the *Wall Street Journal*, are published here, and most of the leading critics of theater, film, art, dance, and music make their pronouncements from Manhattan.

LEFT: according to a recent survey, the most popular girl's name is Ashley; the most popular boy's name is Michael. **ABOVE:** sporty dudes take a break from the bikes in Central Park.

In 2006, Reader's Digest conducted a range of tests across 35 countries. New York was the place they encountered the most courtesy, helpfulness, and civility.

Without any of those publications, important as they are, New York intellectual life would pulse just as vigorously. Outwardly expressed in individual taste and style, at its heart it is little to do with celebrity or vogue. The intellectual sweep is an eclectic striving for search and discovery. So many New Yorkers share a biographical tale that it has become mythic itself. With variations, the story goes like this:

An able young man (or young woman) feels misunderstood, unappreciated, surrounded by what playwright Eugene O'Neill called "spiritual middle-classers," and yearns to escape from small-town minds, to be among people with a broader vision. Perhaps he yearns to reinvent himself, to shake loose the trappings of his youth. Perhaps he has a dream, an aspiration too great or too strange to realize on hometown turf. So

he comes here. Whether or not his dreams are realized even in part, he comes to feel the city has spoiled him for any other place. Despite, or even because of the pressure, the pace, and the grime, he has a vigorous sense of being alive.

Rich stimulation

"New York draws the cosmopolite, the person who wants to be challenged the most, who needs the most varied and rich stimulation," said a well-known Jungian analyst, Dr James Hillman. "It is the person who is full of possibilities, but who needs New York to draw them out. You come to New York to find the ambience that will evoke your best. You do not necessarily know precisely what that might be, but you come to New York to discover it.

"If there were a god of New York it would be the Greeks' Hermes, the Romans' Mercury. He embodies New York qualities: the quick exchange, the fastness of language and style, craftiness, the mixing of people and crossing of borders, imagination." And cosmopolitan, in every sense, is what the Big Apple is. From the lines of sparkly clubbers and diners in Soho and the Meatpacking District to the wild costumes in the Greenwich Village Halloween

New York taxis date from 1907, when John Hertz founded the Yellow Cab Company. He chose this color after reading a study saying that yellow was the easiest to spot.

parade, New York is more than just a melting-pot, it is a hothouse nursery for fantastic hybrids of talent and expression.

A great book store is a hub of imaginative activity, and in New York the Strand Book Store is arguably the best. In a former clothing store at Broadway and East 12th Street in Manhattan, the Strand carries some 2 million volumes of such variety that on a single table titles might range from *The Sonata Since Beethoven* to *Civil Aircraft of the World*.

Writers Anaïs Nin and Saul Bellow, painter David Hockney and poet/rock singer Patti Smith

ABOVE: nearly 170 languages are spoken in the city, and 36 percent of its population is thought to have been born in a country other than the United States.
RIGHT: diners on MacDougal Street, Greenwich Village.

numbered among the Strand's regular customers. Smith was on both sides of the counter, as she also worked at the store.

The complete city

So what stitches the fabric of reinvention and the rigors of intellectual life together? What draws the filmmakers, the flower vendors and the restaurateurs to pack up and move here, and intellectuals to end their contemplations here? Back to the Jungian Dr Hillman: "New York is the city of rampant creativity, of abundant imagination, whether in advertising or the theater or the stock market. Any syndrome that might characterize another city is found in New York: manic energy, depression and hopelessness, the extreme excitement of the hysteric. Psychologically, New York is the complete city."

New Yorkers *do* talk. They talk loud, and they talk a lot – enough to call it a defining characteristic. But here in New York, they also walk the walk. ❑

FACTS THAT FIT

Biggest: the biggest meteorite to hit the earth weighed 34 tons (31,000kg), and is on display at the American Museum of Natural History.

Longest: after Broadway leaves the city, it becomes the Albany Post Road, and travels all the way to New York's state capital – a distance of 175 miles (282km).

Oldest: the oldest grave in New York is located in the back of Lower Manhattan's Trinity Churchyard.

Most clogged: according to the Bureau of Traffic, the city's most congested area is along 42nd Street, between Third and Madison avenues.

Waterlogged: it takes an average of seven hours and 15 minutes to swim around the island of Manhattan.

Making the switch: Radio City's Rockettes make nine costume changes during their annual Christmas show.

Flipping the switch: Thomas Edison turned on New York's first public electric lights on Wall Street, 1882.

City shore: New York City has 15 miles (24km) of beaches. The best known is Coney Island, with its carnival rides and Nathan's hot-dog stand.

City core: how New York got the "Big Apple" nickname is open to debate. Some say it came from a 1920s newspaper column about horse racing called "Around the Big Apple." Others say it was used by jazz musicians to indicate getting to the top of their profession, or reaching "the Big Apple."

THE MAKING OF NEW YORK

Bought for a box of trinkets, New York rose to become the crossroads of the world. Along the way came civil war, riots and recession, terrorism, triumph, and true grit. The Big Apple is a city of constant change, where everything is possible

Local myth has it that New York began in 1626 with a real-estate deal. Peter Minuit, an official for the Dutch, bought Manhattan for a box of trinkets worth 60 guilders, about $24, which wouldn't buy a square inch of today's Big Apple. Minuit came to govern the small village in 1626 and made his deal with the Native Americans, probably where Bowling Green is now situated. Foreign to the notion of land ownership, the Indians may not have understood the deal, but Minuit didn't understand tribal territory, and the group he paid may not have had a claim to Manhattan at all.

New Amsterdam

Despite occasional skirmishes, relations between the Algonquin Indians and European settlers had been cordial, if not exactly friendly, but they deteriorated when the Dutch settled for good. Theft, murder and land disputes turned into a cycle of

The Wiechquaekeck Trail, an Algonquin trade route, ran all the way to the state capital at Albany, crossing the island of Manhattan diagonally. This is now Broadway.

savagery that led to the murder of a Native American woman and the Peach War of 1655.

The Dutch were not the first European arrivals. In 1524, Giovanni da Verrazano was

LEFT: immigrants arrive in the "land of the free."
RIGHT: detail of the painting *Purchase of Manhattan by Pieter Minuit*, 1626, by Alfred Friedericks.

struck by the Lower Bay's "commodiousness and beauty," but Europe paid no regard until Henry Hudson sailed under a Dutch flag into the natural harbor in 1609. Hudson traded, particularly in furs, and in 1621 the Dutch West India Company acquired exclusive trading rights to territory from Cape May (New Jersey) to New England. Trading posts were set along the coast and rivers, and about 50 Walloon Protestants were sent to settle Nut Island (Governor's Island) off the tip of Manhattan. Soon the camp spread to the southern end of Manhattan, which settlers named New Amsterdam.

The Walloons and Dutch were joined by convicts, slaves, religious zealots, and profiteers, with

tribes coming to trade occasionally. In 1647, the company sent Peter Stuyvesant to tame the wild New Amsterdam. He cracked down on smuggling and tax evasion, and kept order with the whip and the branding iron. Stuyvesant got things done, but made few friends in New Amsterdam. In 17 years, he established a hospital, a prison, a school, and a post office. He also erected

Director-general Peter Stuyvesant (1646–64) was known as "Peg Leg" or "Old Silver Nails" because of his wooden leg studded with nails. The bad fit of the prosthesis may have accounted for his notoriously bad temper.

a barricade against the Indians and the British, from river to river on the site of what is now Wall Street, giving the avenue its present name.

Dutch to British

The thriving Dutch town was under pressure from the British on both sides, and in 1664 King Charles II sent four warships to seize New Amsterdam. Stuyvesant was ready for war, but the townspeople were happy for a chance to be rid of him. Without a shot fired, the English raised the Union flag and renamed the town New York, in honor of the king's brother. The Dutch retook the town about 10 years later in the Second Anglo-Dutch War, but quickly negotiated a return to British hands, again without bloodshed.

The seeds of New York's independence were sewn in 1765 with the Stamp Act, among a battery of legislation passed to assert King George III's authority and plump the royal coffers. The Stamp Act levied tax on everything from tobacco to playing cards and brought the cry, "No taxation without representation."

Angry mobs stormed a government stronghold and terrorized officials until the British repealed the act. A later tax on imported items like paper, lead, and tea followed in 1767, this time backed by the English army, the dreaded Redcoats. A battle of nerves rattled until January 1770, when the rebels and Redcoats fought the Battle of Golden Hill.

After Boston's example on April 22, 1774, New Yorkers dumped tea from an English cargo ship into the harbor. A year later, the "shot heard 'round the world" was fired at Lexington, Massachusetts, and the American Revolution began. At the Declaration of Independence's reading in New York, a mob raced to topple King George III's statue in Bowling Green. Legend has it the statue was melted into musket balls, then fired at the British troops.

General George Washington chased the British out of Boston, then came to New York, where he fared poorly. British troops beat Washington's fledgling army from Brooklyn through Manhattan, to a grim defeat at White Plains, New York. A brutal seven-year occupation followed, but in 1785, Washington returned to celebrate an American victory. Four years later he returned again, to place his hand on a Bible for the oath of office as America's first president. For the next 18 months, New York was the nation's capital.

Growing pains

A small town at the turn of the 19th century, New York's population was about 35,000. A yellow fever outbreak scared some residents off to the open spaces of Greenwich Village, but most occupied the crooked lanes south of Canal Street. The public debated the new Constitution; brokers traded in the shade of a buttonwood tree on Wall Street; five people died in a riot against Columbia University doctors who robbed graves for their anatomy labs; and buffalo were brought

FAR LEFT: Lower Manhattan in the 1730s. **LEFT:** George Washington en route to New York to fight the British. **ABOVE:** the Great Fire of 1835 destroyed 674 buildings.

THE GREAT FIRE OF 1835

On the night of December 16, 1835, fire tore through New York's Downtown business district and burned for more than 15 hours. Raging from the East River almost as far as Broad Street, over 600 buildings, including the Merchant's Exchange, the Post Office and, ironically, more than half of the city's insurance companies were destroyed with a cost of over $20 million. The blaze spread, propelled by fierce wind, in just 15 minutes to 50 timber buildings. The volunteer fire department was disorganized and unequal to the task, handicapped by lack of wells or hoses, and the East River being frozen. Fortunately, only two people died in the conflagration.

from the western territories. Politically, the town was split between Democrats, represented by Aaron Burr, who was Thomas Jefferson's vice-president, and Federalists, headed by Alexander Hamilton, the nation's first Secretary of the Treasury. In 1804 their years of feuding were settled in a duel when Burr shot and killed Hamilton.

The 350-mile (565km) Erie Canal from Lake Erie to Buffalo drew cargo from across the globe into the East River Harbor (now South Street Seaport). Business boomed, the population soared to 312,000 (1840), and real-estate prices rocketed. John Jacob Astor and Cornelius Vanderbilt grew rich on property and shipping.

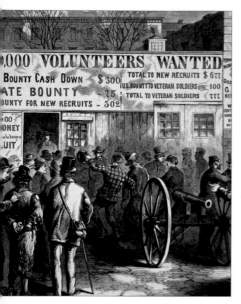

minister Henry Ward Beecher shrieked for "war redder than blood and fiercer than fire," and that is what he got.

In April 1861, Lincoln called for volunteers to put down the rebellious South, and New York sent 8,000 soldiers, including Irish and German regiments. Patriotism swung into vogue. Tiffany & Co. crafted military regalia and Brooks Brothers stitched uniforms.

By the 1850s, the *Evening Post* reported, "The city of New York belongs almost as much to the South as to the North," as Mayor Fernando Wood supported the "continuance of slave labor

Draft riots

The war dragged on, hopes of speedy victory faded, New York's fighting spirit began to sag, and defeatism turned to rage when Lincoln enacted conscription in 1862. When it emerged that the wealthy could buy their way out for $300, the city erupted. One July morning in 1863, a mob of several thousand stormed the Third Avenue draft office, routed police, and torched the whole block. Over several days, an orphanage on Fifth Avenue was burned, 18 black men were lynched, mutilated and left hanging from lampposts, and Union Army regiments were recalled to quell the Draft Riots. (The period of the Draft Riots was dramatically realized in Martin Scorsese's *Gangs of New York*.)

Two years later the Civil War ended, and Lin-

> *Dark-horse presidential candidate Abraham Lincoln made an electrifying speech at a New York college. A year later, the Civil War started. Tiffany & Co. crafted military regalia and Brooks Brothers stitched uniforms.*

and the prosperity of the slave master." When civil war was inevitable, he proposed that the city declare itself independent to protect its business interests with the South.

In February 1860, dark-horse candidate Abraham Lincoln spoke at philanthropist Peter Cooper's free college. Lincoln's words and delivery riveted the audience, and copies of the Cooper Union address crossed the country. Lincoln won the November election without one Southern electoral vote, and five months later Confederate artillery bombarded Fort Sumter. At the Plymouth Church of Brooklyn, abolitionist

LEFT: recruiting New Yorkers for the Civil War, 1864.
ABOVE LEFT: a consultation on the troubled, unfinished Brooklyn Bridge, 1872. **ABOVE RIGHT:** posing during the construction of the Statue of Liberty, 1882.

coln's body was returned to the city to lie in state at New York's City Hall.

After the Civil War, immigrants arrived from Europe. Italians crammed into Mulberry Street and Greenwich Village. Jews fled anti-Semitic pogroms in Russia, flooding the Lower East Side, and Chinese settled around Mott Street.

During the 1860s, the city was run by Tammany Hall, and Tammany Hall was run by William M. "Boss" Tweed. A larger-than-life and highly corrupt figure, Tweed ran the city as his personal piggy bank and fiefdom *(see box below)*. In 1898, the five boroughs formed a single government, bringing New York City's total population to 3.4 million people.

By the end of the 19th century, J.P. Morgan was on the way to creating the first billion-dollar American company (US Steel), John D. Rockefeller struck pay dirt with Standard Oil, and Andrew Carnegie established Carnegie Hall, where Tchaikovsky conducted the opening gala.

Fashion and famine

Abandoning their Downtown haunts to the immigrants, the upper crust began a 50-year march up fashionable Fifth Avenue, leaving a trail of mansions in their wake. This is when the social elite came to be known as the "Four Hundred," from the 400 guests at Mrs

BOSS TWEED AND TAMMANY HALL

During the 1860s, William M. "Boss" Tweed was the most powerful politician in New York state. A man of voracious appetites, he ran the local Democratic Party as though it were his own. The root of Tammany power was the lower classes, who saw Tweed as a Robin Hood figure, robbing the rich and cutting the poor in for a slice.

Tweed did some good for the poor, but most of his energy went into lining his own pockets. City contracts were padded with extra funds, and a percentage of the total – sometimes the largest percentage – fattened Tweed's wallet. On one single morning, Tweed and his cronies raked $5.5 million on a contract for the New York City Courthouse (a.k.a. the "Tweed Courthouse") in Lower Manhattan. After more than a decade as New York's uncrowned monarch and three years of litigation, Tweed was sent to Ludlow Street Prison, which, ironically, he had been responsible for building.

Hardly a typical jailbird, on one of the frequent visits to his Madison Avenue brownstone, Tweed ducked out the back and fled to Spain. He was recaptured and died in prison of pneumonia less than two years later.

A Day in the Life

The Lower East Side went by many names: "the typhus ward," "the suicide ward," "the crooked ward," or simply "Jewtown." The irregular rectangle of tenements and sweatshops crammed between the Bowery and the East River were the New World's ghetto.

Between 1880 and 1920, more than 2 million Eastern European Jews came to the United States, and over 500,000 settled in New York City, mostly on the Lower East Side. With 330,000 people per square

mile and primitive sanitation, yellow fever and cholera were constant threats, and child labor and exploitation were facts of life. Families of six or seven often slept, cooked, ate, and worked in a small room – in hallways, in basements, in alleyways – anywhere they could huddle. Rents were extortionate.

The "needle trade" was a keystone of the economy, and piles of half-sewn clothes cluttered the rooms. Pay was by quantity, hours were long, and the pace was fast and relentless. Sewing machines were typically whining by 6am and droned far into the night.

For the sweatshop workers, conditions were appalling: employees were charged for needles and thread, for lockers and chairs, and fined for damaged material at two or three times its regular value. Wages were minimal – maybe $8 or $10 a week for a family of five or six people, or $14 or $15 for the exceptionally productive. Survival was hand-to-mouth, and every penny saved was precious.

Writer Michael Gold remembered, "On the East Side people buy their groceries a pinch at a time; three cents' worth of sugar, five cents' worth of butter, everything in penny fractions." Compassion for friends had a high personal cost. "In a world based on the law of competition, kindness is a form of suicide."

At the center of the neighborhood was Hester Street market, where Jews not in the garment trade sold meat, produce, or cheap clothes from pushcarts. The area was nicknamed "the Pig Market," probably, as campaigning photo-journalist Jacob Riis said, "in derision, for pork is the one ware that is not on sale."

Eastern European Jews put a high value on education and political organization, and community members were active in the labor movement. Unions were regularly organized, but "strike-busters" were hired by the bosses to intimidate them with threats and violent acts.

Despite Tammany Hall's wooing of their votes for the Democratic Party, East Side Socialists finally saw their candidate in Congress in 1914. Organizations like the Educational Alliance sponsored lectures and demanded libraries; Yiddish theater blossomed on Second Avenue; and religious observances continued as they had in the old country. ❑

LEFT AND ABOVE: portraits of East Side immigrants by photo-journalist/reformer Jacob Riis.

ABOVE: a New York street market in 1908.

William Astor's annual ball. While the Four Hundred gorged themselves at lavish parties, Downtown New York was as wretched as ever. Every day 2,000 immigrants poured into the new Ellis Island immigration station, packing tenements and sweatshops ever tighter. Despite work by reformers like photo-journalist Jacob Riis, it took a tragedy to spur change.

Death trap

On March 25, 1911, as the five o'clock bell rang, fire lapped the top floors of the Triangle Shirtwaist Company near Washington Square. Around 600 workers were inside, and stairways were locked or barred by flames. Girls jumped from the eighth and ninth floors, thudding onto the sidewalk. The blaze lasted only about 10 minutes, but over 140 workers, mostly Jewish or Italian women no older than 20, were killed. The two company owners were acquitted, but the tragedy did stimulate labor reforms.

World War I had little impact on New York City. American infantrymen, known as Dough-boys, returned home to find business booming, the population growing, and an era of good feel-ings in the city. Prohibition was a dreary note to kick off the "Roaring Twenties," though the good times seemed better and the parties wilder now that drinking was taboo.

> *Prohibition backfired in Manhattan even more than in most cities. Twice as many speakeasies were estimated to be in New York City after Prohibition began as there were legitimate bars before.*

The free-spirited Twenties brought free-thinkers, too. Cheap rents and an "old quarter" atmosphere attracted writers, artists, and radi-cals to Greenwich Village. John Reed, Emma Goldman, Louise Bryant, and Edna St Vincent Millay advocated everything from communism to free love. Eugene O'Neill knocked 'em back at a speakeasy called the Hell Hole, and lit up the theater world at the Provincetown Playhouse.

The city may have been in a handbasket, en route to hell, but New York kept on partying – and kept on spending, too. In the 1920s, the city's stock-buying binge didn't look like it would ever

slow down; it didn't matter that trades were on credit, or that the city was being bilked of millions by Tammany Hall. As long as the money kept rolling, the lights burned on Broadway, and Mayor Jimmy Walker was smiling, everything was OK. Gossip columnist and broadcaster Walter Winchell said, "In the 1920s the American people were hell-bent for prosperity and riches. And they wanted a politician who was hell-bent only for re-election… a man who would respect the national rush to get rich, who would accept greed, avarice and the lust for quick gain as a legitimate expression of the will of the people… Walker knew what the people wanted."

Black Thursday

On October 24, 1929 – Black Thursday – the bottom fell out of the stock market, and the goodwill for Mayor Jimmy Walker went with it. The Great Depression hit New

York hard; total income dropped more than half, unemployment leaped to 25 percent and breadlines snaked along Broadway *(see photo on page 119)*. Groucho Marx said the city was on the skids "when the pigeons started feeding the people in Central Park."

Before Walker could ride out a second term, his administration unraveled. Investigations into city government found a nest of corruption second only to the Tweed Ring. Governor Franklin D. Roosevelt reviewed the charges, and Walker knew he couldn't walk away without a political, and personal, skinning. He resigned his office in 1932, and took the next ship to Europe.

About a year later, the new mayor in City Hall was Fiorello LaGuardia – a small, plump man with an animated face, a line in rumpled suits, and none of Walker's finesse. He was quick-witted, savvy, and determined to whip the city into shape. Hard-nosed and almost ruthless, but by turn paternalistic and warm, the man who ordered gangster Lucky Luciano off the streets read comics over the radio every Sunday.

JIMMY AND THE JAZZ AGE

Presiding over Jazz Age New York was Mayor James "Jimmy" Walker. In the 1920s, a blossoming of art and culture throughout the city but especially in Harlem (known as the first Harlem Renaissance) filled the city's streets with an intoxicating sparkle of anticipation. The big bands of Duke Ellington and Count Basie played to audiences at the Cotton Club, Small's Paradise, and other ritzy after-hours clubs, and the alcohol flowed, despite Prohibition. Walker wasn't keen on administration. A gambler, a lady's man, and a former Tin Pan Alley songwriter, he left the running of the city to Tammany Hall hacks. Walker played craps with reporters, hobnobbed with stars, and flaunted his affair with a Broadway actress from his booth at "21" (a speakeasy then, a restaurant now). When he raised his own salary by $10,000, Walker told critics, "Think what it would cost if I worked full-time."

LaGuardia had critics, but for a city ravaged by the Depression, he was their closest thing to a savior. After his 1933 election, LaGuardia joined Franklin Roosevelt's New Deal, launching programs to revive the economy. His government built bridges, highways and housing, and found work for artists and writers in the Federally funded Works Progress Administration.

At the same time, big projects begun in the 1920s came to completion. Art Deco changed the skyline of the city with the Chrysler Building in 1930, the Empire State Building and the Waldorf-Astoria Hotel in 1931, and Rockefeller Center in 1933. The 1939–40 New York World's Fair attracted more than 44 million people to Queens for the "Worlds of Tomorrow," at Flushing Meadows-Corona Park, where the Xerox copier, the electronic computer and television premiered to the American public *(see box on page 36)*.

In 1941, the US entered World War II, and the city swept into the war effort. Actual and supposed German spies were arrested, Japanese families were incarcerated on Ellis Island, and blackouts were ordered – even the torch of the Statue of Liberty was turned off. In the basement of a Columbia University physics lab, Enrico Fermi and Leo Szilard experimented with atomic fission, groundwork for what was later called the Manhattan Project: the atomic bomb.

Postwar boom and bust

The postwar United Nations came to the city in 1947 and Idlewild (now Kennedy) Airport opened in 1948. New York had peace, a healthy economy, and the riches of technology. The glass-walled UN Secretariat Building brought a new sleek look to Midtown and kicked off the 1950s modernity. Glass-box skyscrapers lined Park and Madison avenues, then spread to the West Side and the Financial District. Birdland, the bebop nightclub named for saxophonist Charlie Parker, opened on Broadway, and Franklin National Bank issued the world's first credit card.

Then, as in many northeastern cities, came a postwar decline. The middle class moved to the suburbs, corporations relocated, and poor blacks and Hispanics flocked into a run-down city. Tensions were dramatized in the 1957 version of *Romeo and Jul. t*, the musical *West Side Story*.

FAR LEFT: the Empire State in 1930. **TOP LEFT:** effects of the Wall Street crash of 1929. **ABOVE:** V-E Day in Times Square: May 7, 1945.

In the summer of 1964, a young black man was shot by police under questionable circumstances, and rioters in Harlem raged for six days. Gender and sexual politics also caught light in the '60s. In 1969, gay rights gained momentum from a police raid on the Stonewall Inn in Greenwich Village. The next year, legendary McSorley's Old Ale House was forced to admit women.

The Harlem riots passed, but the bitterness was unresolved. By 1975, the city was on the verge of bankruptcy, and was forced to go cap in hand to the Federal government. President Gerald Ford's response was summarized in the *Daily News*: "Ford to City: Drop Dead."

Ed Koch

In 1976, feisty mayor Edward Koch attempted another financial rescue – this time backed by a Federal government loan guarantee of $1.65 billion. A resurgence of corporate development fed capital into the economy, and the city climbed back onto its feet. Half-empty since their 1973 opening, the twin towers of the 110-story World Trade Center sparkled into life; in 1974, Philippe Petit tightrope-walked between the towers. Three years later, George Willig climbed the South Tower, and was fined one penny per story. Bat-

tery Park City and the South Street Seaport were developed in Lower Manhattan, and the 1977 Citicorp Building led the growth of a forest of new skyscrapers. One UN Plaza, the 37-story AT&T (now Sony) building, and the dark-glass IBM building personified the era.

New York acquired an international reputation for excess. In 1977, Studio 54 exemplified a sybaritic, cocaine-driven culture. A power failure that year led to widespread looting – in contrast to the community spirit around a major blackout in 1965, and the later massive Northeastern blackout in 2003. In December 1980, John Lennon, the former Beatle, was murdered outside his home, the Dakota building.

NEW YORK WORLD'S FAIRS

1829 The American Institute Fair was held every year in New York City from 1829 until around 1900.

1853 The Exhibition of the Industry of All Nations was a World's Fair held in the wake of the highly successful 1851 Great Exhibition in London. It showcased industrial achievements and national pride.

1939 The 1939–40 New York World's Fair, on the current site of Flushing Meadows-Corona Park, was one of the largest World's Fairs. Many different countries participated, and over 40 million people attended its exhibits in two seasons. The NYWF of 1939–40 allowed visitors to take a look at "the world of tomorrow."

1964 The 1964–5 New York World's Fair, again in Flushing Meadows-Corona Park, was held without the approval of the Bureau of International Expositions, the only fair to do so. The Space Age was one of the major themes, and more than 51 million people visited. General Motors, like a number of 1939 exhibitors, updated their *Futurama* show for what proved to be the fair's most popular attraction.

Broadway theatres began their shows an hour earlier to give tourists and out-of-towners a chance to get clear before the late-night mugging shift punched in. The gap between rich and poor widened and the legacy of homelessness was on almost every street corner. Aids and drug abuse pushed the healthcare systems beyond their capacity, and racial conflicts erupted. Manhattan businesses and middle-class workers fled to the suburbs or New Jersey, further weakening the New York tax base.

Good times, bad times

Moguls like Donald Trump snatched up New York real estate like squares on a Monopoly board, and the glitz of conspicuous consumption was lionized on the pages of *Vanity Fair*, a long-defunct magazine revived by Condé Nast in 1983. But by 1987, the good times had turned

---

FAR LEFT: John Lennon in 1974; just six years later he was killed outside his NY apartment building.
TOP LEFT: a 1962 ticker-tape parade for the *Apollo 11* crew. **ABOVE TOP:** Donald Trump: the capitalists' favorite. **ABOVE:** Rudy Giuliani's "get tough on crime" policy paid off, and the city became a safer place. **ABOVE RIGHT:** NY's tallest building from 1973 to 2001.

sour even for the tycoons, with two of Wall Street's biggest share dealers heading for jail and the market taking a record one-day dive of 508 points. On the streets, the annual murder rate

> 200 ticker-tape parades have taken place in Lower Manhattan, along what is known as the "Canyon of Heroes." The Yankees, the Mets, and Nelson Mandela have all been honored.

peaked at 2,245 and the number of citizens on welfare reached a new high. International terrorism arrived in 1993, when a car bomb in the World Trade Center killed six people.

In the 1993 mayoral election, an abrasive New York district attorney, former Department of Justice prosecutor Rudolph ("Rudy") Giuliani promised to get tough on crime. The first Republican mayor for two decades, he more than kept his promise, extending "zero tolerance" on law-breaking and police corruption, jaywalking, begging, graffiti, and non-recyclers. The policy didn't endear him to all, but it did win respect, and the crime rate fell, to make New York one

in 1997 and his ambitions turned towards the US Senate, but in 2000 his luck ran out. Prostate cancer and a messy separation from his second wife forced him out of the contest, which was won by a Democratic candidate, Hillary Rodham Clinton.

Terrorism

On the morning of September 11, 2001, five Boeing 767 passenger planes were hijacked by terrorists. Two of them were crashed into the World Trade Center's towers. New Yorkers and viewers around the world watched the towers collapse, killing 2,603 people, including 343 of the firefighters and 60 members of the police force who raced to the scene.

Smoke at "Ground Zero" hung in the air for three weeks, and the wreckage smouldered for weeks after. More than 20,000 New Yorkers were displaced from their homes near the 16-acre (6.5-hectare) disaster area. Even criminals were subdued; the week following the attack, crime in Manhattan fell 59 percent.

Mayor Giuliani personified New York's resilience. His trademark abrasiveness turned to a straight-talking compassion and earned the town's trust. These qualities were called on again just nine weeks later when an American Airlines morning flight for Santo Domingo crashed in the Rockaway district of Queens. Terrorists were not blamed but, in a bitter twist, the crash site was home to many emergency workers who bore such a toll on 9/11.

Giuliani's popularity was such that he had only to endorse Michael Bloomberg as his successor to win the election for the Republican, self-made media mogul. Bloomberg, a political

of the safer big cities in the US. By 1997, the murder rate had fallen two-thirds from its 1990 high.

Business Improvement Districts (BIDs) sprang up across the city, construction boomed, and seedy areas like Times Square were cleaned up. The economy rebounded from the 1987–92 slump, and unemployment fell. Giuliani was returned for a second term

WORLD TRADE CENTER SITE

In the immediate aftermath of the destruction of the Twin Towers, some believed the site should remain an open space, to commemorate the dead. Others advocated rebuilding the 110-story towers in defiance to terrorism. A competition was held, but the outcome was not without controversy. After years of infighting, a decision was reached: the site will contain four new towers, with the centerpiece, architect Daniel Libeskind's Freedom Tower, currently under construction. Freedom Tower will be 1,776ft (541 meters) in height – 1776 being the date of America's Declaration of Independence from Britain. There will also be a museum and a memorial on the footprints of the original Twin Towers.

novice, put $41 million of his own money into the campaign. Known on Wall Street for his financial data empire, and in the gossip columns for glamorous female companions after his 1993 divorce, Bloomberg inherited daunting tasks. As well as the massive rebuilding program in Lower Manhattan, the city had an $8.7 billion budget shortfall, and New York's social services had already been ruthlessly pruned. Fears of a recession and the effects of the terror attack spiked unemployment numbers. Bloomberg enjoyed a high approval rating and, in 2009, he was re-elected for an unprecedented third term.

Back to the future

But, as always in New York, energy came and rejuvenation began. The Hudson River waterfront was revitalized, Governor's Island reopened as a retreat for visitors, the spectacularly reorganized Museum of Modern Art returned from

Queens and opened its new building to great acclaim. The gleaming Time Warner complex rose over Columbus Circle, with the distinctive triangular facades of the green Hearst Tower climbing nearby to join it in 2006.

> High Line Park is an elevated urban oasis, planted on a disused train track that goes through the Meatpacking District and Chelsea. The first phase opened in 2009.

On the fifth anniversary of the 2001 attack, a memorial visitor center was opened at the south side of the World Trade Center site. Architect Daniel Libeskind's plans to erect Freedom Tower on the site progressed, controversially, of course. The city continues to change: new baseball stadiums opened for both the Mets and the Yankees in 2009; the Lincoln Center renovation was completed; and another museum is scheduled to open on Museum Mile.

New York is still a place of constant renewal, struggle, joy, and ambition, where the air tingles with the promise that everything is possible. ❏

FAR LEFT: the World Trade Center after the terrorist attacks of September 11, 2001. **LEFT:** Michael Bloomberg was re-elected for a third term in 2009. **ABOVE TOP:** RIP James Brown. **ABOVE :** new home of the Mets; the Yankees also have a new stadium. **ABOVE RIGHT:** NY's new skyscraper, Hearst Tower.

DECISIVE DATES

1524
Italian explorer Giovanni da Verrazano, under Francis I of France, sights the territory that is now New York, but doesn't land his ship.

1609
Englishman Henry Hudson weighs anchor on the island, then sails the *Half Moon* up the river that now bears his name.

1624
The Dutch West India Company sets up a trading post on the southern tip of the island at what is now Battery Park.

1626
The provincial director-general of the New Amsterdam settlement, Peter Minuit, purchases Manhattan from the Algonquin tribe for 60 guilders' worth of trinkets – the equivalent of $24 in today's currency.

1630s
Dutch farmers settle land in what is now Brooklyn and the Bronx.

1643
Conflict with local Algonquin tribes leaves at least 80 Indians dead at what became known as the Panovia Massacre.

1647
Peter Stuyvesant becomes director-general and soon suppresses political opposition.

1653
Peter Stuyvesant builds a fence along what is now known as Wall Street to protect New Amsterdam from British incursion.

1660
Nearly half the population is foreign born. Irish-born Americans are the largest group in the city, then German-born Americans.

1664
In the first year of the sea war between England and Holland, Stuyvesant is forced to surrender the town to the British without a fight. New Amsterdam is renamed New York, after King Charles II's brother, James, the Duke of York.

1673
The Dutch recapture New York and rename it New Orange, again without fighting taking place.

1674
New York is returned to the British by the Anglo-Dutch Treaty of Westminster.

1690
With a population of 3,900, New York is now the third-largest town in North America.

1735
Newspaper publisher Peter Zenger is tried for slandering the British

crown. He is acquitted, establishing the precedent for freedom of the press.

1765
In accordance with the Stamp Act, unfair taxes are levied against the early colonists.

1770
Skirmishes between the Sons of Liberty and the British culminate in the Battle of Golden Hill, the first blood to be shed prior to the Revolutionary War.

1776
George Washington loses the Battle of Long Island, and British troops occupy New York until 1783.

1789
New York becomes the capital of the United States of America, but only retains this status for 18 months.

1789
George Washington is inaugurated as President of the United States at the site of the Federal Hall, Wall Street.

1790
A first official census reveals that the city of New York now has a population of over 33,000.

1792
A popular, open-air money market is established beneath a buttonwood tree on Wall Street.

1807
Robert Fulton, sailing along the Hudson River, establishes the first successful steamboat company in the US.

1811
An important decision is made affecting the city's future appearance: all streets are to be laid out in the form of a grid.

1820
An official Stock Exchange replaces the outdoor money market that has been held on Wall Street.

1825
The economic importance of New York increases sharply as a result of the construction of the Erie Canal, which connects the Hudson River with the Great Lakes.

1835
Manhattan, between South Broad and Wall Street, is ravaged by the "Great Fire."

1857
William M. "Boss" Tweed, elected to the County Board of Supervisors, launches a career of notorious corruption.

1858
Calvert Vaux and Frederick Law Olmsted submit plans for Central Park, which is to be the "lungs" of the city.

1860
New York becomes the largest metropolis in the United States; in the previous 30 years, Brooklyn's population increased 10 times over.

1861

The Civil War begins, and many New Yorkers are recruited for the cause.

1863

The Draft Riots rage throughout New York, and it is thought that around 100 people are killed.

1869

The Museum of Natural History opens.

1870s

William M. "Boss" Tweed, of Tammany Hall notoriety, is arrested, tried and taken to a jail he helped to build, before escaping to Spain.

1880

The Metropolitan Museum of Art opens.

1883

The Brooklyn Bridge opens, and there is a first gala performance by the Metropolitan Opera.

1886

The Statue of Liberty, a gift from France, is unveiled on Liberty Island.

1892

Ellis Island in New York Harbor becomes the point of entry for immigrants to the United States.

1898

New York's five boroughs are united under one municipal government.

1902

The Flatiron Building is completed.

1904

An underground subway system is established.

1911

The Triangle Fire alerts the public to the appalling living conditions of immigrants.

1913

Construction of the world's tallest skyscraper, the Woolworth Building, begins. It is superseded in 1930 by the Chrysler Building.

1929

Wall Street crashes, and with it comes the end of the Jazz Age and the start of the Great Depression.

1931

After 14 months of construction, the Empire State Building opens ahead of schedule and is heralded as a great success.

1933

Fiorello LaGuardia is elected mayor and uses Federal money to fight the devastating effects of the Great Depression.

1939

Ten years after its foundation by Abby Aldrich Rockefeller, the Museum of Modern Art moves into its new home on 53rd Street. The World's Fair opens in Flushing, Queens.

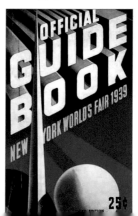

1941
The United States enters
World War II.

1946
The United Nations begins
meeting in New York. The
permanent buildings on
East 42nd–48th streets are
completed six years later.

1959
The Frank Lloyd Wright-
designed Guggenheim
Museum opens. Work
begins on Lincoln Center.

1965
A 16-hour power cut
paralyzes the city.

1970
Economic decline sets in,
which continues until
around 1976.

1973
The World Trade Center
opens. With its 110-story
Twin Towers, it is the tallest
building in the world.

1975
Impending bankruptcy is
avoided only by getting a
bridging loan from the
Federal government.

1977
A 27-hour power cut
occurs, with widespread
looting and vandalism.

1978
Ed Koch becomes mayor of
New York and remains in
office until 1989.

1982
The IBM building opens,
followed by the AT&T
building in 1983.

1986
Battery Park City opens.

1987
"Black Monday" on Wall
Street. Shares suffer a
30 percent drop in value.

1990
David Dinkins becomes the
first African-American mayor.

1993
A bomb explodes below the
World Trade Center. Six
people are killed and over
1,000 are injured.

1997
Mayor Rudolph Giuliani's
"zero tolerance" campaign
is effective, and there are
major declines in crime.

1998
The city celebrates the
Centennial of Greater New

York, marking the
amalgamation of the five
boroughs in 1898.

2001
Terrorists crash two planes
into the World Trade
Center's towers. Nearly
3,000 people are killed.

2003
Smoking is banned in bars
and restaurants. There is
another, huge power cut.

2004
The Museum of Modern Art
moves back to Manhattan.
The Time Warner Center in
Columbus Circle opens.

2006
On the fifth anniversary of
September 11, President
George Bush visits the new
Tribute WTC Visitor Center
in Lower Manhattan.

2009
The renovation of Lincoln
Center is completed, as are
new baseball stadiums for
the Mets and the Yankees.
The Statue of Liberty's
crown reopens. The *Intrepid*
returns to Manhattan.

CULTURE AND THE CITY

New York is both a breeding ground and an international showcase for art and artists of every kind. If you can make it here, they say, you can make it anywhere

New York bristles with world-class performing arts venues, in Lincoln Center, Carnegie Hall, and Madison Square Garden and the whole of Broadway. Big-ticket theaters cluster around Broadway, but the Off-Broadway scene has spawned a thriving and energetic Off-Off-Broadway family.

Parks across the city offer free, fresh-air culture with outdoor performances of the New York Philharmonic, the Metropolitan Opera and the New York Shakespeare Festival. On every New York corner and subway platform, a dreamer or a talented student works the "if I can make it here, I can make it anywhere" refrain. The "if" being key to that kick-step off the city streets.

New York City has over 2,000 arts and cultural organizations and more than 500 art galleries. Lincoln Center is the largest performing arts center in the United States.

One-third of all American independent movies are made here, and great jazz was crafted in clubs like Birdland. Artists of all kinds have thrived in the Big Apple, from Edward Hopper in his Washington Square studio and Andy Warhol's Factory divas, to Bob Dylan and Jimi Hendrix, who was "discovered" in a Village bar by British bass player Chas Chandler.

PRECEDING PAGES: visitors at the Guggenheim Museum. **LEFT:** detail from *Twenty Marilyns,* Andy Warhol, 1962. **RIGHT:** Central Park musician.

Live music
New York is famous for great jazz clubs, like the Blue Note and the Village Vanguard in Greenwich Village. Excellent up-and-coming bands of all kinds play at BAM (Brooklyn Academy of Music), home since 1982 to the innovative Next Wave Festival.

CBGB's on the Lower East Side, birthplace of Talking Heads and the Ramones, has finally slammed its doors, and the Knitting Factory moved from Tribeca to Brooklyn, but Sounds of Brazil (SOB) in Soho is a lively world-music venue, the Mercury Lounge showcases cutting-edge bands, and the Bottom Line in the Village continues to wave the folk-rock flag.

Cultural centers

The Upper West Side's cultural heart is the Lincoln Center for the Performing Arts *(see photo feature on pages 158–61)*, the largest cultural center in the US. The Metropolitan Opera and New York City Opera, and the Philharmonic reside here, with concerts and recitals in Avery Fisher Hall and Alice Tully Hall. The Vivian Beaumont and Mitzi E. Newhouse theaters put on productions and, each September, the New York Film Festival opens at the Lincoln. Jazz at Lincoln Center, a few blocks Uptown at the Time Warner complex, thrives under the artistic direction of Wynton Marsalis.

> *Off-Broadway theater dates back to the Greenwich Village production of four one-act plays by Eugene O'Neill in 1916.*

World-famous Carnegie Hall was opened to the public with Tchaikovsky's American debut in 1891, and later hosted Albert Einstein, Amelia Earhart, Winston Churchill, Frank Sinatra, The Beatles, and Elton John. Charles Dana Gibson drew the Gibson Girls and established

Life magazine in a studio on the premises, and dancer Isadora Duncan lived at the hall. In the late 1950s, developers wanted the plot for office space, but violinist Isaac Stern led a group of citizens to save the site from the wrecker's ball.

In Studio 1011–12, Baroness Hilla von Rebay convinced Solomon Guggenheim to fund promising artists, and established the Guggenheim Foundation, with Alexander Calder and Wassily Kandinsky among the beneficiaries. The baroness's acquisitions formed the core of the Guggenheim collection, housed in the Frank Lloyd Wright building on Fifth Avenue.

Visual arts

Art auctions came to public attention in the 1990s when a Van Gogh sold for $82.5 million at Christie's (Van Gogh once wrote that he wished his paintings were worth what he had spent on the paint). Experts said the auction frenzy was a blip, but in 2004 Picasso's *Garçon*

ABOVE LEFT: Carnegie Hall. **ABOVE RIGHT:** visitors can go to the Queens garden of the late sculptor Isamu Noguchi. **TOP RIGHT:** the innovative P.S.1 has links with MoMA. **FAR RIGHT:** the Tribeca Film Festival is a highlight of New York's spring events.

à la Pipe fetched $104 million at Sotheby's. And in one dizzying week in 2007, Andy Warhol's *Green Car Crash* fetched $71.7 million at Christie's, while Mark Rothko's *White Center* sold for $72.8 million at Sotheby's.

The Metropolitan, the Guggenheim, and others line "Museum Mile" *(see photo feature on pages 136–7)* along Fifth Avenue. The Metropolitan, along with the Museum of Modern Art on West 53rd Street, are the biggest and best. The Frick, once a private Fifth Avenue mansion, shows fine Rembrandts and Vermeers. The New York Public Library on 42nd Street exhibits art in a grand setting, its Reading Room providing an office for many writers.

Moving pictures

Once upon a time in New York, Radio City Music Hall was to movies what Lincoln Center is to ballet and opera. Now it's an Art Deco treasure, and even the ladies' powder room is worth visiting. Designed by a showman who was known for lavish silent-film the-

aters, S.L. "Roxy" Rothafel's Radio City opened for vaudeville shows in 1932 as a "palace for the people." Radio City is still an exciting place to see a movie or catch a gig.

Movie lines often wind around the block in Manhattan, providing eavesdropping and people-watching opportunities. (And, no, the skinny, nervy guy waiting ahead of you isn't Woody Allen.) Space is precious in the city, and multiplex theaters can make movie-going seem like standing in line to watch a TV screen. The Angelika Film Center on West Houston Street

TRIBECA FILM FESTIVAL

First established in 2002 by Robert De Niro *(left)* and producer Jane Rosenthal, the Tribeca Film Festival has rapidly become a major fixture in the moviemakers' calendar. The impetus was originally to lead a Downtown regeneration in response to the 2001 terrorist attacks, but just five years later (in an event that had climate change as a major theme and was opened by the former vice-president Al Gore), 200 titles were screened to an enraptured and ready audience.

The first festival drew crowds of more than 150,000 people, and at least $10.4 million in takings for local Tribeca merchants. The next year, the crowds doubled, takings grew almost fivefold, and screenings featured outdoor drive-in (or sit-in) shows along the banks of the Hudson River. Paul Greengrass's acclaimed *United 93* premiered at the festival, as did *Mission Impossible III*. Tribeca is so successful that *New York* magazine began to wonder if the festival isn't getting too big, and that isn't something New Yorkers often wonder.

in Soho, though, has six screens, an espresso bar, and an atmosphere as good as the coffee. The Film Forum on West Houston Street features movie genres and directors, as do the Museum of Modern Art and the Museum of the Moving Image, aptly located by the Kaufman Astoria film studio complex in Queens.

Lincoln Center's Walter Reade Theater, home of the New York Film Festival, screens foreign and independent films, as do Brooklyn Academy of Music's BAM Rose Cinemas – these with the bonus of Digital Surround Sound. Downtown, the IFC Center opened in 2005 in the Village's historic Waverly Theater, while every spring, the Tribeca

Film Festival, co-launched by actor Robert De Niro, is the high-profile, hot-ticket event at which to be seen and to attend the latest screenings.

Dance

New York's dance boom began in the 1960s, with an infusion of funding and the defection of Russian superstars Rudolf Nureyev, Mikhail Baryshnikov, and Natalia Makarova. The legendary George Balanchine hand-picked the New York City Ballet company, putting them through almost superhuman training. "Mr B" said, "Dancers are like race-horses; they need a jockey on their backs." Balanchine, who designed much of the performance space at the Lincoln Center's New

BUYING BROADWAY TICKETS

A Chorus Line returned to Broadway in 2006 – 16 years after it folded – but with a few useful tips you don't have to wait as long to find good Broadway tickets. The TKTS booth in Times Square has discounted seats (25–50 percent off) for that night's performances. It's open Monday through Saturday 3pm to 8pm for evening performances, Saturday and Wednesday 10am to 2pm for matinees, and Sunday 11am to 7.30pm for both shows. A booth at 186 Front Street near South Street Seaport sells tickets for the following night's shows. Lines form early and are long, so take a book. TKTS booths don't take credit cards.

● Unsold tickets can often be bought at theater box offices an hour or so before show time.

● The Times Square Visitor Center in the Embassy Theater, Broadway between 46th and 47th streets, also sells theater tickets.

York State Theater, died in 1983. The American Ballet Theater occupies the Lincoln Center's Metropolitan Opera House when the opera is out of season. ABT began with a more classical repertory than the New York City Ballet but, under Mikhail Baryshnikov's artistic direction, welcomed contemporary choreographers like Twyla Tharp.

The Dance Theater of Harlem, founded in 1969, performs both classical and contemporary repertories. Other venues for dance, particularly modern dance, range from the Joyce Theater in Chelsea to the Ailey Center and the City Center, both in Midtown West.

Theatrical stories

In 1901, the glare of electric signs earned the theater district of Broadway the name of the Great White Way. Taking in Seventh Avenue and several side streets, its heyday was before talking pictures and long before television. By the 1970s and '80s, the streets were dirty with drugs, pornography, and prostitution, but Times Square today is a twinkly tourist mecca of theaters, hotels, megastores, and restaurants.

The Shubert Theatre (1913) and Shubert Alley are named for the Shubert brothers,

LEFT: enjoying an evening at the Lincoln Center.
BELOW LEFT: the Shubert Theatre near Broadway.
BELOW RIGHT: the Cherry Lane Theatre.

who built dozens of venues. The Palace on West 47th Street was a vaudeville theater until the 1930s, whose boards were trodden by Sarah Bernhardt. Now it's a prime venue for lavish musicals like *Beauty and the Beast* and one-off gigs. The Belasco Theatre, founded in 1907 by flamboyant playwright-actor-director David Belasco, was famously haunted by his ghost until the 1970s production of *Oh! Calcutta*. Perhaps the nudity spooked the spook.

Today, Broadway is in exuberant health. Excellent drama draws crowds, but the big noise is the musicals. Successful musicals often have longer runs, to make back their bigger investments. The original *A Chorus Line* opened in the 1970s and ran for 6,137 performances, before being overtaken by *Cats*, which yowled for more than 20 years.

Off-Broadway venues are a feeding ground for the bigger theaters and a cultural force in themselves. The Lucille Lortel, the Cherry Lane, and the Public Theater: time to take a bow. ❑

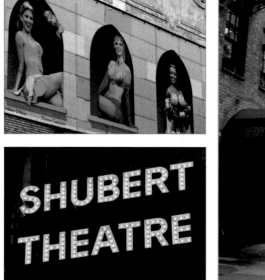

HOLLYWOOD ON THE HUDSON

From the early days of the silver screen, New York has glittered on film

Ever since *The Lights of New York* was released in 1927, the city and its landmarks have been illuminating the big screens of the world's celluloid consciousness. King Kong atop the Empire State Building is an enduring image – although the 1976 remake was so bad it's remarkable that actress Jessica Lange's fledgling career survived the premiere. Peter Jackson's 2005 resurrection of the title with Naomi Watts fared better.

The Empire struck back when New York writer-director Nora Ephron made *Sleepless in Seattle*, itself a pastiche of the 1957 three-hankie weepie *An Affair to Remember*. Director Spike Lee portrayed contemporary life Uptown in *Mo' Better Blues*.

Fonda and Redford went *Barefoot in the Park*, and Scorsese's *Raging Bull* rampaged around Greenwich Village, too. *How to Marry a Millionaire* was set in the apartment of sassy dames Monroe, Grable, and Bacall at 36 Sutton Place South.

Over 200 films are made here each year, and the number continues to rise, so there's no *Escape from New York* to Hollywood just yet.

ABOVE: *Manhattan*: critic Andrew Sarris described Allen's 1979 homage to New York as "a film for the ages by not seeking to be a film of the moment."

TIFFANY

ABOVE: *Breakfast at Tiffany's*: the 1961 comedy based on Truman Capote's darker story. George Peppard and Audrey Hepburn look for love and breakfast.

RIGHT: in 1933, only two years after the Empire State Building opened, King Kong raged on the radio mast.

WOODY ALLEN

From *Annie Hall* to *Manhattan* to *Hannah and Her Sisters*, no filmmaker has portrayed modern New York (and his own personal neuroses) with more acuity and affection than Woody Allen. Born Allen Stewart Konigsberg in Brooklyn in 1935, he started as a comedy writer, became a successful stand-up comic, and segued to writer/director with *Take the Money and Run* in 1969. The city has played a pivotal role in many of his movies since then, including *Crimes and Misdemeanors (1989)*, *Bullets Over Broadway (1994)*, *Small Time Crooks* (2000), and *Melinda and Melinda* (2004). Although some of his films are now made in Europe, when he's in town Allen still drops by to play the clarinet at Café Carlyle in the Carlyle Hotel on East 68th Street. This is where he once turned down a request for an encore because he was coming down with a cold, noting: "People are always saying I'm a hypochondriac, but they're all wrong. I'm more of an alarmist."

RIGHT: *The Seven Year Itch*: Marilyn's then-husband, baseball star Joe DiMaggio, watched the 2am shoot featuring *that* dress over *that* grating at 52nd and Lexington. His distress at the crowd's reaction was thought to have helped break up their marriage. Monroe had been cast in Billy Wilder's 1955 romantic comedy as, simply, "the girl."

ABOVE: *The Godfather:* things get gritty in Little Italy in Francis Ford Coppola's 1972 Mafia tale. The late Marlon Brando *(above)* won an Academy Award, the film was voted best picture, and Coppola's reputation was made by the trilogy.

BELOW: You talkin' to me? Director Martin Scorsese defined a city and a genre in 1976's *Taxi Driver*. Robert De Niro, Cybill Shepherd, Harvey Keitel and Jodie Foster all gave breakthrough performances in a dark tale of obsession and disconnection. Scorsese has gone on to make several movies in the city, among them *New York, New York* (1977), *After Hours* (1985), and *Gangs of New York* (2002).

DINERS, DELIS, AND HIP DELIGHTS

You can get a hot dog for around a dollar, or a double-truffle hamburger for 100 times that price. This is New York, where people eat with attitude

New York is, and always was, a great place to eat. From bagels to corned-beef sandwiches, Italian fine dining to curbside fast food, and from sashimi to sauerkraut, the breadth of cuisines is matched only by the range of prices. It's easy to feast well for a few dollars on a hot dog or banquet at Per Se for – if not a king's, then at least a royal sommelier's – ransom.

Food and fashion

Fashion and trends are vital in all that is New York, and celebrity chefs have left the town peppered with famous-name kitchens (some now leftovers as their famous founders cook up franchises and offshoots elsewhere, like Miami and Las Vegas). Meanwhile, the appetites for star-chef servings are increasingly fed by restaurateurs from out of town, and from as far afield as London, Paris, and Italy. Culinary styles are prefaced by the words

Manhattan restaurants open, close, and are soon forgotten, but two landmarks – Le Cirque and the Russian Tea Room – left and came back again. Who says New Yorkers don't care?

"haute" and "real." "Haute Italian" is elaborate and extravagant, usually found in dressy style palaces like A Voce in the Flatiron District. "Haute Barnyard" (yes, a real phrase)

LEFT: get great dinners at a NY diner.
RIGHT: dining out on the Lower East Side.

also promises cuisine of choking expense, but themed on traditional country cooking with ingredients sourced from impeccable suppliers. Peasant in NoLita presents a Tuscan example of this type, and American rustic heritage is plated and celebrated at Craft. "Real Barnyard" is earthy, country cooking. "Vegetarian" has graduated from a regular option to a mainstay, with vegan diets increasingly available, while the prefix "free" – as in "dairy-free" and "wheat-free" – is sprinkled over all but the very least fashionable menus.

The first visible signs of food are at the street corners on silver carts. In the past, these carts peddled indistinguishable soggy pretzels,

charcoal-burned ears of corn, and overboiled hot dogs. Now *empanadas* (South American savory pastries), chow-fun noodles, whole-grain pancakes, chocolate-truffle cookies, or mango ices are right there at the curb, usually prepared quite well.

Reservation-only cocktail bars, as seen in the hip Lower East Side, are a new trend that deserves to die an undignified death.

Fast and slow pizza

Pizzas range from street-corner slices, often made with a crunchy semolina flour, to the Sullivan Street Bakery, where the slice is about the only thing they have in common. The bakery's Jim Lahey is a passionate campaigner of "slow food" and applies the principles he learned in Tuscany (using only high-grade flour and wild yeast, plus fresh, all-natural ingredients) to his pizzas, which are minimally accessorized. His signature slice is the seductively simple pizza *pomodoro*, with a thin tomato purée. That's it.

Some of the world's finest and most expensive restaurants – the Four Seasons, Le Cirque, and Alain Ducasse at the St Regis to name but a few – are in Midtown. Many Manhattan mainstays are here too, with the the longevity prize going to the excellent nonagenarian Oyster Bar at Grand Central Terminal. For Midtown dining, it pays to do some homework (that's where this guide comes in handy). While spontaneity is fun farther Downtown, in Midtown it's best to make reservations, especially to dine before or after the theater.

Restaurants here, especially the more expensive ones, often have formal dress codes. Men are suited (or at least jacketed) and women go groomed for a glamorous night on the town. Many Midtown restaurants are closed Sundays, and for lunch on Saturdays, as their corporate customers have gone.

The Meatpacking District is good for both dining and posing, even if the patrons are often wafer-thin models who don't look as if they eat, ever. Prepare to eat late, and stay up even later. The nearby Chelsea Market, at Ninth Avenue and 15th Street, is a dreamland for food fetishists – a dozen or so bakeries, meat markets, kitchen suppliers, and

other stores of a gastronomic bent, all based in former warehouses.

Once Soho gained recognition as an artistic center, people began streaming here in search of "the scene." The restaurant tariffs reflect Soho's now-dominant chic-ness, but there's no need to go hungry, or to pay through the nose. You can shell out $35+ for a steak at Balthazar, but you can also eat for plenty less at Jerry's.

Famous diners

Robert De Niro is one of Tribeca's most famous diners. The actor moved here in 1976, and began investing in restaurants: Montrachet, Nobu, and the Tribeca Grill. To avoid these movie-star prices, head for the reasonably priced neighborhood bistro Landmarc, finishing off with frozen yogurt from Emack & Bolio. De Niro promoted his 'hood as a cool area in which to hang out, and it still is.

The once-mean streets of the Lower East Side are now very much the domain of hipsters. An enclave of immigration in the previous centuries, get a taste of the area's heritage at Katz's Delicatessen. To watch Uptown moving to happening Downtown and loving it, head for the Chinatown Brasserie or try Morimoto or Buddakan in the Meatpacking District.   ❏

A list of restaurants appears at the end of each Places chapter, with a map grid reference.

A NEW YORK TRADITION

Weekends are when New Yorkers stroll instead of sprint. On Saturday and Sunday mornings, restaurants are filled with Manhattanites enjoying a slow start to the day, eating brunch in the company of a friend, with a lover or spouse, or alone with the newspaper or a book. Sunday brunch in particular is a local tradition. Most restaurants offer a brunch menu, but there are some standout choices. In the heart of Central Park on the edge of a pond dotted with colorful rowboats, The Boathouse wins the prize for charm. The menu is good, too; try the smoked salmon frittata, French toast, or steak and eggs. For the best French-inspired brunch, head for Balthazar in Soho, and dip your croissant into a gigantic cup of the house "Chocolat Chaud."

LEFT: Sardi's is an old-school, theatrical experience.
ABOVE LEFT: Chelsea Market: everything to eat, drink, or buy. **ABOVE RIGHT:** The Boathouse in Central Park.

FOOD ON THE MOVE

Don't want to make time to sit down and have a full meal? You're in good company in the Big Apple

New York is a city with a rich restaurant scene. But while it seems there's a fabulous new spot opening on every corner, the tasty treats are not just limited to restaurants. This is a city on the go, and many locals can't be bothered to sit down and eat. As a result, you'll find quickie sandwich shops, corner bodegas, and pizza stands selling slices to people who try to eat them without messing up their shirts.

In the morning, many New Yorkers grab their breakfast from a cart on the way to the office, so don't be afraid to give these vendors a go. The coffee is good, and the bagels make a quick meal.

There are a variety of greenmarkets, but none more important than the Union Square Greenmarket. Every Monday, Wednesday, Friday, and Saturday, sidewalks fill up with stands hawking local foods. In winter, start the day with cider and cinnamon donuts; in summertime, there's lemonade and fruit-filled pastries. Or come for a lunchtime picnic, and pick up bread, wine, locally cured meats, and cheese.

ABOVE: you can still buy classic hot dogs from carts all over Midtown. The most coveted ones are seared on cart-top flat grills.

RIGHT: bagels come in sweet and savory flavors. Most New Yorkers get theirs toasted and either buttered or slathered with cream cheese.

KEEP ON TRUCKING

In recent years, a fleet of food trucks has sprung up, moving daily to feed food-loving office workers in largely un-foodie neighborhoods. Other major American cities have their own food-truck scenes, but few can compete with the variety in New York.

So just what can you eat from a truck? Many serve sweets, including Cupcake Stop (www.cupcakestop.com), which offers miniature and full-size versions of its cakelettes, and Treats Truck (www.treatstruck.com), a cart that sells the all-American classics: chocolate chip cookies, brownies, and Rice Krispie squares. Wafels & Dinges (www.wafelsanddinges.com) serves – you guessed it – Belgian waffles. There are fancy ice-cream trucks including The Big Gay Ice Cream Truck (www.biggayicecreamtruck.com) and Van Leeuwen (www.vanleeuwenicecream.com).

There are also plenty of savory foods – look for dumplings (www.rickshawdumplings.com), Taiwanese chicken (www.nyccravings.com), schnitzel (http://schnitzelandthings.com), and burgers (http://lacensebeef.com). Since there are no seats at which to eat these purchases, most people stake out space on public park benches.

To track down a particular food truck, check out the info on the Midtown Lunch website (http://midtownlunch.com) or follow your individual favorites on their websites, Twitter, or Facebook.

TOP: join the crowds at Bryant Park on 42nd Street, a lovely place to eat street-vendor food thanks to its proliferation of tables and chairs.

ABOVE: the Wafels & Dinges truck serves sweet Belgian-style waffles all around the city.

RIGHT: the dumplings at the Rickshaw Dumpling Truck come in a variety of flavors, including pork and chicken. Sometimes they offer duck dumplings as a popular special.

SHOPPING

New York is the shopping capital of the world. If you can't buy it here, you can't buy it anywhere

For anyone who rates shopping as one of life's greater imperatives, New York is the place to be. Manhattan has every kind of shop imaginable. In terms of orientation, a general rule of thumb is that the big department stores are in Midtown. Many of these are opulent – including Barneys and Bergdorf Goodman. Uptown and in Midtown you'll also find stores with world-famous names, like the popular Apple boutique and the powerhouse toy store, FAO Schwartz, on Fifth Avenue.

The more quirky stores are Downtown. Greenwich Village, Soho, NoHo, and the Meatpacking District are places where stylish shoppers go to find the latest fashions from up-and-coming designers, as well as vintage pieces. And the style goes beyond clothing: ABC Carpet and Home offers a mix of luxurious home decor, and more unusual finds. Even the bath goods – like those at Kiehl's – are coveted. So go ahead, take the plunge – just don't forget that sales tax of around 8 percent.

ABOVE: New York institution Bloomingdale's takes up an entire block on Third Avenue in the Upper East Side (there's also a branch in Soho). Bloomies is full of everything you could ever need and a lot you don't, but want to buy anyway. Most of the top designers are here, and the style emporium Barneys is nearby.

ABOVE: the Guggenheim is just one of New York's many museums with great gift shops. Things to buy include posters, books, scarves, ties, T-shirts, caps, and a selection of creative toys for children. There's even Guggenheim china on sale.

BELOW: in Herald Square, at the intersection of Broadway and Sixth Avenue at 34th Street, is a shopping icon – Macy's, whose Thanksgiving Day parade is watched by people all over America. There are now Macy's stores all over the US, but this is the original, built in 1902. The visitor center on the second floor has staff to help people find their way around the store, and also provides tourist information.

THE PRICE IS RIGHT

You can buy anything in New York – for a fee – but smart shoppers know how to get the best for less. New York's city's biggest shopping period is from the day after Thanksgiving (known as "Black Friday") through New Year's Day. During this time, you may find sales (particularly early on the morning of Black Friday) along with festive holiday decorations and, at the department stores, magnificently decorated windows that draw crowds so big they need to put up velvet ropes.

Other than that, the best months for sales are February and August, as the stores clean out their inventory to make way for the next season's wares.

Savvy shoppers who don't like to wait for sales often frequent New York's bargain houses, which include Century 21 and Loehmann's. Here, the clothing won't be well lit and lined up on elegant displays – in fact, you may have to dig through bins, and often you won't find items in many colors or sizes. For some shoppers, it's a frustrating prospect – but for die-hard deal hunters, it's heaven to know there's a bargain waiting if only you're willing to look.

RIGHT: Kiehl's flagship store in the East Village has been providing shampoos, soaps, face creams, and lotions to a discerning clientele for over 150 years. Today this traditional apothecary still offers old-fashioned service and its famous samples.

BELOW: Soho's Dean & Deluca stocks gourmet food and fine wine, wonderful cheeses, charcuterie, chocolate, and freshly ground coffee. The goods aren't cheap, but neither is the quality.

RIGHT: The Zagat guides rank restaurants, bars, and shops in New York based on reader surveys.

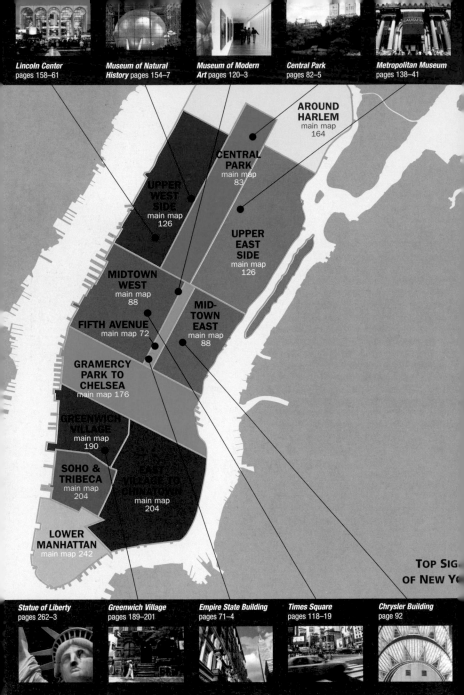

Lincoln Center
pages 158–61

Museum of Natural History pages 154–7

Museum of Modern Art pages 120–3

Central Park
pages 82–5

Metropolitan Museum
pages 138–41

AROUND HARLEM
main map
164

CENTRAL PARK
main map
83

UPPER WEST SIDE
main map
126

UPPER EAST SIDE
main map
126

MIDTOWN WEST
main map
88

MID-TOWN EAST
main map
88

FIFTH AVENUE
main map 72

GRAMERCY PARK TO CHELSEA
main map 176

GREENWICH VILLAGE
main map
190

SOHO & TRIBECA
main map
204

EAST VILLAGE TO CHINATOWN
main map
204

LOWER MANHATTAN
main map 242

TOP SIG
OF NEW Y

Statue of Liberty
pages 262–3

Greenwich Village
pages 189–201

Empire State Building
pages 71–4

Times Square
pages 118–19

Chrysler Building
page 92

PLACES

The cutaway map opposite shows the neighborhoods of
New York, while the Places section to follow details all
the attractions worth seeing, arranged by area. Main
sites are cross-referenced by number to individual maps

New York is synonymous with Manhattan, which is divided into three
areas: Midtown, Uptown, and Downtown. Midtown and Uptown are
crisscrossed by a street grid – avenues travel north and south, streets
travel east and west. Fifth Avenue runs down the center, anchored by huge
Central Park, the "green lung" of the city. It's for this reason that the Places
section of this book begins with Fifth Avenue,
the Big Apple's glamorous, pulsating core.
Midtown is Midtown East, best known for
Grand Central, the United Nations and the
Chrysler Building, and Midtown West, home
of Times Square, Rockefeller Center and the
Museum of Modern Art.

Cool, elegant Uptown is epitomized by the
Upper East Side – between 82nd and 104th
streets are nine cultural treasures so lavish
that this stretch is known as Museum Mile. The Upper West Side is both
more towering (Trump International Tower, the Time Warner Center) and
more family-oriented, witness the number of baby carriages on the small
backstreets. At the top end of Manhattan is Harlem, which is currently
undergoing a cultural renaissance.

Downtown is more of a challenge to navigate, as its smaller streets do
not follow a pattern, and have names instead of numbers. Some of New
York's oldest sites are here, as well as the newest hotspots. Downtown is
Gramercy Park, Chelsea, Greenwich Village, Chinatown, and the hip and
happening Lower East Side. Downtown is also Alphabet City – Avenues A,
B, C, and D   plus NoHo, NoLita, and SoFi: a large-scale map of this area
looks like a kidnapper's ransom note. In a few years these Downtown
neighborhoods will be so familiar the letters will all be the same size, as are
those in the areas previously written as SoHo (South of Houston) and
TriBeCa (Triangle Below Canal).

The southern part of Downtown is the center of financial New York,
where Wall Street banks keep tabs on the money before the Meatpacking
District soaks it up again in its high-end restaurants and boutiques. The
last chapter in the book highlights New York's Outer Boroughs: Brooklyn,
Queens, Staten Island, and the Bronx.

"The Bronx? No thonx," said poet Ogden Nash. You may be surprised. ❏

PRECEDING PAGES: summertime in Central Park; looking over Midtown Manhattan at night.

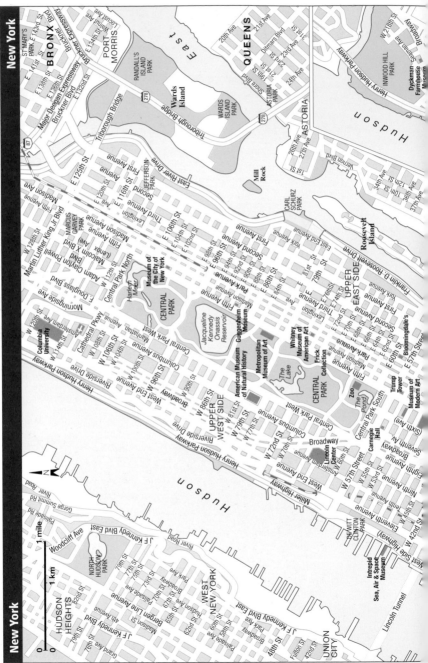

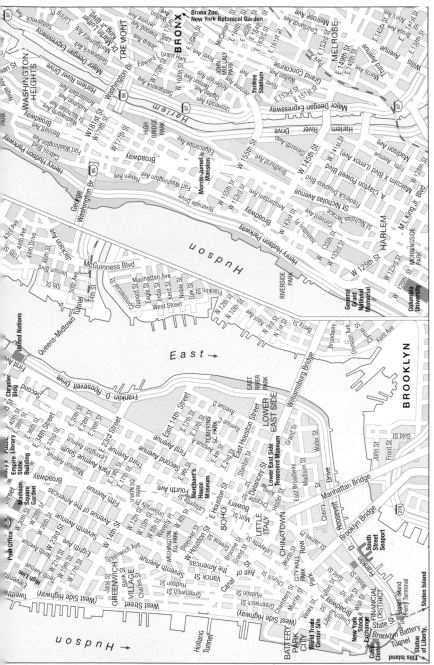

Recommended Restaurants, Bars, & Cafés on pages 80–1

FIFTH AVENUE

Paris has the Champs-Elysées, London has Bond Street, Rome has the Via Veneto, but only New York has Fifth Avenue

There are few streets that evoke the essence of the city as powerfully as Fifth Avenue. It's all here – the audacity of the Empire State Building, the ambition of the Rockefeller Center, and the old-world elegance of the Plaza Hotel.

Fifth Avenue begins at Washington Square, near the crooked streets of Greenwich Village. Rolling up past the Flatiron Building to Madison Square Park – the site of the original Madison Square Garden – the avenue marches past the Empire State Building and the Rockefeller Center, hugs Central Park for 26 scenic blocks, before plunging into "Museum Mile" *(see pages 136–7)*, and some of the city's most important art collections.

Timeline of the city

Continuing past the mansions and embassies of the Upper East Side, Fifth runs a sketchy course through Harlem, bisecting Marcus Garvey Park, before coming to a halt just before the Harlem River. South to north, culturally, socially and economically, few streets in the world can provide a more varied tour of extremes. It's a timeline of the city.

LEFT: looking down Fifth Avenue.
RIGHT: see the view from the 86th and 102nd floors of the Empire State Building.

EMPIRE STATE BUILDING ❶

✉ 350 Fifth Ave (at 33rd and 34th sts), www.empirestatebuilding.com
☎ 212-736 3100 🕒 daily 8am–2am
💲 charge 🚇 34th St/Penn Station

The world's most famous skyscraper rises like a rocket from the corner of 33rd Street. When it was completed in 1931, this was the tallest structure in the world. Presently the city's tallest building, and set to remain so until the Freedom Tower is completed on the site of the World Trade Center – but,

Main attractions
EMPIRE STATE BUILDING
NEW YORK PUBLIC LIBRARY
ROCKEFELLER CENTER
SAKS FIFTH AVENUE
21
ST PATRICK'S CATHEDRAL
TIFFANY & CO.
TRUMP TOWER
GRAND ARMY PLAZA
PLAZA HOTEL
CENTRAL PARK

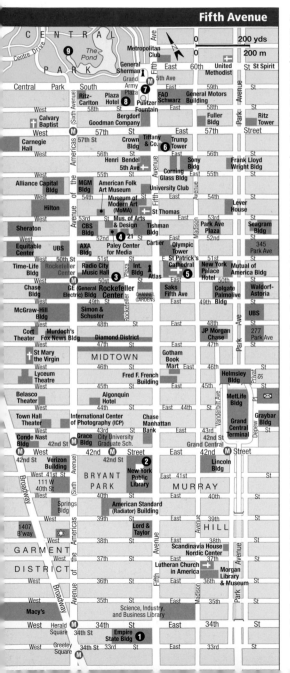

Fifth Avenue

at 1,454ft (443 meters) and with 102 stories, the Empire State now stands in height below buildings in Kuala Lumpur, Taipei, and Chicago's Sears Tower. When it comes to the view, however, the Empire State can't be beaten. On a clear day you can see for as far as 80 miles (130km), while at night, Manhattan spreads out far below, a floating sea of winking, twinkling lights.

The empire strikes back

If you plan to visit during the day, try to get here as early as possible, as the long lines can take something away from the experience. At the concourse level, enter the marble Art Deco lobby, where you are directed to the high-speed elevator that zips straight up to the 86th-floor observation deck. Outside, there are powerful binoculars to peer through, and a couple of souvenir stands in the covered viewing area.

If this is your first visit to New York, it's a good idea to rent the audio tour – an entertaining and informative overview of the city as it spreads out in front of you. Expect a security check on arrival, which involves a lot of waiting around.

Observation deck

For an additional fee, you can ascend to the smaller observatory way up on the 102nd floor, which is just about the spot where in 1933 Fay Wray (and more recently Naomi Watts, in the 2005 remake) made her tearful final farewells to the "tallest, darkest leading man in Hollywood," an ape around 50ft (15 meters) tall by the name of King Kong. Movie posters, photos, and other memorabilia from Wray's private collection are on permanent display in the lobby downstairs.

Kong isn't the only one who met his fate up here. Of the 16 people who have jumped off the building, only two were wearing parachutes,

Recommended Restaurants, Bars, & Cafés on pages 80–1

both of whom were arrested as soon as they landed. On a happier note, 14 lucky couples are given permission to plight their troth at the top of the building every Valentine's Day.

The **New York Skyride** (www.skyride.com; charge), inside the building, offers a simulated flight above the city (this is not recommended for motion-sickness sufferers).

Optimistic design

The Empire State was planned in the optimistic 1920s, but by the time it was completed the United States was in the depths of the Great Depression, and office space was not fetching a premium. In its first year of operation until March 1932, the observation deck took as much as the rent collected on the whole of the rest of the building put together.

The Empire State Building's upper floors are illuminated at night, and special light displays are put on for festivals and holidays, including the Fourth of July, Christmas, and Hanukkah (see the website for a complete schedule).

Illuminated display

The building was first opened on May 1, 1931, with a dazzling display switched on from Washington DC by President Herbert Hoover, and the illuminations have been a feature ever since. The colored floodlights were installed in 1964, and have traditionally signaled events such as Frank Sinatra's 80th birthday; the singer's death was also marked by the crown of the building being bathed in blue light, for Frank's nickname "Ol' Blue Eyes." After the death of *King Kong* actress Fay Wray, the Empire State stood for 15 minutes in complete darkness.

Kong and Fay Wray climb to the 102nd floor in the 1933 movie King Kong.

BELOW: the Empire State Building was completed ahead of schedule.

Empire State Building Timeline

1799 The city of New York sells a tract of land on what is now the Empire State site to a farmer.

1859 John Jacob Astor Jr erects a mansion on the ex-farm site.

1893 Astor's son razes the mansion to build the Waldorf Hotel.

1930 Excavation of the land for a proposed Empire State Building begins on January 22.

1930 Construction begins on March 17. With a peak labor force of 3,000 men, the framework rises at a rate of over 4 stories a week.

1931 On May 1, President Herbert Hoover presses a button in Washington, DC, and officially turns on the lights.

1945 An Army Air Corps B-25 crashes into the building, and 14 people die. The structure of the Empire State remains intact.

1981 The building officially becomes a New York City landmark.

1986 The building officially becomes a National Historic Landmark.

The stone lions in front of the New York Public Library are called Patience and Fortitude.

On Queen Elizabeth II's Golden Jubilee in 2002, the Empire State paid tribute with a display of purple and gold. Mayor Bloomberg said this was also a way of saying thank you for the support Great Britain gave after the September 11, 2001, attacks.

The upper floors of the building are being renovated one at a time, so they might look a little shabby during your visit. All this work should be finished by 2009, when new tourist-friendly 24-hour opening hours will come into effect, along with a much-improved 86th-floor observation area.

Around the Empire State

A few yards north, the less glamorous **Science, Industry, and Business Library** (188 Madison Avenue at 34th Street, tel: 212-592 7000) is a valuable addition to the city's library facilities, with a huge stock of research materials including business and science journals, CD-ROMs, and handbooks for personal or professional study. It's a good place to get online if you've left your laptop behind, with computers for public use.

Five blocks north at Fifth and 39th Street, **Lord & Taylor** is one of New York's best-known department stores; people have been known to line up just to peer into its windows. Lord & Taylor branches in other cities have closed, however, and the future of this flagship store remains uncertain.

New York Public Library ❷

✉ Fifth Ave (at 42nd St), www.nypl.com 📞 212-930 0830 🕒 Mon–Sat 10am–6pm, Tue–Wed until 9pm, Sun 1–5pm 💲 free 🚇 42nd St/Broadway

Directly across the street, in warm weather, office workers and tourists can be found lounging in front of New York's coolest library, under the watchful gaze of two stone lions that flank the marble steps.

Stretching between 40th and 42nd streets, this glorious 1911 Beaux Arts monument is one of the world's finest research facilities, with a vast collection that includes 15 million items and the first book printed in the United States – the *Bay Psalm Book* from 1640 – and the original diaries of Virginia Woolf.

In addition to a fine collection of paintings, which, controversially, the library is in the process of selling off, there is a third space for exhibitions. Topics are varied and have covered everything from Japanese picture books to New York City garbage.

The biggest treasure of all, however, may be the main Reading Room, a vast, gilded gem with windows that overlook **Bryant Park** *(see page 112)*. Ask inside about joining one of the tours of the library; they take place every day but Sunday.

ROCKEFELLER CENTER ③

✉ Fifth Ave (at 47th to 51st sts), www.rockefellercenter.com 📞 212-632 3975 🕐 daily 7am–midnight 💲 Observation Deck; otherwise free 🚇 47th–50th St/Rockefeller Center

At 49th Street, Fifth Avenue lives up to its legend, thanks in large part to the **Rockefeller Center**, one of the world's biggest business and entertainment complexes, and a triumph of Art Deco architecture. The Rockefeller Center has been called a "city within a city," and it's got the numbers to prove it. The center's daily

EAT

Chocolate fans' eyes pop out when they see La Maison du Chocolat, the exquisite French chocolatiers at the foot of the GE Building in Rockefeller Plaza. In the summer months, there's also freshly made ice cream to savor.

LEFT: inside looking out: the Top of the Rock. **BELOW:** Central Park from the Top of the Rock observation deck.

RIGHT: tours of NBC depart every half-hour on weekdays and about every 15 minutes on the weekends.
BELOW: the viewing deck at Top of the Rock.

population (including visitors) is about 240,000, almost the size of a town. It has more than 100,000 telephones, 48,758 windows and nearly 400 elevators.

Add to this a 2-mile (3km) underground concourse, numerous stores and 40 places to eat, four subway lines, a post office, foreign consulates, and airlines, and you've got quite a little metropolis. Indeed, when Rockefeller first envisaged the complex – as a development to house the city's burgeoning TV and radio industry – he called it "Radio City."

The **Channel Gardens** – so named because they separate La Maison Française on the left and the British Building on the right, just as these countries flank the English Channel – draw visitors into the center of the plaza. This is where the famous Christmas tree, lit with countless bulbs, captivates holiday visitors. The *Today* show is broadcast from a glassed-in studio here, too.

Tours of **NBC Studios** (charge) depart every 30 minutes on a weekday, and every 15 minutes at the weekend; tours of the Rockefeller Center (charge) depart hourly (Mon–Sat 11am–5pm, Sun 11am–4pm).

In summer, there are concerts and outdoor movies in the sunken courtyard, while in the winter there's a hugely popular ice-skating rink.

30 Rock

Rockefeller Plaza is dominated by the 70 floors of the soaring 850ft (259-meter) **GE Building**, number 30 Rockefeller Center, or "30 Rock." Formerly known as the RCA Building, it was renamed after the reacquisition by General Electric (GE) of the company, which it had helped to found in 1919. The Rockefeller family retain offices on the 54th and 56th floors.

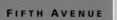

Saturday Night Live

As the headquarters of NBC, the GE building is the home of the comedy show *Saturday Night Live (see page 321)*, and of many of the network's New York facilities. The GE Building was also the setting for a famous photograph taken in 1932 during the construction of the center by Charles C. Ebbets called *Lunchtime atop a Skyscraper*. Sitting astride a steel girder with no harnesses, 11 workers casually lunch and chat, 850ft (260 meters) above the city.

Rockefeller Center's best tourist attraction is the **Top of the Rock** (www.topoftherocknyc.com; daily 8am–midnight; charge). Situated 70 floors above ground, the observation deck offers a different perspective of the city to the Empire State, including terrific sightings of Central Park, and has one major advantage – a clear view of the iconic building itself. The lines for the deck are often shorter, though purists may argue that the experience lacks the class of visiting the Empire State.

Saks, St Pat's, and 21

Back on Fifth Avenue, **Saks Fifth Avenue** (611 Fifth Avenue, tel: 212-753 4000; Mon–Sat 10am–8pm, Sun noon–7pm) is the supremely elegant flagship department store for Saks shops across America, from Dallas to San Diego. There are numerous great shopping opportunities here, including an enormous women's shoe department that has its own zip code, 10022. On the next corner up is the **International Building**, with Lee

Paul Manship's gilded statue called Prometheus Bringing Fire to the World *is the centerpiece of Rockefeller Plaza.*

LEFT: the Rockefeller Center was completed in 1933.
BELOW: skating at the Rockefeller in winter.

Lawrie's monumental bronze figure of Atlas crouching under the weight of the world, over 25ft (8 meters) tall, at its entrance.

Two streets up is another classic dining venue, 21 ❹ (21 West 52 Street, www.21club.com, tel: 212-582 7200; *see page 80*), where every president since FDR has been elegantly entertained. The atmosphere is hushed, the lighting low – and the steak tartare still sets the standard.

St Patrick's Cathedral ❺

✉ Fifth Ave (at 50 and 51st sts), www.saintpatrickscathedral.org
☎ 212-753 2261 Ⓒ daily 6.30am–8.45pm Ⓢ free
Ⓡ 50th St/Rockefeller Center

The site of St Patrick's was purchased in 1810 to build a Jesuit school, and the cornerstone of the church was laid on August 15 – the Feast of the Assumption – 48 years later. Work was suspended during the Civil War, but the first American cardinal, John McCloskey, got construction back underway in 1865, opening the doors in May,

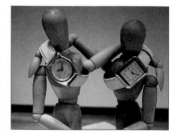

1879. Extensive renovation in 1927–31 included installation of the great organ.

The cathedral is a formidable Midtown landmark, its Gothic facade an intriguing counterpoint to the angular lines and smooth surfaces of the skyscrapers around it. And yet St Pat's is unmistakably New York: where else would one need tickets to attend midnight Mass? Look around the interior, where F. Scott Fitzgerald married his Southern belle, Zelda, before going on to literary fame and domestic hell. Alternatively, take a seat and breathe in the sweet smell of incense – the twinkle of candles and gentle hum of voices makes St Pat's a calm-

ABOVE AND RIGHT: Fifth Avenue shopping.
BELOW LEFT: St Patrick's Cathedral.
BELOW RIGHT: Trump Tower.

ing spot in the middle of the hustle of the city.

Serious shopping

Beyond St Patrick's, Fifth Avenue returns to more worldly concerns, namely, upscale shopping. **Tiffany & Co.** and **Cartier, Gucci,** and **Pucci** are a few that feed into the avenue's élan.

At 57th Street, ladies who lunch totter on stilettos between **Prada, Dior,** and the expensive emporia inside the **Trump Tower** ❻. Now mainly ultra-luxurious condominiums, the tower is worth stopping by for a glimpse of the big-spending opulence synonymous with Manhattan in the 1980s. Viewers of the first series of Donald Trump's TV show *The Apprentice* will recognize its marble atrium and waterfall.

While part of Fifth Avenue has been colonized by chain stores, retail is still a leisurely pursuit at **Henri Bendel** and **Bergdorf Goodman.** Built on the former site of a Cornelius Vanderbilt mansion, Bergdorf is more like a collection of small

boutiques than a department store. Exquisite, and expensive.

Grand Army Plaza ❼ on 59th Street punctuates Fifth Avenue and marks the boundary between Midtown and the Upper East Side. It borders the **Plaza Hotel** ❽ *(see page 298)*, a home-away-from-home for Mark Twain. The Plaza has undergone recent renovation, with some rooms now condominiums or retail spaces. Many have been set aside for visitors, however, and the landmark public rooms remain unaffected.

The views of **Central Park** ❾ *(see photo feature on pages 82–5)* are worth the price of a cocktail in the Plaza's wood-paneled **Oak Bar.** ❑

The perfect place for breakfast.

BELOW: upscale shopping on 57th Street.

BEST RESTAURANTS, BARS, AND CAFÉS

Restaurants

Prices for a three-course dinner per person with half a bottle of wine:

$ = under $20
$$ = $20–$45
$$$ = $45–$60
$$$$ = over $60

21

✉ 21 W. 52nd St (at 5th and 6th aves) ☎ 212-582 7200 ☕ L & D Mon–Fri, D only Sat **$$$$** [p337, D1]
This ex-speakeasy will never be out of style with Manhattan's movers and shakers. Miniature jockeys line the exterior, while other corporate toys hang from the ceiling. A plaque over Table 30 reads "Bogie's Corner." Sip his favorite tipple, Ramos gin fizz, and order the chicken hash.

Adour Alain Ducasse at the St Regis

✉ 2 E. 55th St (at 5th and Madison aves) ☎ 212-753 4500 ☕ D daily **$$$$** [p337, D1]
A match made in cuisine heaven: the five-star hotel marries the five-star French chef at prices to match.

Aquavit

✉ 65 E. 55th St (at Park and Madison aves) ☎ 212-307 7311 ☕ L & D Mon–Sat, Br & D Sun **$$$** [p337, E1]
Savor the sublime Scandinavian cuisine of Marcus Samuelsson, and wonder why you hadn't before.

Bice

✉ 7 E. 54th St (at 5th and Madison aves) ☎ 212-688

1999 ☕ L & D daily **$$$** [p337, D1]
Northern Italian cuisine, served in a very elegant, spacious dining room. It's pretty pricey, but apparently not so much for the high-end Euro and business crowd that frequents the restaurant.

La Bonne Soupe

✉ 48 W. 55th St (at 5th and 6th aves) ☎ 212-586 7650 ☕ L & D daily **$$** [p337, D1]
An old standby that serves up lots more than just soup – try the crepes and the quiche too. Hands down, the best vinaigrette salad dressing anywhere.

Burger Heaven

✉ 20 E. 49th St (at 5th and Madison aves) ☎ 212-755 2166 ☕ B, L, & D Mon–Sat, Br & L Sun **$$** [p337, D2]
Midtown workers are willing to put up with the hellish noontime crush at this burger joint, which has a long, diner-style menu with plenty of options.

DB Bistro Moderne

✉ 55 W. 44th St (at 5th and 6th aves) ☎ 212-391 2400 ☕ B & D daily, L Mon–Sat **$$$$** [p337, D2]
A sleek new take on the bistro concept. Chef

Daniel Boulud's power-lunch spot is awash in culinary surprises and Art Deco glitz, with a clientele to match.

La Grenouille

✉ 3 E. 52nd St (at 5th and Madison aves) ☎ 212-752 1495) ☕ L & D Tue–Sat, D only Mon **$$$$** [p337, D1]
The last of the great French Midtown establishments, where a quenelle is still a quenelle and the flowers are rarely more beautiful. A classic.

Hale & Hearty Soups

✉ 55 W. 56th St (at 5th and 6th aves) ☎ 212-245 9200; ✉ 22 E. 47th St (at 5th and Mad) ☎ 212-557 1900 ☕ L Mon–Sat **$** [p337, D1]
A chain of good, reliable eateries with a long, frequently changing menu.

Harry Cipriani

✉ The Sherry-Netherland Hotel, 781 5th Ave (at 59th and 60th sts) ☎ 212-753 5566 ☕ Br, L, & D daily **$$$$** [p334, C4]
Posh branch of the famed Venice home of the bellini; high-fashion types always welcome.

Katsuhama

✉ 11 E. 47th St (at 5th and Madison aves) ☎ 212-758 5909 ☕ L & D daily **$$** [p337, D2]

LEFT: DB Bistro Moderne.
RIGHT: plates await the night's delights.

No frills here, but an affordable Japanese spot that specializes in *katsu* (Japanese cutlets).

Keen's Steakhouse
✉ 72 W. 36th St (at 5th and 6th aves) ☎ 212-947 3636 ⏰ L & D Mon–Fri, D only Sat–Sun **$$$** [p336, C3]
A classic steakhouse dating back to 1885, a stone's throw from the Empire State Building.

Mangia
✉ 50 W. 57th St (at 5th and 6th aves) ☎ 212-582 5554 ⏰ Br, L, & D Mon–Sat **$** [p334, B4]
Follow the office workers and dine on tasty Mediterranean fare and sandwiches at this noisy, crowded eatery on busy 57th Street.

Michael's
✉ 24 W. 55nd St (at 5th and 6th aves) ☎ 212-757 0555 ⏰ B, L, & D Mon–Fri, D only Sat **$$$** [p334, B4]
Media and publishing movers and shakers sign deals here; it's open for power breakfasts, too.

Prime Burger
✉ 5 E. 51st St (at 5th and Madison aves) ☎ 212-759 4729 ⏰ Br, L, & D Mon–Sat **$** [p337, D1]
This old-school diner-style lunch spot has chairs with individual built-in, tray-style tables. The location is convenient, and the flame-broiled burgers are tasty, but mostly it's just fun to dine in such a nostalgic setting.

Quality Meats
✉ 57 W. 58th St (at 5th and 6th aves) ☎ 212-371 7777 ⏰ D daily **$$$** [p334, B4]
The name of the place really means something here, at a tiptop, high-style New American steakhouse.

Rock Center Café
✉ 20 W. 50th St (at 5th Ave and Rockefeller Pl) ☎ 212-332 7620 ⏰ B, L, & D daily; **The Sea Grill** ✉ 19 W. 49th St (at 5th and 6th aves) ☎ 212-332 7610 ⏰ L & D daily **$$$** [p337, D1]
Two places at the Rockefeller Center, with views of skaters or fun-seekers. The first has a good but general menu; the second has excellent fish.

Sarabeth's
✉ 40 Central Park S. (at 5th and 6th aves) ☎ 212-826 5959 ⏰ B, L & D daily **$$** [p334, B4]
A fancy address for the homey NYC-only chain (Upper East- and Upper Westside locations) making excellent baked goods, preserves, soups, and casual food. Best for breakfast, brunch, or lunch.

'Wichcraft
✉ 555 5th Ave (at 46th St) ☎ 212-780 0577 ⏰ Br & L Mon–Fri **$** [p337, D2]
This sandwich-and-panini shop is a little more expensive than your average deli, but it's also the most casual outpost of Tom Colicchio's restaurant empire.

Bars and Cafés

Cosi Sandwich Bar, 38 E. 45th St (at 5th and Madison aves). Excellent joints offering freshly baked Italian flatbread sandwiches, with many other locations to choose from.

King Cole Bar, 2 E. 55th St. Sipping a drink with the gorgeous Maxfield Parrish mural at the St Regis Hotel as a backdrop can't be beaten. Tea, coffee, and snacks, too.

Morrell Wine Bar & Café, 1 Rockefeller Plaza. A noisy, fun crowd spills out onto a sidewalk café in summer, and in winter there's a great view of the Christmas tree.

Oak Bar at The Plaza, 5th Ave at 59th St, is one of the most elegant of the historic hotel bars, with sumptuous wood paneling, gleaming chandeliers, and a lovely view of Central Park.

Rainbow Grill, 30 Rockefeller Plaza. Food is served here, too, but you only need to order a drink to enjoy an incomparable sunset view over the city.

The Soup Man, E. 42nd St just east of 5th Ave. Slurp on "the soup that made *Seinfeld* famous," according to the shop sign. Fans of the TV show will recall the "soup Nazi."

CENTRAL PARK

Stretching from Grand Army Plaza to Harlem, Central Park is the playground and meeting place of the metropolis

Central Park is a recreational and cultural space, as well as an oxygenating green area in the middle of this crowded, towering city. Frederick Law Olmsted and Calvert Vaux designed the 843-acre (340-hectare) park in 1858. Olmsted's aim was, in his words, to "supply hundreds of thousands of tired workers who have no opportunity to spend summers in the country with a specimen of God's handiwork." The project was known as "Greensward."

In summertime, the New York Public Theater stages *Shakespeare in the Park* at the Delacorte Theater. The New York Philharmonic and the New York Opera give outdoor performances on the Great Lawn, and the musical *Summerstage* brings contemporary acts to an open-air venue at Rumsey Playfield for free concerts. In wintertime, the Wollman Rink provides classes and a picturesque venue for ice skating.

For details, visit www.centralpark.org.

ABOVE: taking a boat on the lake affords serene views of the Majestic apartment building's post-Art Deco twin towers, which stand by the darker, Gothic-style gables of the famous Dakota building. It also provides an afternoon's gentle exercise; rent boats from the Loeb Boathouse, near East 75th Street.

BELOW: by West 72nd Street, across the street from John Lennon's former New York home in the Dakota building, is "Strawberry Fields." This little area is adorned with flowers most of the time, but especially on his birthday, October 9, and the anniversary of his senseless murder, December 8.

ABOVE: Bethesda Fountain was designed with a surrounding terrace to be the park's architectural centerpiece. Along with wonderful views of the lake, the fountain is a perfect spot for romantic meetings.

RIGHT: The Boathouse is a lakeside restaurant with an outdoor grill and an espresso café. Sheep Meadow Café and Ferrara Café are also great spots for refreshment.

LEFT: Hans Christian Andersen takes a seat and prepares to tell a story. Among the statues to delight the kiddies are Mother Goose, Humpty Dumpty, Little Jack Horner, and Little Bo Peep.

Central Park

0 — 500 yds
0 — 500 m

Central Park North
110th St
Central Park North · Duke Ellington
Harlem Meer

East 110th St
Museum for African Art

W. 106th St
West Drive
East Drive

East 107th St
East 106th St

W. 104th St
103rd St
The Loch
Conservatory Garden ★

El Museo del Barrio
East 104th St
Museum of the City of New York

W. 100th St
The Pool
NORTH MEADOW

East 101st St

Recreation House
EAST MEADOW
East 98th St

96th St
W. 96th St
Transverse Rd No 4

East 96th St

C E N T R A L

W. 94th St
South Meadow Tennis Courts
East 94th St

W. 92nd St
Jewish Museum

W. 90th St
Jacqueline Kennedy Onassis Reservoir
Cooper-Hewitt National Design Museum
East 90th St
National Academy Museum

W. 88th St
Guggenheim Museum

86th St
W. 86th St
Transverse Rd No 3
East 86th St
Neue Galerie

W. 84th St
P A R K
East 84th St

GREAT LAWN
Cleopatra's Needle
Metropolitan Museum of Art

W. 82nd St
81st St
W. 81st St
Delacorte Theater
Shakespeare Garden ★
Turtle Pond
Belvedere Castle
Transverse Rd No 2

East 82nd St
East 81st St
American-Irish Historical Society

American Museum of Natural History

W. 77th St
THE RAMBLE
Loeb Boathouse/ The Boathouse Restaurant
East 79th St
Whitney Museum
East 77th St

Alice in Wonderland

W. 74th St
The Lake
Conservatory Water
Hans Christian Andersen
East 74th St

72nd St
W. 72nd Street
Strawberry Fields ★
Bethesda Fountain
East 72nd St
Frick Collection
East 70th St

W. 70th St

W. 68th St
SHEEP MEADOW
The Mall
EAST GREEN

Tisch (Children's) Zoo
East 65th St

Transverse Rd No 1
W. 64th St
The Dairy
Carousel ★
Central Park Zoo
Arsenal Parks HQ

59th St Columbus Circle
Broadway
Wollman Rink
The Pond
Grand Army Plaza
East 62nd St

West 60th St
Maine
Columbus Circle
Central Park South
5th Ave
East 60th St
East 59th St

ABOVE: classic horse-drawn carriages line up along Central Park South between Fifth and Sixth avenues. The vintage buggy rides are available all year round.

CENTRAL PARK ZOO

Central Park Zoo has many exotic creatures in different habitats. The Polar Zone is home to two polar bears, harbor seals, and tufted puffins. The Tropical Zone houses tropical birds as well as lemurs, tamarin monkeys, and innumerable frogs, lizards, snakes, and toads. The Temperate Territory is where California red pandas, Japanese macaques, North American river otters, and mandarin ducks live. Although the present zoo dates only from 1988, the first menagerie was established in 1864. Seventy years later, a "storybook" zoo was created by the Depression-era Works Progress Administration.

LEFT: some of the zoo's ticket receipts are used to fund the Wildlife Conservation Society's international activities.

ABOVE: facilities in Central Park include the Wollman Rink, 30 tennis courts, 26 baseball diamonds, 21 playgrounds, and miles of paths and jogging tracks.

ABOVE AND RIGHT: the charming gingerbread cottages of Old Dairy Milkhouse were built in 1870, as a milking parlor. The dairy now operates as the park's visitor center, offering guides and park information, in addition to providing a station for the park's rangers. Open Tuesday through Sunday 10am–5pm.

ABOVE: this little family of life-sized bronze bears are at the entrance to the Pat Hoffman Friedman Playground, on the east side of the park near the Metropolitan Museum.

ABOVE: the Henry Luce Nature Observatory is housed in Belvedere Castle, which was designed by the park's architect, Frederick Law Olmsted, and constructed in 1872.

TOP RIGHT: the *Maine* monument at Columbus Circle commemorates the US battleship blown up in Havana Harbor in 1898.

RIGHT: on the path to the pond, this bronze bust of Thomas Moore was sculpted in 1879.

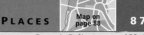

Recommended Restaurants, Bars, & Cafés on pages 100–1

MIDTOWN EAST

The Chrysler Building, Grand Central Terminal, the Waldorf-Astoria, the Chrysler Building, and the United Nations are all here. Midtown East is quintessential New York

Midtown East covers many of the images Manhattan conjures up when people think of New York. This is where the city's corporate heart beats loudest, where power-lunching, power-shopping and sidewalk power-phoning is a daily way of life.

Like its counterpart to the west, Midtown East begins above 34th Street, and rises to a bustling climax between 42nd Street and the Queensboro (59th Street) Bridge, beyond which lies the calmer Upper East Side. Stretching east of Fifth Avenue to the East River, it's a compact, energetic microcosm of Manhattan, encompassing steel-and-glass office towers, historic hotels, familiar landmarks like the Chrysler Building, Grand Central Terminal and the United Nations, and some very exclusive neighborhoods.

HILLS AND BAYS

Along 35th Street is the southern border of **Murray Hill ❶**, a classy residential area in the shadow of sleek Midtown office buildings, its cross-streets lined by brownstone relics of a more genteel era. A plaque on the

south side of 35th Street and Park Avenue marks the center of an 18th-century farm owned by Robert Murray, "whose wife, Mary Lindley Murray (1726–82), rendered signal service in the Revolutionary War." It was said she cleverly delayed a British advance by inviting the officers to tea, but later, doubt was cast on this story. Close by, on Madison Avenue, the lovely **Church of the Incarnation**, built in 1864, has beautiful stained-glass windows by Tiffany, LaFarge, and Burne-Jones, among others.

Main attractions
MURRAY HILL
MORGAN LIBRARY & MUSEUM
MADISON AVENUE
GRAND CENTRAL TERMINAL
CHRYSLER BUILDING
UNITED NATIONS
SUTTON PLACE
CENTRAL SYNAGOGUE
WALDORF-ASTORIA
ST BARTHOLOMEW'S CHURCH
FOUR SEASONS
SEAGRAM BUILDING
SONY BUILDING

LEFT: symbol of a dazzling future, the Chrysler Building's dazzling spire.
RIGHT: the streets of Murray Hill are lined with elegant brownstones.

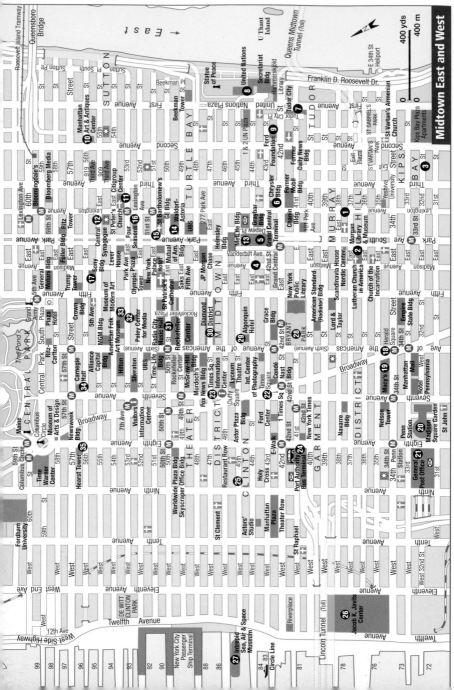

Midtown East and West

400 yds

400 m

Morgan Library & Museum ❷

✉ 225 Madison Ave (at 36th St), www.themorgan.org ☎ 212-685 0008 ⏱ Tue–Thur 10.30am–5pm, Fri 10.30am–9pm, Sat 10am–6pm, Sun 11am–6pm ⓢ charge (free Fri 7–9pm) 🚇 33rd St

Also called the Pierpont Morgan Library, this private collection was opened to the public by J.P. Morgan Jr in 1924. It was amassed by his father, Pierpont Morgan, the most powerful banker of his time and an avid collector whose interests ranged from Egyptian to Renaissance art and Chinese porcelain.

The Morgan has been comprehensively renovated and given a new "campus" by brilliant Italian architect Renzo Piano, which integrates with the original historic buildings while doubling the exhibition space. There are artistic, literary, musical, and historical works, including drawings by Rembrandt and Rubens and original scores from Mozart and Beethoven. The history of writing and printing was one of Morgan's

passions, so the library is strong in this area, with 5,000-year-old carved tablets, three Gutenberg Bibles and manuscripts by Charles Dickens, Mark Twain, and other writers.

The new building on Madison Avenue is "crowned" by a beautiful, naturally lit Reading Room, with excellent facilities for 21st-century researchers. You can see the original pillared entrance on 36th Street.

Sniffin Court

From the Morgan, walk east across Park and Lexington avenues, to reach one of the city's tiniest and most charming historic districts. Behind iron gates and opposite a Yeshiva University building, the red-

KIDS

The Morgan Library has the original manuscript of Charles Dickens's *A Christmas Carol*. On the first Sunday in December each year the library hosts an all-day celebration of the book, with family activities that include storytelling, readings, and dancing.

LEFT: the Morgan has an extension designed by Renzo Piano.
BELOW LEFT: the East Room of the Morgan.
BELOW RIGHT: the West Room, with a portrait of J.P. Morgan.

Grand Central has become a destination for food as well as for taking the train. Besides upscale places like the Oyster Bar and the Campbell Apartment cocktail lounge, there's a food court with lots of kinds of cuisine, like Mexican, Indian, and New York deli, and a market that sells fresh gourmet produce.

BELOW: eat heartily at Michael Jordan's The Steak House.

brick row houses of **Sniffen Court** were constructed in Romanesque Revival style at the time of the American Civil War, and were originally stables for Murray Hill's grander residences (now, of course, very expensive and highly desirable real estate). If you peer through the gates you can make out the horse-relief on the back wall that marks out the former studio of sculptor Malvina Hoffman.

East of Murray Hill, **Kips Bay ③** is a quiet, mainly residential area of apartment buildings, medical offices affiliated to **New York University Medical Center** and local restaurants. There's not much to see here, but it makes an engaging change from the busy Midtown district around Park Avenue.

The area is named for Jacob Kip, a Dutch settler whose farm overlooked a bay, long since filled-in, at the present intersection of Second Avenue and 35th Street. Nearby **St Vartan's Armenian Church** (34th and Second) was modeled on a 5th-century house of Armenian worship. It has a small collection of Armenian antiquities.

AROUND GRAND CENTRAL

Along the west side of Murray Hill is **Madison Avenue ④**. Historically, this has been the spiritual home of the advertising industry, especially the blocks between 42nd and 57th streets. Madison Avenue is one of the city's commercial nerves, where sharp-suited men and women buy their clothes at Brooks Brothers on 44th Street and stop off for cocktails at the Yale Club one block east on Vanderbilt, before running to catch their trains home to leafy suburbs.

Grand Central Terminal ⑤

✉ 42nd St and Lexington Ave, www.grandcentralterminal.com
📞 212-340 2583 🕐 daily 5.30am–1.30am 🚇 42nd St/Grand Central

Recommended Restaurants, Bars, & Cafés on pages 100–1

Often incorrectly referred to as "Grand Central Station," the terminal greeted 150,000 people when it opened at 12.01 on the first Sunday in February, 1913. Today, 750,000 people cross the concourse of the opulent building every day.

Grand Central has bars, a food court, excellent restaurants, shops, and a branch of the New York Transit Museum to entertain those waiting for a train, as well as the iconic clock as a memorable meeting point.

With entrances at Vanderbilt and 42nd Street, and at Park and Lexington avenues, Grand Central is the hub for Metro-North commuter lines reaching deep into the suburbs of Westchester County and neighboring Connecticut. More than 550 trains depart from here. Grand Central was saved from demolition by the Landmarks Preservation Commission, and so this 1913 Beaux Arts reminder of days when travel was a gracious experience remains almost intact.

Vaulted ceilings

It's also undergone a $200 million restoration to return it to its former glory. Advertising signs were removed, new restaurants and stores opened, including an indoor food hall for last-minute purchases, and the glorious illuminated zodiac on the vaulted ceiling of the main concourse – one of the world's largest spaces – gleams like new.

All apart, that is, from a dark patch above Michael Jordan's The Steak House. This was left untouched, to give an understanding of the extent of the restoration effort.

The demolition of Penn Station in 1963 sparked a modern preservation movement. New Yorkers were determined that the decorative features of Grand Central would escape a similar fate.

LEFT: the four clock faces are made of opal. **BELOW:** the Grand Concourse of Grand Central Terminal.

Looking up in Grand Central.

The magnificent astronomical zodiac ceiling was commissioned by the Vanderbilt family from French artist Paul César Helleu in 1912. The constellations were painted back to front, and the Vanderbilts hastily improvised the explanation that it represents a "God's-eye view."

The four faces of the clock over the information desks are made from opal; the clock has a value estimated by Sotheby's and Christie's at between $10 and $20 million. The flag commemorates the terrorist attacks of September 11, 2001.

Grand tours

Grand Central must be one of few commuter hubs that's a tourist destination, too, and you can spot the out-of-towners pretty easily – they're the ones looking up. Tours are given every Wednesday at 12.30pm (for details, check the website or tel: 212-935 3960; suggested donation), and more extensive tours can be booked online or by phone (tel: 212-340 2345; charge). Before leaving, be sure to see the **Oyster Bar** on the

RIGHT: one of many places to stop for a bite at Grand Central.
BELOW: the terminal gears up for Christmas.

lower level, an architectural and culinary landmark.

Chrysler Building ❻

✉ 42nd St and Lexington Ave
🚇 42nd St/Grand Central

One block east on Lexington Avenue, the famed Chrysler Building is one of the jewels of the Manhattan skyline. Erected by William Van Alen for auto tsar Walter Chrysler in 1930, its Art Deco spire rises 1,046ft (319 meters) into the city air like a stainless-steel rocket ship powered by gargoyles.

The building was designated a New York City landmark on September 12, 1979. Three years later,

the stainless-steel arches and triangular windows were illuminated by bright white lights for the first time. This glorious lighting scheme was specified in Van Alen's original plan, but it took the city more than 50 years to implement the scheme.

The Chrysler Building is not open to the public, but visitors are allowed into the lobby. The steel-clad street-level facade is worth seeing up close, while the tower provides classic Manhattan views from any approach in the city.

TOWARD THE UNITED NATIONS AND THE EAST RIVER

Continuing east on 42nd Street, walk on past the crowds and the **Grand Hyatt Hotel** (which adjoins Grand Central, and was built over the old Commodore Hotel), to the former *Daily News* building, between Third and Second avenues. This Art Deco structure, though no longer home to the newspaper, looks so much like the headquarters of the fictional *Daily Planet* that they used it in the *Superman* movies. Check out the gigantic globe in the lobby before continuing

east toward First Avenue, past the steps leading up to **Tudor City** ⑦, a private compound of Gothic brick high-rises that is positioned at a different street level, and has its own tiny park and play area. The development dates from the 1920s, and was designed to attract middle-class buyers out of the suburbs and back into the city. At the time, land along the East River was filled with slums and slaughterhouses, one reason why all

BELOW: the Chrysler Building's soaring tower is a landmark in the real New York and in Batman's home, Gotham City.

Building the Chrysler

In a fantastically theatrical gesture, all seven stories of the steel-clad pinnacle were assembled inside the building, then hoisted into place in an hour and a half. Walter Chrysler's automobile business provided inspiration for much of the spectacular detail, but Van Alen may have regretted his choice of client, since his fee was never paid. The Chrysler was the first building to reach above 1,000ft (305 meters), and was the tallest in the world, until the Empire State Building snatched that title the following year.

Stop in to admire the marble, bronze, and hardwoods in the lobby, quietly busy with office workers and delivery men, but enhanced by epic murals on urban transportation and human endeavor.

The UN flags along First Avenue are those of its member nations. In alphabetical order, the first flag is Afghanistan (48th Street), while the last flag is Zimbabwe (42nd Street).

the windows face west, toward the Hudson River.

United Nations ❽

✉ First Ave and 46th St,
www.un.org/tours 📞 212-963 8687
🕐 tours Mon–Fri 9.45am–4.45pm
Ⓢ charge 🚇 42nd St/Grand Central

RIGHT: Tudor City.
BELOW: tourists on UN Way.

The busy flag-lined entrance of the United Nations is opposite 46th Street. Once inside, the gentle patter of strange languages reminds you that you are now in international territory. Guided tours depart every 30 minutes from the lobby. Apart from an occasional exhibition in the lobby, there's not a lot to see unless you take the tour, but don't miss the Chagall stained-glass windows or the lower-level gift shop, which sells inexpensive handicrafts from all over the world.

On weekdays, the inexpensive Delegates' Dining Room is often open to the public for lunch: jackets are required for men, and reservations must be made a day in advance (tel: 212-963 7625). The view of the river is almost as interesting as the multilingual eavesdropping.

Historic districts

Back on 42nd Street, the lobby garden of the **Ford Foundation** ❾ – glass-enclosed, all lush trees and flowers – is considered one of the city's most beautiful institutional environments. The building's interior offices look over the small oasis, a clever utilization of a usually uninspiring space. This part of town is also home to three of the city's classiest addresses.

The United Nations

The name "United Nations" was devised by United States president Franklin D. Roosevelt, and was first used in the "Declaration by the United Nations" of January 1, 1942, during World War II, when representatives of 26 nations pledged their governments to continue fighting the war in Europe and Asia together. The UN charter was drawn up in 1945, at a conference in San Francisco and signed by delegates from 50 countries; in the new millennium, membership had risen to over 190 countries.

Just like a foreign embassy, the United Nations' grounds, which cover 18 acres (7 hectares) of land along the East River, are not considered a part of the United States, and are outside the jurisdiction of city, state and federal laws. The UN maintains its own independent police force, fire department, and post office. Tours last about 45 minutes, and are available in over 20 languages.

Recommended Restaurants, Bars, & Cafés on pages 100–1

Turtle Bay, once home to privacy-loving celebrities such as Katharine Hepburn, the conductor Leopold Stokowsky, and author Kurt Vonnegut, is a historic district between 48th and 49th streets where 19th-century brownstones share a garden hidden from the public.

Beekman Place, between First Avenue and the East River, is a two-block enclave of elegant townhouses and apartments set along the river. One of its houses was once the home of famed songwriter Irving Berlin.

Sutton Place is an oft-used synonym for luxury, in books and movies. Starting above 54th Street and stretching north for five blocks,

its high-rises are filled with dowagers and poodles. Visual relief is provided by a few still-surviving cul-de-sacs of townhouses, gardens, and promontories offering tantalizing views of the East River.

Nearby is a retail opportunity, the eclectic **Manhattan Art and Antiques Center ❿** on Second Avenue between 55th and 56th streets. It's a strange cross between a museum of curios and a shopping arcade. Over 100 small stores are housed here in glass-fronted rooms, selling everything from antique clocks and furniture to carved tusks. It's really a place to wander around rather than to shop, unless you have a big budget and an even bigger suitcase. On the lower level, you'll find that increasingly rare big-city amenity, public restrooms.

On the way back toward Midtown, another interesting place to call is the **Citigroup Center ⓫**, on 54th Street between Third and Lexington avenues. Its slanted roof makes this a skyline standout, while the indoor atrium lined by shops and cafés makes a pleasant stopping place. Before exiting onto Lexington Avenue, drop by

Stained-glass window by Chagall in the UN building.

LEFT: the Delegates' Dining Room has a view of the East River.
BELOW: Le Corbusier designed the UN's Secretariat building. It opened in 1952.

The globe in the lobby of the former Daily News *building featured in the* Superman *movies; these real-life premises were the offices of Clark Kent's paper, the* Daily Planet.

St Peter's Church, a modern, angular building, which includes a light and airy chapel. St Peter's is respected for its weekly jazz eucharists; it also has frequent concerts.

The **York Theater**, where plays by authors both known and unknown are presented, is on the church's lower level, and operates a program of community-focused events, such as afternoon films for the elderly.

Walking north, note the landmark **Central Synagogue** ⑫, at the corner of 55th Street. Built in 1872, it adds a note of exotic, Moorish-style grace to an otherwise ordinary block. The synagogue was rebuilt and reopened in September 2001, after being severely damaged by a fire.

Boutiques and galleries

There are boutiques and galleries in both directions on **57th Street**, where the prices on both clothes and paintings get more expensive the closer you walk to Fifth Avenue. Toward Third, expensive gadgets galore are on sale at **Hammacher Schlemmer**, while continuing west on 57th you'll find such fashion

fortresses as Turnbull & Asser, Chanel, Hermès, and Burberry.

Along the way to these stores, be sure to notice the **Fuller Building** (41 East 57th Street, at Madison Avenue), which was built in 1929. There's a handbag store at street level, but the building's (separate) main entrance is embellished by a city skyline motif.

The lobby is another glorious example of Art Deco splendor. The floor mosaics depict the Fuller company's original headquarters when it was located in the Flatiron Building. The Fuller's midsection is home to numerous art galleries; the frequent exhibitions are open to the public. A directory is available from reception.

Recommended Restaurants, Bars, & Cafés on pages 100–1

ABOVE GRAND CENTRAL

The view down Park Avenue stops abruptly at the **MetLife Building** ⓭ (originally known as the Pan-Am Building), which was plonked on top of Grand Central Terminal in the early 1960s. Fortunately, beyond it this part of the avenue still retains some of its original glamour.

The **Waldorf-Astoria** ⓮, between 49th and 50th *(see page 300)*, is one of the city's grand hotels, and has attracted guests of the royal and presidential variety ever since it opened on this site in 1931. The Duke and Duchess of Windsor and Cole Porter were only some of the "permanent residents" who lived in the hotel's exclusive towers. The original Waldorf-Astoria on Fifth Avenue, which had brought a new level of luxury to New York's hotel world in the 1890s, had been torn down to make way for the Empire State Building. The hotel retains its air of opulent exclusivity, and the high-ceilinged reception area is populated by wealthy guests lounging in overstuffed armchairs.

The domed **St Bartholomew's Church** ⓯ opened its doors on Park Avenue and 50th Street in 1919, and is a fine example of neo-Byzantine architecture. The church has an evocative program of lighting that changes depending on the religious calendar, meaning that a visit around Christmas will reveal a bright, well-lit interior, while during Lent the church is shrouded in darkness.

One block west, on Madison, the fancy **New York Palace Hotel** *(see page 298)* incorporates as part of its public rooms two of the **Villard Houses**, 19th-century mansions once used as offices by the Archdiocese of New York. Built in 1884 by the architectural firm McKim, Mead, &

The MetLife Building was constructed in 1963, 50 years later than Grand Central, seen in the foreground.

LEFT: the Waldorf's Oscar's Restaurant.
BELOW: Central Synagogue.

White, these half-dozen houses were designed to look like one large Italian palazzo. The owner was the journalist and railway magnate Henry Villard, for whom the houses are named.

Almost 100 years later, when two of the mansions were sold to provide a lavish interior for the Palace, New York historians took exception to the sale. Today, the hotel serves afternoon tea beneath a vaulted ceiling designed by Stanford White.

TIP

There's a feast for the eyes as well as the palate at the fabulous Four Seasons restaurant. The most famous piece is the Picasso tapestry, but other artists have included Miró, Jackson Pollock, and Roy Lichtenstein.

RIGHT: old vs new.
BELOW LEFT: P.J. Clarke's burger bar.
BELOW RIGHT: visit the Sony Wonder Lab for tech toys.

Picasso for a season

There are lines of limos waiting in front of the **Four Seasons ⑯**, on East 52nd Street between Park and Lexington *(see page 100)*, a restaurant so important that its interior has been declared a historic landmark. Picasso's 22ft (6.7-meter) painted curtain from a 1920 Diaghilev ballet, *Le Tricorne*, hangs inside, and luminaries from the worlds of politics and publishing do likewise.

The restaurant is within the distinctive **Seagram Building**. The tycoon Samuel Bronfman, head of Seagram Distillers, had planned to

erect an ordinary office block until his architect daughter introduced him to Mies van der Rohe. The result is one of the most emblematic and influential Modernist constructions of the 1950s.

In the 1980s, some of New York's biggest corporations created public spaces, and contributed significantly to the quality of crowded Midtown life. One of the first was tiny little **Paley Park**, on East 53rd Street between Madison and Fifth avenues, built on the site where the glamorous Stork Club once resided. Slightly raised above street level, the park is

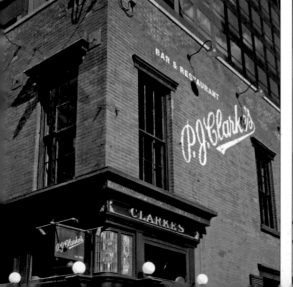

Recommended Restaurants, Bars, & Cafés on pages 100–1

an excellent place to stop off and rest from the outside world. Tables and chairs provide ample seating space, and a water feature provides a calming background noise.

Tech wonders

A short walk away, Philip Johnson's mammoth **Sony Building** (originally built for AT&T), on Madison Avenue between 55th and 56th streets, includes a public arcade squeezed between shops displaying the latest Sony equipment. Drop into the **Sony Wonder Technology Lab** for interactive exhibits and demonstrations of how all this stuff works (tel: 212-833 8100; closed Mon).

At 56th Street and Madison is the former **IBM Building**, a sharply angled tower designed in 1983 by Bauhaus-inspired architect Edward Larrabee Barnes. Its entrance is set back away from the street in a hollowed, cut-out part of the building, the empty space seeming to defy the rest of the structure's enormous height and massive weight. The underground concourse often hosts exhibitions of interest to the public.

Alternatively, head for the atrium, previously a bamboo-filled garden but now stripped of much of its greenery to make way for extra seating or artistic and contemplative sculpture. There's casual dining on the mezzanine, where you can kick back and relax before heading back into the adrenaline-pumping Midtown madness outside. ❑

DRINK

Mixological lore has it that the Bloody Mary was invented at the King Cole Bar in the St Regis Hotel on E. 55th and Madison. We think it originated at Harry's Bar in Paris, but this is still a peach of a place, with a Maxfield Parrish mural, killer cocktails, and lighting that continues to flatter after too many drinks.

LEFT: Manhattan's in the bag.
BELOW: in the production studio at Sony Wonder Technology Lab.

BEST RESTAURANTS, BARS, AND CAFÉS

Restaurants

Prices for a three-course dinner per person with half a bottle of wine:
$ = under $20
$$ = $20–$45
$$$ = $45–$60
$$$$ = over $60

66 Asia de Cuba

⊠ Morgans Hotel, 237 Madison Ave (between 37th and 38th sts) 📞 212-726 7755 Ⓒ L & D Mon–Fri, D only Sat & Sun **$$$** [p337, D3]
A gorgeous room designed by Philippe Starck that attracts pretty people and serves a very fancy form of Asian-Latin fusion cuisine to its devotees.

Avra Estiatorio

⊠ 141 E. 48th St (at Lexington and 3rd aves) 📞 212-759 8550 Ⓒ L & D Mon–Fri, Br & D Sat–Sun **$$$** [p337, E2]
This Greek expense-account fave is especially nice in summer, when you can eat on the terrace. Choose grilled fish, a fresh salad, or platters of Mediterranean dips.

BLT Steak

⊠ 106 E. 57th St (at Park and Lexington aves) 📞 212-752 7470 Ⓒ L & D Mon–Fri, D only Sat **$$$$** [p337, E1]
Chef Laurent Tourondel's flagship (others include BLT Fish, BLT Prime) is a luxury steakhouse that's high on posh style, for when the urge to splurge for fine food hits.

Café Centro

⊠ MetLife Bldg, 200 Park Ave (between 45th St and Vanderbilt Ave) 📞 212-818 1222 Ⓒ Br, L & D Mon–Fri, D only Sat **$$** [p337, D2]
Attracts a busy office lunch crowd near Grand Central, but it's great for a light dinner and drinks.

Caffé Linda

⊠ 145 E. 49th St (at Lexington and 3rd aves) 📞 646-497 1818 Ⓒ L & D Mon–Sat, D Sun **$$** [p337, E2]
This cozy little Italian spot may rely on rustic charm, but the straightforward pastas hit the spot on a cold winter's day.

Chin Chin

⊠ 216 E. 49th St (at 2nd and 3rd aves) 📞 212-888 4555 Ⓒ L & D daily **$$$** [p337, E2]
Sleek and modern, this fave serves the diplomats and business-meeting crowd carefully prepared, if pricey, upscale Chinese food.

Le Cirque

⊠ One Beacon Court, 151 E. 58th St (at Lexington and 3rd aves) 📞 212-644 0202 Ⓒ L & D Mon–Fri, D only Sat **$$$$** [p337, E1]
Legendary restaurant relocated to a drop-dead, sleek location, complete with drive-in, drop-off entrance in the courtyard of the new Bloomberg building. Jackets required.

Convivio

⊠ 45 Tudor City Place (at 42nd St) 📞 212-599 5045 Ⓒ L & D Mon–Fri, D only Sat **$$$$** [p337, E3]
This elegant Italian restaurant made a splash when it opened in 2008. Pasta dishes are modern takes on regional classics. A worthy splurge.

Dawat

⊠ 210 E. 58th St (between 3rd and 2nd aves) 📞 212-355 7555 Ⓒ L & D Mon–Sat, D only Sun **$$$** [p337, E1]
The cuisine of the Sub-continent goes haute amid elegant surroundings at what is arguably the finest Indian eatery in New York City.

Felidia

⊠ 243 E. 58th St (at 2nd and 3rd aves) 📞 212-758 1479 Ⓒ L & D Mon–Fri, D only Sat–Sun **$$$$** [p337, E1]
Italian-American star chef Lidia Bastianich's crown jewel, with a classic menu of pastas, grilled fish, and roasted meats.

Four Seasons

⊠ 99 E. 52nd St (between Lexington and Park aves) 📞 212-754 9494 Ⓒ L & D Mon–Fri, D only Sat **$$$$** [p337, E1]
Since it opened in 1959, the Four Seasons in the landmark Seagram Building has had a clientele that rivals any *Who's Who* listing. The decor is priceless *(see page 98)* and the seasonal classics served in the elegant pool room or the grill room are impeccable.

Good Burger

⊠ 800 2nd Ave (at 42nd and 43rd sts) 📞 212-922 1700 Ⓒ L & D daily **$** [p337, E3]
Located near the UN, this casual burger-and-shake

LEFT: the pool room at the Four Seasons.
RIGHT: fresco at Monkey Bar.

spot is a great option for travelers with limited time (and money).

La Mangeoire

✉ 1008 2nd Ave (at 53rd and 54th sts) ☎ 212-759 7086 ☺ L & D Mon–Sat, Br & D Sun **$$** [p337, E2]
Superbly reliable, in the same location for over 30 years, this traditional French restaurant has the friendly feel of a country inn, but in the heart of NY. Great value.

The Palm

✉ 837 2nd Ave (between 44th and 45th sts) ☎ 212-687 2953 plus branches. ☺ L & D Mon–Fri, D only Sat. **$$$$** [p337, E2]
Huge steaks and lobsters in a narrow space filled with regulars.

Le Périgord

✉ 405 E. 52nd St (east of 1st Ave) ☎ 212-755 6244 ☺ L & D daily **$$$$** [p337, E2]
French classic serving a well-heeled Sutton Place clientele for years.

Pershing Square

✉ 90 E. 42nd St (at Park Ave) ☎ 212-286 9600 ☺ B, L, & D daily **$$$** [p337, D2]
A step away from Grand Central, with crowd-pleasing American fare.

P.J. Clarke's

✉ 915 3rd Ave (at 55th St) ☎ 212-317 1616 ☺ L & D daily **$$** [p337, E1]
Many think Clarke's has the best hamburgers on the East Side. Lately the

historic saloon, dating from the late 1800s and popular in Sinatra's time, has enjoyed a renaissance. A bonus: serves food after 11pm.

Rosa Mexicano

✉ 1063 1st Ave (at 58 St) ☎ 212-753 7407 ☺ D daily **$$$** [off map]
The Rosa is famous for tableside guacamole, as well as an excellent and imaginative modern Mexican menu. East Siders have known it for years.

San Martin

✉ 143 E. 49th St (between Lexington and 3rd aves) ☎ 212-832 0888 ☺ L & D daily **$$$** [p337, E2]
Tasty Italian cuisine in a warm, attractive room.

Smith & Wollensky

✉ 797 3rd Ave (at 49th St) ☎ 212-753 1530 ☺ L & D daily **$$$** [p337, E2]
This NY institution is usually packed with a boisterous crowd of stockbrokers and Midtown executives. For a less expensive food option, try the adjacent Wollensky's Grill.

Tao

✉ 42 E. 58th St (at Madison and Park aves) ☎ 212-888 2288 ☺ L & D Mon–Fri, D Sat–Sun **$$$** [p337, E1]
A gigantically bold spot that features a towering Buddha in the main dining room. Fight past a noisy bar scene for the privilege of ordering from the delectable but pricey pan-Asian menu.

Water Club

✉ East River (at 30th St) ☎ 212-683 3333 ☺ L & D Mon–Sat, Br & D Sun **$$$** [p337, D4]
A floating restaurant on the East River with good fish and great views: booking essential. The Crow's Nest up above is less pricey (open May to Sept only), as is the Sunday brunch.

Zarela

✉ 953 2nd Ave (between 50th & 51st sts) ☎ 212-644 6740 ☺ L & D Mon–Fri, D only Sat–Sun **$$** [p337, E2]
Mexican regional cooking never tasted this good. Share space with its faithful following.

Bars and Cafés

Bogarts, 99 Park Ave (at 39th St), is popular with the young afterwork crowd, a stone's throw from the train.

Bull & Bear, in the Waldorf-Astoria, has a long mahogany bar and a clubby atmosphere that patrons love.

Campbell Apartment at Grand Central Terminal is an elegant hideaway popular with the after-work, before-train crowd or for an after-dinner drink.

Chop't Creative Salad. Ingredients from A to Z are delightfully diced for a fast and healthy lunch. Two locations in the East '50s.

Le Colonial, 149 E. 57th St (between Lexington and 3rd aves), is a romantic meeting spot, with Vietnamese food.

Grand Central Terminal, 42nd St. A noisy collection of ethnic restaurants where food can be eaten on the spot or taken away.

Juan Valdez Café, 140 E. 57th St. Colombian coffee and great pastries. Good before or after shopping.

Monkey Bar, Hotel Elysée (between Madison and Park aves). Noisy but stylish, thanks to Graydon Carter of *Vanity Fair* fame. Think banana daiquiris.

Recommended Restaurants, Bars, & Cafés on pages 116–17

MIDTOWN WEST

The lights of Broadway shine most brightly here,
glittering off tourist-friendly Times Square,
the Museum of Modern Art, and the
dancing queens of Radio City

The West Side shines more brightly than the East, at least in terms of sheer neon wattage, and what Midtown West lacks in finesse it makes up for tenacity. This is where billboards vie with world-class art, and where, as the old saying goes, there's a broken heart for every light on Broadway.

At the center of it all, Times Square has donned new neon baubles like an aging beauty queen with a facelift. Flash and frenzy dazzle the eye. The NASDAQ headquarters in the Condé Nast building dominates with a huge LED display teeming with the latest stock-market quotes. And Broadway – the glamorous Great White Way – has been rejuvenated.

But then, that's the story of Midtown West. It's been bruised, but it's never gone down for the count. The lights that burn on Broadway, and a bevy of new hotels, restaurants, stores, and other businesses, make sure the West Side is alive and booming.

AROUND HERALD SQUARE

Starting at 34th Street, the transition from East to West Midtown begins at **Herald Square ⑱**, where Broadway intersects Sixth Avenue. Named for the *New York Herald* newspaper, whose headquarters once stood here, today this chaotic intersection is best known for its retail temples.

Just south of Herald Square is the slightly faded **Manhattan Mall**, where four of the building's nine floors are occupied by nearly a dozen eateries and a variety of retailers aimed at teenage tastes and corresponding, slimline wallets. The big draw in this area, however, is New York's very definition of a "big store" – Macy's.

Main attractions
MACY'S
MADISON SQUARE GARDEN
TIMES SQUARE
BROADWAY
BRYANT PARK
RADIO CITY MUSIC HALL
PALEY CENTER FOR MEDIA
MUSEUM OF MODERN ART
AMERICAN FOLK ART MUSEUM
CARNEGIE HALL
HEARST TOWER

LEFT: the thronging masses in Times Square.
RIGHT: snack stall on Herald Square.

Search out sample sales and factory floor bargains in the Garment District around busy Seventh Avenue.

Macy's ⑲

✉ 151 W. 34th St (at Broadway), www.macys.com ☏ 212-695 4400
☉ Mon–Fri 10am–9.30pm, Sat 9am–9.30pm, Sun 11am–8.30pm
🚇 34th St/Herald Square

RIGHT: Isaac Singer statue on the corner of Seventh Avenue.
BELOW: Macy's Thanksgiving Day Parade.

A New York institution for more than a century, Macy's is, like the sign says, the biggest department store in the world, and worth seeing for its size alone. The giant building is divided into a men's and a women's store, which can be a little confusing if you get stuck in one but want the other, but staff are always on hand to point you in the right direction. Don't leave without visiting the "Cellar," a gourmet kitchenware emporium with gadgets and accessories that even the most creative chef would covet.

The Garment District

Exiting Macy's on Seventh Avenue puts you right in the middle of the Garment District, a jangly, soot-covered workhorse that still turns out much of America's fashion. There's not much to do or see here, except take in the ambience, but dedicated bargain-hunters have been known to walk away with first-class deals from the factory floor or sample sales.

Showrooms, too, dot the area, where you can find the latest, if not always the greatest, fashions, although you may have to shop around a little, both for the bargains and the showrooms themselves. Keep an eye out for the young men pushing cloth-

Recommended Restaurants, Bars, & Cafés on pages 116–17

According to a recent FBI crime report, New York is the safest big city in America.

ing racks through the streets; they're always in a hurry and definitely not looking out for you.

The structure at Seventh Avenue and 33rd Street is Madison Square Garden, disliked by purists not only for its functional, clumsy design but also for replacing McKim, Mead, & White's magnificent Pennsylvania Station, demolished in 1963. The "new" **Penn Station** is now 50ft (15 meters) beneath it, where it shuttles a quarter-million commuters daily to Long Island and elsewhere.

Madison Square Garden ⑳

✉ Seventh Ave (at 31st and 33rd sts), www.thegarden.com ☎ 212-465 6741 ☯ tours daily 11am–3pm ⓒ charge 🚇 34th St/Penn Station

Once located between Madison and Fifth avenues – that is, in Madison Square itself – this is one of America's biggest entertainment arenas, where rock and pop shows, ice hockey, basketball games, tennis matches, and even circuses are held. Whatever your feelings about the building, there's no denying it fulfills its function, and the behind-the-scenes tour is surprisingly interesting, even visiting the locker rooms of the NY Knicks (tel: 212-465 6080).

The best way to appreciate this building is to attend one of the Garden's events. Last-minute tickets for sports events are often available on the day (don't expect to sit together if there's more than one of you), or you can book ahead online or through Ticketmaster.

There are few New York experiences more authentic than watching a home team play at home. Just don't expect a quiet game.

If you're a Glenn Miller fan, you may want to check out the venerable **Hotel Pennsylvania** *(see page 299)*, across Seventh Avenue at 33rd Street.

BELOW: there's nothing quite like a Knicks game at Madison Square Garden.

If all the neon lights in Times Square were laid end-to-end, they would stretch from New York City to Washington, DC.

RIGHT: Times Square offers plenty of places to eat and drink.
BELOW: the constant kaleidoscope.

This used to be the Big Band era's hottest ticket, immortalized by Miller's hit *Pennsylvania 6-5000* – still the hotel's phone number. Sadly, the busy terminus-style lobby has replaced glamor with function, but at least it's easy for guests to purchase theater tickets and newspapers from the various stands in reception.

Behind Madison Square Garden, the **General Post Office** ㉑ is hardly an attraction, but it *is* impressive, with a monumental Corinthian design that makes your average Greek temple look like a tiki hut. There's also a terrific slogan on the frieze: "Neither snow nor rain nor heat nor gloom of night stays these couriers from the swift completion of their appointed rounds." The motto was stolen from Herodotus, who obviously never mailed a letter in Manhattan.

Heading back to Herald Square, Broadway slices through the Midtown grid up to 42nd Street. This is the Downtown end of Times Square, the garish heart of Midtown West, and one of the city's most dramatic success stories.

TIMES SQUARE ㉒

✉ Broadway (at 42nd to 48th sts), www.timessquarenyc.org
🚇 42nd St/Times Square

Stretching along Broadway to 48th Street, with the **Theatre District** sprawled loosely on either side, Times Square has had long-awaited renovations that have once again made it the "Crossroads of the World" *(see photo feature on pages 118–19).*

Whether you're here for a show or not, be sure to take a stroll down **Shubert Alley**, a busy walkway that runs behind the Booth and Shubert theaters, from 45th to 44th Street.

Recommended Restaurants, Bars, & Cafés on pages 116–17

Sardi's restaurant, at 234 West 44th Street *(see page 117)* is a venerable Broadway landmark. In addition to its fabled dining rooms with star caricatures galore, there's a great bar, abuzz with show talk before or after the theatre. Sadly, Vincent Sardi Jr, son of the founder, died in 2007, but the show, as they say, goes on.

Theatrical nostalgia buffs should head for the **Lyceum Theatre**, a block east on 45th Street. Open since 1903, it is the oldest continually operating theatre on Broadway and – with its elaborate Baroque facade and dramatic mansard roof – probably the most beautiful.

The information hub

The **Times Square Information Center ㉓** (daily 8am–8pm) is a walk-in facility in the landmark **Embassy Theater**, on Seventh Avenue between 46th and 47th streets. There are stands offering information and tickets for Broadway shows, sightseeing tours and many other activities around the city, not just in Times Square. Free leaflets are available in multiple languages, and search engine Yahoo! has a handful of computers for you to check your mail and use Yahoo! Yellow Pages. There is also a post-office stand where you can buy stamps, and public lavatories.

There are advisers on hand to deal with questions, but they often seem so harassed it might be better to grab a handful of leaflets to flip through in the center's theatre-style seats. Free walking tours leave from the center every Friday.

Times Square is changing all the time, and over the past few years or so has started to attract the sort of big-name businesses that first put it on the map: Condé Nast, Reuters,

After years of decline, big-name companies have moved back to Times Square.

LEFT: essential port of call: the Times Square Information Center.
BELOW: the bright lights of Broadway.

Regards to Broadway

Most of the theaters aren't on Broadway itself, and often the most interesting fare can be found in more than 150 smaller Off-Broadway venues

New York theatre, like Miss Jean Brodie, has been going through a prime period for a while. Broadway's 39 theaters sell more than 12 million tickets annually, earning upward of $862 million. Andrew Lloyd Webber's imported musical megahits – *Phantom of the Opera*, *Cats* – dominated the box office for a decade, but American dramas and comedies (often lumped together as "straight plays") are also produced with reassuring regularity. In an average season of 35 new productions, roughly half will be new plays.

In the early 20th century over 100 new plays were staged each season. Playwrights and composers like Eugene O'Neill, Lillian Hellman, Cole Porter, Irving Berlin, Rodgers and Hart, Arthur Miller, and Tennessee Williams all made their names in New York, and their work is often revived. Contemporary American playwrights such as David Mamet,

Wendy Wasserstein, Sam Shepard, and John Guare have also seen revivals in recent years.

Of the 45 theaters known as "Broadway," only a handful are on the Great White Way itself, including the Broadway Theatre, the Palace, and the Winter Garden. The rest are on side streets from 41st up to 65th Street.

One of the oldest and most splendid theaters, the Lyceum (1903), is a neo-Baroque beauty on West 45th Street, just east of Times Square. The New Victory on 42nd Street is even older, but has had a more troublesome history. Built by Oscar Hammerstein in 1900 as the theater Republic, its name was given a patriotic boost during the 1940s. Thirty years later it was reduced to showing porno movies, but now the New Victory presents colorful, fresh productions, often aimed at children.

Broadway may make the headlines, but Off-Broadway is considered by many to be the true soul of New York theater. Some playwrights bypass Broadway altogether in favor of smaller venues. Off-Broadway is also where plays are staged that are unsuitable for the mainstream, whether for their content or for cost reasons. A hit in an Off-Broadway theatre like Playwrights Horizons or the Public Theater provides the confidence backers need to move Uptown. *Rent*, *Bring In 'Da Noise, Bring In 'Da Funk* and *A Chorus Line* started this way.

With limited time on a New York visit, it can be better not to fixate on a particular show, but to have a number of options, and choose the one that offers the best ticket deal. It can also be rewarding to play a hunch and try something relatively unheard of. This may offer the most memorable kind of New York theater experience, as well as giving the chance to see something spectacular before the critics make ticket prices soar. Glittering stars, luscious musical productions and groundbreaking, often controversial drama can all be found on any night in New York. ❏

LEFT: *Mary Poppins* at the New Amsterdam Theatre.
ABOVE: the New Victory Theater.

and Ernst & Young all have office space here. One cultural attraction is the **Ford Center for the Performing Arts**, a relatively new theater with wide aisles and good views of the stage from most seats. The Ford was built on the site of the old Lyric Theater (1903), and has retained some of its elegant facade.

The Ford Center also occupies the site next door, the former premises of the Apollo Theater (1920), and the design has incorporated into its internal decor some of the Apollo The-

ater's embellishments. Appropriately, for several years the Ford Center was the Broadway home of the most recent revival of that perennial musical, *42nd Street*.

Also on 42nd Street is the **E-Walk** entertainment complex, with 13 movie theaters and various chain restaurants, as well as **Ecko Unlimited**, a high-flying hip-hop store.

I want my MTV

At the corner of 44th Street is the **Viacom** building, where the **Times Square Studio** and headquarters of **MTV** are located. Joining the retail roster on the square and keeping with the MTV vibe are **Billabong**, the surf-clothing chain, and **Emerica**, for generic skate style.

Despite the square's transformation, there's still a perceptible sleaze factor seeping over from the few remaining sex shops that are peppered between the discount clothing and cheap food joints on Eighth Avenue, where the **Port Authority Bus Terminal** ㉔ (between 40th and 42nd and now cleaned up) is a major commuter hub.

EAT

For a touch of elegance after the neon wattage of Times Square, head north to 57th Street, and the opulent, recently reopened Russian Tea Room *(see page 117).*

LEFT: billboard babe.
BELOW: MTV is located in the Viacom building.

The Jacob K. Javits Center is growing bigger and better than ever, thanks to state funds granted for expansion.

BELOW: girls just wanna have fun.

This sleazy atmosphere looks set to change, however, with the completion of the new **New York Times Building**, opposite the bus terminal on Eighth Avenue, between 40th and 41st. This gleaming new addition to the NY skyline has been designed by Renzo Piano using ceramic tubes to create a curtain wall effect that acts as a sunscreen, and changes color throughout the day.

WEST OF TIMES SQUARE

Heading west and a little to the north on Eighth or Ninth avenues, things get interesting in the old **Hell's Kitchen** neighborhood, now known as **Clinton** ㉕. At the start of the 20th century, Hell's Kitchen was one of the most notorious slums in the country. Immigrants were crammed into unsafe and insanitary tenements, and Irish gangs governed the streets like petty overlords. The police were afraid to venture into the neighborhood alone.

There's still a certain gut-level edginess to the area, and a new generation of immigrants, but there are also artists and actors, as well as culinary discoveries to be made. Ninth Avenue from 57th Street to 42nd Street is a globetrot for diners, with reasonably priced restaurants offering an atlas of international cuisines.

A stretch of West 46th Street from Eighth to Ninth avenues – known as **Restaurant Row** – is a solid block of brightly colored eateries popular among the pre-theater crowd. During the annual **Ninth Avenue Food Festival** (May), thousands of New Yorkers flock to gorge themselves on a huge variety of delicacies available from street vendors and the restaurants themselves. If you love to eat, this is an event that you should go out of your way to attend.

Off-Broadway

There's also an active Off-Broadway theater scene on 42nd Street between Ninth and Tenth avenues, where the block of small, experimental, or low-budget venues here are known collectively as **Theater Row**. This makes an attractive pairing with Restaurant Row for an evening out.

On the way between Restaurant Row and Theater Row, theater-lovers might consider a quick detour down West 44th Street. Between Ninth and Tenth avenues is the headquarters of New York's most famous acting school – the legendary **Actors' Studio**. Though there's not much to look at, this small building on an otherwise residential street spawned such greats as Marlon Brando, James Dean, Paul Newman, and Robert De Niro – all practitioners of the school's "Method" style of acting.

Harborside

There's little of note to see west of here, except for the **Javits Center** ㉖, at Twelfth Avenue and 34th Street. This is one of the country's largest convention and exhibition spaces, home to the National Boat Show and other events, and is currently being expanded. Phase One is expected to

Recommended Restaurants, Bars, & Cafés on pages 116–17

Intrepid Sea, Air & Space Museum ㉗

✉ Pier 86 (at W. 46th St and 12th Ave), www.intrepidmuseum.org
📞 212-245 0072 🕒 Apr–Sept daily 10am–5pm, Sat–Sun until 6pm, Oct–Mar Tue–Sun 10am–5pm
💲 charge 🚇 42nd St/Port Authority

The museum is centered on one giant exhibit, the USS *Intrepid*, a decommissioned World War II aircraft carrier with a deck the size of a few football fields. It's strewn with aircraft from fighter jets to Concorde, and a retired submarine, the USS *Growler*. The *Intrepid* reopened in 2009 after a two-year, $58 million refurbishment. Farther north, cruise ships berth alongside the Hudson piers.

STROLLING SIXTH AVENUE

For an alternative route, walk east instead of west from Times Square to **Sixth Avenue**. Signs announce the **Avenue of the Americas**, but don't be fooled: to New Yorkers, Sixth Avenue is Sixth Avenue, no matter how many flags hang from the lamp-

be completed by 2011, and will include a 1,000-room hotel on Eleventh Avenue, between 35th and 36th streets. Conventioneers love being here, but unless you have an interest in one of the visiting exhibitions, it's not worth going out of your way to the Javits.

Non-delegates might like to consider a little sightseeing. A bit farther Uptown, at Pier 83 on 42nd Street, **Circle Line** boats depart for delightful cruises around Manhattan *(see right)*.

TIP

Circle Line cruises (www.circleline42.com, tel: 212-563 3200) on West 42nd Street, have been offering tours since 1945 – a three-hour boat trip around Manhattan, with entertaining commentary. Night-time tours are also available, and from May through October you can try The Beast, a hair-raising ride by speedboat.

BELOW: the Intrepid Sea, Air, & Space Museum.

posts. At the corner of 42nd Street is pretty **Bryant Park** ㉘, where fashion shows, summer concerts, and sometimes outdoor movies occur. In winter there's skating on the pond, a pretty sight, especially when the

snow is piled high around the **Bryant Park Grill** *(see page 116)*, which looks out over the park from behind the New York Public Library *(see page 74)*. The Art Deco **Radiator Building** at 40th Street is now the fashionable **Bryant Park Hotel** and bar, and is helping to perk up the square around the park.

At the next corner is the **International Center of Photography** (1133 Sixth Avenue at 43rd Street; www.icp. org, tel: 212-857 0000; closed Mon; charge), which has a permanent collection of over 100,000 photographs – including the archives of *Life* magazine. Visiting exhibitions can include real gems, so if you're interested in photography, make sure to find out what's on while you're in New York.

Clubs and diamonds

Turning right at 44th Street leads to the neighborhood of the **Algonquin Hotel** ㉙ *(see page 297)*, where Dorothy Parker, Robert Benchley, and other distinguished literati traded wit at the famous Round Table. Much has been done to preserve the appearance and atmosphere of this historic hotel.

If you are rich or well connected, West 44th Street has several opportunities for genteel rest and relaxation. No. 27 is the premises of the **Harvard Club**, whose interior can more easily be observed by peering into a back window, rather than shelling out for four years' education; No. 37 houses the distinguished **New York Yacht**

RIGHT: Deco detail from Radio City.
BELOW: Bryant Park.

Club, with an 1899 nautically themed Beaux Arts facade.

Another right turn off Sixth Avenue leads to the **Diamond District** ⓛ, a block-long enclave along 47th Street where close to $500 million's worth in gems is traded every day. Most of the diamond merchants are Hasidic Jews, distinguished by black suits, wide-brimmed hats, and long beards. From 47th Street north, corporate monoliths march up Sixth Avenue. Names change, but the structures stay the same. This stretch of Sixth is really the backyard of the Rockefeller Center and its famous performance space.

Radio City Music Hall ㉛

✉ 1260 Sixth Ave (at 50th and 51st sts), www.radiocity.com
📞 212-247 4777 ⓒ box office Mon–Sat 11.30am–6pm; tours daily 11am–3pm ⓢ charge
Ⓡ 47th–50th St/Rockefeller Center

The world's largest indoor theater graces the west side of the Rockefeller Center. Built in 1932 as a palace for the people, both the exterior and interior are magnificent, and a guided tour is highly recommended. From the massive chandeliers in the Grand Lobby to the

BELOW: Radio City was built to be a palace for the people.

The Rockettes of Radio City

For more than 75 years, four times every day, 365 days a year, the Radio City Rockettes have performed in their Art Deco palace in Rockefeller Center. The Rockettes began in St Louis as the "Missouri Rockets," and were brought to New York by S.L. (Roxy) Rothafel, who adjusted their name to the "Roxyettes" and debuted their high-precision, all-American show at his own Roxy theater. They danced at the opening of Radio City Music Hall on December 27, 1932, and have been resident ever since. The Christmas show at Radio City is an American institution on a par with, say, Krispy-Kreme donuts, and draws an annual audience of over 1 million people. Proficiency in jazz and tap dancing, and a height between 5' 6" and 5' 11" (1.68–1.80 meters) are requirements for ensemble dancers; principals also need strong ballet skills. With one of the largest auditoriums in the world, Radio City is just as much of a treat as the productions themselves.

The American Folk Art Museum has two branches, both on Manhattan's West Side.

BELOW: the MoMA is home to Warhol's Campbell's Soup series.

plush, scalloped auditorium, Radio City was built to impress; it's the last word in Art Deco extravagance. The acoustics are excellent, and even the restrooms were custom-designed. The Stuart Davis mural that graced the men's smoking lounge was thought so important it was acquired by the Museum of Modern Art.

The **Paley Center for Media** ❷ (25 West 52nd Street, www.mtr.org, tel: 212-621 6800; Wed–Sun noon–6pm, Thur until 8pm; charge), formerly the Museum of Television and Radio, is a feast for committed couch potatoes. The vast archive of vintage radio and TV shows can be rented for an hour at a time, and is the perfect rainy-day activity. There are daily screenings, too.

Museum of Modern Art ❸

✉ 11 W. 53rd St (at Fifth and Sixth aves), www.moma.org 📞 212-708 9400 🕐 Mon, Wed, Thur, Sat, & Sun 10.30am–5.30pm, Fri 10.30am–8pm 💲 charge 🚉 53rd St/Fifth Avenue

The Museum of Modern Art, known to culture vultures as MoMA, offers one of the world's most exciting and provocative art collections *(see photo feature on pages 120–3)*. Even if the thought of modern art leaves you cold, the building alone is worth visiting. The ingenious use of light and space means you can be walking along a corridor and suddenly find yourself looking out over a sculpture, or through to the city outside.

Perhaps the most accessible section is the Architecture and Design floor, with groundbreaking designs. It is these imaginative inclusions that, combined with some of modern art's most famous paintings, give MoMA the edge. Be prepared for crowds of fellow art-lovers.

In the same block, the **American Folk Art Museum** (45 West 53rd Street, www.folkartmuseum.org, tel: 212-265 1040; closed Mon; charge) is home to traditional art from the 18th and 19th centuries. The collection has some beautiful and striking pieces of art and textiles that would be equally at home in a gallery at MoMA. The museum has also kept its branch by Lincoln Center *(see page 149)*.

Recommended Restaurants, Bars, & Cafés on pages 116–17

Carnegie Hall ㉞

✉ 57th St and Seventh Ave,
www.carnegiehall.org ☎ 212-247 7800
🅒 box office Mon- Sat 11am–6pm,
Sun noon–6pm; tours Mon–Fri 11am,
2pm, 3pm 🅢 charge 🚇 57th St

As every American knows, there's only one way to get to Carnegie Hall – practice, practice. The joke is about as old as the hall itself, which was built in 1891 by super-industrialist Andrew Carnegie. Ever since Tchaikovsky conducted at the opening gala, Carnegie Hall has attracted the world's finest performers, including Rachmaninov, Toscanini and Sinatra. It would be pleasant if the hall's exterior were as inspiring as its history or acoustics.

Carnegie Hall is, in fact, the umbrella title for three separate halls. The Issac Stearn Auditorium/Ronald O. Perelman Stage is the hall's original space. The auditorium seats nearly 3,000 people and was described by Issac Stearn as "larger than life." Two smaller stages complete the complex, one with 600 seats, and one half that size.

Midtown goes green

Two blocks west is another of the city's spectacular new constructions, the **Hearst Tower** ㉟, soaring up like a giant, glass origami-model, with walls of glass facets that catch the light in ever-changing colors. This is also New York's first recognized "green" skyscraper, low-impact technologies and recyclable materials having been used throughout.

Midtown West wraps up with a flourish on **Central Park South**, famed for luxury hotels and lines of limousines *(see pages 82–5)*. It's a good place to catch a **horse-drawn carriage** and clip-clop around the park – especially in December, when Midtown glistens with holiday lights. ❑

BELOW LEFT: MoMA's Sculpture Garden.
BELOW RIGHT: Hearst Tower, one of New York's new skyscrapers.

BEST RESTAURANTS, BARS, AND CAFÉS

Restaurants

Prices for a three-course dinner per person with half a bottle of wine:

$ = under $20
$$ = $20–$45
$$$ = $45–$60
$$$$ = over $60

Algonquin Hotel, Blue Bar, & Lobby

✉ 59 W. 44th St (at 5th and 6th aves) 📞 212-840 6800 🕐 B, L, T, & D daily **$$$** [p337, C2]
Whether it's Martinis at the Blue Bar or afternoon tea in the wood-paneled lobby, there's a sense of literary history in the air once shared by Dorothy Parker and other members of the Round Table. The people behind a recent renovation worked hard to change nothing.

Angus McIndoe

✉ 258 W. 44th St (at Broadway and 8th Ave) 📞 212-221 9222 🕐 L & D Mon–Sat, Br & D Sun **$$** [p336, C1]
Newer than Joe Allen's and Sardi's, the latest drop-in place provides three levels for various theater stars to unwind after a show.

Barbetta

✉ 321 W. 46th St (at 8th and 9th aves) 📞 212-246 9171 🕐 L & D Tue–Sat **$$$** [p336, C1]
The *grande dame* of "Restaurant Row" has been doing uninterrupted business since 1906. An elegant townhouse plus dreamy garden make for a grand experience of delicious Italian food.

Becco

✉ 355 W. 46th St (at 8th and 9th aves) 📞 212-397 7597 🕐 L & D daily **$$** [p336, C1]
A fixed price, all-you-can-eat pasta paradise. Moderate in price with wine, very cheap without it.

Le Bernardin

✉ 155 W. 55th St (at 6th and 7th aves) 📞 212-554 1515 🕐 L & D Mon–Fri, D only Sat **$$$$** [p334, B4]
Top-of-the-line for fish- and seafood-lovers. One of the best restaurants in the country.

Bryant Park Grill

✉ 25 W. 40th St (at 5th and 6th aves) 📞 212-840 6500 🕐 L & D daily **$$$$** [p337, C2]
There's a busy lunch scene at this terraced eatery behind the New York Public Library; it's a great place for a drink and meeting spot in the early evening too, hosting an attractive after-work crowd.

Café Un Deux Trois

✉ 123 W. 44th St (at Broadway and 6th aves) 📞 212-354 4148 🕐 L & D daily **$$** [p337, C2]
Midtown madness, but with a pre-theater or lunchtime brasserie menu. The *pommes frites* are perfect.

Carnegie Deli

✉ 854 7th Ave (at 54th and 55th sts) 📞 212-757 2245 🕐 B, L, & D daily **$** [p334, B4]
This New York institution provides a tourist-filled version of the authentic deli experience. The lines are long, and the enormous pastrami sandwiches come with an extra charge for sharing.

China Grill

✉ CBS Building, 60 W. 53rd St (at 6th Ave) 📞 212-333 7788 🕐 L & D Mon–Sat, D only Sun **$$–$$$** [p337, D1]
Fabulous nouvelle-Asian restaurant which can be reasonably priced with some careful study of the creative menu.

Daisy May's BBQ USA

✉ 623 11th Ave (at 46th St) 📞 212-977 1500 🕐 L & D daily **$** [p336, B1]
Finger-lickin' barbecue. Serious eaters can order ahead for a whole barbecued hog. It'll cost ya! But everything else is cheap.

Gallagher's Steakhouse

✉ 228 W. 52nd St (at Broadway and 8th Ave) 📞 212-245 5336 🕐 L & D daily **$$$** [p337, C1]
A sometime celeb hangout and a New York tradition since 1927. It's easy to spot; look for beef in the windows.

LEFT: go to Sardi's for a cocktail and theatre talk.
RIGHT: Algonquin Hotel restaurant.

Il Gattopardo
33 W. 54th St (at 5th and 6th aves) [212-246 0412 [L & D daily $$$ [p337, D1]
Tiny restaurant with attractive ivy-covered garden serving authentic Neapolitan dishes. Try the meatballs.

Hourglass Tavern
375 W. 46th St (at 8th and 9th aves) [212-265 2060 [D Tue–Sun $$ [p336, C1]
The gimmick here (a formula that has been popular for years) is that diners must be in and out in 60 minutes.

Joe Allen
326 W. 46th St (at 8th and 9th aves) [212-581 6464 [L & D daily $$ [p336, C1]
Long-time theater hangout serves basic American food with the added bonus of possible celebrity sightings.

John's Pizzeria
260 W. 44th St (at Broadway and 8th Ave) [212-391 7560 [L & D daily $ [p336, C1]
Quality thin-crust pizza, plus much more on the menu, in a former church. What's better, the stained glass or the pie?

McCormick & Schmick's
1285 Ave of the Americas (at 6th and 7th aves, enter on 52nd St) [212-459 1222 [L & D Mon–Sat, D only Sun $$ [p337, D1]
Seafood is the name of the game at this national chain restaurant.

The Modern
Museum of Modern Art, 9 W. 53rd St (at 5th and 6th aves) [212-333 1220 [L & D Mon–Sat $$$$ [p337, D1]
Food really is an art, as is the setting overlooking MoMA's Sculpture Garden. Celebrate a special occasion here.

Russian Tea Room
150 W. 57th St (at 6th and 7th aves) [212-581 7100 $$$ [p334, B4]
The menu will never be the same, but the place is back, right where it always was, just left of Carnegie Hall in a space that is pretty in pink, red, and green all over.

Ruth's Chris Steakhouse
148 W. 51st St (at 6th and 7th aves) [212-245 9600 [L & D Mon–Fri, D only Sat–Sun $$$ [p334, B4]
Scrumptious steaks + loyal customers = a winning formula.

Ted's Montana Grill
110 W. 51st St (at 6th and 7th aves) [212-245 5220 [L & D daily $$$ [p337, D1]
CNN Mogul Ted Turner may not be married to Jane Fonda anymore, but he owns an eatery serving that unique American entrée, organic bison.

Tony's Di Napoli
147 W. 43rd St (at 6th Ave and Broadway) [212-221 0100 [L & D daily $$ [p337, C2]
Family-size portions of

tasty Italian fare. Fresh food draws huge crowds for pre-theater feasts.

Trattoria Dell'Arte
900 7th Ave (at 56th and 57th sts) [212-245 9800 [L & D daily $$$ [p334, B4]
The fabulous antipasti double as a popular main course. This trattoria is always buzzing with culinary cognoscenti.

The View
1535 Broadway (at 45th and 46th sts) [212-704 8900 [D Mon–Sat, Br, & D Sun $$$ [p337, C1]
High atop the Marquis Hotel in Times Square is New York's only revolving restaurant, with a wonderful panoramic view of the skyline. Sunday brunch and early dinner (great for sunsets) are particular favorites.

Bars and Cafés

Café 2 at MoMA, 11 W. 53rd St (at 5th and 6th aves), is the canteen-style eatery at the museum offering tasty tapas-style snacks as well as soups, salads, and desserts. Alternatively try to squeeze into Terrace 5, the museum's full-service café, for views of the Sculpture Garden.

ESPN Zone, 4 Times Square (Broadway at 42nd St). Jocks get off on this triplex sportsbar concept with dizzying screens delivering games galore in the heart of Times Square. Food is incidental.

Heartland Brewery (several locations), W. 43rd St (at Broadway and 6th aves). Although they do a brisk bar biz with the microbrew, there's a little something for everyone on the menu, from crab cakes to basic pub grub.

Sardi's, 44th St (at Broadway and 8th Ave). Of course, lunch and dinner are served at this legendary Theater District mainstay, but a drink at the bar is a must. Sip a cocktail surrounded by the trademark caricatures of every Broadway name. Friendly barmen.

TIMES SQUARE THEN AND NOW

Revitalization marches on at the Crossroads of the World, and the Duffy Square renovation is bringing even better changes

Times Square, named for the *New York Times* offices *(see right)*, has a history as lively as its street life. Theaters, hotels, and restaurants sprang up in the 1920s, when impresarios like the Shubert Brothers staged 250 shows a year. Prohibition brought speakeasies, gangsters, and the characters of Damon Runyon's earthy tales. At the end of World War II, more than 2 million people crowded into the area to celebrate V-J Day. But by the 1960s, Times Square was known mainly for its sleaze, crime, and pornography. In the 1990s, the square was transformed back into a tourist magnet for the more than 20 million visitors who come here each year. The most recent renovations (2007) are of Duffy Square. These include a radical new urban plaza with a stunning red-glass stepped amphitheater, and a new TKTS booth for discounted tickets of that day's Broadway shows.

ABOVE: the Great White Way: free walking tours begin at the Times Square Information Center in the historic Embassy Theater on Broadway between 46th and 47th streets.

BELOW: Lauren Bacall, a former Miss Greenwich Village, seen here 21 years later at Loew's State Theatre for the world premiere of the movie *How to Marry a Millionaire*.

The Essentials

✉ *Broadway between 42nd & 48th sts; www.timessquarenyc.org*
🕐 *Times Square Information Center open daily 8am–8pm. Walking tours every Friday*
Ⓜ *42nd St/Times Square*

THE *NEW YORK TIMES*

Times Square took its name from the *New York Times*, formerly headquartered at the Times Tower, where 42nd Street intersects Seventh Avenue, and now called One Times Square. The *New-York Daily Times*, founded in 1851 (the *Daily* was dropped in 1857), was bought in 1896 by ambitious Tennessee newspaperman Adolph S. Ochs.

The paper moved to 229 West 43rd Street in 1913, where Ochs's great-grandson, chairman Arthur Sulzberger Jr, continued the mission to produce, "an independent newspaper... devoted to the public welfare" under the well-known slogan: "All the News That's Fit to Print."

In a decision that has delighted Manhattanites, the company commissioned architect Renzo Piano to create a new addition to the New York skyline at Eighth Avenue between 40th and 41st streets. This landmark *Times* building changes color with the light.

The *New York Times* has won 95 Pulitzer Prizes, and has a circulation of over 1 million readers.

ABOVE: Times Square's renovations have restored its status as a family-friendly destination. Toys "Я" Us lets kids have their faces projected onto the big screen of the store.

LEFT: Times Square may have been cleaned up, but tricky pick-pockets and con-artists are still drawn to the big crowds, on the small streets especially. Watch your wallets.

BELOW: breadlines on Broadway: during the Great Depression in the 1930s, a city newspaper opened a relief kitchen in Times Square to feed the poor.

MUSEUM OF MODERN ART

Attention and praise is lavished on MoMA's building almost as much as on its world-class collection

"One of the most exquisite works of architecture to rise in this city in at least a generation" was the *New York Times*' welcome to MOMA's Midtown home, when it reopened at the end of 2004 after an extensive refit.

Yoshio Taniguchi, the Japanese architect chosen for the project, said his aim was "the imaginative and disciplined use of light, materials, and space." The new facility offers almost twice the floor space of the former building, with airy galleries on the second floor and more intimate exhibition areas on the levels above. The top floor provides expansive, skylit space for temporary exhibitions.

The much-admired Sculpture Garden follows the original 1953 design, setting Rodin, Picasso and Tony Smith pieces among trees and calm reflecting pools.

ABOVE: *The Starry Night*, 1889, Vincent Van Gogh. "Looking at the stars," he said, "always makes me dream."

BELOW AND BELOW RIGHT: *The Couple*, 1955, and *Woman with Her Throat Cut*, 1932. Gilberto Giacometti's bronzes took inspiration from African tribal art.

The Essentials

✉ *11 West 53rd Street, between Fifth and Sixth aves; www.moma.org*

☎ *212-708 9400*

🕐 *Mon, Wed, Thur, Sat, and Sun 10.30am–5.30pm, Fri 10.30am–8pm*

💲 *charge*

🚇 *53rd St/Fifth Avenue*

MoMA in the Making

The Museum of Modern Art's collection was started by Abby Aldrich Rockefeller, Mary Quinn Sullivan, and Lillie P. Bliss in 1929 with just eight prints and a single drawing. Abby's enthusiasm for the works of modern artists like Matisse, Van Gogh, and Chagall was not shared by her husband, John D. Rockefeller, who decried the work as "unintelligible," and unfit for public viewing. The opening show of works by Cézanne, Gauguin, Van Gogh, and Serrat was held on the 12th floor of a building on 57th Street and Fifth Avenue. After three transfers to larger premises, MoMA moved to its present location in 1939.

The museum's collection, which began so modestly, now includes more than 150,000 works, among them paintings, sculptures, drawings, prints, photographs, architectural models and drawings, furniture, and design objects. MoMA also has around 22,000 films and 4 million film stills. The library and archives are among the premier facilities of their kind in the world.

Top: *The False Mirror*, 1928, René Magritte.

Above: *Side 2*, 1970, by Shiro Kuramata: innovative storage from MoMA's architecture and design collection.

Above Left: *Paimio Chair* 1931–2, Alvar Aalto. The Paimio Chair is a bentwood virtuoso piece that pushed the limits of plywood furniture making.

Museum of Modern Art

- i Information
- ♦ Elevator
- Escalator
- ☐ Public Space

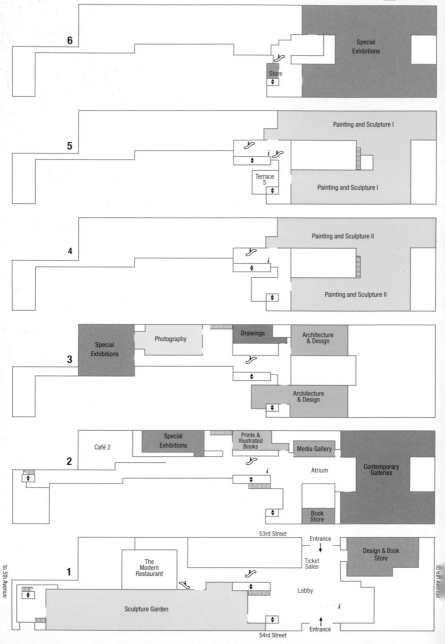

6
Special Exhibitions
Store

5
Painting and Sculpture I
Painting and Sculpture I
Terrace 5
i

4
Painting and Sculpture II
Painting and Sculpture II
i

3
Special Exhibitions
Photography
Drawings
Architecture & Design
Architecture & Design

2
Café 2
Special Exhibitions
Prints & Illustrated Books
Media Gallery
Atrium
Contemporary Galleries
Book Store
i

1
53rd Street
Entrance
Ticket Sales
Design & Book Store
The Modern Restaurant
Lobby
Sculpture Garden
i
Entrance
54th Street

to 5th Avenue

to 6th Avenue

ABOVE: *Sleeping Woman*, 1929. Man Ray was a Surrealist pioneer of photographic techniques like solarization.

LEFT: *Les Demoiselles d'Avignon*, 1907. Pablo Picasso's monumental canvas drew on African masks and Iberian sculpture, and is a landmark in the story of modern art.

BELOW: *La Clownesse assise (The Seated Clowness)*, 1896, Henri de Toulouse-Lautrec. Diminutive Lautrec is best known as a postermaker and chronicler of the Belle Epoque, and the girls of Paris's *fin de siècle* Moulin Rouge nightclub in particular.

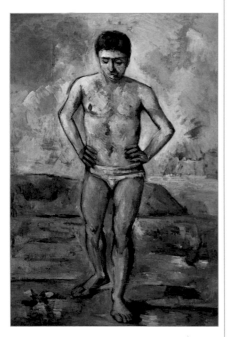

ABOVE: *The Bather*, c.1885, by Paul Cézanne, one of the great Post-Impressionists and the painter whom Henri Matisse described as "the father of us all."

Recommended Restaurants, Bars, & Cafés on pages 134–5

UPPER EAST SIDE

Opulence is in the air here. Old-money New Yorkers glide from Millionaires' Row to Museum Mile before a session of retail therapy at Barneys or Bloomies

The Upper East Side's romance with wealth began in the late 1800s, when the Four Hundred – so called because a social arbiter decreed that in all of New York there were only 400 families that mattered – moved into Fifth Avenue, in order to cultivate roots alongside Central Park.

The homes they built were the most luxurious the city had seen – mansions and townhouses furnished like European palaces and filled with priceless art. Since then, the Carnegies, the Fricks, and the Astors have moved to greener pastures, but the Upper East Side has never lost its taste for the good life, and even the areas east of Lexington Avenue, formerly fairly affordable, are now highly desirable.

An air of wealth

The scent of wealth is, unsurprisingly, most intoxicating on the stretch of **Fifth Avenue ❶** facing the park, known to old-time New Yorkers as **Millionaires' Row**. At the corner of 60th Street is J.P. Morgan's stately **Metropolitan Club ❷**, founded in 1892 after one of the financier's nouveau riche buddies was denied membership of the Union Club. The enormous **Temple Emanu-El ❸** cuts

a brooding figure at the corner of 65th Street, where 2,500 worshippers can gather under its soaring roof, making this cavernous, echoing temple one of the largest reform synagogues in the world.

In the East 70s are a number of splendid old-style mansions. These include the **Harkness House** (1 East 75th Street); the chateau-style **Duke Mansion** (1 East 78th Street), which houses the New York University Institute of Fine Arts; and the **Payne Whitney** house (972 Fifth Avenue),

Main attractions

FRICK COLLECTION
METROPOLITAN MUSEUM OF ART
GUGGENHEIM MUSEUM
NATIONAL ACADEMY MUSEUM
COOPER-HEWITT
  NATIONAL DESIGN MUSEUM
JEWISH MUSEUM
MADISON AVENUE
WHITNEY MUSEUM OF
  AMERICAN ART
PARK AVENUE
MOUNT VERNON HOTEL MUSEUM
GRACIE MANSION
ROOSEVELT ISLAND

LEFT: the Metropolitan Museum of Art.
RIGHT: the Upper East Side's romance with wealth began in the 1800s.

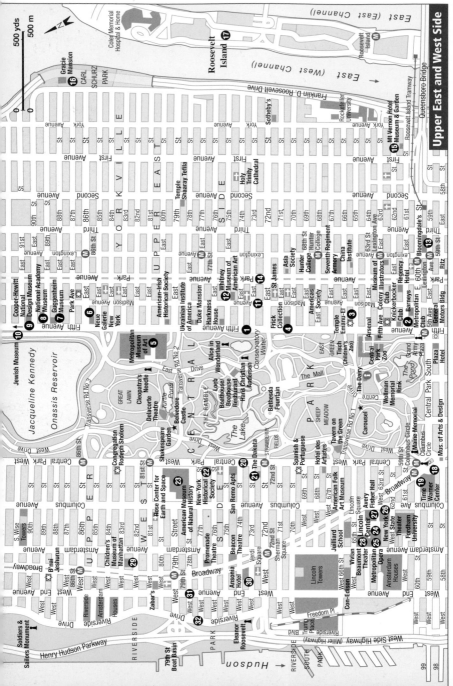

Upper East and West Side

500 yds
500 m

Recommended Restaurants, Bars, & Cafés on pages 134–5

a fabulous Renaissance-style palazzo that now serves as the cultural center of the French Embassy.

International relations are the order of the day on the Upper East Side: the former Stuyvesant mansion at 79th and Fifth is the **Ukrainian Institute**, with the **American-Irish Historical Society** farther up at No. 991. Between 68th and 70th streets, the classic McKim, Mead, & White building at 680 Park Avenue is now home to the **Americas Society**, while the Georgian-style house at No. 686 is the **Italian Cultural Institute**.

Frick Collection ❹

✉ 1 E. 70th St (at 5th and Madison aves), www.frick.org 📞 212-288 0700 🕐 Tue–Sat 10am–6pm, Sun 11am–5pm 💲 charge
🚇 68th St/Hunter College

At the corner of Fifth Avenue and 70th Street, this grand art collection is showcased in the former home of steel magnate Henry Clay Frick, whose passion for art was surpassed only by his ruthlessness in business. It consists mostly of works by great European

masters from the 16th to the 19th century – Vermeer, Velázquez, Goya, Constable, and more. The gallery is also one of the city's more successful marriages between art and setting, with a tranquil garden court, and soft furnishings to luxuriate in when art-lovers' feet are tired from standing in front of the paintings. The Frick's annual concert season showcases young classical musicians (tickets must be booked in advance).

The Frick mansion was purpose-built as a jewel house for the art collection, at a cost (in 1906–13) of $5 million.

LEFT: the *Comtesse d'Haussonville*, by Ingres, from the Frick. **BELOW:** the Garden Court at the heart of the Frick mansion.

The Man and the Mansion

Henry Clay Frick (1849–1919) invested his savings in a coalmine while working in his uncle's store, and by the age of 30 was a millionaire and "the Coke King of Pennsylvania." With his associate (and later bitter rival) Andrew Carnegie, he dominated the US coal and steel businesses for decades. A fierce foe of organized labor, Frick was widely hated for his violent suppression of a steel strike in 1892. After he turned 50, he devoted a little less time to business and more to his other passion – the collecting of art. In 1905 Frick moved from Pittsburgh to New York, after he was told the steel city's air was bad for his paintings, and built this neoclassical mansion as a residence and perfect setting for his Old Masters.

MUSEUM MILE

Between 82nd and 104th streets are nine cultural treasures so lavish that this stretch of Fifth Avenue has become known as **Museum Mile** *(see photo feature on pages 136–7).*

Metropolitan Museum of Art ⑤

✉ 1000 Fifth Ave (at 81st and 82nd sts), www.metmuseum.org
☎ 212-535 7710 ⏰ Tue–Thur, Sun 9.30am–5.30pm, Fri, Sat 9.30am–9pm ⑤ charge 🚇 86th St

Opened on its present site in 1880, the Met is a sprawling Gothic behemoth with the largest art collection in the US. The permanent collection is truly impressive, and the newer galleries will show off its exhibits to even better advantage *(see photo feature on pages 138–41).*

At 86th Street is the **Neue Galerie New York** ⑥ (1048 Fifth Avenue, www.neuegalerie.org, tel: 212-628 6200; closed Tue, Wed; charge), with Austrian and German art, including pieces by Gustav Klimt. The museum

recently started a First Fridays program – they are now open with free admission on the first Friday of each month from 6–8pm.

Guggenheim Museum ⑦

✉ 1071 Fifth Avenue (at 89th St), www.guggenheim.org ☎ 212-423 3500 ⏰ Mon–Wed and Fri, Sun 10am–5.45pm, Sat 10am–7.45pm; closed Thur ⑤ charge 🚇 86th St

Founded in 1937, the Solomon R. Guggenheim Museum – its full name – was relatively new among the city's leading art repositories, but this was no disadvantage. Newcomer though it was, the Guggenheim shared top billing on the cultural marquee thanks largely to Frank Lloyd Wright's fab-

RIGHT: visiting the Neue Galerie.
BELOW: the impressive entrance hall of the Metropolitan Museum of Art.

Recommended Restaurants, Bars, & Cafés on pages 134–5

ulous building, which opened in 1959 to mixed critical reviews but much New York buzz.

The treasures inside are based on Solomon and Peggy Guggenheim's personal collections, showcasing Expressionism, Cubism, and the general trend toward abstraction. Artists given due attention include Klee and Kandinsky, Mondrian and Modigliani, Picasso of course, and later painters like Jackson Pollock and Roy Lichtenstein. The Guggenheim really is a New York masterpiece, and one museum not to miss.

Also on Museum Mile at 89th Street is the **National Academy Museum and School of Fine Arts** ❽ (1083 Fifth Avenue, https://national academy.org, tel: 212-369 4880; closed Mon, Tue; charge) with a collection of over 5,000 19th–21st-century American artworks. Next comes the **Cooper-Hewitt National Design Museum** ❾

(2 East 91st Street at Fifth Ave, tel: 212-849 8400; daily; charge) in the landmark Andrew Carnegie mansion, with displays on the history and process of design and an onsite master's program for students.

Jewish Museum ❿

✉ 1109 Fifth Ave (at 92nd St), www.jewishmuseum.org ☎ 212-423 3200 ⏰ Sat–Tue 11am–5.45pm, Thur 11am–8pm, Fri 11am–4pm Ⓢ charge 🚇 96th St

One of the world's largest centers of Jewish culture contains a vast collection of historical and contemporary Jewish art, as well as the National Jewish Archive of Broadcasting. In observance of the Sabbath the museum is free on Saturdays, and all electronic exhibits are closed.

At the very top of the "Mile" is the **Museum of the City of New York** at 103rd Street and **El Museo del Barrio** at 104th Street, the city's museum of Latino and Caribbean culture. *(For these two museums, see pages 168–9).*

EAT

A special place to stop for coffee and a snack on Museum Mile is the Neue Galerie's Café Sabarsky – an evocation of the great cafés of pre-1914 Vienna, with Art Nouveau decor and sinful pastries.

BELOW LEFT: National Academy Museum and School of Fine Arts. **BELOW RIGHT:** studying a sculpture at the Cooper-Hewitt National Design Museum.

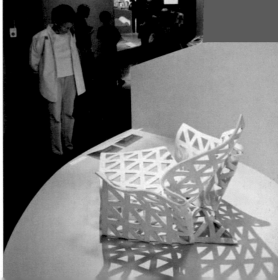

With all the latest designer labels, Barneys is a favorite store for New York fashionistas.

RIGHT: hanging at Barneys New York.
BELOW: bundled up for shopping at Bloomies.

EAST SIDE AMBIENCE

Geographically, Fifth Avenue is only one block away from **Madison Avenue** , but in spirit they're worlds apart. Wave goodbye to the prim and proper salons of the Four Hundred, because Madison Avenue is the land of ritz and glitz – a slick marketplace custom-crafted for the hyperactive, top-of-the-line discriminating consumer. It's a little bit mellower in the pleasant low-90s neighborhood of **Carnegie Hill** than it is in the 60s, but if you cross over from the top of Museum Mile you'll still find plenty of upscale boutiques, gourmet delicatessens, little chi-chi stores and art galleries worth exploring.

Whitney Museum of American Art ⑫

✉ 945 Madison Ave (at 75th St), www.whitney.org ☎ 212-570 3676
🕑 Wed, Thur, Sat, Sun 11am–6pm, Fri 1–9pm ⑤ charge; free Fri 6–9pm
🚇 77th St

In addition to displaying challenging American art, Marcel Breuer's angular, cantilevered structure is a work of art in its own right, second only to the Guggenheim among the Upper East Side's most striking architectural expressions.

The Whitney collection was founded in 1930 by Gertrude Vanderbilt Whitney, whose tastes were for American Realists like Edward Hopper and George Bellows. Since then the museum's policy has been to acquire pieces that represent the full range of 20th-century American art, with works by Georgia O'Keeffe, Willem de Kooning, Jackson Pollock, and Jasper Johns. Every other year it mounts the Whitney Biennial, a survey of provocative new American art. The Whitney is also planning a Meatpacking District location in the future.

Barneys and Bloomies

From the Whitney to 59th Street, Madison is a bacchanalian feast of conspicuous consumption. The names on the store fronts are a roster of the fashion elite: Ralph Lauren, Yves Saint Laurent, Kenzo, Giorgio Armani, Prada, Calvin Klein.

Most of these megastar stores are more for browsing than serious buying, except for those accompanied by a serious bankroll. A quintessentially New York shopping scene is **Barneys New York** on 61st Street, one of the movers and shakers of Manhattan's retail world. In addition to the best designs, there's a chic lower-level restaurant in which to refresh and revive weary wallet-wielders. Barneys Coop, Barneys's smaller sister store, is currently springing up in carefully chosen locations around the city.

Serious shoppers may head straight for one of the city's retail queens: **Bloomingdale's** ⑬ on 59th Street – an institution that dyed-in-the-wool New Yorkers could not live without. Bloomies is almost always crowded – oppressively so at holiday or sale times – but if you only go to one big

A Dylan's Candy Bar mural made from jelly beans.

store, this should be it. Bloomingdale's is so popular, there's now a branch in Soho. As a reward for the kids afterwards, make a stop at **Dylan's Candy Bar**, a sweet dream come true just behind Bloomie's, owned by Ralph Lauren's daughter, Dylan.

Park Avenue style

Skipping east to **Park Avenue** ⑭, the scene changes dramatically. Compared to the flashy indulgence of Madison Avenue, Park seems like a noisy version of a Parisian boulevard.

LEFT: the painting *Lily and the Sparrows*, by Philip Evergood, is on show at the Whitney.
BELOW: cruising on Fifth Avenue.

TIP

Roosevelt Island's
subway station is pre-
ferred by commuters,
but the most enjoyable
way to get there is on
the Roosevelt Island
Tramway, which leaves
from the corner of
Second Ave and 60th
St. On the way, you get
a wonderful view of all
the great towers of the
Upper East Side.

RIGHT: the distinctive
Seventh Regiment
Armory.
BELOW LEFT: the
Mount Vernon.
BELOW RIGHT: Gracie
Mansion is home to
New York's mayor.

A highlight is the **Regency Hotel**, a
favorite for power breakfasts among
big-wheel media types, and where
the elegant library bar serves a jolly
decent afternoon tea. Another is the
Colony Club at 62nd Street, which
has a stately red-brick facade, appropriate to the stately society women
who make up its members' list.

There are several cultural sites: the
Museum of Illustration (128 East
63rd Street between Park and Lexington aves, tel: 212-838 2560;
closed Sun, Mon; free) and the **China
Institute** (125 East 65th Street, tel:
212-744 8181; charge). Their exhibitions cover, respectively, the history
of illustration and Chinese art.

Continuing north, it's near-
impossible to miss the **Seventh Regiment Armory** at Park and 66th. Built
in the 1870s to resemble a medieval
castle, the Armory now serves as an
exhibition hall for art shows.

At 70th Street, the **Asia Society**
(725 Park Ave, tel: 212-288 6400;
closed Mon; charge) houses the Rockefellers' collection of Asian art. There
are also performances, movies, and
other events related to Asian culture.

Yorkville and farther east

East of Park Avenue, the Upper East
Side slips in the prestige department,
but makes up for it with a dash of
self-indulgence. Once dominated by
Eastern European immigrants, much
of the area is now gentrified, but
remnants of the old German and
Czech quarters survive in **Yorkville**,
between 79th and 98th streets.

Between First and York avenues,
the **Mount Vernon Hotel Museum
and Garden** ⑮ (421 East 61st Street,
www.mvhm.org, tel: 212-838 6878;

Recommended Restaurants, Bars, & Cafés on pages 134–5

closed Mon and all Aug; charge), is one of the few 18th-century buildings still standing proud in Manhattan. It's a marvel of survival, as it nestles under the Queensboro Bridge. The house has been furnished with period antiques, reminders of its former incarnation as a hotel. **Sotheby's**, the high-stakes auction house, is 10 blocks away, at York Avenue and 72nd Street.

At 88th Street and East End Avenue is **Gracie Mansion** ⑯, official residence of mayors of New York and another survivor from the 18th century. It was built by Scotsborn Archibald Gracie as a summer home, and was first used in 1942 by Mayor Fiorello LaGuardia. Tours can be arranged by appointment (tel: 212-639 9675).

Gracie Mansion is in **Carl Schurz Park,** a pleasant patch of green overlooking the currents of **Hell Gate,** where the waters of the East and the Harlem rivers flow together.

Hitch a ride on the **Roosevelt Island Tramway** at Second Avenue and 60th Street: the views are unique and lovely, especially at sunset.

ROOSEVELT ISLAND ⑰

Across the water by monorail-tram, Roosevelt Island is a 147-acre (60-hectare) respite from urban living. This tiny (2-mile/3km), tranquil, cigar-shaped island contains one main street, one church, one supermarket, a few restaurants, and one of the city's more recent subway extensions.

This "annexation" made Roosevelt a highly desirable residential neighborhood – witness the sleek apartments of **Manhattan Park.** Amenities include an indoor pool, playgrounds, and five small parks. From the walkways edging the shoreline there are panoramic views of the East Side, and at the north end you can admire a stone lighthouse from 1872. Madison Avenue seems a long way away. ❑

ABOVE: kids on a cold day in Carl Schurz Park.
BELOW LEFT: East Side window dressing.
BELOW RIGHT: Roosevelt Island's tramway.

BEST RESTAURANTS, BARS, AND CAFÉS

Restaurants

Prices for a three-course dinner per person with half a bottle of wine:
$ = under $20
$$ = $20–$45
$$$ = $45–$60
$$$$ = over $60

L'Absinthe
✉ 227 E. 67th St (at 2nd and 3rd aves) 📞 212-794 4950 🅒 L & D daily, D only Sun July, Aug **$$$** [p335, D4]
The etched mirrors, polished brass and French waiters in white aprons are as authentic as the classic brasserie fare.

Beyoglu
✉ 1431 3rd Ave (at 80th and 81st sts) 📞 212-650 0850 🅒 L & D daily **$$** [p335, D2]
This casual Turkish eatery serves a meze-style menu including tasty kebabs and dips like roe-studded tarama and garlicky hummus.

Café Sabarsky
✉ 1048 5th Ave (at 86th St) 📞 212-288 0665 🅒 Br & L daily, D Thur–Sun **$$$** [p335, D1]
This Viennese-style restaurant's Museum Mile location makes it handy. Have eggs at brunch; *spätzle* and goulash for lunch and dinner.

Candle 79
✉ 154 E. 79th St (at Lexington and 3rd aves) 📞 212-537 7179 🅒 L Mon–Sat, Br Sun, D daily **$$$** [p335, D2]
There are plenty of places to "veg out" in New York, but here's one that is elegant and fits the stylish neighborhood, with sophisticated vegetarian and vegan dishes featuring great organic ingredients.

Daniel
✉ 60 E. 65th St (at Madison and Park aves) 📞 212-288 0033 🅒 D only Mon–Sat **$$$$** [p335, C4]
A great chef, Daniel Boulud, presides over this most expensive food kingdom, but gourmets will gladly spend for the unique quality and service he delivers.

Demarchelier
✉ 50 E. 86th St (at Madison Ave) 📞 212-249 6300 🅒 L & D daily **$$$** [p335, D1]
Upper East Side bistro with a sense of style and a moderately priced all-day prix-fixe menu.

E.J.'s Luncheonette
✉ 1271 3rd Ave (at 73rd St) 📞 212-472 0600 🅒 B, L, & D daily **$** [p335, D3]
Anybody longing for a 1950s-style chrome interior will feel they've come home here. Cash only is accepted.

Eli's Vinegar Factory
✉ 431 E. 91st St (at 1st Ave) 📞 212-987 0885 🅒 Br, L, & D daily **$$** [p335, E1]]
This massive grocery store's café is great for soup or sandwiches without all the fuss of a full-service restaurant.

Fig & Olive
✉ 808 Lexington Ave (at 62nd and 63rd sts) 📞 212-207 4555 🅒 L & D daily **$$$** [p335, C4]
Conveniently located for shopping, with a Mediterranean menu, and a raw bar, too.

Gino's
✉ 780 Lexington Ave (at 60th and 61st sts) 📞 212-758 4466 🅒 L & D daily **$$$** [p335, C4]
Watching the regulars, for whom this East Side institution (opened in 1945) is like a club, is as much an experience as eating at this pasta house . A block up from Bloomies.

LEFT: Café Sabarsky.
RIGHT: pretty in pink.

Girasole
151 E. 82nd St (at Lexington and 3rd aves) 212-772 6690 L & D daily $$$$ [p335, D2]
Feel like a pampered Upper East Side regular at this long-established Italian comfort zone.

Heidelberg
1648 2nd Ave (at 85th and 86th sts) 212-628 2332 L & D daily $$ [p335, E2]
Yorkville's last tribute to Germantown. The *wiener schnitzel* and dumplings are the real thing for lovers of tasty, traditional German fare.

Jackson Hole
1270 Madison Ave (at 91st St) 212-427 2820 B, L & D daily $ [p335, D1]
Juicy rare-red or well-done burgers – not for vegetarians. East Side, West Side, a NY tradition.

J.G. Melon
1291 3rd Ave (at 74th St) 212-744 0585 L & D daily $$ [p335, D3]
Upper East Side mainstay for great Bloody Marys and delicious burgers.

JoJo
160 E. 64th St (at Lexington and 3rd aves) 212-223 5656 L & D daily $$$$ [p335, C4]
The rich emerald and burgundy colors, luxurious fabrics, and warm-hued tiles are as inviting as the menu. One of Manhattan's best French food extravaganzas.

Kai
822 Madison Ave (at 68th and 69th sts) 212-988 7277 L & D Tue–Sat $$$$ [p335, C3]
Elegant Asian eatery, specializing in the *kaiseki* multi-course Japanese tradition.

Kings' Carriage House
251 E. 82nd St (at 2nd and 3rd aves) 212-734 5490 L & D daily $$$ [p335, E2]
Cozy two-story Colonial carriage house turned into a restaurant with pre-arranged seatings. A different dining experience.

Nica
354 E. 84th St (at 1st and 2nd aves) 212-472 5040 D daily $$$ [p335, E2]
This cozy place serves Sicilian classics ranging from spaghetti carbonara to braised lamb shank and grilled veal chops.

Pascalou
1308 Madison Ave (at 92nd and 93rd sts) 212-534 7522 L & D daily $$ [p335, D1]
Delicious and excellent value for this expensive area, especially the prix-fixe early dinner.

Sfoglia
135 E. 92nd St (at Lexington Ave) 212-831 1402 L & D Tue–Sat, D Sun–Mon $$$ [p335, E1]
Rustic but hugely popular little northern Italian that serves up such delectable dishes as *fusilli* in *vin santo* cream sauce. Book long in advance for dinner, or go for lunch instead.

Sushi of Gari
402 E. 78th St (at 1st Ave) 212-517 5340 D daily $$$ [p335, E3]
The fish at this small Japanese restaurant is as fresh as can be, and the preparations continue to amaze fans.

Il Vagabondo
351 E. 62nd St (at 1st and 2nd aves) 212-832 9221 L & D Mon–Fri, D only Sat–Sun $$$ [p335, D4]
Complete with its own indoor *bocce* (Italian-style bowls) court, not to mention more than decent Italian food.

Vivolo
140 E. 74th St (at Park and Lexington aves) 212-737 3533 L & D Mon–Sat $$$ [p335, D3]
Charming Italian in an 1875 townhouse that's been serving East Siders for years in a hard-to-please district.

Bars and Cafés

Boathouse in Central Park, enter at 5th Ave and 72nd St and walk north to this scenic spot overlooking the lake; have coffee, brunch, or cocktails on the deck.

Elaine's, 1703 2nd Ave (at 88th and 89th sts), is feted as an old-style celebrity hangout, loved by writers and actors, and best enjoyed with a glass of wine at the bar.

Fred's at Barneys, 660 Madison Ave (at 60th St) is a good coffee recharge stop before hitting a few more of Madison's shopping possibilities.

Le Pain Quotidien, 1131 Madison Ave (at 84th and 85th sts), is good value for excellent French pastries.

Sant Ambroeus, 1000 Madison Ave (at 77th and 78th sts). Elegant espressos to marzipan and more – all is heavenly here.

Serendipity, 3 E. 60th St, around the corner from Bloomies. Dessert delirium is still the specialty here, but light fare for lunch and dinner is also available, and the shop up front is good for kids and grans alike.

MUSEUM MILE

Some of America's finest cultural treasures are housed in fabulous museums that line the east side of Central Park

Museum Mile is a cultural parade of some of the US's finest examples of art, culture, and history, housed in nine, mainly opulent, galleries along Fifth Avenue, from 82nd Street and the Metropolitan Museum of Art, all the way north to the Latin American cultural museum, El Museo del Barrio, at 104th Street.

A newcomer to the auspicious mile, the Museum for African Art, is due to open by the end of 2010 between 109th and 110th streets, the first museum to be built on the mile since 1959. The Neue Galerie features German art and cultural exhibits. The Solomon R. Guggenheim Museum, housed in the remarkable spiral Frank Lloyd Wright building, hosts exhibitions on a grand scale. The Jewish Museum has art and culture from its own perspective at 92nd Street.

The National Academy Museum and School of Fine Arts tutored John Singer Sargent and Thomas Eakins, among other talents, while a branch of the Smithsonian, the Cooper-Hewitt National Design Museum, showcases highly decorative arts in a Beaux Arts mansion.

For opening times and map references to all museums, see pages 128 and 168.

ABOVE: *Pershing Square Bridge*, 1993, by Bascove, can be seen in the Museum of the City of New York.

LEFT: Frank Lloyd Wright's architectural showpiece, the Solomon R. Guggenheim Museum, Fifth Avenue.

ABOVE: the Neue Galerie is devoted to early Austrian and German art, including works by Gustav Klimt. There are also cultural exhibits on show.

RIGHT: the Cooper-Hewitt National Design Museum's international collection includes decorative arts, product design, textiles, and wallpapers, and is housed in this exquisite mansion on the edge of Central Park. The library has more than 70,000 books, and there is an archive of drawings and photographs.

BELOW: *First Night Game, Yankee Stadium, May 28, 1946*, Paolo Corvino, from the Museum of the City of New York. In addition to exhibits, the museum owns an 1851 double-decker fire truck, and organizes excellent walking tours of the city.

MUSEUM MILE FESTIVAL

From 6 to 9pm on the second Tuesday in June each year, the Museum Mile Festival signals that Fifth Avenue is closed to road traffic from the Metropolitan Museum at 82nd Street, and for an entire mile north.

Musicians, street performers, and food stalls line the length of the route, and all of the museums are open to the public for free in what is the city's biggest and most culturally diverse block party.

Special temporary exhibits are often mounted to coincide with the festival, and art activities with kids in mind are held in the street. Live music is performed, some for dancing, some for background listening, and some for contemplation, ranging from jazz to string quartets to Broadway show tunes.

The event has been a highly popular fixture in the New York cultural calendar since the festival's inception in the late 1970s, and regularly attracts a high-spirited crowd of more than 50,000 art-lovers, fun-seekers, and aficionados.

ABOVE: *Goldfish Vendor*, 1928, by Reuven Rubin, from *Culture and Continuity: The Jewish Journey* at the Jewish Museum.

THE METROPOLITAN MUSEUM

The *grande dame* of American museums displays many of the oldest treasures and most important moments in the history of art

The Metropolitan Museum of Art is a palatial gallery with a collection of paintings, sculpture, drawings, furnishings, and decorative arts spanning 10,000 years of human creativity. Featuring exemplary works from major European artists such as Bruegel to Botticelli and from Van Gogh to Velázquez and Vermeer, nearly every civilization is represented. Exhibits feature art objects from Archeulian flints found in Egypt dating to the Lower Paleolithic period (300,000–75,000 BC), right up to 21st-century designs from couturier Alexander McQueen.

The Met has five cafés and bars, ranging from the airy cafeteria to the more formal Petrie Court Café, which offers waiter service. The museum's online gallery has excellent study resources, an art timeline, and podcasts.

ABOVE: the Metropolitan moved to its Fifth Avenue location in 1880, although the facade was remodeled in 1926. In total, the Met houses a collection of more than 2 million pieces.

RIGHT: this 18th-century chest of drawers was made in Philadelphia, and is part of the Metropolitan's American Decorative Arts collection.

BELOW: the Met's collection began in 1870, and one of Central Park's architects, Calvert Vaux, along with Jacob Wrey Mold, designed the museum's first permanent home. The Cloisters, a branch dedicated to medieval art, is in Fort Tryon Park.

The Essentials

✉ *1000 Fifth Avenue at 82nd Street; www.metmuseum.org*
📞 *212-535 7710*
🕐 *Tue–Thur and Sun 9am–5.30pm, Fri, Sat 9.30am–9pm*
💲 *charge; audioguides also available for a fee.*
🚇 *86th Street*

GREEK AND ROMAN GALLERIES

The Greek and Roman galleries opened in 2007 and were built specifically to house and display the Metropolitan's art *c*.900 BC to the early 4th century AD. The collection is a monumental showcase that describes the parallel developments of Greek art in the Hellenistic period and the arts of southern Italy and Etruria, culminating in the rich and varied world of the Roman Empire.

The museum's Greek and Roman pieces have not been seen together since 1949. Many of the thousands of works that are now displayed in the spacious galleries have not been on view to the public since their creation, which was up to 3,000 years ago. The galleries bring under one roof the very foundations of Western artistic civilization.

RIGHT: the Iris and B. Gerald Cantor Roof Garden provides a summertime setting for large sculptures, with Central Park and the Upper West Side as backdrops. Wine and light food is available, too.

ABOVE: the André Mertens Galleries display the Metropolitan's handsome collection of musical instruments, which includes early flutes, Baroque organs, and electric guitars, in addition to this fine Flemish virginal, which dates from the 16th century.

ABOVE: *Young Woman with a Water Jug*, 1660, was painted by the Dutch Master, Johannes Vermeer.

ABOVE: *Madame X (Madame Pierre Gautreau)*, by John Singer Sargent, painted in 1883–4.

ABOVE: among the works of artists on display in the American Paintings and Sculpture Gallery is *The Lighthouse at Two Lights*, by Edward Hopper, 1929.

RIGHT: the Met's rich decorative arts collections include medieval works in stained glass, lamps from Tiffany, and wall hangings from William Morris of the English Arts and Crafts movement.

Metropolitan Museum of Art

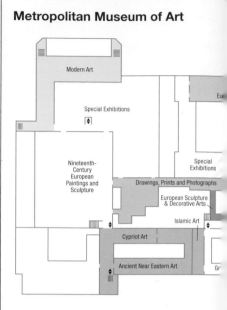

Modern Art

Special Exhibitions

Eu

Nineteenth-Century European Paintings and Sculpture

Special Exhibitions

Drawings, Prints and Photographs

European Sculpture & Decorative Arts

Islamic Art

Cypriot Art

Ancient Near Eastern Art

Gr

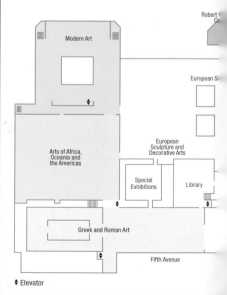

Robert
Co

Modern Art

European S

Arts of Africa, Oceania and the Americas

European Sculpture and Decorative Arts

Special Exhibitions

Library

Greek and Roman Art

Fifth Avenue

↕ Elevator

Second Floor

The American Wing

The American Wing

Musical Instruments

pean Paintings

Japanese Art

Chinese Art

Chinese Art

Asian Art

Arts of Korea

Arts of Korea

Asian Art

South Asian Art

Southeast Asian Art

First Floor

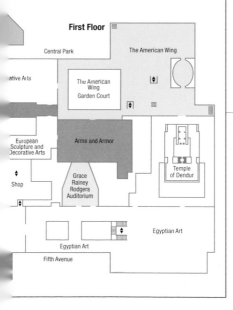

Central Park

The American Wing

The American Wing Garden Court

ative Arts

European Sculpture and Decorative Arts

Arms and Armor

Temple of Dendur

Shop

Grace Rainey Rodgers Auditorium

Egyptian Art

Egyptian Art

Fifth Avenue

ABOVE: *The Great Wave at Kanagawa*, by Katsushika Hokusai, is a paper print made between 1830 and 1832. The artist said of this period in his life, "Nothing I did before the age of 70 was worthy of attention."

ABOVE: relief of Nebhepetre Mentuhotep II from the Egyptian Middle Kingdom, Dynasty 11, created between 2051–2000 BC. Painted limestone.

LEFT: the Met's collection of Islamic arts includes Anatolian, Ottoman, and Turkoman rugs, with decorative as well as devotional pieces on display. After eight years of construction, the museum will open a new 19,000-sq-ft (1,765-sq-m) gallery for the collection in late 2011.

Recommended Restaurants, Bars, & Cafés on pages 152–3

UPPER WEST SIDE

The Upper West Side is laid out a little like a pepper
sandwich: it looks tempting on the outside,
and has some spicy delights in the middle

The highlights of the Upper West Side tend to be around Broadway, Columbus and Amsterdam avenues, a sort of 24-hour circus squeezed between the calm of Riverside Drive and Central Park West. The entrance to all this is **Columbus Circle** , with its hustling bustle of cars, pedestrians, and skateboarders, and the Time Warner Center, whose asymmetric glass towers loom over and almost dwarf the stately statue of Christopher Columbus.

High-flyers

The southern part of the neighborhood has moved up in the world in recent years, due in great part to the Time Warner Center, but also to the growth of residential apartment towers in the far west, home to prosperous young hedge-funders and their starter families.

On the south side of Columbus Circle, look for the striking concrete-and-glass building which is the new home of the **Museum of Arts and Design**. The museum opened in 2008, with double its previous space. On the north side is the gleaming **Trump International Hotel and Tower** (*see page 301*). The hotel is across from the gateway to Central Park, which is usually thronged with people playing music, eating lunch, passing through, or just plain hanging out. Vendors crowd the sidewalks, and pedicab drivers troll for passengers.

The **Time Warner Center** has made space for dozens of new stores aimed squarely at affluent shoppers, and some very pricey restaurants, including an eatery that is currently New York's most expensive, **Masa**. The center does have less expensive

Main attractions

COLUMBUS CIRCLE
MUSEUM OF ARTS AND DESIGN
TIME WARNER CENTER
CENTRAL PARK WEST
THE DAKOTA
STRAWBERRY FIELDS
AMERICAN MUSEUM
OF NATURAL HISTORY
LINCOLN CENTER
METROPOLITAN OPERA
AVERY FISHER HALL
AMSTERDAM AVENUE
ANSONIA HOTEL
RIVERSIDE PARK

LEFT: the view from the Time Warner
Center over Columbus Circle.
RIGHT: the Trump International Hotel and
Tower, with its gleaming globe.

Aiming for the Top

**The Big Apple is a Type-A town –
the driven, the dreamers, and the
high achievers all gravitate here**

New Yorkers may not have many obvious things in common, apart from a particular fondness for black clothes, but one thing they all do have is an energetic drive. A drive to succeed, to excel, to reach to the top.

It may be more than a coincidence that this city has been spiritual home to the most literally concrete symbol of aspiration, the skyscraper; those steel-and-glass fingers stretching for the sky also serve as metaphors for the New York spirit. Not just "Get up and go," but more. More like, "Get up. Now get higher up."

"New York is a city that loves what has been called the 'Type A' personality: always feeling the press of time, aggressive and competitive, a workaholic, dedicated to achievement," says Dr Anthony Zito, a psychiatrist engaged in stress research, with artists and performers among his patients.

The Type-A pattern (competitive, impatient, and averse to seeking help) was first identified in 1959 by American physiologists Meyer Friedman and Ray Rosenham, as an indicator of likely cardiac disease. A pattern which may make some people successful, but could also kill them earlier. Later studies focused on what the differences are that enable some people to thrive under the very pressures that can make others terminally ill.

What draws these Type As to compete in New York City, rather than settle for what could be greater relative success in a smaller town? Psychotherapists familiar with the syndrome think that the drive to compete on the grandest scale is important. From the clinical perspective, the kind of person drawn to that challenge is a narcissist, and that some degree of narcissism may be essential for aspects of their mental wellbeing.

The urge to be great

Zito said, "The urge to be great is in the spectrum of healthy narcissism. That spectrum includes those who simply do their thing well and live productive lives. They don't dream of writing the Great American Novel; they are satisfied just doing their work. Another group has higher aspirations; they work much harder, push themselves more. Finally, there are narcissists who really aspire to be great. Some really do have talent, and it makes sense for them to aim high. But others just want people to declare them great. They have no intention of doing the hard work. That is where pathological narcissism begins."

A Jungian analyst, Dr James Hillman said, "I believe the city is good for the soul." Credited with returning the concept of the soul and the importance of mythology to the realm of psychoanalysis, Hillman said, "It is as if there were a human need for cities to manifest the richness, including the darkness, of human nature. But the city, as [urban historian] Lewis Mumford observed, is a living work of art. It manifests the human imagination." ❑

LEFT: Type-A man Donald Trump. **ABOVE:** Michael Bloomberg with California's Arnold Schwarzenegger.

Recommended Restaurants, Bars, & Cafés on pages 152–3

options, including a branch of the organic produce chain Whole Foods, where you can pick up something to eat in the food court or as a picnic in Central Park.

CNN is on the third floor of the Time Warner Center, and you can peek through the windows at the studio. On the north side of the complex at the corner of 60th Street and Broadway is the entrance to the home of **Jazz at Lincoln Center** (tel: 212-258 9800), a world-class concert venue *(see pages 147–9 and 158–61)*.

CENTRAL PARK WEST ⑳

Central Park West takes over from Eighth Avenue, branches off Columbus Circle and heads up into the West Side's most affluent residential section. The apartment houses overlooking the park are among the most lavish in the city – like the famous twin towers of the **San Remo Apartments**, built in 1931 – and the cross streets, especially 74th, 75th, and 76th, are lined with equally splendid brownstones. At the corner of West 67th Street, the **Hotel des Artistes** has numbered Valentino, Isadora Dun-

can, Noel Coward, and Norman Rockwell among its tenants, and was once home to the **Café des Artistes**, an exquisite hideaway on the first floor with the perfect ambience for a rendezvous – unfortunately, it closed in 2009.

The most famous apartment building on this stretch is **The Dakota ㉑**, built in 1884 by Henry Hardenbergh, who also designed the Plaza Hotel.

LEFT: the San Remo Apartments and Central Park West in wintertime.
BELOW: outside the Time Warner Center.

Founded in 1869, the American Museum of Natural History is constantly refreshed with new exhibits.

BELOW: exhibits from the AMNH.

At the time, people joked that it was so far outside the city, "it might as well be in the Dakota Territory," which explains the Indian's head above the entrance.

Imagine

Urban streets caught up with The Dakota soon enough, and over the years the building has attracted tenants like Boris Karloff, Leonard Bernstein, and Lauren Bacall, and was the setting for the 1968 movie *Rosemary's Baby*. Most famously, John Lennon lived at The Dakota and was shot outside it in 1980. **Strawberry Fields**, a touching knoll dedicated to his memory, is across the street a few steps into Central Park *(see pages 82–5)*.

These days, foreign students buy Lennon merchandise from the surrounding stands, and visitors converse on memorial benches bordering Strawberry Fields' *Imagine* mosaic.

From 72nd Street, it's a short walk Uptown, past the somber facades of the Universalist Church and the **New-York Historical Society ㉒** (170 Central Park West, www.nyhistory.org, tel: 212-873 3400; closed Mon; charge), New York's oldest museum, with permanent exhibitions on the city's history, to the 79th Street entrance of the American Museum of Natural History, the *grande dame* of Manhattan museums, which sprawls over several blocks of the city.

American Museum of Natural History ㉓

✉ 79th St (at Central Park West), www.amnh.org ☎ 212-769 5100
🕐 daily 10am–5.45pm
💲 charge 🚇 81st St

Guarded by an equestrian statue of

Theodore Roosevelt, the museum's main entrance is one of many additions built around the original structure *(see photo feature on pages 154–7)*. The original facade – a stately Romanesque arcade with two towers – was built in the late 1800s, and can be seen from 77th Street. The front steps have become a regrouping point, where families and school groups study guidebooks and maps.

For children, a visit to the museum

is a must, but with 45 exhibition halls housed in 25 buildings, there's plenty for grown-ups to see, too. Some of the exhibits are more successful than others, but choice is the main problem here.

Highlights include a 34-ton (31,000kg) meteorite, the largest blue sapphire in the world, and a full-sized model of a blue whale. The world's tallest dinosaur – the 50ft (15-meter) Barosaurus – is in the Theodore Roosevelt Rotunda. The museum also includes a gigantic screen **Imax Theater**, in addition to the **Rose Center for Earth and Space**, which houses the **Hayden Planetarium**.

From October to May the **Butterfly Conservatory** provides a popular opportunity to see some rare and beautiful tropical butterflies as they flutter around a temporary enclosure erected inside the building.

Don't even think about doing the whole museum in one shot, and expect to spend some of your time trying to find your way around, despite having a floor plan.

THE BROADWAY CULTURE TOUR

If culture is high on your list, try this route through the Upper West Side. From Columbus Circle, Broadway swerves west toward Columbus Avenue and nicks the corner of Lincoln Center, flanked on one side by the Juilliard School and on the other by **Fordham University**. Even to be accepted at the **Juilliard School** is an honor, as the highly selective enrollment and small classes draw some of the most talented students in America. Trumpeter Miles Davis was an alumnus, and for a while lived a few blocks north on West 77th Street.

Lincoln Center ㉔

✉ Columbus Ave (at 65th St), www.lincolncenter.org
📞 see page 148
🕐 tours daily 10.30am–4.30pm
💲 charge 🚇 66th St/Lincoln Center

Construction of the **Lincoln Center for the Performing Arts** *(see photo feature on pages 158–61)* began in 1959 as part of a massive redevelopment plan to clean up the slums that occupied the site. Now, the cen-

TIP

On the first Friday of each month, the American Museum of Natural History hosts a "Starry Nights" series of jazz concerts in the unique setting of the giant glass shell of the Rose Center for Earth and Space.

BELOW: sizzling sounds under the stars at the Natural History Museum.

ter is one of the city's most popular venues, with attendance running at about 5 million people a year.

Around Lincoln Center

ABOVE: smooth sounds from Frederick P. Rose Hall. The venue is part of Lincoln Center, but is housed in the Time Warner Center.
BELOW: the New York City Ballet performs to *Symphony in C* by the Ringer Martins Group.

The black marble fountain in the middle of the plaza is surrounded by the glass-and-white-marble facades of the center's three main structures. The **Metropolitan Opera** ❻ (tel: 212-362 6000) is directly in front, with two large murals by Marc Chagall behind the glass wall – *Le Triomphe de la Musique* to the left, *Les Sources de la Musique* to the right.

The Met is home to the Metropolitan Opera Company from September to April, and the American Ballet Theater from May to July. Although marvelous, its productions and performers carry a hefty price tag, but the tiny **Gallery Met** just off the main foyer has a collection of paintings which you can see free of charge.

To the left of the central fountain, the **New York State Theater** ❼ (tel: 212-870 5570) is shared by the New York City Opera and the New York City Ballet – both more adventurous than the Met, and less expensive. The third side of the main plaza is occupied by **Avery Fisher Hall** ❽ (tel: 212-875 5030), home of the New York Philharmonic and the Mostly Mozart summer concert series.

Two secondary courtyards flank the Metropolitan Opera. On the right, the **Vivian Beaumont Theater** ❾ (tel: 212- 362 7600) is fronted by a shady plaza and reflecting pool, around which office workers gather for lunch. The oxidized bronze sculpture in the center of the pool is by Henry Moore. A spindly steel sculpture by Alexander Calder is

near the entrance to the **Library of the Performing Arts**. The Bandshell in **Damrosch Park** is used for free concerts in summer. These are usually around lunchtime, but there are occasional performances in the early evenings too. Over the next few years the Lincoln Center complex will be gradually transformed, with new street-level entrances for many venues and a major overhaul of **Alice Tully Hall**, used for chamber music, so expect building work around the area.

Following Columbus

After soaking up culture at Lincoln Center, cross **Columbus Avenue** for the **American Folk Art Museum** (2 Lincoln Square, www.folkartmuseum.org, tel: 212-595 9533; closed Mon; charge). This smaller branch of the main museum *(see page 114)* has a lovely collection of Amish quilts, as well as a more recent addition – a patchwork-quilt memorial to the victims of the attack on the World Trade Center. The museum also has a great little gift shop.

Head Uptown for some high-grade browsing. Shopping along this end of Columbus Avenue can be a pleasant, almost small-town activity in comparison with the Midtown mayhem of Macy's and other places. Trees line the sidewalks, while dog-walkers spilling over from Central Park contribute to a gentler pace.

Classic and organic

The Uptown branch of **Kiehl's** (150 Columbus Avenue), a generations-old natural cosmetics and perfume apothecary, is worth visiting. New editions to the classic range include lip-glosses and SPF-rated face cream, all in traditionally simple packaging. Hair-accessory headquarters **Boyd's of Madison Avenue** also has a West Side branch, at 309 Columbus, with children's clothes and toys as well as organic shampoos.

There are far too many clothes stores to list by name, but those that deserve special mention are north of 68th Street. There's outrageous fashion at **Betsey Johnson** (248 Columbus), upscale women's wear at **Eileen Fisher** (341 Columbus), and equally upscale men's wear at **Frank Stella** (440 Columbus).

Columbus's proximity to Central Park – the Uptown dog-walker's playground – is recognized at various pet stores, none more deliciously over-the-top than **Canine Ranch** at No. 452. Here you can pick up

ABOVE: the Upper West Side's proximity to Central Park makes it a dog-walker's delight.
BELOW: Lincoln Center and the Metropolitan Opera building.

everything from freshly baked bone-shaped cookies to New York Knicks jackets for your furry friend. There's also a wide selection of funky vintage wear (and wares) at a flea market every Sunday between 76th and 77th streets. Here, locals like to browse before or after brunch with friends or family.

THE FAR WEST

Skipping west to **Amsterdam Avenue**, the scene is dressed down but still trendy: restaurants, boutiques, and bars with a twentysomething clientele dominate, though there are a few remaining Latino-flavored grocer's stores and traditional neighborhood shops like **West Side Kids** at 84th Street, with its unusually intelligent toy inventory.

At 80th and Broadway, **Zabar's** is the gourmet store against which gourmet stores are measured. Even if you're not in the mood for buying, it's worth elbowing your way to the counter for a free taste of all the goodies; visiting the store is worthwhile for the smells alone. On the opposite corner, and appearing to

share the same 1970s color scheme, is **H&H Bagel** – considered by some to sell the best bagels in New York.

At 212 West 83rd Street, the amusing **Children's Museum of Manhattan** (www.cmom.org, tel: 212-721 1234; closed Mon; charge) is a brightly colored multilevel kiddy kingdom with interactive exhibits and special events. The noise level is high, so arrive very calm or come equipped with earplugs.

And at West 89th Street, just off Amsterdam Avenue, spare a thought for the Claremont Riding Academy, the last surviving riding stables in Manhattan, which after 115 years in business closed in April, 2007.

Off-Off-Broadway

In recent years, new meaning has been added to the term "Off-Broadway," with an Upper West Side scene that includes performances and literary readings at **Symphony Space**, on Broadway between 94th and 95th streets, and the **Beacon Theatre**, 2124 Broadway at 74th Street, a popular music venue where you might catch James Taylor (either one) one night and a gospel group the next.

Shopping continues on Broadway with the appearance of **Barneys Co-op** at 2151, the "neighborhood-sized" and more laid-back relation of the upscale department store that is popping up at desirable locations throughout the city. Thrift-store fans with an aversion to actual thrift stores can find cute and kooky things at **Urban Outfitters**.

SHOP

Grab a bag of bagels from H&H Bagel, top it off with some white-fish dip from Zabar's and head off to the park or the river for a real New York-style picnic.

RIGHT: taking religion to the streets.
BELOW: the lavish interior of the Beacon Theatre.

Occupying the entire block between 73rd and 74th streets is the **Ansonia Hotel** ㉚, and while it's a little worn around the edges, this is still the *grande dame* of West Side apartment buildings, with a resident list that over the years included Enrico Caruso, Igor Stravinsky, Arturo Toscanini, and Theodore Dreiser.

The hotel was particularly popular with singers and musicians because its thick internal walls allowed them to practice without disturbing the neighbors. Although retailers now dominate the first floor, the Ansonia's mansard roof, towers, and fabulous terracotta detailing still add up to a Beaux Arts fantasy that captures the gaze and won't let go.

Down by the Riverside

A tour of the far west of New York finishes nicely by taking 72nd Street to **West End Avenue** ㉛, then on to Riverside Drive. North of 72nd Street, West End Avenue is affluent and strictly residential; a great place to live, but not a particularly fascinating place for visitors. Humphrey Bogart lived for a while in Pomander

Walk, an English-style mews situated between 94th and 95th streets, West End Avenue, and busy Broadway.

South of 72nd Street, a mini-city of high-rise apartments has altered the Hudson River skyline on Riverside Boulevard, not to be confused with **Riverside Drive** ㉜, which winds along the edge of Frederick Law Olmsted's **Riverside Park**. The 72nd Street entrance has a bronze sculpture of Eleanor Roosevelt, one of only four statues of real-life women gracing New York's parks.

This is a picturesque corner of Manhattan, with sweeping views of the Hudson River. In warm weather, Manhattanites come to the **79th Street Boat Basin** for drinks and burgers. ❏

KIDS

Kids' stores on Columbus are good value. Kidville is a "boutique" and hair salon with fire trucks, airplane, and car-shaped seats to entice the under-5s in for a haircut.

BELOW: alfresco dining at the 79th Street Boat Basin.

BEST RESTAURANTS, BARS, AND CAFÉS

Restaurants

Prices for a three-course dinner per person with half a bottle of wine:

$ = under $20
$$ = $20–$45
$$$ = $45–$60
$$$$ = over $60

Artie's Deli
✉ 2290 Broadway (at 82nd and 83rd sts) ☎ 212-579 5959 ⓒ B, L, & D daily **$$** [p334, B1]
Hang out among the hanging salamis in this gentrified, kid-friendly deli.

Bar Boulud
✉ 1900 Broadway (at 63rd and 64th sts) ☎ 212-595 0303 ⓒ L & D daily **$$$** [p334, B3]
Daniel Boulud's wine-and-charcuterie restaurant, across from Lincoln Cen-

ter, is a great place to get a lardon salad or a plate of pâté before a show.

Barney Greengrass
✉ 541 Amsterdam Ave (near 86th and 87th sts) ☎ 212-724 4707 ⓒ B & L Tue–Sun **$$** [off map]
This old-school smoked-fish spot is the real deal – it has been open for more than 100 years. Barney serves up some of the best sturgeon, white fish, and Nova on the Upper West Side.

Boat Basin Café
✉ W. 79th St on the Hudson River ☎ 212-496 5542 ⓒ L & D daily May–Oct **$$** [p334, B1]
Hands-down the most popular Upper West Side outdoor eating spot, with

a boisterous Thursday-night bar scene. Mainly grills, but unbeatable Hudson River sunsets more than make up for the food.

Bouchon Bakery
✉ 10 Columbus Circle ☎ 212-823 9366 ⓒ B, L, & D daily **$$** [p334, B3]
Affordable bistro/boulangerie in the Time Warner Center. Takeout also available.

Café Frida
✉ 368 Columbus Ave (at 77th and 78th sts) ☎ 212-712 2929 ⓒ L & D daily **$$$** [p334, B1]
Rich-tasting Mexican cuisine at a bar-restaurant behind the Museum of Natural History.

Café Luxembourg
✉ 200 W. 70th St (at Amsterdam and West End aves) ☎ 212-873 7411 ⓒ B, L, & D daily **$$$** [p334, B2]
This classic French bistro is within walking distance of Lincoln Center. With a lovely Art Deco dining room, this is a long-running success.

Calle Ocho
✉ 446 Columbus Ave (at 81st and 82nd sts) ☎ 212-873 5025 ⓒ D Mon–Sat, Br & D Sun **$$** [p334, B1]
Regular young professionals dine well on innovative versions of classic

Cuban and Latin dishes, washed down with what many claim are New York's best mojitos.

Gennaro
✉ 665 Amsterdam Ave (at 92nd and 93rd sts) ☎ 212-665 5348 ⓒ D daily **$** [off map]
Upper West Siders love the casual vibe and hearty Italian dishes (gnocchi, braised lamb) here almost as much as they love the surprisingly low prices.

Isabella's
✉ 359 Columbus Ave (at 76th and 77th sts) ☎ 212-724 2100 ⓒ L & D daily, Br Sun **$$** [p334, B1]
Crowded at brunch for all the right reasons: great food and a great location on a Columbus Avenue corner; outdoor tables when possible.

Jean-Georges
✉ 1 Central Park W. (at 60th and 61st sts) ☎ 212-299 3900 ⓒ L & D Mon–Sat **$$$$** [p334, B3]
Chef Jean-Georges Vongerichten's four-star experiment in ultra-chic surroundings is well worth the price. For the ultimate, try the seven-course tasting menu; for the experience of just being here, order the prix-fixe lunch at a frac-

LEFT: Ouest has stylish food to match its clientele.
RIGHT: Oysters Rockefeller originated in New Orleans.

tion of the cost. "Prepare to be open-mouthed whenever you're not chewing," raves *New York* magazine.

Land
✉ 450 Amsterdam Ave (at 81st and 82nd sts) ☎ 212-501 8121 ☯ L & D daily $–$$ [p334, B1]
Called the best Thai on the Upper West Side, and now with an Upper East Side branch, too.

Luzia's
✉ 429 Amsterdam Ave (at 80th and 81st sts) ☎ 212-595 2000 ☯ L & D Tue–Sun, Br Sun $$ [p334, B1]
Amsterdam's affordable Portuguese: home-style cooking with robust and pungent flavors.

Niko's Mediterranean Grill
✉ 2161 Broadway (at 76th St) ☎ 212-873 7000 ☯ B, L, & D daily $$ [p334, B1]
Huge menu of fish and meats at excellent value – a neighborhood find.

Ocean Grill
✉ 384 Columbus Ave (at 78th and 79th sts) ☎ 212-579 2300 ☯ L & D daily $$$ [p334, B1]
Excellent West Side fish house, but the volume of noise can detract from the culinary experience – best at lunchtime.

Ouest
✉ 2315 Broadway (at 83rd and 84th sts) ☎ 212-580 8700 ☯ D daily, Br Sun $$$$ [off map]

This smart eatery is a place to be "scene." The clubby atmosphere says it all, but its food should not be missed or dismissed.

Porter House New York
✉ 10 Columbus Circle (at Broadway and 60th St) ☎ 212-823 9500 ☯ L & D daily $$$$ [p334, B3]
The fourth floor of the Time Warner Center is as special as the food prepared here by Michael Lomonaco, former chef at Windows on the World. Expect the best aged beef at prices called "reasonable" – at least compared to TWC's neighboring **Masa**, NY's priciest tab.

Rack and Soul
✉ 258 W. 109th St (at Broadway) ☎ 212-222 4800 ☯ L & D daily $$ [off map]
A menu rich in fried chicken, fried catfish, and baby back ribs complete with biscuits and honey is sinfully delicious. Go for it!

Saigon Grill
✉ 620 Amsterdam Ave (at 90th and 91st sts) ☎ 212-875 9072 ☯ L & D daily $ [off map]
The Vietnamese dishes are carefully prepared – consider crispy spring rolls served with mint and lettuce wrappers, pork chops marinated in lemongrass, or shrimp and scallops fried and tossed with a tangy-sweet glaze. Takeout too.

Shake Shack
✉ 366 Columbus Ave (at 77th and 78th sts) ☎ 646-747 8770 ☯ L & D daily $–$$ [p334, B1]
Down the block from the Natural History Museum; kids and adults alike feast on burgers, fries, and milkshakes.

Telepan
✉ 72 W. 69th St (at Columbus Ave and Central Park W.) ☎ 212-580 4300 ☯ D daily, L Wed–Fri, and Br Sat–Sun $$$$ [p334, B2]

A real purist, the chef here uses only the freshest locally grown ingredients, in a New American cuisine with the silly name "haute barnyard."

Bars and Cafés

Alice's Tea Cup
102 W. 73rd St (between Columbus and Amsterdam aves), is a whimsical place for light lunch, tea, and intimate conversations.

Bin 71, Columbus Ave at 71st St. An intimate modern Italian wine bar frequented by Upper West Side regulars.

Buttercup Bake Shop, 141 W. 72nd St, at Columbus and Amsterdam. Yummy cupcakes, just as they are. Also at 2nd Ave and E. 51st St.

Edgar's Café, 255 W. 84th St (between Broadway and West End Ave). Edgar Allen Poe once haunted this neighborhood. A hideaway in his memory (bright, rather than dark and scary) serves light fare, teas, and coffees.

Hudson Bar, Hudson Hotel, W. 58th St off 8th Ave. Very sleek and chic bar in a Philippe Starck-designed hotel.

Gray's Papaya
2090 Broadway (at 72nd St). A two hot-dog dinner with a fruit-juice chaser. Stand-up only. Whaddya expect for three bucks?

O'Neal's, 49 W. 64th St (opposite Lincoln Center). A fixture in the Lincoln Center area for drinks and food.

Popover Café, 551 Amsterdam Ave (between 86th and 87th sts). A great place for breakfast or brunch.

Stone Rose, 10 Columbus Circle, a bar in the soaring Time Warner Center with intoxicating views.

THE AMERICAN MUSEUM OF NATURAL HISTORY

From whales in the depths of the oceans to fragments of far-distant worlds, AMNH makes natural history fun. There's live music, too

The Natural History Museum on the Upper West Side has one of the most popular collections in New York City. It's also one of the United States' largest, and takes weeks to explore. The museum has many features other than its 45 permanent exhibition halls. These include a monthly lecture series – on everything from birds to wine – several traveling exhibitions, an Imax theater, monthly music events, and SonicVision, a digitally animated music show produced in conjunction with MTV.

LEFT: in addition to this prehistoric creature, the museum's collection includes a 50ft (15-meter) Barosaurus skeleton, said to be the world's highest free-standing mount dinosaur.

TOP: a dramatic, full-size model of a blue whale dominates the Milstein Family Hall of Ocean Life. Marine ecosystems, including coral reefs, are depicted along with dioramas and exhibits on vertebrates and invertebrates.

ABOVE: the museum's dioramas of habitats depict the environs, habits, and behavior of innumerable species of animals, reptiles, insects, and aquatic life. Kids love the elephants in particular.

The Essentials

✉ *79th Street and Central Park West; www.amnh.org*
☎ *212-769 5100*
🕐 *daily 10am–5.45pm*
💲 *charge; audioguides also available.*
🚇 *81st St*

(Map: West 83rd St, West 82nd St, West 81st St, 81st St M, Rose Center for Earth and Space, W. 79 St, American Museum of Natural History, West 77th St, West 76th St, West 75th St, West 74th St, West 73rd St, Columbus Avenue, Central Park West, West Drive, The Lake)

A MAN'S PASSION

Naturalist Dr Albert S. Bickmore had a passion for a museum of natural history, and lobbied tirelessly for one to be established in New York. In 1869 he was successful, and a museum was founded in the Arsenal building in Central Park. Ground was broken for the museum's home at its present site in 1874. The original building is almost subsumed among later extensions, between the Gothic steps and turrets at the rear entrance and the white neoclassical Roman-style facade by Central Park West.

At the northern end of the museum's grounds, and dramatically lit at night, is the most recent addition, the $210-million glass cube housing the Rose Center for Earth and Space.

ABOVE: the Rose Center for Earth and Space includes a spiral walking tour of the growth of the universe, vividly demonstrating the concepts of cosmic scale.

ABOVE AND RIGHT: two of the main features of the Rose Center for Earth and Space are housed within the Hayden Sphere, which itself acts as a scale model of the sun, orbited by comparably sized planets of our solar system. Inside the top half of the sphere, the Hayden Planetarium's unique Zeiss Star Projector creates a powerful virtual-reality planetarium. The bottom half of the Hayden Sphere houses the Big Bang exhibit, which takes visitors on a multisensory re-creation of the big bang and recreates the beginnings of the universe.

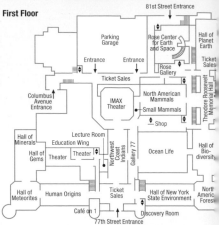

First Floor

ABOVE: vivid representations of animals from all seven continents inform, educate, and delight visitors. This diorama in the Akeley Hall of African Mammals, called *Water Hole*, features giraffes and antelope.

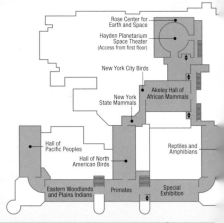

Third Floor

ABOVE: the museum has nearly 1 million fossil specimens, and more than 600 of them are on view. Most displays are of actual fossils, as opposed to the more commonly seen casts.

RIGHT: in addition to displaying one of the world's largest hunks of space rock – the 34-ton (31,000kg) Cape York meteorite – the Arthur Ross Hall of Meteorites has moon rocks and interactive exhibits, with computer animations of the formation, journeys, and final impact of these gigantic cosmic tourists.

Second Floor

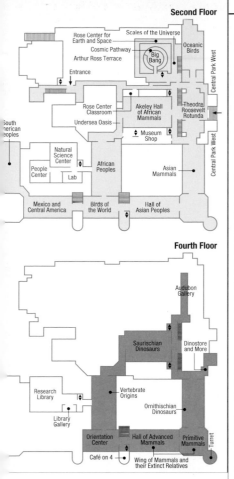

Rose Center for Earth and Space
Scales of the Universe
Cosmic Pathway
Big Bang
Oceanic Birds
Arthur Ross Terrace
Entrance
Central Park West

Rose Center Classroom
Akeley Hall of African Mammals
Theodore Roosevelt Rotunda
Undersea Oasis
Museum Shop
Central Park West

Natural Science Center
People Center
Lab
African Peoples
Asian Mammals

South American Peoples

Mexico and Central America
Birds of the World
Hall of Asian Peoples

Fourth Floor

Audubon Gallery

Saurischian Dinosaurs
Dinostore and More

Research Library
Vertebrate Origins
Ornithischian Dinosaurs

Library Gallery

Orientation Center
Hall of Advanced Mammals
Primitive Mammals
Turret

Café on 4
Wing of Mammals and their Extinct Relatives

HUMAN ORIGINS

The museum's Anne and Bernard Spitzer Hall of Human Origins exhibits remains and artifacts from our ancestor's progression to humanity and the birth of civilization. Using fossil records, carbon dating, and the latest gene technology, mankind's development from a threatened hunter-gatherer to a dexterous toolmaker and gregarious mass communicator is traced and described.

The oldest human finds, the 93,000-year-old remains of a woman and child buried near Nazareth in Israel, give clues to the progress of civilization at that time, significantly from the very fact that they were buried, depicting a formal ritual.

ABOVE AND RIGHT: exhibits tell the histories of man and civilization, drawing from cultures all over the world, including these rarities from Asia and South America.

BELOW LEFT: the Hall of Human Origins presents human evolution from our earliest ancestors, through the rise to *Homo erectus* and the development of tools, hunting, and farming.

LINCOLN CENTER

Lincoln Center for the Performing Arts is a massive cultural village, with companies from opera to jazz and two dozen excellent performance venues

A meeting place, an outdoor space in which to relax, a plaza with sculptures, and a mini-metropolis of concert venues: Lincoln Center is all of these and more. New York City's capital of culture is a community of 12 institutes, teaching, commissioning, and showcasing almost all forms of musical and theatrical art.

Permanent home to both the Philharmonic and the Metropolitan Opera, the center is also a place of study, encompassing the Juilliard School, the School of American Ballet, and both the Film and Chamber Music societies.

TOP RIGHT: Lincoln Plaza: kasbah of culture.

The Essentials

✉ *between West 62nd and 65th sts and Columbus and Amsterdam aves;*
www.lincolncenter.org
📞 *various box offices;*
see page 152
🕐 *tours daily*
10.30am–4.30pm
💲 *charge for performances*
🚇 *66th St/Lincoln Center*

ABOVE: the director of conducting and orchestral studies at the Juilliard School, James DePriest is also permanent conductor of the Tokyo Metropolitan Symphony Orchestra.

TOP LEFT: under the directorship of Wynton Marsalis, Jazz at Lincoln Center's home is the Frederick P. Rose Hall in the Time Warner Center. The hall encompasses three performance spaces and the Irene Diamond Education Center.

THE METROPOLITAN OPERA

The first performance of the Metropolitan Opera was of Charles Gounod's *Faust*, which took place on October 22, 1883. Tenor Enrico Caruso and conductor Arturo Toscanini graced the stage of the opera house's first premises, on 39th Street and Broadway.

The Met's new home opened in 1966 with the world premiere of Samuel Barber's *Antony and Cleopatra*. The company is committed to bringing opera to a wider audience. Initiatives include reduced-price tickets, live high-definition broadcasts to theaters in the US and in Europe, streaming internet transmissions, and satellite radio broadcasts.

For anyone with shaky Italian or German, there are simultaneous translations to individual screens at every seat in the opera house.

TOP LEFT: at the core of the Juilliard Jazz Orchestra are 18 musicians following a two-year jazz studies program, with an annual performance stipend also awarded.

LEFT: soprano Renée Fleming as Tatiana in Tchaikovsky's opera *Eugene Onegin*, in the Met's 2007 production.

ABOVE: in the 1995 production of *Aida*, Robert McFerrin was the first black male soloist in the Metropolitan Opera's (then) 112-year history. McFerrin died in St Louis in 2006.

ABOVE: tickets for Lincoln Center performances go on sale up to a year in advance, and can be booked from the website. As of 2007, the entire outdoor space of Lincoln Center is now covered by free broadband Wi-Fi internet access. Be careful if using your laptop by the fountains, though.

ABOVE: classical and modern architectural styles blend to make the airy plaza a relaxing place to be.

LEFT: a popular public space both day and night, the computer-controlled fountains in the plaza are adjusted according to the wind, in order to prevent visitors sitting nearby from being drenched with water.

IMPROVEMENTS TO LINCOLN CENTER

Since 1959, when President Dwight D. Eisenhower broke ground for the new Lincoln Square Urban Renewal Project, this cultural village within New York has continued to grow and mature. Ongoing improvements occur regularly; the most recent ones include a new book store for Juilliard to replace a temporary street-level trailer, and modernization to Juilliard's Alice Tully Hall and Peter J. Sharp Theater. These plans were completed in time for the center's 50th anniversary in 2009.

ABOVE: Lincoln Center and the Juilliard School are known for their dance troupes. The New York City Ballet is made up of 92 young dancers who perform mainly contemporary works, most commissioned especially for the company. George Balanchine was the co-founding director.

TOP RIGHT: Alexander Calder's sculpture *Le Guichet (The Ticket Window)* stands in front of Avery Fisher Hall, and was presented to the center in 1965.

RIGHT: *Reclining Figure*, a two-piece bronze sculpture, was commissioned for Lincoln Center Plaza in 1963 from English artist Sir Henry Moore, and unveiled in 1965.

Recommended Restaurants on page 171

AROUND HARLEM

Fidel Castro and The Beatles couldn't wait to visit. Artists and professionals are moving into historic brownstones. The first Harlem Renaissance was in the 1920s, but a new one is coming up fast

An Alabama-born, African-American professor recalled being an 18-year-old in Europe in the late 1950s. He was asked repeatedly about Harlem, a place he'd never been in his life. His inquisitors didn't want to hear this. The man was black; he lived in the United States; therefore he had to be from Harlem. What they didn't know was that the only thing he "knew" was based on the same stereotypes shared by the Europeans, that Harlem was full of naughty nightlife, devilish dancing, mind-blowing music, dangerous dudes, and wicked women.

Harlem heritage

That heritage is palpable up and down the neighborhood's avenues. But there was, and is, much more to Harlem. As well as the area's well-documented attractions, urban pioneers driven out of the rest of Manhattan by rising prices have discovered Harlem's handsome buildings – even ex-president Bill Clinton has an office on 125th Street. These are now being restored to their former elegance, and real-estate prices are climbing. Harlem is recapturing some of its classy heyday.

In the early 1900s, black people began moving into homes on 135th Street, west of Lenox Avenue. From then on, Harlem became a place where Americans of African descent made their presence felt. Poet Langston Hughes *(see page 167)* and writer Zora Neale Hurston, along with musicians Duke Ellington, Billie Holiday, and Ella Fitzgerald, all launched their careers here in the 1920s and '30s, during what was termed the Harlem Renaissance.

Later, Harlem, or more precisely, a restaurant called Sherman's Barbeque at 151st Street and Amster-

Main attractions
125TH STREET
APOLLO THEATER
STUDIO MUSEUM IN HARLEM
SCHOMBURG CENTER
EAST HARLEM
EL MUSEO DEL BARRIO
MUSEUM OF THE CITY OF NEW YORK
COLUMBIA UNIVERSITY
JUMEL TERRACE HISTORIC DISTRICT
MORRIS-JUMEL MANSION
THE CLOISTERS
DYCKMAN FARMHOUSE MUSEUM

LEFT: Harlem legend: the Apollo Theater.
RIGHT: succinctly named Harlem Deli.

 TIP

Among the best of all the tours to Harlem are those organized by Harlem Heritage, tel: 212-280 7888, led by local residents and with a light-hearted, lightly scholarly approach. Visitors come away with a real feeling for the streets.

dam Avenue, was where music producer Phil Spector's all-girl singing group The Ronettes brought The Beatles in 1964. More headlines were made in the mid-1970s when Cuba's Fidel Castro took up residence in Harlem's Hotel Teresa, where he brought in live chickens and made his own food for fear he might be poisoned while attending UN functions in Midtown.

New attractions

Two cultural institutions have continued Harlem's post-millennium Renaissance. **The Gatehouse** (150

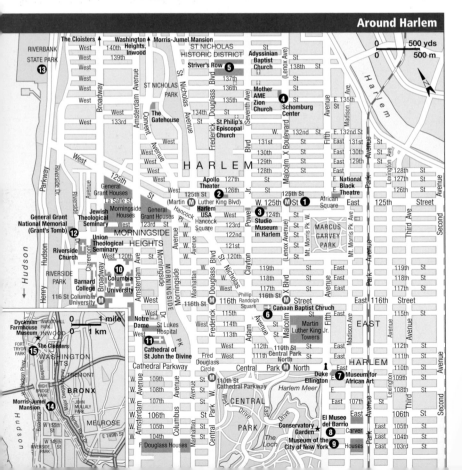

Around Harlem

Convent Avenue at 135th Street; www.harlemstage.org; tel: 212-650 7100; *see photo on left*) opened in 2006 in a renovated building, and showcases new theater and dance groups and musicians. And in late 2010, a long-anticipated permanent home for the **Museum for African Art** will be completed *(see page 168)*.

Geographically, the area is divided into Central Harlem (which includes 125th Street), East Harlem (sometimes called Spanish Harlem), and West Harlem, encompassing Morningside and Hamilton Heights. The most enjoyable way to see this part of the city is to take an organized tour.

125TH STREET ❶

A good place to begin is Harlem's famous main drag. It's Fifth Avenue and Times Square compressed into one river-to-river street, a street where every north–south Manhattan subway stops and several north–south buses cross over. A main shopping area, it's vibrant with throngs of people, street vendors, and music blasting from record stores. Officially, 125th Street is now known as **Martin Luther King Boulevard**, and it's home to many of Harlem's foremost attractions.

Apollo Theater ❷

✉ 253 W. 125th St (at Frederick Douglass Blvd), www.apollotheater.com
☎ 212-531 5305 ⓒ box office Mon–Fri 10am–6pm, Sat 10am–8.30pm, Sun noon–6pm 🚇 125th St

This is where the presence of singers Billie Holiday, Mahalia Jackson, Dinah Washington, and Ella Fitzgerald can still be felt, especially during the Apollo's weekly Amateur Night (every Wednesday). Other music stars whose careers have been launched at the Apollo include Stevie Wonder and Marvin Gaye.

The experience of seeing rising young talent, while at the same time being a part of the highly responsive, and sometimes harshly critical Apollo audience, is not to be missed. The legendary James Brown lay in state here in December 2006, before his funeral in Georgia. Thousands of fans filed past his onstage coffin, as tracks from the singer's *Live at the Apollo* were broadcast to the crowds outside. For information on Apollo tours, tel: 212-531 5337.

There's more nightlife at the old-style **Showman's Bar** at No. 375, a jazz club that still hosts live acts, and at the **Cotton Club**, which moved to No. 565. The **Lenox Lounge** at 288 Lenox Avenue, home to Billie, Miles, and Coltrane, offers a great night in its famous, refurbished Zebra Room.

Harlem hasn't been this good in years. Try El Rincón Boricua (above) on 119th for Puerto Rican cooking, and the top-notch, refurbished Lenox Lounge on Lenox Avenue for great jazz and drinks.

BELOW:
the St Nicholas Historic District.

RIGHT: the Studio Museum hosts the best new exhibitions.
BELOW: striding down 125th Street.

Studio Museum in Harlem ❸

✉ 144 W. 125th St (near Adam Clayton Powell Jr Blvd), www.studio museum.org ☎ 212-864 4500 ⏰ Wed–Fri, Sun noon–6pm, Sat 10am–6pm 💲 charge 🚇 125th St

This dynamic museum hosts changing exhibitions in addition to a permanent collection of contemporary work by artists of the African diaspora. There are extensive archives, including those of James Van Der Zee, who photographed Harlem's jazzy dancing days of the 1920–40s. The Studio Museum also holds workshops and shows films. A short distance away, at 2031 Fifth Avenue, the **National Black Theatre** is an innovative performing arts complex that hosts music, dance, and drama performances.

From 125th Street, walk up one of the neighborhood's north–south streets, like **Malcolm X Boulevard** (also called Lenox Avenue) or **Adam Clayton Powell Jr Boulevard** (also Seventh Avenue). Malcolm X Boulevard is probably central Harlem's best-known street after 125th Street.

Schomburg Center ❹

✉ 515 Malcolm X Blvd (at 135th St), www.nypl.org/research/sc ☎ 212-491 2200 ⏰ Mon–Wed noon–8pm, Thur–Fri 11am–6pm, Sat 10am–5pm 💲 free 🚇 135th St

The landmarks along Malcolm X Boulevard include this Center for

Recommended Restaurants on page 171

Research in Black Culture. Here lie, interred beneath the foyer, the ashes of the acclaimed poet Langston Hughes. There is no more fitting spot than this library, a goldmine of books, records, films, and photos about black Americans in general and Harlem in particular, and where Alex Haley did much of the research for his book, later a TV epic, *Roots*.

From the Schomburg it's a short distance to the **St Nicholas Historic District**, rows of 19th-century townhouses situated between 137th and 139th streets, known as **Striver's Row** ❺ in honor of the professionals who moved here in the 1920s.

Along the side streets are evidence of the regeneration being achieved by this new era of Harlem professionals.

On a Sunday morning in Central Harlem, don't miss the opportunity to attend services at a local church. The fervor of the singing and the response of the congregations is stirring; it's a spiritual experience that is hard to replicate elsewhere.

Sunday gospel

To judge by the diversity of the congregation who show up at **Canaan Baptist Church** ❻ on 116th Street every Sunday, visitors from all over the world have made this discovery already, as non-New Yorkers are as much in evidence as Harlemites.

Harlem's churches have long played a significant role in its political, economic, and cultural life. In addition to the Canaan, the **Abyssinian Baptist Church**, the **St Philip's Episcopal Church**, and the **Mother AME Zion Church** have all been influential since the early 1900s.

Gospel tours are conducted by **Harlem Spirituals-New York Visions** (www.harlemspirituals.com; tel: 212-391 0900). Evening jazz tours can be arranged, too.

Jazz poet Langston Hughes's works made him a light of the Harlem Renaissance of the 1920s and '30s. His earthy sketches of black life were controversial: "I knew only the people I had grown up with," he wrote, "and they weren't people whose shoes were always shined, who had been to Harvard, or who had heard Bach."

LEFT: poet Langston Hughes, whose ashes are interred at the Schomburg Center.
BELOW: the Abyssinian Baptist Church.

TIP

The Greater Harlem Chamber of Commerce is at 200A West 136th Street, tel: 212-862 7200. Website: http://harlemdiscover.com tells you what's going on whatever month you're visiting.

EAST HARLEM

Traditionally, this was considered Spanish Harlem, its residents having close ties with Puerto Rico. But East Harlem also includes a strong Haitian presence, as well as the remnants of an old Italian section along First and Pleasant avenues, above 114th Street. Frank Sinatra enjoyed the pizzas at **Patsy's**, 2287 First Avenue (between 117th and 118th streets) so much that it's said he used to have stacks of them flown across the country to his mansion in California. Patsy's still does a mean pizza today; the secret is a coal-fired oven.

Three other East Harlem attractions are part of the famous "Museum Mile" *(see pages 128–9 and 136–7)* that begins on the Upper East Side and, with a stately march of cultural awareness, continues north into Harlem.

The **Museum for African Art** ➐ (www.africanart.org), which has had a nomadic existence since it opened in 1984, has finally found a permanent home on Fifth Avenue between 109th and 110th Street. It will be the first new museum to be built along Museum Mile since the Guggenheim, in 1959. Celebrating and showcasing the cultural life and heritage of Africa, there will be a tower of luxury condos built above, facing Central Park, while the museum itself will have a shimmering glass wall on one side, and a soaring wall of wood from Ghana on the other. It is scheduled to open in late 2010.

RIGHT: Harlem is still made up of family businesses, despite new people moving in.
BELOW: the Museum for African Art will open on Museum Mile in 2010.

El Museo del Barrio ➑

✉ 1230 Fifth Ave (at 104th Street), www.elmuseo.org ☎ 212-831 7272
🕐 Wed–Sun 11am–5pm Ⓢ charge
🚇 103rd St

New York's leading Latino cultural institute was originally founded by Puerto Rican educators and artists, but now covers the artistic impact of the Caribbean, too. After an extensive renovation, the museum reopened in October 2009. Festivals and workshops held throughout the year are designed to involve the immediate community as well as visitors in projects that usually relate to its four special exhibitions. The museum's permanent collection of paintings and sculpture is particularly strong on works from the 1960s and '70s.

Recommended Restaurants on page 171

Museum of the City of New York ❾

✉ 1220 Fifth Ave (at 103rd Street),
www.mcny.org ☎ 212-534 1672
🕐 Tue–Sun 10am–5pm 💲 charge
🚇 103rd St

Founded in 1923 and originally housed in Gracie Mansion, now the mayor's home *(see page 133)*, the museum has amassed a collection of over a million artifacts and artworks related to the city's ever-changing character and phenomenal growth. Antiquated fire trucks, antique toys, elegant bedroom furniture that once belonged to the Rockefellers – this is no dry and dusty slog through history, but a museum as vibrant and exciting as the city it chronicles.

WEST HARLEM TO WASHINGTON HEIGHTS

West Harlem extends from around Amsterdam Avenue to Riverside Drive, taking in the Convent Avenue and Sugar Hill areas, along with Hamilton and Morningside Heights. Many of Harlem's white residents live in this district, which encompasses **Columbia University** ❿ and **Barnard College**, as well as the Jewish Theological and Union Theological seminaries. All these are located on or near upper Broadway.

At 112th Street and Amsterdam Avenue, the impressive **Cathedral of St John the Divine** ⓫ is home to the city's largest Episcopal congregation;

it is said to be the world's second-largest Gothic cathedral. At Riverside Drive and 120th Street, the non-denominational **Riverside Church** has the world's largest bell carillon atop its 22-story tower. Both churches host special religious and cultural events throughout the year.

Grant's Tomb ⓬

✉ Riverside Drive (at 122nd Street),
www.nps.gov/gegr ☎ 212-666 1640
🕐 daily 9am–5pm 💲 free
🚇 116th St

Officially the General Grant National Memorial, this granite mausoleum is the final resting place of Civil War general and former president Ulysses S. Grant and his wife, Julia; it was dedicated in 1897 as a national-park site, and is said to be inspired by Les Invalides in Paris, which contains Napoleon's tomb.

Parks and historic homes

Farther north on Riverside Drive, Manhattan's only state park opened in 1993 on the 28-acre (11-hectare) site of a former sewage-treatment

Both Columbia University and Barnard College are highly regarded for their excellence in education.

LEFT: external wall of El Museo del Barrio.
BELOW: Columbia University, where numerous Pulitzer Prize winners were educated.

ALMA MATER

EAT

Among the upscale eateries moving Uptown is Billie's Black (271 W. 119th St). The menu is soul food, and the prices are relatively moderate. In keeping with the neighborhood, Sunday brunch goes gospel.

RIGHT: Grant's Tomb, the largest memorial to one man in America.
BELOW: The Cloisters is a branch of the Metropolitan Museum.

plant alongside the Hudson between 137th and 145th streets. Today, the swimming pools, skating rink, and spectacular views of **Riverbank State Park** ⑬ are enjoyed by an estimated 3 million people every year.

West and north Harlem have many other historical attractions. Around 160th Street is the **Jumel Terrace Historic District**, built up in the 1880s and 1890s. **Jumel Terrace**

itself is a street of 20 beautifully presented row houses; the famous singer and activist Paul Robeson had a home nearby, on **Sylvan Terrace** on 161st.

Morris-Jumel Mansion ⑭

✉ 65 Jumel Terrace (at 162nd Street), www.morrisjumel.org
☎ 212-923 8008 ◉ Wed–Sun 10am–4pm ⓢ charge ⑧ 163rd St

Built in 1765, this lovely Palladian-style mansion served as George Washington's headquarters during the American Revolution, and was visited by Queen Elizabeth II during the American Bicentennial of 1976.

Cultural complex

Audubon Terrace, back on Broadway between West 155th and 156th streets, is lined by stately neoclassical structures built as cultural institutions between 1905 and 1923. Admission to both of them is free: the **American Academy and Institute of Arts and Letters** (tel: 212-368 5900), whose members have included luminaries from Mark Twain to Toni Morrison;

Recommended Restaurants listed below

and the **Hispanic Society of America** (www.hispanicsociety.org, tel: 212-926 2234), with a superb collection including El Greco and Goya. The Hispanic Society was renovated in early 2010; additions included new decorative arts galleries and early 20th-century masterworks by Spanish artists such as Sorolla.

Once mainly Irish, today far-northern **Washington Heights** is pleasantly ethnically mixed, as Dominicans, Puerto Ricans, Haitians, and others claim it for their own. (New York's largest Jewish educational institution, **Yeshiva University**, is on 185th Street).

Frederick Law Olmsted designed lovely **Fort Tryon Park** (62 acres/ 25 hectares) on West 192nd Street, which includes The Cloisters, a branch of the Metropolitan Museum of Art.

The Cloisters is an inspiring spot, built to showcase the Metropolitan's collection of medieval art. French and Spanish monastic cloisters, a 12th-century chapterhouse, and Gothic and Romanesque chapels were shipped from Europe and reassembled on this site, stone by stone. The prize of the collection is the six handwoven 15th-century Unicorn Tapestries.

The pretty **Dyckman Farmhouse Museum** (tel: 212-304 9422; closed Mon, Tue; charge) is in **Inwood**. A Dutch-Colonial cottage from 1785, it was restored in 1915 *(see page 228)*.❏

EAT

Eat well and do good: the New Leaf Café, nestled in the wooded approach to The Cloisters, serves New American food in a rustic setting. A portion of the profits goes toward the upkeep of Fort Tryon Park.

The Cloisters ⑮

✉ Fort Tryon Park, www.met museum.org ☎ 212-923 3700 ⏰ Tue–Sun Mar–Oct 9.30am– 5.15pm, Nov–Feb 9am–4.45pm 💲 charge 🚇 190th St

BEST RESTAURANTS

Amy Ruth's
✉ 113 W. 116th St (at Lenox and 7th aves) ☎ 212-280-8779 ⏰ B, L, & D daily **$**
The restaurant *(shown right)* attracts political, sports, and entertainment luminaries, but the big pull is the Southern food.

Londel's Supper Club
✉ 2620 Frederick Douglass Blvd (at W. 138th and W. 140th sts) ☎ 212-234 6114 ⏰ L & D Tue–Sat, Br Sun. Closed Mon **$$–$$$**

Weekend jazz nights are a big attraction at this friendly soul-food haven with a most welcoming owner presiding.

Melba's
✉ 300 W. 114th St (at Frederick Douglass Blvd) ☎ 212-864 7777 ⏰ D daily, Br Sat–Sun **$$–$$$**
Start with one of the luscious rum cocktails, then move on to ribs or select one of the other yummy soul-food items on Melba's menu.

Miss Maude's Spoonbread Too
✉ 547 Lenox Ave (at 137th and 138th sts) ☎ 212-690 3100 ⏰ L and D daily **$**
One of Harlem's most inviting restaurants. Most diners come for the fried chicken, Southern-style.

Rao's
✉ 455 E. 114th St (at Pleasant Ave) ☎ 212-722 6709 ⏰ D only Mon–Fri **$$$$**
Family-owned since 1896, this small southern Italian eatery has a celebrity clientele, so Rao's can be impossible to get into.

Sylvia's
✉ 328 Lenox Ave (at 126th and 127th sts) ☎ 212-996 0660 ⏰ L & D daily, B Mon–Sat **$$**
Soul food, Harlem-style. It's a good idea to book.

Terrace in the Sky
✉ 400 W. 119th St (at Amsterdam Ave) ☎ 212-666 9490 ⏰ L Fri, D Tue–Sat, Br Sun **$$$$**
The ultimate in romance: food, views, atmosphere.

● ● ● ● ● ● ● ● ● ● ● ●
Price includes dinner and half a bottle of wine. **$** = *under $20,* **$$** = *$20–45,* **$$$** = *$45–60,* **$$$$** = *over $60.*

Recommended Restaurants, Bars, & Cafés on pages 185–7

GRAMERCY PARK TO CHELSEA

Genteel Gramercy, the area south of the Flatiron Building, wired-for-action Union Square and gallery-hopping Chelsea are some of Downtown's most innovative neighborhoods

The area from Madison Park to Union Square – loosely referred to as the Flatiron District – is home to writers, photographers, ad agencies, publishers, new restaurants, and new media firms. Chelsea has a thriving art gallery scene, a thriving gay scene, and a riverside sports and entertainment development that attracts an estimated 8,000 visitors a day. Even Gramercy Park has shed its usual well-heeled reserve and become the destination *du jour*.

GRAMERCY PARK ❶

On the East Side between 20th and 21st streets, Gramercy Park is a genteel square that punctuates Lexington Avenue and Irving Place with welcome leafy greenery. This is Manhattan's sole private park, established in the 1830s, a place where immaculately kept beds and gravel paths sit just out of reach behind an ornate fence. Only residents of the surrounding townhouses have keys, although there are a limited number for guests of the Ian Schrager-led **Gramercy Park Hotel** *(see page 302)*.

Once a faded relic from the Jazz Age, the building has been gutted and redesigned as a lavish, idiosyncratic hotel draped in rich velvets, deep reds and azures and decorated with antique-framed modern art and glittering chandeliers. The Gramercy's "21st-century bohemia" has scored well with the reviewers that matter, and if celebrity-spotting is your thing, head for the resident Rose or Jade bars. Part of the previous building has been put aside as condos, the popularity of which will soon bring a new generation of monied residents to Gramercy Park.

Main attractions

GRAMERCY PARK
PETE'S TAVERN
MADISON SQUARE PARK
FLATIRON BUILDING
SoFi
THEODORE ROOSEVELT BIRTHPLACE
UNION SQUARE
CHELSEA HOTEL
CHELSEA MARKET
GENERAL THEOLOGICAL SEMINARY
CHELSEA ART MUSEUM
CHELSEA GALLERIES
CHELSEA PIERS

PRECEDING PAGES: couples mingle with George Segal sculptures in the West Village.
LEFT: relaxing on the High Line.
RIGHT: lobby of the Gramercy Park Hotel.

EAT

Vegans need despair no more: Pure Food & Wine at 54 Irving Place *(see page 186)* serves dishes that look great and taste even better. All food is raw and fresh, and most of the wines are organic.

On the park's southern perimeter, look at the elaborate 19th-century facades of the **National Arts Club**, home to the Poetry Society of America, and the **Players Club** next door, where members have included leading American theater actors, as well as Mark Twain, Winston Churchill, and Frank Sinatra.

Change is afoot on the other side of the Arts Club, at the former Parkside Evangeline Residence for Young Women. Until recently this attractive

RIGHT: the National Arts Club is housed in the Tilden Mansion, design in part by Calvert Vaux of Central Park fame.

corner building provided inexpensive, dorm-style accommodation to women attempting to find their feet in New York. Unfortunately its owners, the Salvation Army, put it up for sale at the end of 2006, prompting a clamor to own one of the last developable properties on the park.

Irving Place, which Samuel Ruggles named for his friend Washington Irving, runs south from Gramercy Park to 14th Street, and is lined by pretty brownstones that continue with particular charm along East 19th Street.

At 18th Street, **Pete's Tavern** is a dark, historic bar where the atmosphere reeks of speakeasies and spilled beer. Its interior has featured in several beer commercials, as well as in episodes of *Seinfeld* and *Sex and the City*. Short-story scribe O. Henry is said to have written *The Gift of the Magi* here. Down at 15th Street, the **Fillmore at Irving Plaza** (tel: 212-777 6800; www.irvingplaza.com) is one of the

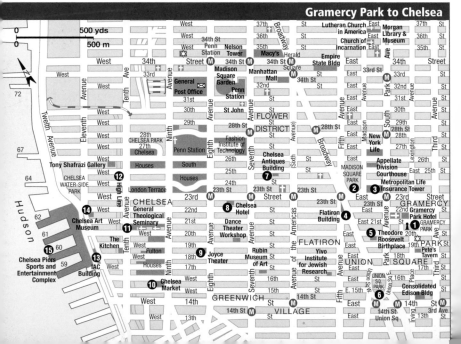

Gramercy Park to Chelsea

Recommended Restaurants, Bars, & Cafés on pages 185–7

A block south, the **Metropolitan Life Insurance Tower ❸**, completed in 1909, was briefly considered the world's tallest building at 54 stories. Until its recent incarnation as a place to meet and greet like-minded fashion and media types in a number of watering holes, however, the Madison Park area was noted mainly for its proximity to one of Manhattan's favorite architectural whimsies, which rises from the corner where Broadway crosses Fifth Avenue below 23rd Street.

FLATIRON DISTRICT

The triangular Fuller Building raised eyebrows and hopes for a bright future when it was erected in 1902. It soon became known as the **Flatiron Building ❹** because of its distinctive shape, and is considered by most to be the oldest skyscraper in New York City. Rising 285ft (87 meters) into the air, the Fuller was immortalized in 1903 with a classic black-and-white shot by photographer Alfred Stieglitz, who described the building as "looking like a monster steamer." The architect was

TIP

On Location Tours runs the TV & Movie Tour of New York, the *Sopranos* Tour, and a tour called *Sex and the City* Hotspots. Most last about three hours. For more information, go to www.screentours.com.

city's best small rock music venues. Drifting northward, the often overlooked green space between Madison Avenue and Broadway from 23rd to 26th streets is **Madison Square Park ❷**. In summer, Shake Shack sells the city's best burgers and hot dogs.

LEFT: the Flatiron Building was once described as "looking like a monster steamer."
BELOW: statue in Madison Square Park.

Theodore "Teddy" Roosevelt was the first US president to own a car, fly in an airplane, go underwater in a submarine, have a telephone installed in his house, and entertain an African-American in the White House (Booker T. Washington, in 1901).

Daniel Burnham, of the influential Chicago firm of the same name that specialized in early skyscrapers.

Word got around the offices and bars of New York that the building produced particular eddies in the wind that caused women's skirts to fly around as they walked along 23rd Street. Large groups of young men were interested enough to gather in the area to find out. To disperse them, the story goes, cops would chase them away with the words "23, skidoo."

The neighborhood immediately south has been dubbed **SoFi** by realtors, which stands, not surprisingly, for **S**outh of **Fi**atiron. From here, Broadway follows the old "Ladies' Mile," a shopping route that, during the latter part of the 19th century, ranged along Broadway and Sixth Avenue, from 23rd Street down to 9th Street. Lord & Taylor, which began as a small shop Downtown on Catherine Street and opened on the southwest corner of Broadway and 20th Street in 1872, moved Uptown to 38th and Fifth in 1914, where it is still open for business (*see page 78*).

RIGHT: the 26th US president, Theodore Roosevelt, lived here.
BELOW LEFT: Union Square's Greenmarket.
BELOW RIGHT: Union Square style.

Roosevelt Birthplace ❺

✉ 28 E. 20th Street
(at Park Ave South and Broadway),
www.nps.gov/thrb 📞 212-260 1616
🕐 Tue–Sat 9am–5pm
⑤ charge 🚇 23rd St

Just east of Broadway is the place where Theodore Roosevelt, 26th President of the United States (from 1901–9) was born in 1858. Unlike some US presidents, Theodore Roosevelt came from one of the East Coast's wealthiest families, and in the 1850s the house at 28 East 20th Street was a fashionable residence. The current building is actually a 1920s replica of the house in which "Teddy" Roosevelt spent his child-

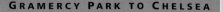

hood: the original was knocked down in 1916, but after his death in 1919 it was faithfully recreated as a memorial. About 40 percent of the furnishings come from the original home; the rest was either donated by family members or are authentic period pieces. The living quarters are only accessible as part of the tour, which is worth taking simply to see how a rich family like the Roosevelts would have lived in the mid-19th century, when this part of New York was considered the wealthy suburbs.

UNION SQUARE ❻

Named for the busy convergence of Broadway and Fourth Avenue, Union Square sits comfortably between 17th and 14th streets. A stylish prospect in the mid-1850s, later it was more or less deserted by genteel residents and became a thriving theater center. Eventually the theaters moved to Midtown, and the square became known for political meetings – in the years before World War I, anarchists and socialists regularly addressed sympathizers here.

Rallies continued to draw crowds throughout the 1930s, but finally even radicalism dwindled, and the area went into a decline that lasted until the 1980s.

Today, Union Square brims with life, a resurgence that might be attributed to the **Greenmarket**, which brings farmers and their produce to the northern edge of the square four days a week. While there are other fruit and vegetable markets in other parts of the city, this is the biggest and the best. *Wired* magazine have made Union Square fit for Wi-Fi, and Manhattanites with portable computers can be seen leisurely surfing the web near the market porters.

BELOW: colorful produce at the Greenmarket.

The land that makes up the Chelsea Historic District (between Eighth and Tenth avenues from 19th to 23rd streets) was inherited in 1813 by Clement Clarke Moore. He sold the land but imposed restrictions that kept its elegance intact. Moore is better known for writing A Visit from St Nicholas, *which became the modern-day* 'Twas the Night Before Christmas.

RIGHT: Himalayan art at the Rubin Museum.
BELOW: Chelsea transportation.

Food for the soul can be found at the **Union Square Theatre**, 100 East 17th Street, a historically appropriate locale in light of Union Square's 19th-century theatrical past.

A huge Barnes & Noble and Whole Foods dominate the outer edges of Union Square. In the evening, young tourists and skateboarders congregate around their doors.

CHELSEA

West of Fifth Avenue to the Hudson River, from 14th up to about 30th Street, Chelsea borders the Midtown Garment District and includes the **Flower District**. In the spring and summer, these blocks are crowded with leafy vegetation and bathed in a sweet loamy odor.

Fifth Avenue between 14th and 23rd streets has stores like Emporio Armani and Paul Smith, while the Avenue of the Americas (**Sixth Avenue**) is lined by modern chains that have continued the fashion tradition by moving into the historic Ladies' Mile buildings.

If you have a big yen for vintage accessories and goods, head for the

Chelsea Antiques Building ❼ at 110 West 25th between Sixth and Seventh avenues. There are fine scavenger opportunities here, with an enticing jumble of items like gilded chairs, metal lamps, and bathtubs.

Chelsea Girls

Walking west on long, busy 23rd Street (or better yet, a ride on the M23 crosstown bus) will take you past the **Chelsea Hotel ❽** *(see page 303)*. One of the city's most famous residential hotels, this 12-story, red-brick building is where Dylan Thomas died in 1953, Andy Warhol filmed *Chelsea Girls* in 1967, and punk rocker Sid Vicious allegedly murdered his girlfriend before dying of a drugs overdose in 1978. Join the hotel's eclectic collection of residents in the lobby, and have a look at the unusual artwork (done by guests and changed at a whim), or stop in the basement restaurant **El Quijote** *(see page 186)*.

A 2008 change in management, however, has brought consternation to some of the hotel's longer-term residents. As Chelsea itself becomes more and more gentrified and property prices and desirability soar, the unique character of the hotel is increasingly under threat. Watch this space for further details.

Recommended Restaurants, Bars, & Cafés on pages 185–7

Art Deco and dance

The Art Deco sign to the **Joyce Theater ❾** (175 Eighth Avenue at 19th Street) is easily spotted from the street. The Joyce presents some of the city's most innovative dance performances, from Spanish Gypsy flamenco to classical ballet, and Native American troupes.

Other original work is staged at the **Dance Theater Workshop** (219 West 19th Street). The lobby has a welcoming coffee shop where you can kick back with specialty hot chocolate and a big cookie.

Before or after indulging, stop by the **Rubin Museum of Art** at 150 West 17th Street. The Rubin is the first museum in the Western world dedicated to the art of the Himalayas and surrounding regions. The emphasis is on educating visitors about the region, and there are wall notes and interactive displays.

Continue on to the striking architecture of the **Chelsea Market ❿**, at 75 Ninth Avenue between 15th and 16th streets, where an ambitious renovation transformed what were once 18 buildings erected between 1883 and 1930 into a hugely popular indoor food market. Much of the original brickwork and steel has been left bare, giving the food court an artsy, industrial feel.

The interior of the Chelsea Market has a waterfall and sculptured seating, around which are scattered more than 20 locally owned stores selling specialty foods and home design items, as well as plenty of tempting places to eat.

The area is trendy and stylish, so much so that this neighborhood is almost indistinguishable from the cool and gritty Meatpacking District, which stretches west along 14th Street to the Hudson in the West Village *(see page 197)*.

Fans of architecture will also love the blocks between Eighth and Tenth Avenues, from 19th to 23rd streets. This is the **Chelsea Historic District**.

SHOP

Many of the stores in the Chelsea Market have glass walls that back onto a walkway. Too tempting to resist is Amy's Bakery. Watch as the bread is kneaded, shaped, and then placed in an oven, and chances are you'll leave with a loaf under your arm.

BELOW LEFT: lobby of the Chelsea Hotel.
BELOW RIGHT: Chelsea Market.

The Chelsea Art Museum is just one of many galleries in the area. Most are closed on Mondays.

RIGHT AND BELOW: hanging out on the High Line.

General Theological Seminary

✉ 175 Ninth Ave (at 20th and 21st sts), www.gts.edu 📞 212-243 5150
🕐 Mon–Sat noon–3pm 💲 free
🚇 23rd St/Eighth Ave

This lovely seminary was established in 1817, and prepares students for ordination into the Episcopal Church. Among its best buildings are the Chapel of the Good Shepherd and St Mark's Library; among its most important buildings is the **Desmond Tutu Center**, which emphasizes peace and reconciliation. The seminary's tree-lined quadrangle is one of New York's best-kept secrets: a calm oasis amid the busy urban streets all around, where visitors can sit under a tree and listen to the sound of birds.

Walking east on 20th and 21st streets from Tenth Avenue brings you to one of the Chelsea Historic District's most scenic stretches of Greek Revival and Anglo-Italianate townhouses, the tree-lined streets a

reminder of Chelsea's desirability as a residential area. A block farther south, between Tenth and Eleventh avenues, **The Kitchen** (512 West 19th Street) is a long-standing center where video, dance, and performance art are staple fare.

Parallel to Tenth Avenue and stretching to the West Village is the **High Line ⑫**, a disused railroad line that has been transformed into a sky-high green promenade for walkers. In 2009, the sections between Chelsea and the Meatpacking District opened. In time, the High Line will extend all the way to 34th Street *(see also page 198)*.

Dominating the space between West 18th and 19th streets at Eleventh Avenue is the Frank Gehry-designed **IAC Building ⑬**. This is the acclaimed architect's first NYC office building. Not everyone is pleased with the enormity of the edifice, which is way out of scale for low-key Chelsea, but few can fault its impressive facade.

Galleries galore

Once Soho became overrun with boutiques and restaurants, gallery owners moved north to Chelsea. One of the best is the **Tony Shafrazi**

Recommended Restaurants, Bars, & Cafés on pages 185–7

Gallery, 544 West 26th Street, between Tenth and Eleventh avenues (tel: 212-274 9300). The gallery may hold only two or three exhibitions each year, but they are always worth seeing. Past exhibits have focused on names as famous as Andy Warhol, Picasso, and Keith Haring.

Although galleries are scattered throughout the neighborhood, **22nd Street** between Tenth and Eleventh avenues is particularly packed with light, converted warehouse-style galleries, spearheaded by the Chelsea Art Museum at the end of the street.

Chelsea Art Museum ⑭

✉ 556 W. 22nd Street (at Tenth and Eleventh aves), http://chelseaart museum.org 📞 212-255 0719 🕐 Tue, Wed, Fri, Sat noon–6pm, Thur noon–8pm 💲 charge 🚇 23rd St/Eighth Ave

One of the larger spaces in the area, the museum showcases international and abstract art that might not otherwise be exhibited in New York. Depending on the exhibition, at any time the gallery could be showing a mixture of film, photography, painting, and interactive installations. A rooftop sculpture garden makes a welcome respite for summertime relaxation, and the museum also has an excellent gallery store, with a large selection of artist-produced fanzines and literature.

Gallery-hopping

This activity is particularly popular on Thursday nights, when most venues keep later hours, but note that all galleries tend to close on Mondays. Despite the avant-garde nature of some of the work, the galleries themselves are mainly unintimidating places, and inquiries are met with friendly, informed responses.

The **PaceWildenstein Gallery**, opposite the Chelsea Art Museum, is worth seeing, the size of the space allowing for some impressive works. The main room has an attractive wood-beamed ceiling. There's another PaceWildenstein gallery on 25th Street. The appearance of Comme des Garçons and Balenciaga on 22nd Street hint that change might be afoot as art turns

DRINK

Calling all smokers: the patio of the cocktail bar Glass, 287 Tenth Avenue, between 26th and 27th sts, is a pleasant place to blow the rings without being run out of town. Sadly, it's legal here, which takes some of the fun away.

BELOW LEFT: Chelsea girl.
BELOW RIGHT: Frank Gehry's IAC Building.

Map on page 176

TIP

When visiting Chelsea Piers, ask someone to tell you about the site's history. One fascinating fact is that the *Titantic* was scheduled to dock at the piers on April 16, 1912. Of the 2,000 passengers onboard, only 675 were rescued. The survivors arrived at Chelsea Piers four days later.

RIGHT: detail from a mandala painted on cotton, the Rubin Museum.
BELOW: the view over Chelsea Piers.

into retail, but for now galleries still dominate.

In the early days of moving pictures, the Famous Players Film Studio was located on West 26th Street; today, the **Silver Screen Studios** at Chelsea Piers are where such popular TV shows as *Law and Order* have been in post-production.

Chelsea Piers 15

W. 23rd Street (at Twelfth Ave and Hudson River), www.chelseapiers.com
212-336 6666 daily, various opening hours charge
23rd St/Eighth Ave

The last stop on the crosstown 23 bus is **Pier 62**, the hub of this huge sports and entertainment complex, which sprawls south along the Hudson from 23rd to 17th streets, and which has brought such a wealth of leisure opportunities to the city.

A Fitness Club is open to members only, but there are other facilities the public can use for a fee. The development includes **Pier 61**, with the double Sky Rink, **Pier 60**, which has a fabulous spa with a range of treatments including facials and massages, and **Pier 59**, which offers a golf-driving range. Other activities include bowling, indoor soccer, dance classes, and basketball.

The Chelsea cruise

The transformation of Chelsea's dilapidated piers has given new access to the Hudson River. Passenger boats (**World Yacht**, tel: 212-630 8100, www.worldyacht.com; and **Spirit Cruises**, tel: 866-483 3866, www.spiritcitycruises.com) offer day and evening cruises, with dinner included. For non-passengers, the walkway by the piers weaves around for more than a mile, providing great riverside views and fine sunsets. ❑

BEST RESTAURANTS, BARS, AND CAFÉS

Restaurants

Prices for a three-course dinner per person with half a bottle of wine:

$ = under $20
$$ = $20–$45
$$$ = $45–$60
$$$$ = over $60

A Voce
41 Madison Ave (at 26th St) 212-545 8555 L & D Mon–Fri, D only Sat **$$$** [p337, C4]
Italian country cuisine. The veal *agnolotti* with a soffritto sauce is outstanding, as are the rustic potato wedges.

Bar Jamón
125 E. 17th St (at Irving Pl) 212-253 2773 L & D daily **$$$** [p339, D2]
Lusty Spanish tapas and snacks served up by Mario Batali.

Blossom
187 9th Ave (between 21st and 22nd sts) 212-627 1144 D daily, L Fri–Sun **$$** [p336, A4]
The best in mock pastas and spicy starters. Dishes perfect for vegans who want to indulge in guilty pleasures.

Blue Smoke
116 E. 27th St (at Park and Lexington aves) 212-447 7733 L & D daily, Br Sun **$$** [p339, D1]
Great BBQ (with the Jazz Standard club located downstairs). There's also a kids' jazz brunch.

Blue Water Grill
31 Union Sq W (at 16th St) 212-675 9500 L & D daily **$$$** [p339, C1]
Big, beautiful fish house; excellent seafood in a converted bank building.

Boquería
53 W. 19th St (at 5th and 6th aves) 212-255 4160 L & D daily **$$** [p338, C1]
Flavors of Spain from tiny tapas to mid-week suckling-pig platter specials to share. Small space and always crowded Flatiron hotspot.

Buddakan
75 9th Ave (at 16th St) 212-989 6699 D daily **$$$** [p338, B1]
On the border between Chelsea and the Meat-packing District, Buddakan is hugely popular for the food and its vast, chandeliered dining room.

Chat 'n Chew
10 E. 16th St (at 5th Ave and Union Sq) 212-243 1616 L & D daily, Br Sat–Sun **$** [p339, C1]
American comfort food and prices to match in a room with a nice, funky line in retro decor.

Co.
230 9th Ave (at 24th and 25th sts) 212-243 1105 L & D Tue–Sun, D only Mon **$$** [p336, A3]
This Chelsea place is one of a new wave of Neapolitan pizza hotspots.

Cookshop
156 10th Ave (at 20 St) 212-924 4440 B, L, & D daily **$** [p336, A4]
Marc Meyer's experimental menu changes daily and serves up fashionably sustainable treats, including a local favorite – fried spicy hominy. Fine dining without ethical sacrifices.

Craft
43 E. 19th St (between Broadway and Park Ave S) 212-780 0880 D daily **$$$$** [p339, C1]
The menu is split into sections (vegetable, sides, meat, and fish), and you concoct your own meal – a nightmare for the indecisive, but wildly popular otherwise.

Craftbar
900 Broadway (at 20th St) 212-461 4300 L & D Mon–Fri, L only Sat–Sun **$$$** [p339, C1]
Craft's informal sister offers airy and spacious dining and a vivacious bar. An eclectic menu includes tasty, simple bites, while desserts such as red-velvet cake tickle the tastebuds.

Del Posto
85 10th Ave (at 16th St) 212-497 8090 D daily, L Wed–Fri **$$$$** [p336, A4]
Haute modern Italian on a grand scale with matching prices. Glitzy Roosevelt-era decor and big meaty dishes served with largesse. Extravagance at its best.

Prices for a three-course dinner per person with half a bottle of wine:
$ = under $20
$$ = $20–$45
$$$ = $45–$60
$$$$ = over $60

Eleven Madison Park

11 Madison Ave (at 24th St) ☎ 212-889 0905 ⊙ L & D Mon–Fri, D only Sat **$$$$** [p337, C4]
There's a vaulted ceiling, an elegant atmosphere, expensive and excellent New American food on the menu here, including the ever-popular suckling pig.

Gramercy Tavern

42 E. 20th St (at Broadway and Park Ave) ☎ 212-477 0777 ⊙ L Mon–Fri, D daily **$$$$** [p339, C1]
A fave for its food, service, great New American cuisine, and the high-ceilinged dining room.

Les Halles

411 Park Ave S. (at 28th and 29th sts) ☎ 212-679 4111 ⊙ B, L, & D daily **$$$** [p337, C4]
This steakhouse packs in the crowds, who come to soak up the French atmosphere.

Mesa Grill

102 5th Ave (at 15th and 16th sts) ☎ 212-807 7400 ⊙ L Mon–Fri, D daily, Br Sat–Sun **$$$** [p338, C1]
Sophisticated Southwestern fare that put energetic Bobby Flay on the culinary map. Still hot after all these years.

Morimoto

88 10th Ave (at 15th and 16th sts) ☎ 212-989 8883 ⊙ L & D Mon–Fri, D only Sat–Sun **$$$$** [p336, A4]
Excellent sushi, maki, and modern Japanese dishes like braised black cod.

Naka Naka

458 W. 17th St (at 9th and 10th aves) ☎ 212-929 8544 ⊙ D Tue–Sun **$$** [p336, A4]
Tatami mats greet you at this shoebox-sized Japanese restaurant. A quiet spot in a busy neighborhood, the modest menu serves sushi and soba dishes.

Old Homestead

56 9th Ave (at 14th and 15th sts) ☎ 212-242 9040 ⊙ L & D daily **$$$$** [p336, A4]
A classic, old-school steakhouse if ever there were one. Watch out for the "colossal" crab cakes.

Pongal

110 Lexington Ave (at 27th and 28th sts) ☎ 212-696 9458 ⊙ L & D daily **$$** [p337, C4]
This kosher vegetarian restaurant, specializing in the food of Gujarat, Punjab, and southern

India, is a very good choice on a block filled with many Indian eateries.

Pure Food and Wine

54 Irving Pl (at 17th and 18th sts) ☎ 212-477 1010 ⊙ D daily **$$$** [p339, D2]
There's nothin' cookin' at this all-raw food restaurant – healthy and unusual for sure.

El Quijote

226 W. 23rd St (at 7th and 8th aves) ☎ 212-929 1855 ⊙ L & D daily **$$** [p336, B4]

Old-time Spanish main-stay beneath the Chelsea Hotel, with a great bargain: the lobster dinner. Portions are huge and the bar can get crowded.

Red Cat
227 10th Ave (at 23rd and 24th sts) 212-242 1122 L & D Tue–Sat, D only Sun–Mon $$$ [p336,A3]
Hipsters love the Red Cat. Great room, excellent food, cool clientele – a stylish place before or after gallery-hopping.

Republic
37 Union Sq. W. (at 16th and 17th sts) 212-627 7172 L & D daily $$ [p339,C1]
There are oodles of tasty noodles at this noisy Asian eatery. Communal tables are fun.

Rickshaw Dumpling Bar
61 W. 23rd St (at 5th and 6th aves) 212-924 9220 L & D daily $ [p336,B4]
Chinatown comes to Chelsea at a delicious spot that serves up tasty little packets of dumplings. Order them steamed or fried; they're extremely affordable.

Rub
208 W. 23rd St (at 7th and 8th Ave) 212-524 4300 L & D daily $$ [p336,B4]
Best low-down, hoe-down barbeque in Chelsea. Cheap, too. Ask for the burned ends.

Shaffer City Oyster Bar and Grill
5 W. 21st St (at 5th Ave) 212-255 9827 L & D Mon–Fri, D only Sat $$ [p336,C4]
Whether it's the raw bar or seafood main courses, quality is king here in a neighborhood over-crowded with options.

Shake Shack
Madison Square Park 212-889 6600 L & D daily $ [p336,C4]
The first in the empire remains as popular as ever. Some say the spectacular burgers, dogs, shakes, and fries are the best in America.

Tabla
11 Madison Ave (at 25th St) 212-889 0667 L Mon–Sat, D daily $$$$ [p337,C4]
Unique Indian/New American fusion food, like Vermont baby lamb with tandoori eggplant, or soft-shell crab with chilled mung-bean noodles. There's a great prix-fixe lunch at the downstairs Bread Bar, and cheaper options for dinner, too.

Tocqueville
1 E. 15th St (at 5th Ave) 212-647 1515 L & D Mon–Sat $$$ [p338,C1]
Fans swear by this trendy French-American just around the corner from Union Square. Particularly noted are the seared sirloin or roast chicken.

Union Square Café
21 E. 16th St (at 5th Ave and Union Sq) 212-243 4020 L & D daily $$$$ [p339,C1]
Despite its cramped rooms, year after year this is voted one of the best restaurants in NYC for its winning formula of four-star food, wine, and service. The menu is New American, with dishes like lobster shepherd's pie, or rock shrimp in garlic, almond and tomato sauce.

Bars and Cafés

71 Irving Place Coffee and Tea Bar (between 18th and 19th sts) is a great alternative to the ever-present Starbucks. Order the signature Irving Farm Blend.

Brick Oven Pizza 33, 268 W. 23rd St, just down from the Chelsea Hotel, is good for a slice before the galleries.

Chop't Creative Salad 24 E. 17th St (at 5th Ave and Broadway). It's fun to watch as selected salad-bar ingredients are minced and tossed into big bowls for eat-in or take-out. Two branches in the 50s, too, but this is the original.

City Bakery, 3 W. 18th St (between 5th and 6th aves), is a popular Flatiron hang-out with pastries, soups, sandwiches, and more.

Lady Mendl's, Inn at Irving Place, 56 Irving Pl (between 17th and 18th sts), is an elegant tea salon in a Gramercy Park townhouse.

Los Dos Molinos, E. 18th St near Irving Place, serves a mighty margarita. No wonder, then, that they're near a few hospitals. Closed Sun and Mon.

Old Town Bar and Restaurant, 45 E. 18th St (between Broadway and Park Ave S.), has a wonderful long bar and great hamburgers.

Pete's Tavern, 129 E. 18th St (at Irving Pl), is a long-running establishment that's better for drinks than dinner, but there's loads of atmosphere.

PRECEDING PAGES: Tabla. **LEFT:** Chelsea dining.
RIGHT: enjoying an urban evening near Union Square.

Recommended Restaurants, Bars, & Cafés on pages 200–1

GREENWICH VILLAGE

Greenwich Village was the country's first true bohemian neighborhood, a place where Dylan Thomas and Bob Dylan found inspiration. Now, Stella McCartney and Alexander McQueen are doing the same in the Meatpacking District

Writers and poets, artists and radicals, runaway socialites, and others seeking freedom from conventional lifestyles have long flocked to Greenwich Village, spotlit in recent history by poets and musicians of the 1950s and '60s.

Today, as other neighborhoods set the trends, New Yorkers often think of "the Village" as one big tourist attraction. Untrue. A commercial element exists, serviced by double-decker tour buses, but many streets are as quietly residential as they were in the 18th and early 19th centuries, when the village of Greenwich was first settled by pioneers fleeing illness and epidemics at the tip of the island.

Success and the city

Spiraling real-estate prices have forced out all but the most successful, but the Village (both Greenwich and the West Village) is still where many people would choose to live: witness the "Gold Coast" buildings facing the Hudson River, home to stars like Meryl Streep and Nicole Kidman.

Bordered by 14th Street to the north, the Hudson River to the west, and Broadway to the east (where the East Village begins), this is where the offbeat and the fashionable mingle

with ease, and where the annual Halloween Parade is a riotous spectacle attended by both.

AROUND WASHINGTON SQUARE

Walking south on Fifth Avenue, **Washington Arch** rises in the distance. Designed in wood by Stanford White to commemorate the 1889 centennial of the first president's inauguration, the imposing marble arch from 1918 is the entrance to **Washington Square ❶**, the symbolic heart of Greenwich Village.

Main attractions
WASHINGTON SQUARE
GRACE CHURCH
WASHINGTON MEWS
MACDOUGAL STREET
BLUE NOTE
JEFFERSON MARKET LIBRARY
CHRISTOPHER STREET
VILLAGE VANGUARD
HUDSON STREET
WHITE HORSE TAVERN
BLEECKER STREET
BEDFORD STREET
MEATPACKING DISTRICT
WEST 14TH STREET

LEFT: summertime in Washington Square.
RIGHT: the *Village Voice* began in the 1950s.

"Book Row" started in the 1890s and ran from Union Square to Astor Place. In its heyday, there were 48 book stores. Nowadays, the Strand, named after the famous street in London, is the only remaining survivor.

ABOVE: the Strand Book Store has 18 miles of used books.
ABOVE RIGHT: there are thousands of toy soldiers on display at the Forbes Galleries.

Booksellers and collectors

A walk east from the square and then north up Broadway will lead you to the **Strand Book Store** (www. strandbooks.com, tel: 212-473 1452; open to 10.30pm every night; rare books room closes at 6.20pm). Dusty and delightful, the Strand was started in 1927 and is the perfect place to track down that elusive edition.

Grace Church ❷, just to the south, is one of New York's loveliest ecclesiastical structures. Built in 1846, its exterior white marble, now a muted gray, was mined by convicts from the infamous Sing Sing prison in upstate New York.

Turn right at 10th, and walk toward Fifth Avenue crossing **University Place**, which runs parallel to Fifth

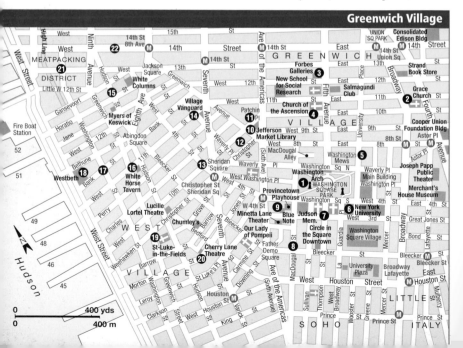

Greenwich Village

Recommended Restaurants, Bars, & Cafés on pages 200–1

for several blocks, to West 12th Street, where a block-shaped building houses the **New School for Social Research**, which offers classes in everything from Arabic to screenwriting.

At Fifth Avenue and 12th Street, the **Forbes Galleries** ❸ (www.forbes galleries.com, tel: 212-206 5548; Tue–Sat 10am–4pm, Thur groups only; free) hold the late Malcolm Forbes's collections of tin soldiers and other collectibles. The toys are organized in entertaining displays across themed rooms, while the air is filled with appropriate sound effects, from military marches to war cries. The galleries also host art shows.

The nearby **Salmagundi Club**, at 47 Fifth Avenue, is the country's oldest artists' club, founded in 1870. Its facilities are for members only, but there are walk-in classes (tel: 212-255 7740) should you fancy joining the artistic fraternity for a few hours.

Washington Square sites

Take a stroll along 9th and 10th streets, two of the most picturesque in the city. Lined by stately brick and brownstone houses, they have been

home to numerous artists and writers (Mark Twain lived at 14 West 10th). The **Church of the Ascension** ❹ on the corner of Fifth and 10th was designed by Richard Upjohn in 1840, and features a marble altar relief by sculptor Augustus St-Gaudens.

Pretty **Washington Mews** ❺ runs between Fifth and University Place, just above Washington Square. Originally built as stables for the townhouses along Washington Square North, the pretty row houses here and along nearby **MacDougal Alley**

DRINK

Can't finish it? A new law in New York permits taking that expensive, half-empty bottle of wine home from restaurants. The law requires the bottle be "securely sealed" before being bagged.

LEFT: chess has been a Washington Square pastime for decades.
BELOW: all that jazz in Washington Square.

were converted to artists' studios after the arrival of the motor car put stables out of business. The painter Edward Hopper lived and worked at 3 Washington Square North for 54 years, from 1913 until his death in 1967. Washington Mews has retained much brickwork cobbling, and on a winter's day when the snow settles between the bricks in the road, the setting is particularly lovely.

RIGHT: MacDougal Street today.
BELOW RIGHT: Bob Dylan in the Village.

All this eventually leads to **Washington Square** itself. Originally a potter's field, where the poor and unknown were buried, it later became a parade ground, and still later a residential park.

Though it's lost the cachet it had in the days of Henry James – who grew up nearby and based his novel *Washington Square* on his childhood memories – on weekend afternoons the park fills with musicians and street performers playing to appreciative crowds of Japanese camera crews, out-of-town students, tourists, chess hustlers and pot dealers. During the school term, NYU students congregate on the grass, and the atmosphere is generally less frantic.

With two blocks of Greek Revival townhouses, **Washington Square North** retains a 19th-century elegance, at odds with the monolithic **New York University ❻** buildings across the park. Past NYU's busy Kimmel Student Center, Bobst Library, and Catholic Center (all on Washington Square South), is **Judson Memorial Church ❼**. Designed in 1890 by Stanford White in Romanesque Revival

Village Voices: Bob Dylan

In the 1950s and '60s, the café scene of Greenwich Village drew poetic, artistic, and politically inquisitive newcomers to New York. Low rents may well have been a factor, together with a boho-artistic aura that had been gaining strength since the 1920s. Deep in the Village, major musical moments of the mid-20th century took place in MacDougal Street, many at an unpromising little coffee bar called the Cafe Wha? David Barry, a musician who frequented and played at the café, said, "It was a grubby, awful scene there."

In spite of this, a number of careers in the American folk revival began and grew. On first reaching New York on January 24, 1961, Bob Dylan took a subway straight to Greenwich Village and blew into the Café Wha? in a flurry of snowflakes. Barry remembered those times well. "Although Dylan could neither sing or play the guitar, he clearly had something on stage that none of the rest of us did."

Recommended Restaurants, Bars, & Cafés on pages 200–1

style, the church has been a cultural and religious center in the Greenwich community for decades.

Beat streets

Turn off Washington Square South onto **MacDougal Street ❽**, into the heart of what was once a beatnik haven, where world-weary poets wore black, sipped coffee, and discoursed on the meaning of life late into the night. These days, the area is a magnet for out-of-towners, drawn by ersatz craft shops and "authentic" ethnic restau-

rants. Only a handful of Beat-era establishments remain, however, including **Café Wha?** on MacDougal between Bleecker and West 3rd, once a hangout of Allen Ginsberg.

Nevertheless, a stroll around these streets offers the pleasure of a pilgrimage down passageways of past grooviness and cloisters of cool. Some nights echoes of the young Bob Dylan or Jimi Hendrix seem to drift around the intersection of Bleecker and MacDougal streets. And there's still plenty of entertainment, from performances by jazz greats to contemporary drama at the **Minetta Lane Theater** (tel: 212-420 8000), towards Sixth Avenue.

Blue Note ❾

✉ 131 W. 3rd St (between MacDougal St and Sixth Ave), www.bluenote.net 📞 212-475 8592 Ⓒ music nightly 8pm and 10.30pm with an occasional extra set at 12.30am, also jazz brunch Sun 12.30pm Ⓢ charge 🚇 W. 4th St

This club has been drawing jazz fans to Greenwich Village for over 25 years. It's comforting to think that no matter what transformations take place on the surrounding streets, inside the Blue Note the beat goes on.

THE WEST VILLAGE

The area west of the Avenue of the Americas (Sixth Avenue) and a few blocks north is where the Village hosts the annual Halloween Parade; witnessed the gay-rights riots at the Stonewall Inn in the late 1960s; and where attractive, quiet knots of streets wind around confusingly between the major avenues.

A good place to start is the striking **Jefferson Market Library ❿** at 10th Street and Sixth Avenue. Part of a complex that included the old Women's House of Detention, it was built as a courthouse in 1877. This is where Harry Thaw went on trial for shooting America's then-most famous architect, Stanford White, in 1906, after White had an affair with Thaw's wife, in one of New York's most celebrated scandals. The upstairs rooms

The Village's very own Italian-Gothic fantasy, Jefferson Market Library.

LEFT AND BELOW: fans will happily queue up at the Blue Note for the chance to see jazz stars like Bilal.

The Village Vanguard helped to launch the careers of jazz greats Miles Davis and John Coltrane; see their photographs inside.

RIGHT: chatting on Christopher Street.
BELOW: the West Village eatery Mexicana Mama.

still have a court-like feel, with dark wood and stained-glass windows. Next door is a pretty community garden, open to all.

Walk west on 10th Street to **Patchin Place** – a mews where Eugene O'Neill, journalist John Reed, and poet e.e. cummings all lived. Continue on **Christopher Street** ⑫, symbolic center of the gay community and a main cross-street that slants across the West Village to a renovated pier, walkway, and bike path that, on a sunny day, make New York seem like a brand-new city. (At night, however, it's still the haunt of hustlers, so be alert.)

Just past **Waverly Place**, with its curved row of small Federal-style houses, is the **Northern Dispensary**. A non-profit health clinic from 1831 up until fairly recently, it's one of the oldest public buildings in the city. A few doors up, and nearly four decades ago, the modern gay-rights movement got its spontaneous start one night in 1969 at the **Stonewall Inn** (53 Christopher Street), a gay bar whose habitués got tired of being rousted by police. Today, there's a

bar with the same name operating next door, with a gay-pride flag.

Just across the street, tiny fenced-in **Christopher Park** has a statue of Civil War general Philip Sheridan. **Sheridan Square** ⑬ itself isn't a square at all, it's actually at the triangular junction where Grove, Christopher, and West 4th streets meet.

At 121 Christopher Street is the **Lucille Lortel Theater** (tel: 212-924 2817, www.lortel.org), a theater that for many years has been the friend and supporter of new writers.

Village Vanguard ⑭

✉ 178 Seventh Ave S. (at W. 11th St), www.villagevanguard.com 📞 212-255 4037 🕐 music nightly at 9pm and 11pm, occasional extra set Sat 12.30am 💲 charge 🚇 14th St

If it's music that gives a cultural *frisson*, this is the right neighborhood: the tiny Vanguard has been in business over 70 years, and pictures of its musical alumni line its walls. With a capacity of just 123, the historic basement venue has kept the sort of intimacy most jazz clubs – and musicians

Recommended Restaurants, Bars, & Cafés on pages 200–1

– only dream of. If you are lucky enough to get tickets, be warned that it's meant for jazz and jazz alone – conversation or, heaven forbid, cell ringtones during a performance are a throw-out-able offence. On Mondays, the house jazz orchestra plays.

West of 4th Street

The nearer to the river you head, the deeper you go into the oldest part of Greenwich Village, which makes up for any lack of the chic-and-glitz found in nearby districts with a nicely low-key neighborliness.

Flowing north–south is **Hudson Street ⑮**, its main artery. Over the past few years, this area has acquired curious British connections, with a clutch of British businesses on Greenwich Avenue *(see page 196)*.

A favorite is **Myers of Keswick** (634 Hudson St, www.myersofkeswick. com, tel: 212-691 4194), a British specialty shop where Keith Richards and Elton John have stocked up on pork pies and bags of Walkers crisps. Their sausage rolls are spectacular and, although there isn't any seating, they'll heat them up for you.

White Horse Tavern ⑯

✉ 567 Hudson St (at W. 11th St)
☎ 212-243 9260 🕒 daily 11am–3am
🚇 Christopher St

The White Horse has been serving drinks at the corner of 11th Street since 1880, and is one of the last remaining wood-paneled bars in New York. The Horse was a haunt of Dylan Thomas, where he had several too many (some say 18) whiskies, before dragging himself back to the Chelsea Hotel. The next day, he died. Although on the tourist route, the White Horse retains much charm. Weekends are manic, so try to visit during the week.

Pretty thoroughfares

Near the White Horse, cute little **Abingdon Square** leads to the start of newly chic **Bleecker Street**. This end of the street has fallen hard to the onslaught of high-fashion stores (Marc Jacobs, Prada, luxury leather specialists Mulberry), and many locally owned businesses have been forced out by escalating rents.

Nevertheless, Bleecker is bisected

TIP

Note the Playwrights Sidewalk in front of the Lucille Lortel Theater, replete with names like Eugene O'Neill and Sam Shepard, whose celebrated work has been performed here.

BELOW: the Village people.

RIGHT: Dylan Thomas drank (and drank) here.
BELOW: the Cherry Lane Theatre.

by some of the Village's prettiest thoroughfares. **Bank Street** is particularly scenic, with its cobblestones and pastel houses, and lies in the center of the **Greenwich Village Historic District**'s finest 19th-century architecture.

Toward the west end of Bank Street, **Westbeth** is a sprawling, government-funded artists' enclave (sometimes open for performances), that looks out over the Hudson. It's only a short walk from the church of **St-Luke-in-the-Fields** , built in 1821. **Number 17 Grove Street**, built in 1822, is a wooden home that brims with character, as does **Grove Court**, a gated alleyway with a cluster of attractive brown-brick houses. Grove Street intersects **Bedford Street**, one of the oldest Village byways. At No. 102 is the original "Twin Peaks," built in 1830 as an artists' residence, with two peaks in its gabled roof.

Byways and speakeasies

A left turn leads to the former site of **Chumley's**, a speakeasy turned bar and restaurant, where novelist John Steinbeck and playwright Eugene O'Neill were regulars. A leftover from Prohibition, it had an unmarked entrance around the corner on Barrow Street – until it closed in 2008.

Tiny poet Edna St Vincent Millay was a tenant at **75 Bedford Street**, Manhattan's narrowest house at just over 9ft (3 meters) wide. A bigger tenant was John Barrymore, of the theatrical dynasty. And before her break into stardom, Barbra Streisand

Recommended Restaurants, Bars, & Cafés on pages 200–1

worked as an usher at the **Cherry Lane Theatre** ⑳ (38 Commerce Street, www.cherrylanetheatre.com, tel: 212-989 2020), a nurturing space for American playwrights since 1924.

St Luke's Place is lined by gracious Italianate row houses. New York's Jazz Age mayor Jimmy Walker *(see page 34)* lived at No. 6, and two lamps – a sign of mayoral honor – are at the foot of the steps.

MEATPACKING DISTRICT ㉑

Up until a decade or so ago, the Meatpacking District was just what it sounded like – a warehousing, wholesale meat market, and distribution area for butchered goods making their way into the city's restaurants

and grocery stores. Located on Manhattan's west side, to the west of the West Village and just south of Chelsea, it's bordered to the north by **West 14th Street** ㉒ (or even a couple blocks further north, depending on who you ask), to the south by **Gansevoort Street**, and from Hudson Street to the east to the Hudson River at the west. In fact, it is so well located (with decent subway and bus access) that it should have seemed inevitable that such prime real estate would eventually be developed for more fashionable pursuits. But, back when this was a red-light district (and the streets were literally stained red from the cow carcasses in the slaughterhouses) there was nothing cool about this stretch of Manhattan.

First came the lounge-style nightclubs, in the late 1990s, lured by the promise of large warehouse spaces – then came the crowds of Manolo- and Jimmy Choo-clad fashionistas, making their way to Pastis restaurant at night and high-end boutiques by day. At its peak, the neighborhood became a symbol of *Sex and the City*-style trendiness, with late-night crowds of

The Meatpacking District: it's hard to go hungry here.

BELOW: Pastis is an iconic Meatpacking District haunt.

The High Line

Get away from the bustle and soar above street level in Manhattan's new city park – it's as lovely as it is unique

The city's most famous green space is easily Central Park – but its coolest is one of its newest, the High Line. Opened in 2009, this innovative city park is located on an elevated train track that was used between the 1930s and 1980 to ship meat from the Meatpacking District to Chelsea's refrigerated warehouses.

Enter at the corner of Gansevoort Street and Washington Street, where a set of stairs rises up from the street level, just east of 10th Avenue, to the elevated line. Immediately, you'll heave a sigh of relief as you escape this industrially designed part of the city, and the crowds of shoppers that fill West 14th Street during the day.

Up on the old rail line, a walking path has been landscaped, and lined with the type of plant life that grew here naturally after the rail was abandoned – tall grasses, wild flowers, and low bushes. There are gaps in the walkway, so bikes and dogs are not allowed up there, and in the wintertime the High Line feels eerily hushed and removed from the noise of the city.

Make your way north, and you'll pass the site of a future outpost of the Whitney Museum. You'll also pass under the glamorous new Standard Hotel, the only building that crosses directly over the High Line.

The next area you come to is designed with seating: lounge chairs are built into the rail lines, with train wheels that allow them to slide along. In the evenings, crowds gather here to watch the sunset over the Hudson River. Further on, at the point where the path passes Chelsea Market, there are food vendors in the summertime, and in winter, you can duck into the market for Thai food, brownies, baked goods, and other treats.

Pay attention as you continue to walk down the path – in some places the railings that held the meat hooks remain, and in others you can see the newer bricks indicating where the trains used to pass through buildings.

You'll feel very aware of the fact that the High Line is, in fact, not a straight line – it is a meandering, winding path. In some areas where it widens, there are benches, and an amphitheater has been set up for lectures, discussions, and use as outdoor classroom space for the High Line's programs for schoolchildren.

The first section of the park to open runs from Gansevoort Street, in the West Village, to 20th Street in Chelsea; the second stretch (20th Street to 30th Street) is expected to open in late 2010. For more information, go to www.thehighline.org or tel: 212-500 6035. There is no charge, and park hours change seasonally. ❑

LEFT AND ABOVE: getting back to nature on the High Line.

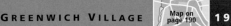

Recommended Restaurants, Bars, & Cafés on pages 200–1

fabulous people posing on the cobblestone street – right next to the last remaining meatpacking plants.

Over the next few years, the Meatpacking District went mainstream. Trading in the "insider's secret" pedigree for a more broad popularity, you're as likely to see bachelorette parties and bridge-and-tunnel (Manhattan speak for those from New Jersey and the outer boroughs) club kids in for a night of dancing as you are to glimpse the Manhattan elite at night.

That said, during the day the exclusive boutiques (Alexander McQueen, Diane von Furstenberg, Stella McCartney, a gorgeous glass-encased Apple shop) remain a draw for everyone who loves to be current and fashionable.

Sleeping and eating

Two major hotels – the **Hotel Gansevoort** *(see page 304)*, with its rooftop pool, and **The Standard** hotel – bring crowds of visitors, and the exclusive Soho House (a private club of British origins, with an even harder-to-access rooftop pool) continues to add cachet to the district.

And the restaurant scene here continues to grow as well *(see pages 200–1)*. Celebrity chefs like Jean-Georges Vongerichten, who opened **Spice Market** in 2004, and Mario Batali, who launched **Del Posto** in 2006, have outposts here. And, because of the club scene, many restaurants keep their kitchens open late into the night.

The **High Line** *(see left)*, a major new park built on an elevated railroad track, has brought a lot of attention to the area. Now, you can sit on this path-in-the-sky and watch the sunset over the river, without having to buy a loft space – something unimaginable before.

Things change quickly around the Meatpacking District, so there's little point in picking out more specific highlights. (The closing of popular Florent restaurant taught everyone that.) However, a growing number of galleries signal the movement of Chelsea's art scene further south, as will the Whitney Museum of Art branch, when it opens in a few years – heralding the Meatpacking District's next act. ❏

A meatpacker on the job.

BELOW LEFT: glamorous Hotel Gansevoort.
BELOW RIGHT: dining in the Meatpacking District.

BEST RESTAURANTS, BARS, AND CAFÉS

Restaurants

Prices for a three-course dinner per person with half a bottle of wine:

$ = under $20
$$ = $20–$45
$$$ = $45–$60
$$$$ = over $60

AOC

⊠ 314 Bleecker St (at Grove St) ☎ 212-675 9463 ☺ B, L, & D daily **$$** [p338, B2]
The dishes are served here as simply and perfectly as in a Paris bistro. Unlike other hurried New York spots, here *le savoir-vivre* reigns, and you can linger and talk all night if no one needs your table. There's a little garden patio for summer, too.

Babbo

⊠ 110 Waverly Pl (at MacDougal St and 6th Ave) ☎ 212-777 0303 ☺ D only daily **$$$$** [p338, B2]
Make a reservation days in advance for Mario Batali's top-of-the-line Italian gem. Some say it now has the best, most elegant Italian cuisine in New York City.

Barbuto

⊠ 775 Washington St (at W. 12th St) ☎ 212-924 9700 ☺ L & D daily **$$** [p338, A1]
Another great restaurateur, Jonathan Waxman, forges into the Meatpacking District at – what's this? – reasonable prices. He presents imaginative American cuisine using seasonal ingredients.

Blue Hill

⊠ 75 Washington Pl (at 6th Ave and Washington Sq W.) ☎ 212-539 1776 ☺ D only daily **$$$$** [p338, B2]
A mellow, sophisticated spot with rave reviews for its finely conceived American dishes created with fresh produce from the proprietors' own farm in upstate New York.

Café Asean

⊠ 117 W. 10th St (at Greenwich and 6th aves) ☺ L & D daily ☎ 212-633 0348 **$** [p338, B2]
Cash only, but worth it when the priciest item on the Southeast Asian menu is little over $20. A local secret.

Caliente Cab Company

⊠ 61 7th Ave S. ☎ 212-243 8517 ☺ L & D daily **$$** [p338, B2]
A friendly Mexican with tiled tables, (sometimes too loud) music, but with good guacamole.

CamaJe

⊠ 85 MacDougal St (at Bleecker and Houston sts) ☎ 212-673 8184 ☺ L & D daily **$–$$** [p338, B3]
Chef Abigail Hitchcock prepares top-notch French bistro dishes with imagination and heart. The casual atmosphere and reasonable prices make this a real find.

Chow Bar

⊠ 230 W. 4th St (at W. 10th St) ☎ 212-633 2212 ☺ D daily **$$$** [p338, B2]
Pan-Asian, trendy, and utterly delicious.

Da Silvano

⊠ 260 6th Ave (at Bleecker and Houston sts) ☎ 212-982 2343 ☺ L & D daily **$$$** [p338, B3]
You're pretty much guaranteed a celebrity sighting at this Tuscan hotspot, which is always in the gossip columns.

Fatty Crab West Village

⊠ 643 Hudson St (at Horatio and Gansevoort sts) ☎ 212-352 3592 ☺ L & D daily **$$** [p338, A1]
This trendy Malaysian fusion restaurant serves up whole, shell-on crabs swimming in addictive red chili sauce. Also consider ordering the porkbelly tea sandwiches and pork-filled steamed buns. In the summer, watermelon juice hits the spot.

Gavroche

⊠ 212 W. 14th St (at 7th and 8th aves) ☎ 212-647 8553 ☺ L Tue–Fri, D daily, Br Sun **$$$** [p338, B1]
Excellent straightforward French bistro on the fringes of the Meatpacking District and, to its credit, lacking a high-fashion attitude.

LEFT: Caliente Cab Company.
RIGHT: trusty condiments.

Little Owl

✉ 90 Bedford St (at Grove St) █ 212-741 4695 ☺ L & D daily $$$ [p338, B2]
A memorable name for a small Village hotspot known to serve the best pork chops around.

Macelleria

✉ 48 Gansevoort St (at 9th Ave) █ 212-741 2555 ☺ L & D daily $$$ [p338, A1]
The name is Italian for "butcher's shop," as befits this chic dining room in a former meat warehouse. Reservations essential at weekends.

Mercadito

✉ 100 7th Avenue S. (at Grove St) █ 212-647 0830 ☺ D daily, L Sat–Sun $$ [p338, B2]
This Mexican hotspot has plenty of taco options, but it's hard to resist the allure of *ancho*-rubbed pork topped with pineapple.

Mexicana Mama

✉ 525 Hudson St (at Charles and W. 10th) █ 212-924 4119 ☺ L & D Tue–Sun $$ [p338, A2]
This tiny Mexican gem is worth the wait to get in. The menu is limited, but the boldly flavored and beautifully presented dishes are a far cry from your average Tex-Mex fare. A taco here is timeless. Cash only.

Minetta Tavern

✉ 113 MacDougal St (at Bleecker and W. 3rd sts) █ 212-475 3850 ☺ D daily $$$ [p338, B3]
Old-time, comfy landmark. Recently relaunched with much buzz and a brasserie menu.

Il Mulino

✉ 86 W. 3rd St (at Sullivan and Thompson sts) █ 212-673 3783 ☺ L & D Mon–Fri, D only Sat $$$$ [p338, B3]
A loyal clientele has made this Italian Village classic almost like a club. Endless courses justify the expensive tab, and, after decades of excellent service, no one complains.

Paradou

✉ 8 Little W. 12th St (at 9th Ave) █ 212-463 8345 ☺ D only Mon–Fri; L & D Sat–Sun $–$$ [p338, A1]
What might seem like just another Meatpacking District bistro is a real gem – although the small, bright room and lovely garden are no longer a secret.

Pastis

✉ 9 9th Ave (at Little W. 12th St) █ 212-929 4844 ☺ B, L, & D daily $$$ [p338, A1]
There's food for most tastes most hours at this ultra-fashionable Meatpacking District brasserie, as tempting as the pretty people who come here.

Pearl Oyster Bar

✉ 18 Cornelia St (at Bleecker and W. 4th sts) █ 212-691 8211 ☺ L & D Mon–Fri, D only Sat $$ [p338, B2]
Raw-bar discovery in a Village side street full of tiny restaurants. Chowder is served perfectly, as is the lobster roll.

Risotteria

✉ 270 Bleecker St (at Morton St) █ 212-924 6664 ☺ L & D daily $ [p338, B2]
Nestled in the Italian heart of Bleecker Street, this casual restaurant knows its *arborio* from its *canaroli*; this is the place to come for risotto.

Spice Market

✉ 403 W. 13th St (at 9th Ave) █ 212-675 2322 ☺ L & D daily $$$ [p338, A1]
Exotic Meatpacking District duplex that really does feel like a Southeast Asian bazaar, serving four-star Malay cuisine. Part of the Jean-Georges Vongerichten stable.

The Spotted Pig

✉ 314 W. 11th St (at Greenwich St) █ 212-620 0393 ☺ L & D daily $$ [p338, A2]

A trendy gastro-pub, open late and always full. Great sandwiches, then New Wave Italian for dinner.

The Waverly Inn

✉ 16 Bank St (at Waverly Pl) █ 212-929 4377 ☺ D daily $$ [p338, B1]
A landmark since 1844, this is now the virtual private dining room of owner and *Vanity Fair* editor Graydon Carter. Booking can be tricky.

Bars and Cafés

Buddha Bar, 25 Little W. 12th St (at 9th Ave) The Meatpacking District bar scene on a Las Vegas level.

Caffè Reggio, 119 MacDougal St (at Bleecker and W. 3rd sts). Best of the Village Italian coffee houses.

Chocolate Bar, 19 8th Ave (at Jane and W. 12th sts), exists for all your chocolate needs.

Grom, 233 Bleecker St (at Carmine St), has some of the best *gelato* in New York.

Peanut Butter & Co., 240 Sullivan St (at Bleecker and W. 3rd sts). Anything and everything ever imagined with this staple of the American diet, from milkshakes to peanut butter/fluffernutter sandwiches, and much, much more.

Slaughtered Lamb Pub, 182 West 4th St (at Great Jones St). Steaks, hamburgers, and over 50 varieties of beer, in a horror-theme pub inspired by the movie *An American Werewolf in London*.

Recommended Restaurants, Bars, & Cafés on pages 224–5

THE EAST VILLAGE TO CHINATOWN

From historic synagogues on the Lower East Side to the newest style shops in NoLita; from garlicky food in Little Italy to cutting-edge clubs in Alphabet City – this is Manhattan's melting pot

Bordered by 14th Street to the north and Houston Street to the south, and roughly centered between Third Avenue and Avenue B, the **East Village** is a place that stays up late, where fashion and politics have always been more radical than elsewhere in the city, and whose residents have included Beat icons like Allen Ginsberg and William Burroughs, as well as Yippies and Hell's Angels.

Beneath its scruffy avant-garde surface, the East Village is also a neighborhood of immigrants, with Ukrainian and Puerto Rican social clubs next to cutting-edge boutiques, and free health clinics not far from expensive co-op buildings. Like other Downtown neighborhoods, old and new are juxtaposed here in an ever-changing mosaic.

EAST VILLAGE

At the beginning of the 20th century, lower Broadway around 9th Street was part of the "Ladies' Mile" of fashionable retailing that extended north to 23rd Street. Later, it was just a dingy pause away from Soho (when that area was still known as SoHo), but all that changed when Tower Records and other consumer meccas moved in. Unofficially known as **NoHo** ❶ (**N**orth of **Ho**uston), this stretch of the East Village includes Broadway from Astor Place down to Houston Street, a place crowded with fashion, art, and design stores.

Some interesting home furnishing emporia also tempt along Lafayette Street, where the huge **Chinatown Brasserie** (380 Lafayette, at Great Jones Street) serves up Asian food with a helping of trendy, Downtown attitude *(see page 224)*.

Main attractions

NoHo
MERCHANT'S HOUSE MUSEUM
ASTOR PLACE
ST MARK'S PLACE
"LITTLE INDIA"
TOMPKINS SQUARE PARK
ALPHABET CITY
LOWER EAST SIDE
LOWER EAST SIDE TENEMENT
    MUSEUM
NEW MUSEUM OF
    CONTEMPORARY ART
LITTLE ITALY
CHINATOWN

LEFT: Lower East Side folk.
RIGHT: NoHo knitwear.

East Village to Chinatown, Soho, and Tribeca

Recommended Restaurants, Bars, & Cafés on pages 224–5

Merchant's House Museum ❷

✉ 29 E. 4th St (at Lafayette St and the Bowery), www.merchantshouse.com
☎ 212-777 1089 ◷ Thur–Mon noon–5pm ⓢ charge 🚇 Astor Place

A block up from Great Jones Street on West 4th Street (just above Lafayette), drop in and see the city as it used to be at the "Merchant's House," a compact Greek Revival-style brick townhouse built in 1832. The same family, the Tredwells, lived here for generations until Gertrude Tredwell died in 1933, in the house where she was born. Their furnishings and personal effects have been preserved as they would have looked in the 19th century.

This is a good opportunity to see how wealthy New Yorkers lived – a nice companion to the slightly later Theodore Roosevelt Birthplace near Gramercy Park *(see page 178)*. Visitors are free to walk around the house, and a booklet provides information on its history and the Tredwell family; groups requiring a tour guide need to book in advance.

NoHo residents catch up over a drink.

NoHo arts

A detour east along 4th Street will take you to the slightly shabby **La MaMa** experimental theater (74A E. 4th St; tel: 212-475 7710, www.lamama.org). A pioneer of the avant-garde since 1961, the theater has three performance spaces and an art gallery.

Continuing north on Lafayette Street, **Colonnade Row** was originally a group of nine columned

LEFT AND BELOW: the Merchant's House gives a glimpse into how wealthy New Yorkers lived in the 1800s.

homes, built in 1833 when this was one of the city's most elegant neighborhoods. Only four of the houses still stand: current occupants include the perennially stylish **Indochine** restaurant at No. 430 *(see page 224)* and the **Astor Place Theatre** (No. 434), where the Blue Man Group is currently resident.

Across the street is the **Joseph Papp Public Theater ❸** (tel: 212-539 8500, www.publictheater.org), a red-brick, five-theater complex that originally housed the Astor Library. Since 1967, the theater has been the home of the

city's Shakespeare Festival (with free performances in Central Park during the summer), as well as more contemporary productions – from the world premiere of *Hair* to *A Chorus Line* to *Bring in 'Da Noise, Bring in 'Da Funk* – that have gone on to be bit hits on Broadway.

For great live music, spend an evening in **Joe's Pub** (425 Lafayette Street, tel: 212-539 8778), an innovative small venue, bar, and satellite of the Joseph Papp Public Theater. You can have dinner here, too.

Around Astor Place

Lafayette ends at **Astor Place ❹**, where a large Kmart reflects a departure from the Village's counter-culture roots. The area's most notable landmark, besides the handsome **Astor Place subway kiosk** and the glassy condo building by Gwathmey Siegel, is the giant black cube by Tony Rosenthal called *The Alamo*. One of the first abstract sculptures installed on city property, it stands at the intersection of Astor Place, St Mark's Place, and Lafayette Street, largely unnoticed by local workers as they hurry by.

The imposing brown Italianate **Cooper Union Foundation Building ❺**, between Third and Fourth avenues, opened in 1859 as one of the country's earliest centers of free education. Now well known as an

ABOVE: *The Alamo*, by Tony Rosenthal.
ABOVE RIGHT: the popular Astor Place Theatre. **BELOW:** the cast-iron Astor Place subway kiosk is one of New York's finest.

art school (varied exhibitions, tel: 212-353 4100, www.cooper.edu), this is also where Abraham Lincoln gave the popular speech said to have launched his presidential campaign.

A statue of the schools' founder-philanthropist Peter Cooper by Augustus St-Gaudens, who was a student here, stands behind Cooper Union at **Cooper Square**, where Third and Fourth avenues converge at the top of the Bowery.

Historic Fish

Walking from the Cooper Union to Third Avenue, you'll come across Stuyvesant Street, which veers off at an angle toward Second Avenue. **St Mark's Bookshop** (tel: 212-260 7853, www.stmarksbookshop.com), at the corner of Third and Stuyvesant, is a long-established store stocked with obscure new fiction, art books, and political tomes – its peaceful aisles provide a refreshing break.

The red-brick Anglo-Italianate houses on Stuyvesant Street and on East 10th Street form the heart of the **St Mark's Historic District**. The handsome home at 21 Stuyvesant

is the **Stuyvesant-Fish House**, a national historic landmark built by former Dutch governor Peter Stuyvesant's great-grandson by marriage, Hamilton Fish, which is now owned by the Cooper Union.

St Mark's-in-the-Bowery ⑥

✉ 131 E. 10th St (at Second Ave), http://smhlf.org 📞 212-228 2781 🕒 daily, times vary 💲 free 🚇 Astor Place/Third Ave

The second-oldest church building in Manhattan (after St Paul's Chapel, *see page 252*), St Mark's was nearly destroyed by fire in 1978, and was restored with the help of local residents. It has suffered a little again in the intervening years and is in need of attention, but when you consider its age this is hardly surprising. St Mark's has a long history of liberal religious thought – a reflection of the neighborhood that manifests itself in such long-standing community programs as the Poetry Project – and holds art shows in the parish hall.

St Marks-in-the-Bowery was built in 1799 on land that belonged to Peter Stuyvesant.

BELOW LEFT: long-established La MaMa is just one of the area's Off-Broadway venues.
BELOW: on the fire escape looking down over St Mark's Place.

Veniero has been owned and operated by the same family since 1894.

RIGHT: love and temptation in St Mark's.
BELOW: savor the labors of the bakers at Veniero – there have been four generations of them so far.

East Village North

Continuing on 10th Street into the East Village, toward First Avenue, the **Theater for the New City** (tel: 212-254 1109, www.theaterforthenewcity.net) on First Avenue was founded in 1971 as a venue for experimental Off-Broadway productions. Today it continues to put on new plays, as well as providing a performance space for theater groups that don't have their own.

If you feel the need for an energy rush, there's espresso and pastries at **Veniero** on 11th Street near First Avenue, testimony to an Italian enclave that flourished here in the early 1900s. You can't miss the red neon sign (even though a few of the letters have ceased working); once inside choose from a toothache-inducing array of tiny Italian pastries to take out, or sit down and enjoy one in the high-ceilinged café.

Not far away, **St Nicholas** ❼ Carpatho-Russian Orthodox Greek Catholic Church is a reminder of this ethnic and religious melting pot. Originally built for a predominantly Episcopal parish as St Mark's Chapel,

inside it has tiled walls and a beamed ceiling dating from 1894.

Over on 9th Street, Performance Space 122, better known as **P.S.122** (First Avenue at 9th Street, tel: 212-477 5288, www.ps122.org), is a multi-arts organization set up to nurture young and mid-career artists. The East Village has been a center for live performances ever since Second Avenue was lined by Yiddish theaters in the 1890s; a reminder of those times is the venerable **Orpheum Theater** situated at 126 Second Avenue.

Velvet Underground

St Mark's Place ❽, a continuation of 8th Street between Third Avenue and Avenue A, is the East Village version of Main Street. In the 1960s, this was the counter-culture center of the East Coast, where Andy Warhol presented Velvet Underground "happenings" and, later, barefoot freaks tripped out at the Electric Circus. It's now a gentrified condo/retail center of stores and residences.

The Fillmore East, which presented the East Coast's most psychedelic concerts, is also gone, but St Mark's Place is still one of the city's liveliest thoroughfares. Sidewalk cafés and restaurants heave with cus-

Recommended Restaurants, Bars, & Cafés on pages 224–5

tomers, and the bazaar-like atmosphere is augmented by street vendors selling T-shirts, leatherwear, jewelry, and bootleg CDs and DVDs.

Shop for retro, punk, or retropunk gear here, then pause for refreshment around the corner – down Third Avenue to East 7th Street – at a true drinking-man's pub.

McSorley's Old Ale House ❾

✉ 15 E. 7th St (between Second and Third aves), www.mcsorleysnew york.com 📞 212-474 9148
🕐 Mon–Sat 11am–1am, Sun 1pm–1am 🚇 Astor Place/8th St

McSorley's has been in business since the 1850s, although women weren't allowed inside until more than a century later. This was a favorite New York hangout of the Irish writer Brendan Behan, among other luminaries. The decor hasn't changed much over the past 150 years – there's still sawdust on the floor and standing-room only at the bar – but space *has* been made for a ladies' bathroom.

Every last patch of wall is covered with photos, posters, cartoons, and

other curios; eagle-eyed patrons might spot an original wanted poster for Abraham Lincoln's assassin. As with New York's other remaining 19th-century saloons, McSorley's can be a little bit of a tourist trap, but it's so much a part of the area's history that it still has its regulars – all of whom must abide by the McSorley motto: *Be Good, Or Be Gone.*

Music legends

Back on St Mark's, the block between Second and Third is lined by a motley array of music stores, tattoo parlors, and places to get piercings in a variety of body parts. CBGB-OMFUG, previously at 315 The Bowery, was the city's coolest live-music venue and the birthplace

Testimony to the East Village's Eastern European heritage can be found at the Ukrainian Museum (tel: 212-228 0110; www.ukrainian museum.org), which is now in an elegant new building at 222 East 6th Street, between Second and Third avenues.

BELOW: McSorley's Old Ale House dates from 1850, but only opened to women in 1970.

new (more expensive) restaurants are opening all the time. However, if cheap and spicy is your preference, you can't do much better than head for "**Little India**" ⑩, a strip of Indian restaurants on 6th Street between First and Second avenues. In the evening the air is filled with enticing smells, and visitors drift from menu to menu in the attempt to make a decision. All the restaurants here are inexpensive, most stay open pretty late, and some have live Indian music on weekend evenings.

of the New York punk scene. The club was forced to close at the end of 2006 – joining the roll-call of local businesses forced out by rising property prices. In 2008, the space reopened as a John Varvatos clothing boutique. The poster- and sticker-covered walls were left intact, and are behind glass.

Down the block, Daniel Boulud's sausage-and-beer restaurant, DBGB, opened to rave reviews in 2009.

Cheap and spicy

Once upon a time you used to be able to find just about any cuisine in the East Village, and while some of its old stalwarts have been forced on,

Farther east on 6th Street is Avenue A, and a café-lined stretch that continues to **Tompkins Square Park** ⑪. Formerly reclaimed swamp that was used as a drill ground and recruiting camp during the Civil War, it was later the center of the *Kleine Deutschland* (Little Germany) community that thrived here 100 years ago. The park was an infamous gathering place for hippies and runaways in the 1960s, and became a focal point for conflicts between homeless activists and police in the 1980s. Today, however, it's a generally peaceful place, frequented by

ABOVE AND BELOW:
I ♥ New York dogs.

Tompkins Square Dog Run

Dogs are popular with New Yorkers, and vice versa. Uptown, the price of apartment space is visible from the huge number of pocket-sized pooches, and the obvious wealth of the proud owners of large, aristocratic afghans. A common sight is the wage-earning dog-walker, leading five or six hounds around town.

For even super-rich Manhattanites, though, a safe place to let dogs off the leash isn't easy to find. Sufficient space where the dog won't be at risk, or threaten others, is rare. Hence, Tompkins Square Park First Run – celebrated in an episode of *Sex and the City* – was started by Lower East Siders in the 1980s. Separate runs keep small and large dogs apart (otherwise the little breeds start fights). Dogs over six months must be neutered, no toys are allowed, nor is anyone who arrives without a pooch. Hours vary seasonally, but are typically before 9am, and between 5 and 7pm.

young mothers with kids and neighborhood folk exercising their pets in the specially enclosed dog-friendly area. Many of the homes have been renovated (the 19th-century row houses on 10th Street are a good example), fueling a hike in rents as in other "reclaimed" parts of the city, and creating resentment from the locals fighting to stay in the area.

Alphabet City

Nowhere is this urban reclamation more evident than in the area known as **Alphabet City** ⑫ (Avenues A, B, C, and D). For decades the very name was synonymous with crime and little punishment, but now slums and barbed wire have been surplanted by bars and restaurants with a young, hip clientele.

Tiny community parks have been divested of drug dealers and twinkle at night with fairy lights, while former bodegas have metamorphosed into fashion boutiques with Soho prices. Avenue A in particular is on the up, and although still a little rough around the edges, now wears its graffiti like a badge of honor.

As in other cutting-edge neighborhoods, though, it's wise to exercise a degree of caution, and here it's easy – just follow the alphabet. Avenues A, B, and C are fine anytime. Avenue D is fairly safe until midnight, but just for now it's an idea to avoid it after that.

Dining possibilities in the area are seemingly limitless, but an inexpensive stalwart has always been **Odessa** (119 Avenue A at 7th Street, open 24 hours), a survivor of the neighborhood's Eastern European past, where specialties include home-cooked *pirogi*, *blintzes* and *borscht*.

LOWER EAST SIDE

Technically, this area starts east of Tompkins Square Park, where Avenue C unofficially becomes Losaida Avenue (*Losaida* is Puerto Rican "Spanglish" for "Lower East Side"). But the traditional Lower East Side, with its Jewish-immigrant roots still in place, is south of East Houston Street, bordered by the Bowery and the East River. This is

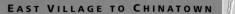

BELOW: two views of Alphabet City.

where the narrow streets are lined by tenements that date back 150 years.

These days you'll see stores with Jewish names and Chinese or Hispanic owners, a reminder that this neighborhood has always welcomed new arrivals. Modern newcomers are the bohemian-minded bars, clubs, and shops thriving along Ludlow, Orchard, and other streets, a trend that was kicked off in 1993 when **Mercury Lounge** – one of the city's best small music venues – kicked open its doors at 217 East Houston Street (check out listings in the free sheet, the *Village Voice*).

Today, you can shop for exotic foods from family stores that have been here for decades, then stroll along next door for a cutting-edge outfit – evidence of the gentrification of an immigrant neighborhood, but also of the vibrancy of change.

Delis and designers

Walk along East Houston to the top of **Orchard Street** to reach a favorite Lower East Side retail destination. Serious shoppers may want to stop first at **Katz's Delicatessen**

(205 East Houston, near Ludlow Street) for a little sustenance. The menu here has hardly changed since opening day in 1898 – and their pastrami sandwich has long been a New York culinary landmark.

New customers include the many construction workers currently working on the apartment blocks and fashionable hotels that are springing up in the area.

Once crowded with peddlers selling old clothes and cracked eggs, today the top of Orchard from East Houston to Rivington is being heavily redeveloped, with stylish new stores selling an intriguing mix of

TIP

The Lower East Side Business Improvement District (LES BID) has a visitor center at 54 Orchard Street (between Hester and Grand sts, www.lowereastsideny.com; daily), with information on the area, walking tours, and discounts at many neighborhood businesses.

BELOW LEFT: the all-glass and über-cool Hotel on Rivington.
BELOW RIGHT: WD-50, the foodie's favorite.

Recommended Restaurants, Bars, & Cafés on pages 224–5

marked-up second-hand clothing, bespoke jewelry, street-smart sneakers, and designer clothes.

In the company of cool

The crowning glory of this upscale takeover is **The Hotel on Rivington**, by Ludlow Street *(see page 304)* – a 21-story glass tower with unrivaled views over the Lower East Side. Bouncer-like doormen guard the entrance to the über-designed interior, and sharply dressed urbanites toy with French-fusion cuisine at **Thor**. The arrival of this hotel loudly proclaimed the Lower East Side's new status of cool, and more hotels are planned for the future.

Three blocks west of The Hotel, proof of the area's continuing role as a center for immigrants is the 19th-century **University Settlement House** on Eldridge Street (at Rivington). The first settlement house in the US, the organization continues to provide advice and assistance to local immigrants and low-income residents today.

Farther south along Orchard Street, the lifestyle stores and boutiques give way to the Lower East Side's famous discount premises, selling bargain fashions, fabrics, linens, and shoes. The scene is frenetic at times, and bargaining is encouraged, but make sure you know what you want beforehand to ensure you get a good price.

Old favorites

Old favorites include Giselle at 143 Orchard, with four floors of discounted women's fashion (labels include Escada, Laurel, and Valentino), Ben Freedman at 137 Orchard, for 75 years the purveyor

A sign of old times: the Lower East Side's Jewish heritage dates back to the mid-1800s.

LEFT: Orchard Street.
BELOW: the menu at Katz's Deli has hardly changed since 1898.

The Sunshine, 143 E. Houston between First and Second avenues, is housed in an old vaudeville theater. There are five screens and Dolby sound. Tel: 212-330 8182.

RIGHT AND BELOW: the Lower East Side Tenement Museum.

of bargain men's apparel, and Sam's Knitwear at 93 Orchard, where Polish immigrant Sam Goldstein has provided vintage and modern suits to snappily dressed men since 1969.

Head west on Delancey Street for some old-world comfort food at **Sammy's Roumanian Steak House** (175 Chrystie Street, just north of Delancey), a memorable, if not inexpensive, place to feast, and where a traditional pitcher of chicken fat comes with every meal. On a corner of Delancey is a well-known tribute to the area's first immigrant families.

Lower East Side Tenement Museum ⓴

✉ 108 Orchard St (at Delancey and Broome sts), www.tenement.org
☎ 212-431 0233 ⏱ tours 10.30am–5pm daily ⓢ charge Ⓜ Delancey St/Essex St

This museum is dedicated to the story of what life was like for poor immigrants in New York at the end of the 19th century. The address at 108 Orchard is the visitors' center and the starting point for tours of the

tenements, which can only be visited with a guide.

Tours cover different themes, but all last one hour, during which visitors explore the recreated apartments of families who lived in the cramped quarters at 97 Orchard Street – each arranged to provide insight into the families' ethnic backgrounds and daily lives. What is remarkable is the imagination and resilience with which they sought to combat poverty and assimilate into New York society. The museum's tours are very popular, so be sure to book in advance. From April to December the museum also

Recommended Restaurants, Bars, & Cafés on pages 224–5

conducts weekend walking tours of the Lower East Side.

Designer tenement

The **Blue Moon Hotel** on Orchard *(see page 304)* has tried to bridge the gap between the tenement experience and the area's modern-day desirability by converting a traditional tenement building, empty since the 1930s, into a fashionable hotel. Many of the building's original features have been restored, and items recovered during the renovation – including newspapers and Yiddish sheet music – have been put on display. Room prices are *very* contemporary, though.

Farther down Orchard Street you'll find Il Laboratorio del Gelato, an artisanal maker of Italian-style *gelati*, with surprising flavors like wasabi and rose petal. Around the corner, on Broome, you'll see the trendy Babycakes bakery. Sadly, as in other parts of the city, soaring rent prices are forcing many of the traditional stores and eateries to close; the Tenement Museum publishes a list of all surviving specialty food shops in

the area. Unfortunately a local fave, Guss' Pickles, closed in 2009.

Living history

The Lower East Side's Jewish population produced an extraordinary number of famous actors and comedians. Oscar-nominated actor Sam Jaffe was born in an apartment at 97 Orchard Street – the 1863 tenement now run by the Tenement Museum – while a couple of blocks south, Grand Street's Seward Park High School (at Ludlow Street) counted Tony Curtis and Walter Matthau among its graduates. The high school closed in 2006, and has been divided up into five different schools, offering courses in a variety of fields.

Marching, marching, marching to the shopping.

LEFT: TG-170, on Ludlow Street.
BELOW LEFT: vintage fashion at Marmalade on Ludlow Street.
BELOW RIGHT: East Side watering hole.

DRINK

An enjoyable drinking spot in the smartened-up Lower East Side is 'inoteca at 98 Rivington Street, a stylish wine bar with over 300 quality Italian wines. Plates of tasty Italian nibbles keep hunger at bay while you pop another cork.

In the 19th century, the area's sub-standard working and living conditions (ably chronicled by Jacob Riis, *see page 32*) were instrumental in spawning anarchist and socialist movements. Emma Goldman preached her gentle anarchism on the Lower East Side, radical newspapers such as the *Jewish Daily Forward* flourished, and settlement houses offering immigrants health and education assistance were established.

Landmark buildings

The faces of Karl Marx and Friedrich Engels peer from a frieze above the entrance to the landmark building at **173 East Broadway** (between Pike and Rutgers) where the old *Daily Forward* was published, which has been converted into condos. A block south, the glorious red-brick **Henry Street Settlement** (265 Henry Street), founded in 1893 as the country's first volunteer nursing and social-service center, continues to serve the immigrant community and offers classes, health clinics, and after-school clubs.

Religion played an important role in the lives of immigrants. Although many of the synagogues in the area are no longer used, the **Eldridge Street Synagogue**, an 1887 Moorish-style landmark close to Division Street, has been the recipient of a 20-year restoration. Guided tours are available Sun–Thur, tel: 212-219 0302; charge.

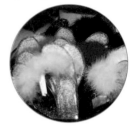

NoLita ⑮

Dubbed **NoLita**, for **N**orth of **Li**ttle I**ta**ly, the retail heart of this area, with its good-looking, arty residents and one-off (but pricey) fashion boutiques, is Mulberry Street, particularly between Houston and Kenmare. The best way to enjoy NoLita is simply to stroll around and drink in its exuberant atmosphere – a laid-back mix of the traditional and the

BELOW: a hat hawker does her thing on Prince Street.

Recommended Restaurants, Bars, & Cafés on pages 224–5

New Museum of Contemporary Art ⑰

✉ 235 the Bowery (at Prince St), www.newmuseum.org
📞 212-219 1222 🕐 Wed, Sat, Sun noon–6pm, Thur, Fri noon–9pm
💲 charge 🚇 Bowery/Broadway-Lafayette St

In contrast to the Beaux Arts beauties around it, the New Museum of Contemporary Art is designed to make an emphatic statement in this historic neighborhood. Consisting of a series of cubes and rectangles, like a giant stack of boxes, the building provides a spectacular purpose-built home for the museum, which highlights the latest contemporary art and design.

Art timeline

The location of the New Museum is a timeline of New York artistic trends. From its beginnings in 1977 on Fifth Avenue, it moved to Soho during the 1980s, then followed Soho's artists to Chelsea. The museum's arrival on the Lower East Side seals the status of the neighborhood for all to see.

TIP

Here we go 'round Mulberry Street... if you head for Little Italy and walk north looking for NoLita (North of Little Italy), you'll end up in NoHo. NoLita is a misnomer: the neighborhood is really "NoSLita", the Northern Section of Little Italy, but this doesn't sound nearly as cool.

trendy – before stopping off for a drink and a tasty tidbit in one of the watering holes on Elizabeth or Mott streets, now also with their share of fashionable stores.

Old St Patrick's Cathedral ⑯, on the corner of Mott and Prince streets, was the seat of New York's Catholic archdiocese until 1879, when the "new" St Patrick's Cathedral on Fifth Avenue was completed. Construction of the cathedral began in 1809, was interrupted by the War of 1812, and was eventually finished three years later. It was rebuilt in 1868 after being destroyed by fire, and remains a unique landmark.

Across Mott Street from the cathedral graveyard, a plaque on the wall of a red-brick Victorian building explains that this was the School of the Children's Aid Society, created for the care and education of immigrant children. Designed in 1888 by Calvert Vaux, the English architect who also designed Jefferson Market Library and helped create Central Park, it's now one of NoLita's most coveted apartment blocks.

Farther south on Centre Street are more desirable apartments; one in particular is the **Police Building**. This Beaux Arts edifice served as a police headquarters until 1973 (the current doormen do not look unlike the building's former employees).

LEFT AND BELOW:
the New Museum of Contemporary Art.

LITTLE ITALY ⑱

Crowds – led along by tantalizing food stands and raucous games of chance – are an integral part of the festivals that draw visitors to the streets of Little Italy. The **Feast of St Anthony** takes place on Mott Street between Grand and Canal streets in late May, while Mulberry Street from Canal to East Houston becomes a lively pedestrian mall during the 10-day **Feast of San Gennaro**, held in September.

This area has been an Italian neighborhood since the 1880s, when large numbers of immigrants arrived in New York, mainly from southern Italy. The most pleasant part is along **Mulberry Street**, north of Canal, where the atmosphere abruptly changes from boisterous to almost mellow, and the sidewalks are lined by cafés and social clubs.

Buon appetito!

Little Italy used to be about the food, but now it is mostly a touristy spot, and good Italian restaurants are hard to find. **Umberto's Clam House**, now on Broome near the corner of Mulberry Street, is a good spot. The restaurant's previous Mulberry Street location was where gangster Joey Gallo met an abrupt and bloody end over dinner in 1972.

Walking north on Mulberry past the headquarters of the Society of San Gennaro, you come to one of the oldest houses in Little Italy, a small white Federal-style building erected in 1816 for Stephen Van Renssellaer, a member of one of New York's oldest families. Originally at 153 Mulberry Street, the

ABOVE AND BELOW:
dining out in Little Italy.

Recommended Restaurants, Bars, & Cafés on pages 224–5

entire house was moved to its present site at No. 149 in 1841.

At the corner of Grand and Mulberry, **E. Rossi and Co.** has gifts, novelties, and religious relics to browse through, before it's time to sample the delicacies at **Ferrara**, a pastry shop and café since 1892.

CHINATOWN ⑲

One of the largest Chinese-American settlements in America, Chinatown got its start in the 1870s, when Chinese railroad workers drifted east from California in the wake of anti-Asian sentiment. Once squeezed into a three-block area bordered by Mott, Pell, and the Bowery, today's Chinatown encompasses around 40 blocks, swinging around Little Italy to Houston Street. Although Chinatown is now a little faded in some areas, half of its appeal is in negotiating the vendors, tourists, and residents that fill its busy streets.

Chinatown's heart lies south of Canal, where Worth Street, East Broadway and the Bowery meet at **Chatham Square** ⑳. Though the square is named after William Pitt – the Earl of Chatham – the **Kim Lau Memorial Arch** was built in honor of a Chinese-American pilot who died in World War II.

Nearby **Confucius Plaza** ㉑ is a lightly dilapidated concrete high-rise with apartments, stores, and a school. A bronze statue of the philosopher Confucius stands in front, facing the square.

Tucked in among all the Chinese banks lining the Bowery is a remnant

of old New York: built in 1785, **No. 18 Bowery** – or the Edward Mooney house, after its first owner, a prosperous meat wholesaler – is a Federal-style house and the oldest surviving row house in Manhattan. It's now occupied by a mortgage bank. Another striking Bowery landmark is the elegant, pagoda-style building that was until recently an HSBC bank, but is currently unoccupied.

Long-ago gangland

Walk west to **Columbus Park** – a pleasant space with basketball courts, benches, and a children's play area – to reach the bottom of busy **Mulberry Street**, one of Chinatown's two main thoroughfares, the other being **Mott Street**. In the mid-19th century, this was part of the notorious Five Points slum district, evoked at length in Martin Scorsese's 2002 epic, *Gangs of New York*, where street gangs ran rampant and squatters' huts formed an equally notorious shantytown (later cleared to make way for Columbus Park).

The best place to learn about the neighborhood is at an old (1900s)

Chinatown has spread from a three-block area to one that sprawls more than 40 blocks, growing larger with each decade.

BELOW: shop for flowers and food in Chinatown.

City of Immigrants

Getting started may be tough, but Lady Liberty's legendary call still beckons far across the globe

The US Census Bureau estimated in 2005 that there were 8,143,197 people in New York. Of these, 36 percent were born outside the United States, and 34 different regions of the globe were represented in the population. The common term "melting pot" was first used by Israel Zangwill, an immigrant himself, to describe the masses huddled on the Lower East Side.

The New York migrant groups challenge city planners: the standard four-part categories – white, black, Hispanic, Asian – are hopelessly inadequate for the kaleidoscope of culture, race, and nationality of the people who live in the city. There's as much diversity within ethnic groups as there is between them, and the social and political splits within a group are often the most divisive.

A sample of Asians, for example, is as likely to include Taiwanese financiers or Indian doctors as a Chinese immigrant smuggled in by boat. Foreign-born blacks may

resemble African-Americans, but black immigrants include French-speaking Haitians, plus English-speaking Barbadians, Trinidadians, and Jamaicans, Senegalese and Ghanians.

Among Latino groups, bound together by a common language, are deep-rooted cultural differences. Mexicans and Chileans, Cubans and Puerto Ricans keep their cultural distinctions in the city's neighborhoods, just as they did back home. Little wonder, then, that the 2 million Latinos, easily the city's largest ethnic group, have yet to consolidate a unified political voice.

Syncretism

In the end, it doesn't matter where people come from: they are here, and more arrive every day. New York's immigrants don't boil into a homogeneous cultural stew; they keep their identities and languages, and build new institutions and alliances. Nor is New York an example of pluralism – a multiethnic society where everyone has an equal say.

That tag is too static, and doesn't account for the dynamism, or for the possibilities of confrontation and conflict. The right term for New York's cultural mix is probably syncretism; a continuous state of cultural collision, blending, and overlapping, where groups and individuals influence each other to create something new.

New York is a city of immigrants, and has been since the Dutch shared the town with English, French, and Scandinavian settlers as well as with free Africans, black slaves, and Native Americans. The give-and-take – and often the push-and-shove – between cultures is what gave the city its vitality and a rough-cut worldliness.

Although immigrants come from farther away and speak languages never heard by New Yorkers 300 years ago, the same explosive energy runs through the city today. ❑

LEFT AND ABOVE: 34 different parts of the world are represented in New York's population.

Recommended Restaurants, Bars, & Cafés on pages 224–5

school building on the corner of Mulberry and Bayard, now the Chinese community museum.

Museum of Chinese in the Americas ㉒

✉ 215 Centre St (between Howard and Grand sts), www.mocanyc.org
☎ 212-619 4785 ⏲ Tue–Sun noon–6pm 💲 charge, free on Fridays
🚇 Canal St

Founded in 1970, when the area's population began to explode, this tiny museum features a permanent exhibit on the Chinese-American experience, with many items donated by residents or salvaged from demolitions. It also has a research library and a gift shop, and organizes regular walking tours and lectures. The exhibitions are located in a brand-new museum as of 2009.

Shiny restaurants

From the museum, walk south to Canal Street and turn left. As you enter Chinatown, you'll pass stands selling fruit, vegetables, and snacks, including leaf-wrapped packets of sticky rice. Crowded with vendors hawking Taiwanese DVDs and stores stocked with designer "knock-offs," this is a scene that feels far removed from the rest of Manhattan. From Canal Street, turn south down Mott Street to find shiny Singapore-style restaurants with marble facades and plastic signs. These are part of the "new" Chinatown built by recent, wealthier immigrants from Hong Kong and Shanghai; some are excellent, and surprisingly cheap.

Signs of the "old" Chinatown are still visible, however, especially at the **Chinese Community Center**, which

Columbus Park in Chinatown has been the recipient of Federal funding to renovate its Grand Pavilion, which stands on the northern edge of the park. The pavilion was built in 1897.

LEFT: Museum of Chinese in the Americas.
BELOW: seeing red in Chinatown.

first opened on Mott Street in 1883. Next door, in the **Eastern States Buddhist Temple** , there's a multi-armed statue of the Goddess Kuan-Yui. The air is thick with the scent of sweet incense.

Farther along, the **Church of the Transfiguration** was built for a Lutheran congregation in 1801 and was sold to the Roman Catholic Church in 1853. Today it offers Catholic services in Cantonese and runs a school for local children.

Turn right down **Pell Street** and you'll see the shop-front facade of the **First Chinese Baptist Church**. Above Ting's Gift Shop on the corner of Doyers Street and Penn is the Sun Wui District Association. This type of organization afforded Chinese immigrants a means of coping with the New World. Unlike others, it chose an edifice more traditionally Chinese, maybe to combat homesickness, or maybe to establish home here.

The pagoda roof is topped by two "good luck" ceramic fish. Nearby is the headquarters of the Hip Sing Association, one of Chinatown's many *tongs*, or fraternal organizations. From the 1870s until the 1930s, these groups were involved in often-violent disputes that were sensationalized as "*tong* wars" by the non-Chinese press.

The Chinatown grapevine

The narrow lane off to the right is the most crooked street in Manhattan; in the 1600s it was a cart track leading to one of the first breweries. Later, **Doyers Street** became an important communications center, where men gathered to get the latest news from China and to drop off letters and money for home with the

---

EAT

Although it's possible to find Chinese food anywhere in New York, one of the best places is the Nom Wah Tea House, 1 Doyers Street at Chatham Square, tel: 212-962 6047. Serving dim sum in a tiny space, this is the oldest teahouse in Chinatown.

BELOW: Chinatown's bustling Mott Street.

Recommended Restaurants, Bars, & Cafés on pages 224–5

small shopkeepers who served as combination banks and post offices.

In keeping with this tradition, the current Chinatown post office was built on the site of the old brewery. Nearby is the **Nom Wah Tea House**, the neighborhood's oldest restaurant. Unlike many places in the area, it generally closes early (around 8pm), but has some of the best dim sum in Chinatown. The interior is much as it was in 1921 when it opened, with sagging red-leather banquettes, linoleum floor, and ceiling fans. Prices are as old-fashioned as the decor.

Food and festivals

Food is one of the main attractions of Chinatown and, with hundreds of restaurants to choose from, the hardest part is picking where to eat. Options range from the extremely cozy five-table Malaysia Restaurant in the **Chinatown Arcade** to the Golden Unicorn on East Broadway, where house specialties are served in luxurious surroundings, or the Peking Duck House on Mott Street, a favorite of former New York mayor Ed Koch *(other food options on pages 224–5).*

For a deeper taste and sense of Chinese culture, drop in at one of the movie theaters that show films from Taiwan and China, or visit the **Asian-American Arts Center** (111 Norfolk Street), which features ongoing exhibits. Inside, the **Asian-American Dance Theater** presents traditional and contemporary dance productions here, too.

Chinese New Year combines feasts, dance, and music, and begins with fanciful parades. The festivities start around the end of January, and go on for several days, usually into February, but the street decorations tend to hang around a little bit longer. ❑

Finding refreshment is never more than a few steps away in Chinatown.

BELOW: Happy Chinese New Year.

BEST RESTAURANTS, BARS, AND CAFÉS

Restaurants

Prices for a three-course dinner per person with half a bottle of wine:
$ = under $20
$$ = $20–$45
$$$ = $45–$60
$$$$ = over $60

Angelica Kitchen
✉ 300 E. 12th St (at 1st and 2nd aves) 📞 212-228 2909 ☕ L & D daily **$$** [p339, D2]
Veg out on organic vegetarian cuisine, run by people with a retro mindset.

Angon
✉ 320 E. 6th St (at 1st and 2nd aves) 📞 212-260 8229 ☕ L & D Tue–Sun **$** [p339, D3]
One of the better places on this bargain strip known as "Curry Row."

Caracas Arepa Bar
✉ 91 E. 7th St (at 1st Ave and Ave A) 📞 212-228 5062 ☕ L & D daily **$** [p339, D3]
Locals flock to this casual Venezuelan restaurant for *arepas*: warm cornmeal pancakes topped with savory meat and vegetable options, and served with hot sauce.

Chinatown Brasserie
✉ 380 Lafayette St (at Great Jones St) 📞 212-533 7000 ☕ L & D daily **$$** [p338, C3]
One of the big new Downtown "in" spots for Asian cuisine. Big and brassy, with a noisy scene.

I Coppi
✉ 432 E. 9th St (at 1st Ave and Ave A) 📞 212-254

2263 ☕ D daily **$$$** [p339, D3]
This Tuscan restaurant oozes authenticity thanks to its brick walls, terracotta floors, wood-burning oven, and pretty garden. Dishes are rustic but sophisticated. It's pricey for the casual neighborhood, but highly romantic and very enjoyable.

Da Nico
✉ 164 Mulberry St (at Broome and Grand sts) 📞 212-343 1212 ☕ L & D daily **$$** [p341, C1]
Old-style Little Italy restaurant, where former mayor Rudy Giuliani can be seen eating.

DBGB Kitchen and Bar
✉ 299 Bowery (at 1st and 2nd sts) 📞 212-933 5300 ☕ L & D daily **$$$** [p339, C3]
This sleek restaurant elevates the humble – hot dogs, sausages, and burgers – to the elegant, with smooth service and prices to match.

Excellent Dumpling House
✉ 111 Lafayette St (at Canal and Walker sts) 📞 212-219 0212 ☕ L & D daily **$** [p340, C1]
Chinatown standard, serving up fine scallion pancakes along with the dumplings.

Freeman's
✉ Freeman Alley (off Rivington St, at Bowery and Chrystie St) 📞 212-420 0012 ☕ L & D daily **$$$** [p338, C4]
Devils on horseback anyone? American and English classics in a trendy spot; great cocktails.

H.S.F.
✉ 46 Bowery (at Bayard and Canal sts) 📞 212-374 1319 ☕ L & D daily **$$** [p341, C2]
One of the originators of dim-sum dining in NYC. Rolling tables of tiny delectables makes the rounds of the room.

Indochine
✉ 430 Lafayette St (at Astor Pl and 4th St) 📞 212-505 5111 ☕ D daily **$$$** [p338, C3]
Trendy, tropical decor, French-Vietnamese food, still sexy after all these years. It's located across from the Public Theater, and offers a decently priced pre-theater deal.

Itzocan
✉ 438 E. 9th St (between 1st Ave and Ave A) 📞 212-677 5856 ☕ L & D daily **$** [p339, D3]
Cheap and chic Mexican with French-accented preparations in a tiny intimate spot on the edge of Alphabet City.

LEFT: I Coppi – rustic, Tuscan, and romantic.
RIGHT: dumplings and dim sum.

Jewel Bako

✉ 239 E. 5th St (at 2nd and 3rd aves) ☎ 212-979 1012 ☻ D Mon–Sat **$$$$** [p339, C3]

A tiny "Tiffany" of sushi, where you don't need to cash in diamonds to eat.

Katz's Delicatessen

✉ 205 E. Houston St (at Ludlow St) ☎ 212-254 2246 ☻ B, L, & D daily **$$** [p339, D4]

This old-style Jewish deli is a New York institution. The huge space is often packed, especially on Sunday mornings. Portions are huge, and the service is friendly. A must for any first-time NY visitor.

Lombardi's Pizza

✉ 32 Spring St (at Mulberry and Mott sts) ☎ 212-941 7994 ☻ L & D daily **$$** [p338, C4]

Descended from the first pizzeria in the USA (opened in 1897), this is a Little Italy classic. It's open late: join the crowds, line up for a table (no reservations are taken), and be ready to pay cash.

Mermaid Inn

✉ 96 2nd Ave (at 5th and 6th sts) ☎ 212-674 5870 ☻ D daily **$$$** [p339, C3]

Winning formula of kitsch and great seafood makes this a popular, fun place.

Momofuku Noodle Bar

✉ 171 1st Ave (at 10th and 11th sts) ☎ 212-475 7899 ☻ L & D daily **$$** [p339, D3] This shrine to Korean haute cuisine also has two sophisticated sib-

lings: Momofuku Ssam a few blocks north on 2nd Ave and nearby, reservation-only Mamofuku Ko.

Peasant

✉ 194 Elizabeth St (at Prince and Spring) ☎ 212-965 9511 ☻ D only Tue–Sun **$$$** [p338, C4]

Like eating in a sophisticated Italian country place, with hearty flavors matched only by the wine list. A romantic setting.

Peking Duck House

✉ 28 Mott St (at Pell and Mosco sts) ☎ 212-777 1810 ☻ L & D daily **$$$** [p340, C2]

The crisp-skinned duck is served tableside with scallions, hoi sin sauce and rice-flour pancakes.

Pho Bang

✉ 157 Mott St (at Broome and Grand sts) ☎ 212-966 3797 ☻ L & D daily **$** [p341, C1]

Vietnamese noodle shop (several locations) that can't be beaten for value.

Prune

✉ 54 E. 1st St (at 1st and 2nd aves) ☎ 212-677 6221 ☻ L & D daily **$$$** [p339, C4]

Uptowners venture here for a foodie's dream. Chef Gabrielle Hamilton always makes culinary news with her tasty dishes.

Puglia

✉ 189 Hester St (at Mulberry St) ☎ 212-966 6006 ☻ L & D daily **$$** [p340, C1]

The Little Italy of old has survived here since

1919. Apparently things get "pretty crazy" at night, but group tables, a singer called "The Fat Lady," plus lots of red wine make for a party every time.

The Redhead

✉ 349 E. 13th St (at 1st and 2nd aves) ☎ 212-533 6212 ☻ D Mon–Sat, Br Sat–Sun **$$** [p339, D2]

A bar serving gastropub cuisine. Try the fried chicken with cornbread.

Schiller's Liquor Bar

✉ 131 Rivington Street (at Norfolk St) ☎ 212-260 4555 ☻ B, L, & D daily **$$** [p341, D1]

A hipster scene at affordable prices, and good grub to boot. Open late.

WD-50

✉ 50 Clinton St (at Rivington and Stanton) ☎ 212-477 2900 ☻ D daily **$$$$** [p341, D1]

WD stands for Wally Dufresne, who presides over a brilliant American-eclectic menu. A place (and prices) appreciated by all New York foodies.

Bars and Cafés

Acme Bar and Grill, 9 Great Jones St (at Broadway and Lafayette St), looks like a truck stop, but is worth closer examination.

ChickaLicious, 203 E. 10th St (at 1st and 2nd aves), is a tiny dessert bar serving yummy sweets with sweet wines.

De Robertis, 176 1st Ave (at 10th and 11th sts), is an Italian *pasticceria* and café established over a century ago.

Lucky Cheng's, 24 1st Ave (at 1st and 2nd sts), has a late-night scene, with the main

attraction being the colorful, cross-dressing wait staff.

Momofuku Milk Bar, 207 2nd Ave (next door to Momofuku Ssam), serves cakes and pies filled with candy bars, and milk and shakes sweetened with cereal (yes, really).

Max Fish, 178 Ludlow St (at E. Houston and Stanton sts). A rowdy rocker-art bar with its own gang of hipsters.

Veniero, 342 E. 11th St (between 1st and 2nd aves), is a lovely spot for an espresso, but we dare you not to order the *cannoli*, too.

Recommended Restaurants, Bars, & Cafés on pages 238–9

SOHO AND TRIBECA

Great shopping, good food, landmark buildings, and the chance to carouse in the heart of Manhattan's hippest movie arena – Soho and Tribeca are cast-iron cool

Soho, an acronym for **South of Houston**, is bordered by Canal Street to the south, Lafayette Street to the east, and the Avenue of the Americas (Sixth Avenue) to the west. When Abraham Lincoln made his first campaign speech at nearby Cooper Union, the area was the center of the city's most fashionable shopping and hotel district. By the end of the 19th century, however, the narrow streets were filled by factories, their imaginative cast-iron facades masking sweatshop conditions so horrific that the city fire department dubbed the entire region "Hell's Hundred Acres."

Temples of industry

The neighborhood could have been razed to the ground in the 1960s if local artists hadn't started moving into the old lofts, and the city hadn't changed zoning laws to allow them to do so legitimately.

Around the same time, determined conservationists established the **Soho Cast Iron Historic District** to protect the appearance of these elaborate "temples of industry." As a result, apartments are now too expensive for all but the most successful (or those who got in when prices were low), and most of Soho's remaining art galleries have relocated above street level to avoid the exorbitant rents. Others have absconded completely – to Chelsea or Brooklyn. If Soho is no longer the artists' neighborhood of old, it does maintain a New York combination of grit and blatant commercialism, where burly men unload trucks right by outrageous window displays, and double-decker tour buses lumber and wind slowly through the cobblestoned streets.

Main attractions

SOHO
WEST BROADWAY
CHILDREN'S MUSEUM OF THE ARTS
HAUGHWOUT BUILDING
WOOSTER STREET
NEW YORK CITY FIRE MUSEUM
TRIBECA
DUANE PARK
MERCANTILE EXCHANGE BUILDING
TRIBECA FILM CENTER
HARRISON STREET
WASHINGTON MARKET PARK

LEFT: sunshine and shopping on Soho's Prince Street.
RIGHT: hot sounds from the hot club on Varick Street, S.O.B. (Sounds of Brazil).

EAT

For fast, tasty Mexican food, try the Calexico stand, at the corner of Wooster and Prince streets. Its many fans consider it one of the best food carts in New York.

THE STREETS OF SOHO

The main drag is **West Broadway** , lined by stores offering everything from jewelry to quirky household wares. On Saturdays in particular, it's packed with crowds of tourists loaded down with shopping bags. From Houston to Canal are a generous selection of designer and top-end boutiques including US giants Tommy Hilfiger, Ralph Lauren, and DKNY, interspersed with European designers such as Missoni and Prada, which is housed in a Rem Koolhaas design.

At the end of a hard day's credit-card abuse, the best-dressed shoppers head to the **Soho Grand Hotel** (310 West Broadway, at Grand and Canal streets, *see page 304*). When it opened in 1996, this was the first new hotel in this part of town since the mid-1800s, when the fashionable American House Hotel stood at the corner of Spring Street, and the white-marble St Nicholas on Broadway and Broome held gala polka parties.

Rising 15 stories above the neighborhood, the Soho Grand manages to fit in with the "temples of industry,"

thanks to its industrial-chic decor and cozy bar and lounge, a meeting place for fashion and entertainment-industry types. It's also one of the few hotels where pets are not only welcome but are as pampered as their owners (witness the dog statues in the foyer). If you check in without an animal, you can request a complimentary bowl of goldfish.

Prince Street ㉕

Cutting across the top of West Broadway, Prince Street has all but forsaken galleries and turned into

RIGHT: eating at Bread, east on Spring Street.
BELOW: Soho is a shopper's paradise.

Recommended Restaurants, Bars, & Cafés on pages 238–9

prime shopping territory, and the surrounding streets have been swift to follow suit. It now carries a mix of familiar designer brands – including Calvin Klein Underwear at No. 104 – as well as more unusual stores such as Kid Robot at No. 126, selling a selection of Japanese toys and gadgets aimed equally at kids and graphic-designer adults.

Housed in an attractive former post-office building at the corner of Prince and Greene streets, **Station A** (103 Prince) is Apple's suitably stylish retail temple. Fight your way through the mainly European crowd to aesthetically pleasing iPods and other Apple products – you can even browse the internet on one of the display models. The upstairs theater holds free seminars on how to get the best from your tech toy.

The Romanesque Revival-style building on the opposite corner dates from the same period, but a century or so later has been transformed into the small, luxurious **Mercer Hotel** *(see page 306)*. Beneath it is a highly acclaimed basement-level restaurant, the **Mercer Kitchen**.

Broadway and beyond

Once home to the city's most elegant stores, and later to textile outlets, discount stores, and delis, the stately cast-iron buildings on Broadway below Canal Street reacquired cachet in the 1980s, first as museums, then as galleries, and then as stores like Crate & Barrel and Banana Republic. A Downtown **Bloomingdale's** (504 Broadway) has added more shopper traffic to the busy sidewalks.

Despite the presence of Bloomies and a handful of upscale stores, the Soho stretch of Broadway is best seen as West Broadway's younger, more mainstream cousin. Here you can find stores selling the latest jeans, sneakers and casual daywear. Recent imports H&M, Topshop, and Uniqlo are proving particularly

BELOW LEFT: air kisses at the Mercer.
BELOW RIGHT: Prada is housed on the premises of the former Guggenheim Museum.

popular with Soho's young trendsetters looking for style on a budget.

A 1904 cast-iron confection called the **Little Singer Building**, designed by Ernest Flagg (and now housing classy stationers Kate's Paperies), stands across Broadway from **Dean & Deluca**  (560 Broadway), at the opposite corner of Prince Street. Dean & Deluca has been described by the *Washington Post* as "a combination of Paris's Fauchon, London's Harrod's Food Halls and Milan's Peck all rolled into one," and presents food as art: a cornucopia of fruits, vegetables, and imported gourmet grocery specialties. This has proved to be so successful a formula that Dean & Deluca stores have

branched out. The stand-up coffee bar is stocked with delectable pastries, and is a perfect place for a quick snack – although if you arrive before 10am, expect a long line of pre-work coffee drinkers.

If the Harry Potter novels made J.K. Rowling a millionaire, evidence that it did even more for her US publisher **Scholastic Books** is their huge and colorful book store at 555 Broadway. Aisles of kids' books, arts and crafts, and free Saturday events make this a good family stop.

Walking east on Prince leads to Lafayette Street, where urbanites can pick up hip-hop-influenced streetwear from stores such as Triple Five Soul, Wesc, or Brooklyn Industries.

BELOW AND RIGHT: something for everyone at Dean & Deluca.

Leo Castelli

Leo Castelli's gallery at 420 West Broadway (now DKNY) gave a shop window to the 1960s and 1970s Pop Art movement, and a massive boost to the Soho arts scene. Leo and his wife Ileana first had a gallery in Paris in 1935, but as World War II broke out they decamped to New York. It wasn't until 1954, when Leo saw some of Robert Rauschenberg's work, that he re-entered the art world, wanting only to work with art that inspired him with "pure enthusiasm." In the 1960s, Andy Warhol and Roy Lichtenstein led the way in treating commercial objects and comics as artistic symbols. The Pop Art movement exploded, and Castelli championed these and many other groundbreaking artists. He died in New York on August 22, 1999.

Children's Museum of the Arts ㉗

✉ 182 Lafayette Street (at Broome and Grand sts), www.cmany.org
☏ 212-274 0986 ◷ Wed, Fri–Sun noon–5pm, Thur noon–6pm ⑤ charge
🚇 Spring St/Canal St

A successful cross between a museum and a particularly lively crèche, the Children's Museum aims to encourage tiny artists through inspiration – it has a collection of 2,000 works of children's art from around the world – and through interactive exhibits and artist-led classes for kids. Group activities are tailor-made for specific age groups – for example, the "Wee Arts" program allows children aged 10 months to 3½ years to explore art (or make a mess) using playdough, paints, and a variety of other child-friendly materials, while for older kids, a highlight is the Performing Arts Gallery – a mock, child-size theater with the making of costumes and improvised performances.

Flora and Miss Lizzie

Back on Broadway, the **Haughwout Building** ㉘ is the palazzo-style structure near Broome Street. The Haughwout is one of Soho's oldest – and most striking – cast-iron edifices. Designed by John Gaynor, it was constructed in 1857 as one of the country's first retail stores, complete with its first elevator.

Named after a Revolutionary War general, **Greene Street** ㉙, like Mercer and Wooster streets, runs parallel to West Broadway and Broadway. In the late 19th century this was the center of New York's most notorious red-light district, where brothels with names like Flora's and Miss Lizzie's flourished behind shuttered windows. Now the same windows attract a very different sort of browser –

Fashionista earns her stripes on the busy shopping streets of Soho.

BELOW: a friendly zebra welcomes visitors to the Children's Museum of the Arts.

splendor at **72–76 Greene Street**, just opposite. This impressively ornate structure was designed and built by Isaac Duckworth in 1873.

Wooster Street arts scene

For more shopping and a selection of Soho's few remaining galleries (which seem to hop from street to street on a regular basis), walk across to stone-cobbled **Wooster Street 30**. The long-established **Dia Center for the Arts** has managed to stay anchored to the second-floor space at 141 Wooster Street with the *New York Earth Room*, a room interior filled with real earth, by Walter De Maria (Wed–Sun noon–6pm, closed 3–3.30pm). The Dia Center also has a major gallery space at Beacon in the Hudson valley.

In addition to galleries, this end of Wooster also has the **Ohio Theater** at No. 66, where the Soho Think Tank presents independent theater productions, and, near the corner of Grand Street, the ever-popular and experimental **Performing Garage** (33 Wooster, tel: 212-966 9796), which has presented the Wooster Group's unique brand of theater, dance, and performance art since 1967.

Food for thought

John Broome was a successful merchant who imported tea and silk from China at the end of the Revolutionary War, so he might have appreciated the fresh produce and other goods sold at the **Gourmet Garage** (453 Broome, at Mercer Street), an indoor market serving the restaurant trade and Soho locals.

In general, Broome Street is one of Soho's least jazzed-up thoroughfares, unless you count the ornate Calvert Vaux-designed edifice at No. 448, built in 1872. A lunch treat awaits a little farther on at the corner of West Broadway in the characterful **Broome Street Bar**. Situated in a pretty, 18th-century

gazing longingly over summer dresses in bright, '80s-influenced colors at Anna Sui (No. 113).

As befits one of the Soho Cast Iron Historic District's prime thoroughfares, Greene Street also offers a rich concentration of this uniquely American architecture at its best, including (at the Canal Street end) the city's longest continuous row of cast-iron buildings.

At the corner of Broome Street, the 1872 **Gunther Building** is particularly worthy of notice. Before continuing, stop and admire the cream-colored architectural "king" of cast-iron

ABOVE: ladies who lunch do it in Soho.
BELOW: late-nite sounds in a late-nite part of town.

house, the Broome Street Bar with its friendly staff has been serving sandwiches, soups, and burgers at its wooden tables since Soho was involved in the arts scene.

Crossing West Broadway, you're on the fringe of the South Village, where chic little shoe salons and boutiques nestle among places like the **Birdbath Bakery** on Prince between West Broadway and Thompson Street, which, until very recently, had been run as the Vesuvio Bakery by the same family since the 1920s. Vesuvio had locals lining up for its freshly baked bread, and now Birdbath follows in its footsteps.

Milady's, another neighborhood bar and restaurant (162 Prince) has been around for close to half a century, and is one of a dwindling number of Soho eateries left from less fashionable times.

One of these refreshment stops should provide the stamina for a detour down Thompson to Spring Street, then west across Sixth Avenue to the New York Fire Department's museum, on one of Spring Street's last blocks before it meets the river.

New York City Fire Museum ③①

✉ 278 Spring Street (at Varick and Hudson sts), www.nycfiremuseum.org
☎ 212-691 1303 Ⓒ Tue–Sat 10am–5pm, Sun 10am–4pm
Ⓢ charge 🚇 Spring St

It's worth the walk to Engine Company No. 30's former headquarters to visit this charming museum. The restored fire house's original features include the brass sliding pole and apparatus doors, providing a perfect setting for one of the country's largest collections of firefighting apparatus and memorabilia. Highlights include the shiny red antique hand- and horse-pulled wagons – especially popular with children. A special extension houses a permanent 9/11 exhibit, with powerful images from that sad day.

Canalside

Back on West Broadway, Soho comes to a halt at **Canal Street** ③②, where stores sell plastic odds and ends, rubber tubing, neon signs,

BELOW: Engine Company No. 30's former headquarters.

TIP

TOAST stands for the **T**ribeca **O**pen **A**rtist **S**tudio **T**our, when over 100 artists throw open their doors. This four-day event is usually held in spring. Details from: www.toastartwalk.com.

RIGHT: a NY minute at the Tribeca Grand.
BELOW: Tribeca, looking toward City Hall.

household appliances, and barrels of peculiar industrial leftovers. It's all mixed together in a bedlam of hot-dog carts and street vendors displaying old books, new CDs and DVDs, and, from time to time, a few bona fide treasures.

TRIBECA

In the late 1970s, artists in search of lower rents migrated south from Soho to Tribeca – the **Tri**angle **Be**low **Ca**nal – which runs south of Canal Street to Chambers Street, and west from Broadway to the Hudson River. Called Washington Market in the days when the city's major produce businesses operated here (before they moved to Hunt's Point

in the Bronx), this part of the Lower West Side is one of Manhattan's most pleasant neighborhoods.

Now an eclectic blend of renovated commercial warehouses, Corinthian columns, condo towers, and celebrity restaurants, Tribeca was where artists like David Cale or Laurie Anderson showed their early works, at venues like the Alternative Museum and Franklin Furnace (both now closed).

Change of pace

Today's Tribeca scene has more to show in the culinary than in the fine arts, but its largely residential atmosphere makes a pleasant change of pace from Soho's tourist-packed streets. A block south of Canal, the Tribeca Grand Hotel, rising from the triangle bordered by Sixth Avenue, Walker and White streets, looms over one of the area's oldest survivors: an 1809 brick house at **2 White Street,** just off West Broadway, which dates back to an earlier era when this was one of the city's original residential enclaves.

Grand designs

The **Tribeca Grand** hotel *(see page 304),* younger sister to the Soho Grand, keeps the residential tradition alive with its hip, trendy hos-

Recommended Restaurants, Bars, & Cafés on pages 238–9

pitality. Features for glamorous guests include an atrium lounge and 203 ergonomically designed rooms, with extra-large windows and great amenities.

The handsome **Clocktower Building** at 108 Leonard Street – named for its ornate tower – is the former New York Life Insurance Building, which was remodeled by Stanford White in 1898.

The building now houses the studio for **WPS1 Art Radio**, the internet-based radio station affiliated with the P.S.1 arts center in Queens. WPS1 does cool things like broadcast from an Italian barge during the Venice Biennale.

On the corner of Thomas Street and West Broadway, two blocks below Leonard Street, a red neon sign spells out "Cafeteria," but don't be fooled. This 1930s mock-stone building has housed **Odeon**, one of Downtown's hippest restaurants since it opened in 1980 *(see page 239)*. Unlike many trendy spots, it shows no signs of fading away and is still a favorite with the cognoscenti, especially late into the night.

Across the street, Tribeca über-chef David Bouley's recent venture, the **Bouley Bakery & Market** (130 West Broadway) has yummy pastries, pizza, salads, and soups at street level, meats, cheeses, and seafood piled high in the basement, and a dining room for more grown-up meals upstairs.

Duane and Staple

Below Thomas is **Duane Street**. Named for New York's first post-Revolution mayor, it meets Hudson Street at tiny triangular **Duane Park ㉝** – all that's left of a farm that the city bought for $5 in 1795, and now bordered by cute clothes stores.

Staple Street, a narrow strip of cobblestone where "staple" produce

BELOW LEFT: trio on a Tribeca corner.
BELOW RIGHT: the terrace of the grand suite at the Tribeca Grand.

Young diners at the Tribeca Grill.

was once unloaded, connects the park with the ornate, brick **Mercantile Exchange Building** ㉞, on the corner of Harrison and Hudson streets.

The neighboring 1920s **Western Union Building** ㉟ at 60 Hudson Street soars 24 stories above the rest of the neighborhood like a layered missile, and is made of 19 different shades of brick. Its lobby, where even the letterboxes are marvels of Art Deco artistry, is also stunning. Unfortunately you can no longer walk through it to West Broadway, but you can still get a good glimpse through the gate by the main doors.

Old and new

Greenwich Street is where much of Tribeca's new development is centered, but you can still find authentic early remnants – like the 19th-century lantern factory between Laight and Vestry streets, which now houses million-dollar lofts. In the new non-smoking New York, the wine and cigar club provides a growing niche.

The corner of Greenwich and Franklin streets is the place where

actor Robert De Niro transformed the old Martinson Coffee Factory into the **Tribeca Film Center** ㊱. On the first floor is the **Tribeca Grill** *(see page 239)*. Many come here in the hope of seeing De Niro or film-biz luminaries from the upstairs offices. Chances are, the closest you'll get to a sighting is one of De Niro's dad's paintings on the walls, and while you do occasionally see people talking "back-end" and

RIGHT: Bubby's on Hudson serves "food like Mom makes."
BELOW: cool pool in a Tribeca club.

Recommended Restaurants, Bars, & Cafés on pages 238–9

reading scripts, most of the clientele are regular business types and star-struck tourists. The food, however, rarely disappoints.

The late 18th- and early 19th-century brick houses on **Harrison Street** look incongruous, like a stage set in the shadow of **Independence Plaza**'s gargantuan 1970s apartment towers, but like the house on White Street, they're evocative survivors of Tribeca's residential beginnings.

Just off Harrison, **Bazzini's** at 339 Greenwich Street is a hardy remnant of the area's old commercial incarnation; it has been a fruit and nut wholesaler since 1886. While Bazzini's has since branched into standard deli fare, it's still the most authentic place to buy huge bags of pistachios.

Grass and a gazebo

Opposite the big line of condo dwellings stretching between Duane and Chambers streets, **Washington Market Park** ③⑦ has a thick grassy meadow to stretch out on, and even a fanciful gazebo to daydream in. Public School 234 – its wrought-iron fence embossed with Spanish galleons in full sail – is across from the park, and worth noting.

From Chambers and West Street, you can reach **Hudson River Park** via a pedestrian bridge that stretches across the West Side Highway. Walkways and bike paths extend north along the river beyond Pier 25, and south to connect to Battery Park City. If you continue south, there's a scenic riverside walk, complete with views of the Statue of Liberty.   ❏

Brandy Library, 25 North Moore Street at Varick, appeals to an upscale crowd who like their couches low and their drinks long. To complete the sophistication, cigar smokers can light up on the heated terrace.

LEFT: the Odeon keeps on going year after year.
BELOW: actor Morgan Freeman at the Tribeca Film Festival.

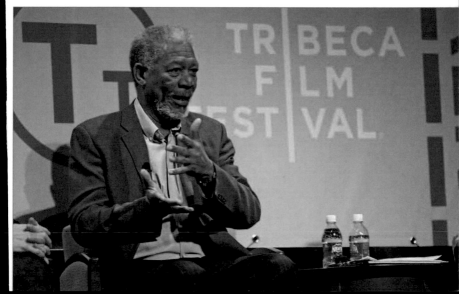

BEST RESTAURANTS, BARS, AND CAFÉS

Restaurants

Prices for a three-course dinner per person with half a bottle of wine:
$ = under $20
$$ = $20–$45
$$$ = $45–$60
$$$$ = over $60

Balthazar
✉ 80 Spring St (at Broadway and Crosby sts) 📞 212-965 1414 🕐 B, L, & D daily **$$$** [p338, B4]
Parisian-style brasserie; hard to imagine Soho without it.

Blaue Gans
✉ 139 Duane St (at W. Broadway and Church St) 📞 212-571 8880 🕐 L & D daily **$$$** [p340, B2]
Locals love the neighborhood feel of this Viennese-style restaurant, as well as the European fare, including schnitzel, goulash, and bratwurst.

Blue Ribbon
✉ 97 Sullivan St (at Prince and Spring sts) 📞 212-274 0404 🕐 D daily, until 4am **$$$** [p338, B3]
The first in a mini-empire of Downtown "Blue Ribbons." At all the outlets (**Blue Ribbon Sushi** a few doors north, **Blue Ribbon Bakery**, 33 Downing St, and **Blue Ribbon Downing St Bar** next door), there's exceptional quality food and service for a price. All are open late.

Bouley
✉ 163 Duane St (at W. Broadway and Hudson St) 📞 212-964 2525 🕐 L & D daily **$$$$** [p340, B2]

David Bouley's "new French" food experience transcends price, and his flagship restaurant is undoubtedly one of New York's Top Ten. Bouley moved into this new space in 2008, and the restaurant is better than ever.

Bread
✉ 20 Spring St (at Elizabeth and Mott sts) 📞 212-334 1015 🕐 B, L, & D daily **$** [p338, C4]
Follow Spring Street due east for a snack that doesn't smack of Soho prices. Hot sandwiches come with pesto, chicken and avocado, goat's cheese and shiitakes, or fresh sardines and tomatoes. There's pasta and a very good antipasti plate, too.

Bubby's
✉ 120 Hudson St (at N. Moore St) 📞 212-219 0666 🕐 B, L, & D daily **$$** [p340, A4]
Funky joint, kid-friendly but also a celeb-spot from time to time. Comfort food is top of the menu.

Capsouto Frères
✉ 451 Washington St (at Desbrosses and Watts sts) 📞 212-966 4900 🕐 L & D Tue–Sun, D only Mon **$$$** [p338, A4]
French in the most tradi-tional sense, this far-West Side bistro serves *escargots*, onion soup gratinée, and duck confit.

Centrico
✉ 211 W. Broadway (at Franklin St) 📞 212-431 0700 🕐 D only **$$$** [p340, B1]
Zarela Martinez (of Zarela's, at 2nd Ave and 50th St) brought the true regional cuisines of Mexico to NYC. Her son succeeds her in this stylish Downtown location.

Ecco
✉ 124 Chambers St (at Church St and W. Broadway) 📞 212-227 7074 🕐 L & D, Mon–Fri, D only Sat **$$$** [p340, B2]
Longtime Italian favorite way Downtown.

The Harrison
✉ 355 Greenwich St (at Harrison and North Moore sts) 📞 212-274 9310 🕐 D daily **$$$** [p340, B1]
The creative menu continues to impress hard-to-impress New Yorkers. Try lamb ragu with mint and ricotta, or cod poached in olive oil and served with white balsamic caramel. Dessert could be a black-and-white pear bread pudding, or an ode to peanut butter and jelly using peanut mousse and concord grapes.

LEFT: David Bouley, king of Tribeca cuisine.
RIGHT: long cocktails for a cool crowd.

Landmarc

179 W. Broadway (at Leonard and Worth sts)
212-343 3883 L & D Mon–Fri, B & D Sat–Sun $$ [p340, B1]
This chic bistro has become a restaurant "landmark" in NY's Gold Coast territory: it's got both style and unpretentious prices. Food is mostly Italian, but with French influences too. Reservations only taken for parties of six or more.

Locanda Verde

377 Greenwich St (at Franklin and North Moore sts) 212-941 8900 B, L, & D daily $$$ [p340, B1]
An Italian media darling, it's as good for breakfast as it is for lunch and dinner.

Lucky Strike

59 Grand St (at W. Broadway and Wooster St) 212-941 0479 L & D daily $$ [p340, B1]
Hip and seasoned bistro fare, always a good bet. Affordable and late-nite.

Megu

62 Thomas St (at W. Broadway) 212-964 7777 D daily $$$$ [p340, B2]
Extravagant Japanese. Megu's menu is overwhelming and maybe overpriced, but it's much talked about around town.

Nobu

105 Hudson St (at Franklin and N. Moore sts) 212-219 0500 L & D Mon–Fri, D only Sat–Sun $$$$ [p340, B1]
Tribeca celeb-spot, unique for its Japanese-Peruvian cuisine and near-impossibility of getting a booking. **Nobu Next Door** is a second-best, and does not accept reservations.

Odeon

145 W. Broadway (at Duane and Thomas sts)
212-233 0507 B Sat, Sun, L & D daily $$$ [p340, B2]
Great bar atmosphere, and a tasty French-American menu: a strongpoint of the Tribeca scene.

Raoul's

180 Prince St (at Sullivan and Thompson sts) 212-966 3518 D daily $$$ [p338, B3]
French bistro with 25 years of serving the international chic set.

Savoy

70 Prince St (at Crosby St) 212-219 8570 L & D Mon–Sat, D only Sun $$$ [p338, B4]
Stylish but comfy corner house serving creative food using only fresh farmers' market products.

Tribeca Grill

375 Greenwich St (at Franklin St) 212-941 3900 L & D Mon–Fri & Sun, D only Sat $$$ [p340, B1]
Co-owned by actor Robert De Niro and chef Drew Nieporent, the Grill is still packing them in almost 20 years later.

Bars and Cafés

Bar Artisanal, 268 W. Broadway at 6th Ave, is a cheese bar serving *pissaladières* and charcuterie trays.

Café Borgia II, 161 Prince St at Mercer St, is where espresso and an Italian pastry can really perk up a Soho shopping spree.

Cupping Room Café, 359 W. Broadway (between Broome and Grand sts), is a cozy place for brunch.

Emack & Bolio, W. Houston and W. Broadway. For high-end ice cream and frozen yoghurt in as many flavors as Crayola crayons, this place can't be beaten. Locations on the Upper East and West Sides, too.

Fanelli's, 94 Prince St at Mercer, is where trendy Soho grew up, around this down-to-earth corner hangout.

Le Pain Quotidien, at Grand and Mercer. One of many branches of a Belgian farmhouse-style café chain, with communal tables, newspapers, and excellent eggs, coffees, breads, and so on.

Puffy's Tavern, 81 Hudson St (at Harrison and Jay sts). Open 'til 4am, this is one of Tribeca's most laid-back bars.

Recommended Restaurants, Bars, & Cafés on page 259

LOWER MANHATTAN

Lower Manhattan is where New York began. Now it's an area of high finance and poignant memories, Wi-Fi parks and South Street Seaport. Plus Ellis Island, the Statue of Liberty, and the Staten Island ferry, of course

Below Chambers Street to the west and the Brooklyn Bridge to the east is the original New York, where the Dutch and the English first settled, the country's first hotel was built, the first president was sworn in, and the city's first theatrical opening night took place. Clipper ships bound for the California Gold Rush sailed from Lower Manhattan's piers in the 1850s, and by 1895 the first skyscraper stood 20 stories above lower Broadway.

Financial powerhouses

Over a century later, New York's financial powerhouses and city government areas are bracketed by out door recreations like the South Street Seaport and Battery Park. Some of the landmark office buildings on or near Wall Street have been converted to high-tech business use and residential apartments.

But Manhattan's oldest neighborhood also has some of its most moving history, being the site of two memorials to modern tragedies. Just as events in the 20th century shifted the area from a maritime economy to one of financial commerce, so, too, have events early in the 21st century changed the face of Lower

Manhattan once again. The changes have been absorbed with typical New York energy – adapting and reconstructing, facing the future, without missing a beat.

PLACES OF PILGRIMAGE

Between West Street and Trinity Place is **Ground Zero**, the site of the former World Trade Center. Rising an impressive 110 stories into the sky, the Twin Towers were the most prominent structures in a 16-acre (6.5-hectare), seven-building complex

Main attractions
TRIBUTE WTC VISITOR CENTER
MUSEUM OF JEWISH HERITAGE
BATTERY PARK
CASTLE CLINTON
NATIONAL MUSEUM OF
THE AMERICAN INDIAN
FRAUNCES TAVERN MUSEUM
WALL STREET
MUSEUM OF AMERICAN FINANCE
ST PAUL'S CHAPEL
CITY HALL
BROOKLYN BRIDGE
SOUTH STREET SEAPORT
ELLIS ISLAND
STATUE OF LIBERTY

LEFT: South Street Seaport.
RIGHT: the view from the Brooklyn Bridge.

New Yorkers died as the result of suicide terrorist attacks. Nearby St Paul's Chapel *(see page 252)* offered aid in the crisis, and acted as an unofficial spot where grief-stricken families could mourn their loss.

The grounds of the World Trade Center are now a construction site, as work continues on its redevelopment *(see page 38)* and the center-piece **Freedom Tower**, a 1,776ft (541-meter) skyscraper which is due to open around 2018. And at the southern end of the site, a tribute center now provides a space for all to share memories and to remember.

ABOVE: *An Icon of Hope,* in Battery Park, is a memorial to the victims of the World Trade Center atrocity.

that took 17 years to complete. It was a classic piece of 1970s architecture, and the view from the South Tower's 107th-floor Observation Deck was one of the best in the city.

On September 11, 2001, a day few will forget, and witnessed on TV screens around the globe, 2,603

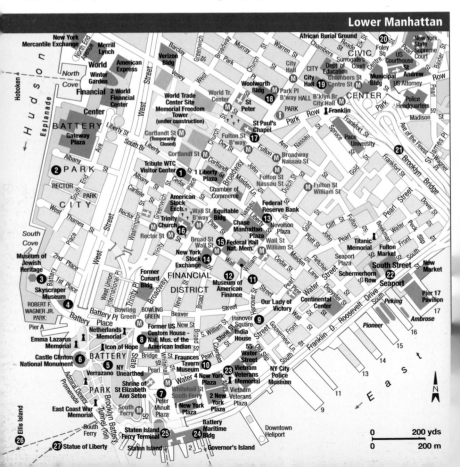

Lower Manhattan

Recommended Restaurants, Bars, & Cafés on page 259

Tribute WTC Visitor Center ❶

✉ 120 Liberty Street (between Greenwich and Church sts)
☎ 866-737 1184
🕒 Mon and Wed–Sat 10am–6pm, Tue noon–6pm, Sun noon–5pm
💲 charge 🚇 World Trade Center/ Rector St

Opened in late 2006, the WTC Tribute Visitor Center is a project of the September 11th Families' Association, a non-profit organization set up in the aftermath of the tragedy to allow those most affected to stay in touch. The purpose-built center is comprised of five themed galleries: a running documentary on life before the attack has testimonies from former employees and local residents describing life as part of the WTC community, while other galleries focus on the day's events as they unfold, and the subsequent rescue and clean-up operation.

Understandably, the center is very moving, and no matter how many documentaries are aired on television, little can prepare visitors for the stark reality of salvaged items, including a battered but instantly recognizable airplane window, or the variety of faces that peer out from the wall of "missing people" posters. A rolling list of names provides an intense reminder of the scale of the loss, while a collage of personal photos and mementoes ensures that we remember the victims' lives and not just their deaths.

LEFT: 9/11 mourners at St Paul's Chapel.
BELOW LEFT: fireman memorial at the Tribute WTC Visitor Center.
BELOW RIGHT: towers of light: a haunting tribute at Ground Zero.

People from the world of finance on the streets of the Financial District.

The **World Financial Center**, with its towers and elegant waterfront **Winter Garden**, was repaired after structural damage during the attacks, and high-profile occupants such as Dow Jones and the *Wall Street Journal* were soon able to move back in.

Art events

The World Financial Center has become a new focus in the area, with stores, restaurants, and regular arts events held in the Winter Garden. An annual event in June, the "Bang on a Can" marathon, is a 26-hour nonstop art event that begins at 8pm on Saturday and continues until 10pm on Sunday.

Ultimately, the center is a tribute not only to the lives lost, but to those coping with being left behind. A wall in the final gallery allows visitors to add their thoughts and wishes for the future.

Another, outdoor memorial lies in the leafy confines of Battery Park. Fritz Koenig's huge bronze sculpture *The Sphere* had stood for more than 30 years in the World Trade Center Plaza, and withstood the tons of metal and concrete crashing down on top of it. In 2002, the battered globe was moved to Battery Park and re-titled *An Icon of Hope*, at the foot of a bed of roses called Hope Garden. An eternal flame burns in memory, and it is a fine spot for contemplation.

Battery Park City ❷ is a huge, 92-acre (37-hectare) development stretching along the Hudson River, and is highly desirable residential property. A third of the area around Battery Park City is public space, and linked to Manhattan's riverfront expansion by scenic walkways that meander north to Tribeca and beyond. Running alongside the Hudson River is the pretty, green, and

BELOW: strolling along Battery Park Esplanade.

Recommended Restaurants, Bars, & Cafés on page 259

leafy **Battery Park Esplanade**, which stretches for more than a mile. It's a fine place to stroll and reflect (look out for the skateboarders). There are also benches that offer relaxing vantage points for enjoying the splendid views over the Hudson River and across to the Statue of Liberty.

Another memorial to the past lies on the southwestern tip of Manhattan Island.

The Museum of Jewish Heritage ❸

✉ 36 Battery Place (at 1st Place), www.mjhnyc.org ☎ 646-437 4200
🕒 Sun–Tue and Thur 10am–5.45pm, Wed 10am–8pm, Fri 10am–3pm
💲 charge 🚇 Bowling Green/Rector St

With more than 2,000 photographs, artifacts, and original documentaries, the museum provides an insight into the experiences of Jewish people through the Holocaust and into the present day. In 2003, the building was extended by a new wing with a digitally equipped performance center which runs a program of film, theater, music and the spoken word. Steven

Spielberg contributed video testimonies from Holocaust victims compiled while directing *Schindler's List*.

Beyond the museum, pathways wind through **Robert F. Wagner Jr Park**, which has attractive landscaped gardens, deck-topped brick pavilions, and places to sit with fine views of New York Harbor. Here are opportunities to meditate on the Jewish Museum's aim, which is to provide a thoughtful and moving chronicle of history, keeping the memory of the past alive and offering hope for the future.

TIP

Members of the Alliance for Downtown New York conduct free, 90-minute walking tours of the area every Thursday and Saturday at noon. Meet on the front steps of the National Museum of the American Indian; reservations are not required, so just turn up.

LEFT AND BELOW: the Museum of Jewish Heritage.

Tall Towers

New York has always aimed high, and with landmark new buildings, is still reaching for the sky

New York is a vertical city. The first skyscraper was Daniel Burnham's 1902 Flatiron Building, which is 285ft (87 meters) high. Mapping the shape of its knife-edge lot at Broadway and Fifth Avenue, the Flatiron gained instant élan from its height and classical styling, and romance from its look of sailing up Broadway.

Napoleon LeBrun styled the 700ft (210-meter) Metropolitan Life Insurance tower (Madison Avenue at E. 23rd Street) after St Mark's Campanile in Venice, while, 11 years after the Flatiron, architect Cass Gilbert set out to give the tallest-building title to retail tycoon F.W. Woolworth. The Woolworth Building soared for 792ft (241 meters), but nevertheless harked back to Gothic styles.

New York's iconic 20th-century skyline was wrought more by politics than art. As buildings rose up and up, planners feared that city streets were becoming lightless canyons. A 1916 zoning formula capped street-level facades by the width of the street, so towers

of unlimited height rose only over a quarter of a building plot. This led to the "setback" feature of architectural plots.

The boom and confidence of the 1920s led to the classic era, none finer than William Van Alen's Chrysler Building. The gleaming spire of the 1,046ft (319-meter) 1930 Art Deco masterpiece tops a pinnacle of stainless-steel automotive motifs and gargoyles. The 1,454ft (443-meter) Empire State Building (Shreve, Lamb, & Harmon) took the "world's tallest" title from the Chrysler in 1931. Raymond Hood's 1934 RCA Building in the Rockefeller Center is more muted Art Deco, softer than the monolithic skyscrapers.

Behind the glass curtain

The postwar International style arrived in Mies van der Rohe's 1958 Seagram Building (375 Park Avenue), graceful glass curtain walls rising from an open plaza. Many anonymous 1950s and '60s glass boxes showed the same style with less aplomb. Far above the crowd, the 1,368ft (417-meter) Twin Towers of the World Trade Center (1976) were a New York icon on a par with the Empire State – a status tragically confirmed by the towers' destruction on September 11, 2001.

Recent architectural efforts have again brought imaginative elements to the skyscraper. The triangular panels of the 2006 Hearst Tower, by English architect Norman Foster, are integral to the heat, light, and air management system of the city's first "green" tower, while Renzo Piano's new tower for the *New York Times* has sunscreen-walls of ceramic tubes. The Freedom Tower being built on the former World Trade Center site has been altered from Daniel Libeskind's original design to become more of a modern statement of the classic Empire State style. In all these awesome structures, New York is always building, always soaring.   ❑

LEFT: the HSBC Bank building on Lower Broadway.
ABOVE: Lower Manhattan cityscape.

Skyscraper Museum ❹

✉ 39 Battery Place (at West St), www.skyscraper.org ☎ 212-968 1961 ⒸWed–Sun noon–6pm Ⓢcharge ℝBowling Green

Visitors with an interest in modern architecture may enjoy this museum, which is on a mission to convert us to tall buildings in this, the most vertical of modern cities. Through exhibitions, programs, and publications, the small museum explores tall buildings as objects of design, products of technology, sites of construction, investments in real estate, and places of work and residence. The interior itself is a dazzling example of the form, with mirrored floor and ceiling offering a bewildering perspective.

EARLIEST NEW YORK

At the island's tip, **Battery Park ❺** is where New Amsterdam was first settled by Europeans, and New York's history began. Named for the battery of protective cannons that once stood here, this is famously where Manhattan begins, or ends – as the song goes, "...the Battery's down." The park, as well as having wonderful views and many memorials, now contains a lovely natural garden, the **Bosque**. It also includes a reddish-stone former fort built as a defense against the British in the war of 1812.

Castle Clinton ❻

✉ Battery Park, www.nps.gov/cacl ☎ 212-344 7220 Ⓒdaily 8.30am–5pm Ⓢfree ℝBowling Green/South Ferry

In 1824, as Castle Garden, this was the city's premier place of amusement, where Samuel Morse gave his first public telegraph demonstration and Swedish singer Jenny Lind made her American debut in a tumultuously acclaimed concert in 1850 (for which some wealthy New Yorkers paid a then-unheard-of $30 a ticket). Not long after, the area was joined to the mainland by landfill and served as the New York State Immigration Station, where more than 8 million immigrants were processed between 1855 and 1890.

For two years, potential settlers were processed on a barge moored in the Hudson, but when the new headquarters opened on Ellis Island in 1892, the tide of immigration shifted. Home to the New York Aquarium until 1941, Castle Clinton was made a national monument in 1950 and opened to the public in 1975.

EAT

For a choice of cafés and restaurants, head for cobblestoned Stone Street, said to have been the first paved street in New York City. This tiny alley, tucked away in the concrete canyons of Lower Manhattan, is situated off Hanover Square, between South William and Pearl streets.

LEFT: lunch among the skyscrapers in cobblestoned Stone Street. **BELOW:** Castle Clinton, built as a defensive fort, is the place to buy tickets for the Statue of Liberty and Ellis Island.

RIGHT: National Museum of the American Indian.
BELOW: Shrine of St Elizabeth Ann Seton.

New York Unearthed

Peter Minuit Plaza ❼, east of Battery Park, is named for the first governor (director general) of New Amsterdam. In a tiny park nearby, a plaque commemorates some of the city's lesser-known arrivals: 23 Sephardic Jews, dropped off by a French ship in 1654, who founded New Amsterdam's first Jewish congregation, Shearith Israel.

Turn left on State Street, once lined by wealthy merchants' houses, to come to the **Shrine of St Elizabeth Ann Seton** (7 State Street), in the only 1790s Federal-style mansion still standing here, now surrounded by giant glass towers. The chapel by the shrine is dedicated to the first American-born saint, who founded the Sisters of Charity in 1809 and was canonized in 1975 by Pope Paul VI.

Herman Melville, author of Moby Dick, was born in a house near 17 State Street, where today **New York Unearthed** (www.southstreet seaportmuseum.org, tel: 212-748 8600; Mon–Fri noon–5pm, at other times by appointment; free) offers a glimpse of what actually lies beneath the city streets. It's run from South Street Seaport *(see page 255)*, from where tours can be arranged. The site includes relics gleaned from ongoing digs in the Lower Manhattan area, and an archeological lab.

On the other side of State Street from Battery Park, the former **US Custom House** was designed by Cass Gilbert and built in 1907. A magnificent example of Beaux Arts architecture, with a facade embellished by ornate limestone sculptures

Recommended Restaurants, Bars, & Cafés on page 259

that represent four of the world's continents and "eight races" of mankind, this grand edifice also has striking Reginald Marsh murals on the rotunda ceiling inside.

And, in what could seem an ironic twist, this spot where Peter Minuit is believed to have given goods to the value of $24 to local Indians for the purchase of Manhattan Island is now a major museum to tribal culture.

National Museum of the American Indian ❽

✉ George Gustav Heye Center, 1 Bowling Green, www.nmai.si.edu
☎ 212-514 3700 ◷ Fri–Wed 10am–5pm, Thur 10am–8pm
⑤ free ⒭ Bowling Green

Operated by the Smithsonian Institution, the museum details the history and cultural legacy of America's native peoples through artifacts, costume, artworks, and online resources. The glass-cased exhibits seem dwarfed by the grand surroundings of the Custom House, but the museum is a worthy achievement nevertheless, and often presents music and dance performances in addition to its permanent displays.

Bowling Green and Hanover Square

From **Bowling Green Park**, New York's first public park, you can wander up Beaver Street to Broad Street, or take a quick detour back to State Street before following Pearl Street to **Hanover Square** ❾.

The square burned to ashes in the Great Fire of 1835, one of many fires that destroyed virtually all remnants of Dutch New Amsterdam. According to one eyewitness who was watching from Brooklyn, "the sparks from that fire came over the river so thick that the neighbors… were obliged to keep their roofs wet all night." The square recovered to become a thriving commercial center, and includes **India House** (1 Hanover Square), an 1850s Italianate brownstone that's been home to a private club (at lunchtime) for maritime movers and shakers since 1914. You don't have to be a member, however, to drop in for a drink

Costume from the National Museum of the American Indian.

BELOW: Bowling Green was New York's first public park.

Samuel Fraunces opened his tavern in 1763 as the Queen's Head, but because of mounting anti-British sentiment, changed the pub's name.

RIGHT: the Fraunces Tavern: George Washington ate here. Several times.
BELOW: dine with captains of industry at Delmonico's.

at the **Blue Bar at Bayard's** upstairs (Tue–Fri from 4.30pm).

Captains of industry have dined at **Delmonico's**, at the corner of Beaver and William streets, since the 1830s, when two Swiss brothers established the city's first formal French-style restaurant. Stop and admire the impressive marble columns at the entrance, reputedly shipped over from Pompeii, or venture inside for a drink and a bit of market eavesdropping at The Grill *(see page 259)*.

Fraunces Tavern Museum ⑩

✉ 54 Pearl Street (at Broad St), www.frauncestavernmuseum.org
☎ 212-425 1778 🅒 Tue–Sun 10am–5pm ⑤ charge
🚇 Whitehall St/Broad St

Farther south, at the corner of Pearl and Broad streets, is one of Old New York's oldest buildings. Built in 1719 for a French Huguenot merchant, the house was extended and made into a tavern by Samuel Fraunces in the 1760s. The New York Chamber of Commerce got its start over a few mugs of ale here, and George Washington gave an emotional farewell address to his officers in 1783 in the Long Room. The tavern was restored to its 18th-century appearance and opened again in 1907.

The wood-paneled tavern is still an atmospheric bar-restaurant, with dining rooms for private rental. On the two floors above is the intriguing **Fraunces Tavern Museum**, where exhibits include a lock of Washington's hair, the Long Room complete with period furniture, a fragment of one of Washington's teeth (not, contrary to legend, wooden), and a shoe that belonged to his wife, Martha. The cases housing the exhibits were built by Tiffany & Co. in 1907.

WALL STREET

Walk north on William Street (its twists and turns a reminder of when it was known as Horse and Cart Street) to **Wall Street** ⑪, traditional hub of the financial world, where the narrow stone canyons are lined by towering banks, brokerage houses, and law offices.

A worldwide symbol of wealth, power and deal-making, remembered for traumatic scenes during the 1929 stock market crash, the street took its name from the 17th-century wall – or, more accurately, a wooden blockade built by the Dutch as protection against the threat of

Recommended Restaurants, Bars, & Cafés on page 259

Indian and English attacks. The country's first stock exchange began just in front of **60 Wall Street** in 1792, when 24 brokers gathered beneath a buttonwood tree. The building at **55 Wall Street** is a massive columned landmark that dates to 1841 and served as the original Merchants' Exchange, and later as headquarters for the influential First National City Bank.

Financial history

A few buildings south at the corner of William Street is the former Bank of New York, founded by Alexander Hamilton in 1784 and the new home of the **Museum of American Finance** ⑫ (48 Wall Street, www.financialhistory.org, tel: 212-908 4110, Tue–Sat 10am–4pm; charge). Affiliated with the Smithsonian, the museum is dedicated to the trading and financial industries, with a collection of antique stocks and bonds, ticker tape from the 1929 crash, and memorabilia from the era of the robber barons, a group that included Messrs Carnegie, Frick, and Rockefeller.

Following William Street to Maiden Lane will lead to **Nevelson Plaza**, with seven tall abstract sculptures by the late Louise Nevelson, a long-time New York resident.

Money may not be art, but there's a lot of it at the **Federal Reserve Bank** ⑬ (33 Liberty Street, www.newyorkfed.org, tel: 212-720 5000), west of Nevelson Plaza. Constructed in 1924, as well as wheelbarrows-full of old and counterfeit cash this imposing edifice is said to house a quarter of the world's gold reserves. Tours are available, but security is tight and visits must be booked ahead *(see page 252)*.

Easy Street

Double back to Wall Street and the corner of Broad Street, where the **New York Stock Exchange** ⑭ was constructed in 1903, its building fronted by an impressive facade of Corinthian columns. Since 9/11, though, the Stock Exchange's Visitors' Gallery is no longer open for spectators to observe the speculators. The exchange has an annual trading volume of over $5 trillion.

The Greek temple-style **Federal Hall National Memorial** ⑮ (26 Wall Street, www.nps.gov/feha, tel: 212-825 6990; Mon–Fri 9am–5pm) is, however, open to the public. It's on the

Wall Street was named for the wooden barrier that was erected by the Dutch against the English in the mid-1600s.

BELOW: stars and stripes at the New York Stock Exchange.

TIP

The Federal Reserve Bank offers tours every Monday through Friday starting at 9.30am and continuing hourly until 2.30pm. For security reasons, you must book the tour in advance, and arrive 20 minutes before the tour begins. The vaults store more than one-quarter of the world's gold bullion.

RIGHT AND BELOW:
Trinity Church – a slice of Old New York.

site of the original Federal Hall, where on April 30, 1789, George Washington was sworn in as the first President of the United States (there's an impressive statue of him on the steps); it later became a branch of the US Treasury Department. Today it's run by the National Park Service and includes historical memorabilia, plus the suit that George Washington wore at his inauguration.

Trinity Church ⑯

✉ 89 Broadway (at Wall St), www.trinitywallstreet.org 📞 212-602 0800 🕒 Mon–Fri 7am–6pm, Sat 8am–4pm, Sun 7am–4pm
Ⓢ free Ⓡ Wall St/Rector St

At the very top of Wall Street where it meets Broadway, pretty Trinity Church is a serene survivor of early New York. First established in 1698, the present 1846 church is the third one built on the same site. **Trinity Church graveyard** contains some of the oldest graves in the city – including that of Alexander Hamilton, the US's first Secretary of the Treasury, who owned a house at 33 Wall Street and was killed in a duel with Aaron Burr. A small **museum** offers a look at the original charter, among other historic artifacts.

St Paul's Chapel ⑰

✉ 209 Broadway (between Fulton and Vesey sts), www.saintpaulschapel.org
📞 212-233 4164 🕒 Mon–Fri 10am–6pm, Sat 8am–3pm, Sun 7am–3pm
Ⓢ free Ⓡ Fulton St/Broadway

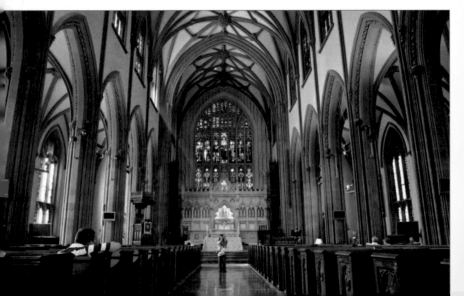

Recommended Restaurants, Bars, & Cafés on page 259

St Paul's Chapel, part of the Trinity Church Parish, is situated five blocks north on Broadway, between Fulton and Vesey streets. Built in 1766, this Georgian-style landmark is the only church left from the Colonial era, when luminaries like Prince William (later King William IV) and Lord Cornwallis worshipped here. George Washington's personal church pew is also preserved.

Although it is located just one block east of the World Trade Center, remarkably, the building was not damaged on September 11, 2001, and was used as a shelter for many of the volunteers and workers who helped in the aftermath. The chapel is now the site of a permanent 9/11 exhibit: *Unwavering Spirit: Hope and Healing at Ground Zero*, honoring the eight-month long volunteer effort of its parishoners during and after the tragedy *(see also page 242)*.

CITY HALL AREA

The handsome, gargoyle-topped **Woolworth Building ⓲** (233 Broadway) was known in its heyday as the "cathedral of commerce." Designed by architect Cass Gilbert, from 1913 until 1930, when the Chrysler Building was completed, its 60 stories and soaring height of almost 800ft (245 meters) made it the tallest building in the world. The Gothic Revival tower cost five-and-dime baron Frank W. Woolworth $13 million, and was officially opened by President Woodrow Wilson, who pushed a button in Washington that successfully lit up all of the floors.

Since 1910, New York has honored everyone from Teddy Roosevelt to Nelson Mandela (and, of course, the New York Yankees) with ticker-tape parades that conclude at handsome **City Hall ⓳**. At the junction of Broadway and Park Row, this French Renaissance/Federal-style edifice has been the seat of city government since DeWitt Clinton was mayor in 1812, and was co-designed by French architect Joseph-François

BELOW AND LEFT:
St Paul's Chapel and the *Unwavering Spirit* 9/11 memorial.

TIP

Stockbrokers and other wired types can be seen surfing the net in City Hall Park and seven other places, taking advantage of Lower Manhattan's free wireless internet hotspots. For a map, log on to www.downtownny.com/wifi.

Mangin, responsible for the Place de la Concorde in Paris.

Protests and politicking

City Hall Park, a triangular, tree-shaded former common in front of City Hall, has played an important role throughout the city's history: as the site of public executions, almshouses for the poor, and a British prison for captured Revolutionary soldiers. It's also where Alexander Hamilton led a protest against the tea tax in 1774, and where, two years later, George Washington and his troops heard the Declaration of Independence for the very first time.

Behind City Hall stands the former New York County Courthouse, dubbed on its completion in 1878 the **Tweed Courthouse**. This was after the revelation that "Boss" Tweed and his Tammany Hall cronies *(see page 31)* had pocketed some $9 million of the final $14 million construction costs.

After extensive refurbishment, the courthouse is now the home of the New York City Department of Education. Tours can be arranged by appointment (tel: 212-639 9675).

Past sumptuous **Surrogate's Court** (31 Chambers Street), with its eight Corinthian columns, **Foley Square** ⑳ is named for another Tammany Hall politician. It's also the site of worthy civic structures like the 1936 Cass Gilbert-designed **United States Courthouse** (1 Foley Square), and the **New York State Supreme Court** (60 Centre Street), built in 1913, where New Yorkers are summoned for jury duty.

RIGHT: City Hall.
BELOW: construction of the Brooklyn Bridge (1867–83) was marred by tragedy.

The Brooklyn Bridge

The Brooklyn Bridge was the inspiration of engineer John Augustus Roebling. The span of almost 1,600ft (488 meters), from City Hall across the East River to Brooklyn's Cadman Plaza, was the world's longest ever conceived. Steel-cable suspension gave unmatched stability and strength, as well as a striking image.

Construction began in 1867 and took 16 years to complete *(see photo on page 30)*. Building was marred by tragedy. Two years into the project, Roebling was killed by a ferryboat. His son, Washington Roebling, took over, but fell victim to the bends during riverbed excavation. An invalid the rest of his life, Roebling Jr monitored the works by telescope as his wife, Emily, supervised the project. When the bridge opened in 1883, 12 people were trampled to death in a panic, fearing a collapse. Despite its beginnings, the Brooklyn Bridge was dubbed the "new eighth wonder of the world," and has inspired artists ever since.

Recommended Restaurants, Bars, & Cafés on page 259

When workers were excavating the foundations of a new Federal courthouse building, the skeletons of African slaves were discovered. Now a city, state, and Federal landmark, the **African Burial Ground** is commemorated by a memorial at the corner of Duane and Elk streets.

The **Municipal Building** (1 Centre Street), slightly to the south, is an enormous, ornate 1914 McKim, Mead, & White confection. In the second-floor civil wedding chapel you can tie the knot in about five minutes (after the proper preliminaries, of course).

In the lobby of the Municipal Building, **City Store** (www.nyc.gov/citystore; Mon–Fri 9am–6pm) is a place for unusual gifts (manhole cover mat or genuine New York taxi medallion, anyone?) and can provide a wealth of information on the city.

BRIDGE AND HARBOR

For one of the best of all views of the **East River** and Lower Manhattan, walk down Frankfort Street or along Park Row. Both lead to the pedestrian walkway that leads onto the **Brooklyn Bridge ㉑**, one of the world's first suspension bridges *(see box on left)*. As the pointed arches of the bridge's great Gothic towers come into view, recognition is immediate, for this is another icon of New York that has etched itself into the world's visual vocabulary.

Alternatively, walk toward the East River along **Fulton Street**, to the place from where (until the Brooklyn Bridge was built) ferries carried New Yorkers to Brooklyn, from the Fulton Street pier. In the 1800s, this part of town was the center of New York's maritime commerce, where spices from China, rum from the West Indies, and whale oil from the Atlantic were bought and sold, where ships were built, and where sailors thronged to enjoy a seedy red-light district. All

that ended after the Civil War, when the old East River port fell into a decline, and big ships no longer sailed here.

South Street Seaport ㉒

✉ Fulton Street (at South St), www.southstreetseaport.com 📞 212-732 7678 🕐 Mon–Sat 10am–9pm, Sun 11am–8pm 💲 charge 🚇 Fulton St/Broadway-Nassau

South Street Seaport bills itself as a 12-block "museum without walls." Near the **Titanic Memorial Lighthouse**, at the corner of Fulton and Water streets, **Schermerhorn Row** is

TIP

There are dozens of stops on the free, seven-days-a-week Downtown Connection bus service in Lower Manhattan. Buses run from near South Street Seaport to Battery Park City, via Battery Park, from 10am to 7.30pm, roughly at 10-minute intervals (www.downtownny.com).

BELOW: the Brooklyn Bridge: the "new eighth wonder of the world."

South Street Seaport has historic vessels on Pier 16, and lots of other attractions that kids will enjoy. Don't miss the retail opportunities on Pier 17.

lined by the last surviving Federal-style commercial buildings in the city, part of a block of early 19th-century warehouses.

Cannon's Walk is another block of restored buildings, between Fulton and Beekman streets. Around the corner on Water Street, the **Herman Melville Gallery** and **Whitman Gallery** are on either side of **Bowne and Co.** (211 Water Street), a 19th-century printing shop.

Pier 17 is a three-story pavilion that juts over the East River at the end of Fulton Street. In addition to the third-floor food court's ethnic delicacies, there are dozens of stores.

In summertime, on the north side of Pier 17, is Water Taxi Beach, one of the city's newly developed man-made beaches. From May through October, it's a family-friendly environment during the day with food stands and plenty of sand (trucked in from New Jersey) on which to sun. At night, DJs spin tunes for an adult-only crowd. Check the website (www.watertaxibeach.com) for opening and closing dates as they change each season.

In summer, catch free evening concerts on Pier 16. The adjacent booth sells tickets for one-hour **Downtown Liberty Harbor Cruises**, operated by Circle Line (tel: 866-782 8834).

The sloop *Pioneer*, the *Peking*, a four-masted sailing barque, and the *Ambrose*, last of the city's lightships, are just a small part of the Seaport Museum's impressive collection of **historic vessels**, graceful ships that occasionally cast off to conduct elegant cruises around Manhattan.

RIGHT: "Give me your tired, your poor..."
BELOW: fun in the sun on Water Taxi Beach.

Recommended Restaurants, Bars, & Cafés on page 259

Back toward Battery Park

The last few sites extend around the tip of the island, offering wonderful views along the way. South of South Street Seaport – past Pier 11, and just beyond **Old Slip**, a landfilled inlet where 18th-century ships berthed to unload their cargo – is a park where stranded sailors used to congregate. Today, at the foot of a brick amphitheater near the corner of Coenties Slip and Water Street, is a monument to other young men.

A 14ft (4-meter) monument erected by the city in 1985, the **Vietnam Veterans Memorial** ㉓ is made of green glass etched with excerpts of letters written to and from soldiers in Vietnam. It is movingly illuminated at night. Nearby is the **New York City Police Museum** (100 Old Slip, www.nyc policemuseum.org, tel: 212-480 3100), with exhibits on the many aspects of policing New York.

A few blocks away, the rusting **Battery Maritime Building** ㉔ (11 South Street), a steel landmark Beaux Arts structure built in Whitehall Street in 1909, is the boarding point for ferries to **Governor's Island**

each spring and summer. The island is also the site of corporate parties and special events that the public can join.

On the next pier down from the Maritime Building is the refurbished **Staten Island Ferry Terminal** ㉕ (1 Whitehall Street, www.nyc.gov for schedule). The 25-minute cruise to Staten Island not only offers close-up views of the Statue of Liberty but is also free, making it the best bargain in town. There are rumors the ferry will be forced to charge in future because of its huge costs. In the meantime, however, the shiny new terminal and

ABOVE: the ever-ready Staten Island ferry.
BELOW: South Street Seaport calls itself "a museum without walls."

Map on page 242

TIP

Romantics should look at Shearwater Sailing, www.shearwater sailing.com, tel: 212-619 0885, which offers a variety of trips on a 1929 double-masted schooner, including harbor cruises that sail close to the Statue of Liberty and Ellis Island. There's a bar on board, or you can book for the excellent brunch cruise.

BELOW: taking in the view of Manhattan from the Staten Island ferry.

a new fleet of ferries make this a trip you really should make.

Another essential cruise departs a little farther around the waterfront. **Ferries** leave for Ellis Island and the Statue of Liberty a few steps from the East Coast War Memorial in Battery Park. Tickets and schedule information are available from **Statue Cruises** (http://statuecruises.com, tel: 877-523 9849), or at Castle Clinton.

Ellis Island 26

✉ Ellis Island, www.ellisisland.org
☎ 212-561 4588 ⏰ Ferries daily approx. 9.30am–5pm 💲 free, charge for ferry 🚇 South Ferry/Whitehall St

Ellis Island *(see also photo feature on pages 260–1)* was known as the "Island of Tears" because of the medical, mental, and literacy tests applicants had to undergo in the 32 years that it served as gateway to the United States. Today, it is a national monument and one of the city's most popular tourist destinations. Outside the museum, a promenade offers wonderful views of the Statue of Liberty and the Manhattan skyline.

Statue of Liberty 27

✉ Liberty Island, www.nps.gov/stli
☎ 212-363 3200 ⏰ Ferries daily approx. 9.30am–5pm 💲 free, charge for ferry 🚇 South Ferry/Whitehall St

The Statue of Liberty *(see also photo feature on pages 262–3)* was completed in France in July 1884, and arrived in New York Harbor in June of 1885 on board the French frigate *Isère*. In transit, Lady Liberty and her crown, torch, tablet, and other accessories were reduced to 350 pieces and packed in 214 crates, but it took only four months to reassemble the statue in its entirety. On October 28, 1886, the dedication took place in front of thousands of spectators. ❑

BEST RESTAURANTS, BARS, AND CAFÉS

Restaurants

Prices for a three-course dinner per person with half a bottle of wine:
$ = under $20
$$ = $20–$45
$$$ = $45–$60
$$$$ = over $60

Au Mandarin
✉ World Financial Center, 200-50 Vesey St
☎ 212-385 0311 🕐 L & D daily **$$** [p340, A2]
Upscale Chinese, one of many reasonable restaurants in the WFC.

Battery Gardens
✉ Battery Park (opposite 17 State St) ☎ 212-809 5508
🕐 L & D Mon–Sat, L only Sun **$$$** [p340, A4]
Multileveled dining rooms facing the Statue of Liberty. Touristy, but still worth stopping by.

Bennie's
✉ 88 Fulton St (at Gold St)
☎ 212-587 8930 🕐 L & D daily **$** [p340, B3]
It's nothing to look at, but this Downtown Thai café is the best-tasting bargain in the South St Seaport neighborhood.

Bon Chon Chicken
✉ 98 Chambers St (at Church St and Broadway)
☎ 212-227 2375 🕐 L & D daily **$** [p340, B2]
Come here for Korean-style spicy fried chicken wings, which have plenty of heat but no sauce, not for the atmosphere.

Bridge Café
✉ 279 Water St (at Dover St)
☎ 212-227 3344 🕐 L & D daily **$$$** [p340, B3]
Located "under" the Brooklyn Bridge, this hideaway has been here since the 1790s.

Carl's Steaks
✉ 79 Chambers St (at Church St and Broadway)
☎ 212-566 2828 🕐 L & D daily **$** [p340, B2]
This Philadelphia-style cheesesteak sandwich shop may not compete with Pat's in Philly, but for Downtown New York it will do just fine.

Delmonico's
✉ 56 Beaver St (at William St) ☎ 212-509 1144 🕐 L & D Mon–Fri **$$$$** [p340, B3]
The place for power lunches; a club-like steakhouse that closes at weekends.

Fraunces Tavern
✉ 54 Pearl St (at Broad St)
☎ 212-968 1776 🕐 L & D Mon–Sat **$$$** [p340, A4]
Historic, welcoming dining rooms and a good museum too. Great for lunch or a drink.

Gigino at Wagner Park
✉ 20 Battery Place (at West St) ☎ 212-528 2228 🕐 L & D daily **$$** [p340, A4]
Gorgeous sunsets with a view of Lady Liberty at this moderately priced Italian spot – the terrace is ideal in summer.

Harbour Lights
✉ South St Seaport, Pier 17, 3rd Flr (at Fulton and South sts) ☎ 212-227 2800 🕐 L & D daily **$$$** [p340, B3]
Spectacular view of the East River and the Brooklyn Bridge while enjoying pleasing seafood.

Harry's Café
✉ 1 Hanover Sq (at Pearl and Stone sts) ☎ 212-785 9200 🕐 L & D Mon–Sat **$$** [p340, B3]
Folks refused to accept that the original Harry's closed, so the owners reopened it, offering great steaks and seafood.

Ise
✉ 56 Pine St (at William and Pearl sts) ☎ 212-785 1600
🕐 L & D daily **$$** [p340, B3]
Follow the Japanese expats for authentic gyoza, yakitori, and katsu.

Lili's Noodle Shop & Grill
✉ 102 North End Ave (at Vesey St) ☎ 212-786 1300
🕐 L & D daily **$** [p340, A2]
A huge menu and quick service make this yum on the run.

Steamer's Landing
✉ 1 Esplanade Plaza (at Albany St) ☎ 212-432 1451 🕐 L & D daily **$$** [p340, A2]
Eat facing the Hudson, as cruise ships set sail.

Bars and Cafés

The Bar, 2 West St, is in the lobby of the Ritz-Carlton Battery Park – expensive, but the comfy setting is worth it.

Paris Café, 119 South St (at Peck Slip). A long-time seaport hangout with a great wood bar.

SouthWest NY, at 225 Liberty St, has good terrace food in warm weather, and is great all the year round for cocktails.

St Maggie's Café, 120 Wall St (between Front and South sts), has a fine Victorian feeling and serves food too.

Stone Street Tavern, 52 Stone St (at Coenties Alley). Cozy café with an outdoor terrace in this cobblestoned alleyway of eateries.

Ulysses, 95 Pearl St (off Hanover Square). A gathering spot for young Wall Street tycoons.

ELLIS ISLAND

More than 100 million Americans trace the history of their families' US citizenship back to the Grand Hall of Ellis Island

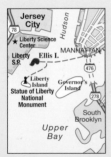

Visitors arrive by boat in front of the Ellis Island Immigration Center's main building, exactly as thousands of hopeful migrants did during the center's operation from 1892 to 1954. The grand red-brick exterior and the high, vaulted ceiling of the Great Hall were meticulously restored and reopened in 1990, after nearly four decades of decay since the facility's closure. The daunting reconstruction effort was driven mainly by public subscription, to which more than 20 million Americans donated. In addition to historic exhibits, Ellis Island houses an archive of records of the millions of immigrants who were processed through its halls.

ABOVE: an Italian family arrives at Ellis Island, *c*.1900.

The Essentials

✉ *www.nps.gov/elis*
📞 212-363 3200
🕐 *daily 9.30am–5.15pm, seasonal variations*
💲 *free, but fee for ferry*
🚢 *Circle Line-Statue of Liberty ferry from the pier at Battery Park*

TOP: the Ellis Island Immigration Museum is operated by the National Park Service. The immigration archive, compiled from passenger manifests of ships docking at the island during its operation, is also available online at www.ellisisland.org.

ABOVE: reliving history: on January 1, 1892, the first immigrant processed at Ellis Island was Annie Moore. Annie arrived from Ireland on the SS *Nevada*, on her 15th birthday.

A NEW LIFE IN THE NEW WORLD

The promise of a new life called to more than 22 million people from all over the world. Among these were Irving Berlin, Bob Hope, and the singing von Trapp family, all of whom entered the United States via the immigration center on Ellis Island. Applicants were taken through a selection process intended to sift out the physically and mentally infirm and the criminal, who were returned to the ships on which they came. These unfortunates gave the island its nickname: The Island of Tears.

ABOVE RIGHT: in the early 1900s, more than 2,000 people arrived at Ellis Island every day.

RIGHT: young visitors to the island are catered for with a self-guided tour and a Junior Ranger program, run by the National Park Service.

ABOVE: the restoration of Ellis Island, backed by public generosity, was inspired by the energetic work of Lee Iacocca, the chairman of the Chrysler corporation.

RIGHT: the tiling of the Great Hall is a legacy of Rafael Guastavino (1842–1908), himself an immigrant from Catalonia in northern Spain. Already a successful builder when he came to the US, his specialty was Catalan vaulting. His work can also be seen over the Oyster Bar at Grand Central Terminal (see page 92).

THE STATUE OF LIBERTY

A potent icon in the United States for more than 120 years, the Statue of Liberty is still the most evocative sight in New York City

Like millions of other immigrants, Italian-born writer Edward Corsi's first glimpse of America was the heroic figure of Lady Liberty, her hand thrust skyward with a torch to light the way. He wrote: "Looming shadowy through the mist, it brought silence to the decks of the *Florida*. This symbol of America – this enormous expression of what we had all been taught was the inner meaning of this new country – inspired awe in the hopeful immigrants."

Partly because of the statue's significance as a symbol of freedom and democracy, security measures have been implemented since 9/11. Visitors are screened before boarding the ferry, and backpacks and large bags are not permitted. You can climb as far as the top of the pedestal, where a glass ceiling allows a view upwards. To go to the recently reopened "crown" level, you'll need to buy special tickets in advance.

The Essentials

✉ *www.nps.gov/stli*
📞 *tel: 212-363 3200*
🕐 *daily 9.30am–5pm; seasonal variations. Time-pass reservations required; pick up with ferry ticket, first-come first-served.*
💲 *free, but fee for ferry*
🚢 *Statue Cruises*

ABOVE: the tablet that Liberty holds in her left hand reads (in Roman numerals) "July 4, 1776," the date of America's independence from Britain.

RIGHT: there are 25 windows in Liberty's crown which symbolize gemstones found on earth. The seven rays of the crown represent the seven seas and continents of the world.

A GIFT FROM FRANCE

The Statue of Liberty was a gift from the people of France to the United States to symbolize the spirit of successful revolutions in both of their countries.

In 1865, Edouard-René Lefèvre de Laboulaye, an intellectual, politician, and admirer of America, suggested to a young sculptor named Auguste Bartholdi that he make a large monument in honor of French and American brotherhood. By 1874, enough money had been raised by the French – through lotteries, subscriptions, and entertainment – to construct the statue. Funding for the pedestal was slower to materialize in the United States, however, and it took a concerted campaign from Joseph Pulitzer through his newspaper, *The World*, to raise the necessary finance.

Gustave Eiffel, who later built the Eiffel Tower, designed the ingenious framework that supports the thin copper skin. In 1885 Bartholdi's statue, called *Liberty Enlightening the World*, was shipped to the US, and was formally dedicated in a ceremony on October 28, 1886.

ABOVE: the statue is situated on 12-acre (5-hectare) Liberty Island, which is owned by the Federal government. The observation platform in the pedestal allows great views of New York and the harbor.

Recommended Restaurants, Bars, & Cafés on page 291

THE OUTER BOROUGHS

Today's pioneers in art and real estate
are beating a path to the Outer Boroughs,
attracted by green fields, watery vistas, excellent
museums, and 18th- and 19th-century enclaves

Staten Island, Queens, Brooklyn, the Bronx: these are places some visitors to Manhattan simply don't go to, except maybe to see the zoo or a ballgame, or to take the ferry.

They're missing out. The Outer Boroughs offer parks, cafés and gourmet restaurants, museums, and history. Cool bars buzz around Williamsburg in Brooklyn; woodlands and the Verrazano-Narrows Bridge beckon on Staten Island; New York's oldest – and thriving – movie studios are in Queens; and the home of Edgar Allen Poe engages the mind in the Bronx. There are architectural sites of Old New York. As well as the zoo and Yankee Stadium, of course.

Being so overlooked, these attractions – all less than an hour from Broadway, and accessible by public transportation – have the added plus of being (with few exceptions) uncluttered by other out-of-towners.

Neighborhoods
The key word in the Outer Boroughs is "neighborhood." Neighborhoods change, overlap, and can be a bazaar of ethnic delight. Stroll through Middle Eastern stores selling frankincense and myrrh, order pasta in Italian, and have *kasha* served in Yiddish.

Some new neighbors are artists and young professionals in search of affordable rents. As the prices of Manhattan soar, a new generation has turned to former industrial zones, like Long Island City in Queens and Williamsburg in Brooklyn, to live. Coops flourish where warehouses once thrived. Burned-out buildings become galleries or restaurants. Then real-

Main attractions
DUMBO
BROOKLYN ACADEMY OF MUSIC
BROOKLYN MUSEUM OF ART
PROSPECT PARK
RED HOOK AND WILLIAMSBURG
CONEY ISLAND
FLUSHING MEADOWS CORONA PARK
MUSEUM OF THE MOVING IMAGE
LONG ISLAND CITY
STATEN ISLAND
HISTORIC RICHMOND TOWN
BRONX ZOO
EDGAR ALLAN POE COTTAGE
CITY ISLAND
YANKEE STADIUM

PRECEDING PAGES: Hasidic Jewish families in Williamsburg.
LEFT: New York City Marathon starts on Staten Island's Verrazano-Narrows Bridge.
RIGHT: the Enid A. Haupt Conservatory in the Bronx's New York Botanical Garden.

ABOVE:
cruise to Brooklyn
from Lower Manhattan
by water taxi.

the late 19th century. Architects like Frederick Law Olmsted and Calvert Vaux found open space here unavailable in Midtown. With sweeping gestures, they decked the boroughs with buildings inspired by the domes and gables of Parisian boulevards.

Despite this grandeur, however, one thing "the boroughs" lack is Manhattan's easy grid system. Off the parkways, they are a maze of streets and expressways. With a little attention, though, it's easy to uncover neighborhoods that can be explored at a comfortable pace on foot – places where the boroughs really breathe.

estate values skyrocket, and the artists turn their sights elsewhere.

Amid the new is the older side of the boroughs: the avenues, parks, and palazzi built as grand civic projects in

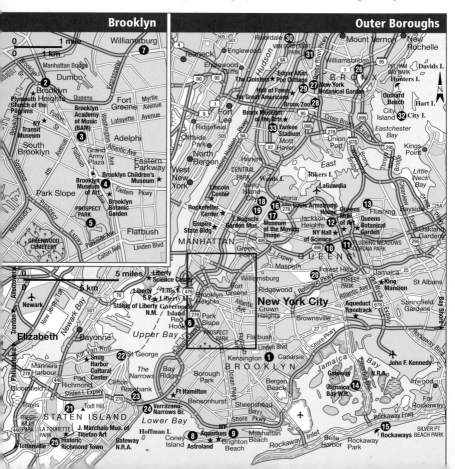

Manhattan will take you out to Williamsburg or Prospect Park.

Another scenic way to escape from Manhattan is via the **Brooklyn Bridge**. A stroll across the walkway leads to **Fulton Ferry Landing**, where cobblestone streets are coming back to life after lying dormant for decades. It was here that the borough inaugurated its first mass transit, to Wall Street. In 1814 Robert Fulton's steam ferry, the *Nassau*, replaced the East River's earlier rowboats, sailboats, and vessels powered by horses on treadmills. Ferries remained the main way to cross until the Brooklyn Bridge opened in 1883.

BROOKLYN ❶

The over 70 sq miles (180 sq km) at the southeast tip of Long Island encompass the second-most populous borough of New York City, Brooklyn. More than 2.4 million people live here, which would make it the fourth-largest metropolis in the United States if it weren't a part of New York City. Just a 20-minute ride on the subway from the heart of

DUMBO

Brooklyn's modern-day renaissance began in now-classic New York style – following the trail of artists. When Soho got too expensive, they moved over the water to lofts in DUMBO (for Down Under the Manhattan Bridge Overpass), now a thriving neighborhood that includes the innovative cultural hub **St Ann's Warehouse** (38 Water Street, www.stannswarehouse.org, tel: 718-254 8779).

TIP

Over the next few years, Brooklyn's East River waterfront is set to undergo the same upscale transition as has the Hudson River in Manhattan. Oh-so-cool Red Hook is hard to reach by subway or bus, but it's easy by water taxi. Go to www.nywatertaxi.com.

LEFT: ice cream on sale by Brooklyn Bridge.
BELOW LEFT: DUMBO.
BELOW RIGHT: DUMBO flea market.

The neighborhood of DUMBO stands for Down Under (the) Manhattan Bridge Overpass.

Young families followed – so many that nearby **Brooklyn Bridge Park**, now completing its first phase of regeneration, incorporated into its designs a children's playground, open grass fields, and a rock beach on the East River. When DUMBO became too expensive, the artists moved to Williamsburg, and now that they are priced out of Williamsburg, they are colonizing Red Hook.

Wherever artists went, they left behind a series of neighborhood revivals when they moved on. For instance, you can listen to chamber music, jazz, and avant-garde music at **Bargemusic** (Fulton Ferry Landing, Brooklyn, www.bargemusic.org, tel: 718-624 4061), a converted old coffee barge that's moored at the end of Old Fulton Street.

It's on the other side of the Fulton Ferry Landing from the **River Café** *(see page 291)*, considered one of the city's most romantic restaurants. Around the bend to the east is the old **Brooklyn Navy Yard** (now an industrial park, not open to visitors), where ships like the USS *Missouri* were built during World War II.

RIGHT: Brooklyn street scene.
BELOW: elegant Brooklyn Heights.

Brooklyn Heights ②

Directly inland from the Fulton Ferry, the property has always been hot. In **Brooklyn Heights**, where streets are lined with narrow row houses, brownstones change hands for sums in the million dollars.

Along the river edge of the Heights is the **Brooklyn Heights Promenade**, a walkway that overlooks the East River and the Brooklyn Bridge, and offers a movie-star view of the Manhattan skyline. A stroll along here and through the Heights can be extremely pleasant. Each block is iced with wrought-iron flourishes, stained-glass windows, stone busts, and fancy trims. On the corner of **Willow Street** and **Middagh** is the oldest wooden house in the district, dating to 1824.

Before the Civil War, **Plymouth Church of the Pilgrims** (tel: 718-624 4743; tours available by appointment), on **Orange Street** between Henry and Hicks, served as a stop on the Underground Railroad, while Henry Ward Beecher (Harriet Beecher Stowe's brother) preached abolitionism to the congregation.

Many streets in the Heights, like Middagh and Hicks, take their names from the neighborhood's early gentry. Five, however, are

Recommended Restaurants, Bars, & Cafés on page 291

Trinity church. Dating to the 1840s, it has the oldest stained-glass windows made in the US.

On the southern slope of Brooklyn Heights is the **Civic Center**, with its Greek Revival **Borough Hall** (209 Joralemon Street, tel: 718-802 3846; free tours Tue). From here, it's a short walk down Boerum Place to the fun **New York Transit Museum** (Boerum Place and Schermerhorn Street, www.mta.info/mta/museum, tel: 718-694 1600; closed Mon; charge). In a classic 1930s-era subway station, the museum has exhibits on the city's transportation systems, along with vintage subway cars and buses.

Keep walking south past State Street and turn right on **Atlantic Avenue**. Between Court and Henry streets, stores bulge with imported spices, dried fruits, olives, and halvah. Some bakeries cook their filo pastries in coal-burning ovens. This Middle Eastern bazaar shares the sidewalk with a number of antiques shops. These have plenty of interesting stock (Victorian, Art Deco, 1930s, 1940s), and are usually open on weekends, if not every day.

Brooklyn has its own microbrewery.

named after flora – **Pineapple, Cranberry, Orange, Poplar,** and **Willow** streets.

The **Brooklyn Historical Society** (128 Pierrepont Street, www.brooklynhistory.org, tel: 718-222 4111; closed Mon and Tue; charge) is in a landmark building. Browse and enjoy its rich mix of "Old Ebbett's Field" baseball memorabilia, maritime artifacts, and Coney Island exhibitionism. A block away is **St Ann and the Holy**

LEFT: out for a jog on Henry Street.
BELOW: the Brooklyn Heights Promenade provides movie-star views of Manhattan.

TIP

The free, hour-long Heart of Brooklyn trolley tour (www.heartof brooklyn.org; Sat, Sun and hols noon–6pm) leaves from Wollman Rink in Prospect Park on the hour and makes stops throughout the park, as well as calling at the Brooklyn Museum, the Botanic Garden, and Grand Army Plaza.

RIGHT AND BELOW:
One Hanson Place houses the Brooklyn Flea Market.

Fort Greene

On the other side of Brooklyn's not terribly attractive downtown is another cache of worthwhile sights. From Brooklyn Heights, walk east on Atlantic Avenue, and turn left on Flatbush Avenue.

At Flatbush and Hanson Place, one block down, you'll find the **Brooklyn Flea Market** housed in One Hanson Place, a former bank. The schedule and location of the market change frequently, so check the website (www.brooklynflea.com) before setting out.

Just a few blocks down, you'll find **Junior's**, home to Brooklyn's original claim to cheesecake fame, and BAM, the Brooklyn Academy of Music.

Brooklyn Academy of Music (BAM) ❸

✉ Peter Jay Sharp Building, 30 Lafayette Ave, www.bam.org 📞 718-636 4100 🕐 Mon–Fri 10am–6pm, Sat noon–6pm 💲 charge 🚇 Atlantic Ave, Nevins St, Fulton St

At the corner of Lafayette Avenue and Ashland Place is this innovative school and performance space for music and the performing arts. Its spectrum has included multimedia maestro Laurie Anderson, Martha Clarke's performance art, and the music of minimalist composer Philip Glass. Home to the experimental Next Wave Festival since 1982, it includes the beautifully restored **BAM Harvey Lichtenstein Theater** (formerly known as the Majestic Theater), the lively **BAM Café**, and four screening rooms, known as the **BAM Rose Cinemas**. Just around

Recommended Restaurants, Bars, & Cafés on page 291

the corner is a massive new shopping mall, **Atlantic Terminal**.

Prospect Heights and Park Slope

Follow Flatbush Avenue in the other direction from Fort Greene, and you'll make your way on the road that separates **Park Slope**, to your right, and **Prospect Heights**, to your left. Here you'll find, at Grand Army Plaza, the entrance to Brooklyn's foremost green lung, Prospect Park. The neighborhood of Park Slope runs along Prospect Park's western border, and is filled with Victorian row houses, many of which have been divided up into apartments. It has become a popular neighborhood for Manhattan defectors and young

families. Seventh Avenue, wall-to-wall with stores and restaurants, is two blocks west of the park.

Make a left from Grand Army Plaza onto Eastern Parkway, and you'll see a number of cultural attractions lining the boulevard.

Brooklyn Museum of Art ❹

✉ 200 Eastern Parkway, www.brooklynmuseum.org ☎ 718-638 5000 ⊙ Wed–Fri 10am–5pm, Sat–Sun 11am–6pm ⑤ charge 🚇 Eastern Parkway/Brooklyn Museum

This marvelous museum – the second-largest in New York after the Metropolitan – has an Egyptian collection considered by many the best outside of Cairo and London.

Wonderfully eclectic, the Brooklyn museum displays an array of world-class exhibits, including 28 period rooms and an unusual outdoor sculpture garden of New York building ornaments. There are many other highlights in addition to its celebrated Egyptian relics. A global museum, it has lovely artifacts from Polynesia, Africa and

BAM is one of NYC's dynamic performing arts centers.

LEFT: Grand Army Plaza and the Soldiers' and Sailors' Memorial Arch.
BELOW: BAM now features dance, film, and theater, in addition to music.

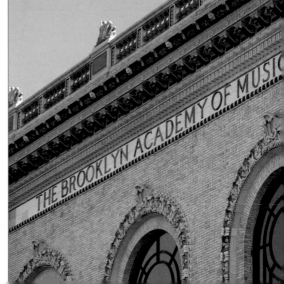

Southeast Asia, Japanese ceramics and an *Art in the Americas* section with highlights from ancient Peruvian textiles to modern bowls from New Mexico's Pueblos.

American art
The kaleidoscope of American art continues with Colonial decorative art, including a reconstructed 1675 Dutch interior from Brooklyn itself, and a comprehensive display of 18th- and 19th-century American paintings with contemporary masterpieces by artists such as Georgia O'Keeffe. Lastly, there's an impressive stock of European – especially French and 19th-century – art, including sculptures by Rodin and major paintings by Degas, Cézanne, Monet, and Matisse, and a photography collection that is excellent.

Grand Army Plaza
Beside the museum is the **Brooklyn Botanic Garden** (1000 Washington Avenue, www.bbg.org, tel: 718-623 7200; closed Mon; charge), covering 52 acres (21 hectares). The Japanese gardens alone are worth a visit, especially when the cherry trees bloom in spring, but it's pleasant in any month.

The huge traffic circle at the western end of the Parkway is **Grand Army Plaza**, where the **Soldiers' and Sailors' Memorial Arch** – a Civil War memorial designed by John H. Duncan, architect of Grant's Tomb, with sculptures by Frederick MacMonnies – provides a formal entrance to the

Recommended Restaurants, Bars, & Cafés on page 291

585 acres (237 hectares) that make up **Prospect Park** ❺. The park, plaza, and boulevards were all designed by Frederick Law Olmsted and Calvert Vaux, and are considered to be their best work, even better perhaps than Central Park.

Prospect Park

Grand Army Plaza is their most literal tribute to Paris – an Arc de Triomphe at the focal point of the borough. Roam dreamily through the romantic park: the **Long Meadow**, the **Ravine** and **Nethermead**. For details, check www.prospect-park.org, tel: 718-965 8951. At the **Children's Corner** (near Prospect Park Subway), as well as an antique carrousel, there is the **Lefferts Historic House** (Apr–Nov Thur–Sun, Dec–Mar Sat–Sun; free), a two-story Dutch farmhouse built in 1777–83. Interactive exhibits portray African and Native American life in 19th-century Flatbush.

Red Hook

Hop in a cab, or take a ferry from the Fulton Ferry Landing to **Red Hook** ❻, one of the latest communities to break out of the old industrial mold, with art studios and performance spaces, as well as cute little restaurants and boutiques. Creative businesses as well as high-end store complexes are putting down roots among the restaurants and galleries, although the advent of

Barnum's Circus (later the Barnum & Bailey Circus) opened in Brooklyn in 1871. "The Greatest Show on Earth" was an instant success. By taking the circus on tour (in 65 railcars), the show was playing to 20,000 people a day by 1874.

ABOVE: Gilbert Stuart's *George Washington.* **BELOW:** John Singer Sargent's 1889 painting *An Out-of-Doors Study.*

Colorful graffiti in Williamsburg, one of Brooklyn's most happening spots.

RIGHT: boy on a bike in Crown Heights.
BELOW: shopping on Bedford Avenue.

a large IKEA store and a cruise ship terminal have been greeted with mixed feelings by residents. On the one hand is the growth in local employment; on the other are worries about the increase in popularity and traffic.

Williamsburg

To the left instead of right from the Brooklyn and Manhattan bridges, up the East River, there's another connection to Manhattan, the **Williamsburg Bridge**, which is, naturally, also the entryway to **Williamsburg** . At the foot of the bridge is the **Peter Luger Steakhouse** *(see page 291)*. Across Broadway, the lovely, Renaissance-style **Williamsburg Savings Bank** building was constructed in 1875, while north up Driggs Avenue, the onion-domed Russian Orthodox **Cathedral of the Transfiguration** (228 N. 12th Street, tel: 718-387 1064), dating from 1922, demonstrates the area's ties to Eastern Europe. This part of Brooklyn is hopping right now. **Bedford Avenue** is the main drag, with clothes stores and cafés neighboring happily.

One block west is **Berry Street**, another place with hip restaurants, cafés for people-watching, and some intriguing street-corner galleries and eclectic stores. Williamsburg has a vibrant arts community, and some of the outdoor murals and graffiti are of a high quality. The center for all this creativity is the **Williamsburg Art & Historical Center** (135 Broadway at Bedford, tel: 718-486 7372).

Crown Heights and East Brooklyn

East of central Brooklyn in **Crown Heights**, Hasidic Jews and immigrants from the West Indies are building communities that are worlds apart, but only a few doorsteps away. Also

Recommended Restaurants, Bars, & Cafés on page 291

here is **Brooklyn Children's Museum** (145 Brooklyn Avenue, at St Mark's Avenue, www.brooklynkids.org, tel: 718-735 4400; Wed–Fri 11am–5pm, Sat–Sun 10am–5pm; charge). Founded in 1899, this is the oldest children's museum in America and very much a hands-on learning experience, with thousands of interesting artifacts to wonder at – and almost as many buttons and knobs to twiddle. Child-powered vehicles, too.

Even farther east is **Brownsville**. Before World War II, this was a mainly Jewish slum, where local legend locates the headquarters for Murder Inc. – the notorious 1930s gangster ring – in a candy store on Livonia Avenue. (For a Brownsville classic book, check out *A Walker in the City* by Alfred Kazin.)

Coney Island ❽

On the coast to the south is Coney Island, which is not actually an island, but a peninsula. The famous name of Coney Island really belongs to what was once New York's premier vacation center, and urbanites have been escaping here ever since the summers

of the 1840s. Get a **Nathan's Famous** hot dog at the stand on Surf and Stillwell, where fans insist the mass-produced sausages were invented in 1916. The grills sizzle up to 1,500 dogs an hour on a hot summer's day.

Tempt fate aboard the **Cyclone**, the grand-daddy of roller coasters, with 2,640ft (805 meters) of steel-and-wood track and cars speeding at 68mph (109kph). It's the centerpiece of **Astroland Amusement Park** (1000 Surf Avenue, corner of W. 10th Street, www.astroland.com, tel: 718-265 2100). Then, take a calming stroll along the boardwalk, and watch the seagulls swooping over the ocean.

The popular **New York Aquarium** (www.nyaquarium.com, tel: 718-265 3474; charge) is located just behind the beach, at West 8th Street and Surf Avenue. With an outdoor theater where frisky and lovable sea lions perform, this metropolitan home for ocean life is one of the borough's best-known attractions.

Farther east on the boardwalk is **Brighton Beach ❾**, which for years was an enclave of elderly Jews, made famous by playwright Neil Simon.

After that Nathan's hot dog, why not finish with some cotton candy?

BELOW LEFT: the big wheel at Astroland Amusement Park.
BELOW RIGHT: Nathan's Famous hot dogs are a Coney Island essential.

TIP

Queens was the home of Louis Armstrong, Dizzy Gillespie, Count Basie, Billie Holiday, Ella Fitzgerald, and John Coltrane. Queens Jazz Trail tours can be booked through Flushing Town Hall, tel: 718-463 7700.

RIGHT AND BELOW: images of jazz legend Louis "Satchmo" Armstrong's home.

But in the 1970s a new wave of migrants, mainly Russians and Ukrainians, began moving into the area, which soon became known as "**Little Odessa.**" Today Russian restaurants, book stores, markets, and other businesses have infused the neighborhood with vitality. Dance the night away at one of the exuberant nightspots on **Brighton Beach Avenue**.

QUEENS ⑩

Visitors taking taxis from JFK International Airport into Manhattan pass as swiftly as traffic allows through Queens, but the borough is more than just a point of arrival. Named for Queen Catherine of Braganza, wife of Charles II of England, it is a diverse community, with one of the largest Greek neighborhoods outside of Athens, and immigrants from all around the world.

The area between **Northern Boulevard** and **Grand Central Parkway**, once a swamp and later the "Corona Garbage Dump," ended up as the glamorous grounds for the 1939 and 1964 World's Fairs. Now known as **Flushing Meadows Corona Park ⑪**,

it is an expanse of 1,255 acres (508 hectares) that includes museums, sports facilities, and botanical gardens. On display in what was the 1939 and 1964 World's Fair's New York City Building – now the **Queens Museum of Art** (www.queensmuseum. org, tel: 718-592 9700; closed Mon and Tue; charge) – is the **Panorama of the City of New York**, a scale replica of the city in meticulous detail.

The **New York Hall of Science** (www.nyscience.org; tel: 718-699 0005; Sept–Mar closed Mon; charge), near the park's 111th Street entrance, is

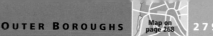
Recommended Restaurants, Bars, & Cafés on page 291

well known for its hands-on exhibits and rocket ships in the outdoor Rocket Park. The park also has a theater, a zoo, an indoor skating rink (in the same building as the Museum of Art), and an antique carrousel.

Close by are two nationally recognizable sports arenas, the **USTA Billie Jean King National Tennis Center**, open to public players but also home of the US Open; and the new **Citi Field**, which became home of the Mets in 2009 (http://newyork.mets.mlb.com; *see page 288*). Also in the neighborhood, the 38-acre (15-hectare)

Queens Botanical Garden (43–50 Main Street, www.queensbotanical.org, tel: 718-886 3800; closed Mon; free) has the largest rose garden in the northeast, and is a good spot for weddings.

Louis Armstrong House ⑫

✉ 34–56 107th St (at 34th and 37th aves), Corona, www.satchmo.net
☎ 718-478 8274 🕐 Tue–Fri 10am–5pm, Sat–Sun noon–5pm 💲 charge
🚇 103rd St/Corona Plaza

Louis and Lucille Armstrong came to live in this modest house in 1943, a year after they were married, and stayed here for the rest of their lives, despite Louis being one of the world's most famous faces. Louis died in his sleep here in 1971, and Lucille stayed on until her own death in 1983.

Lucille had much more to do with the decoration of the house than Louis did – he was often on tour – but "Satchmo's" den has been restored to look exactly as it did in his lifetime. Also part of the museum are the **Louis Armstrong Archives** (Queens College, 65–30 Kissena Boulevard, tel: 718-997 3670; by

DRINK

On the east side of Queens in Bayside, there's a restaurant and bar scene along Bell Boulevard. The NoNo Cocktail Lounge (at No. 42–32, tel: 718-428 6666) has a garden and is credited with bringing Soho style to Queens' outer fringes.

LEFT AND BELOW: the Queens building called 5 Pointz, a labor of love by local writer Meres.

Long Island City in QNS (as residents like to define their area), promotes itself as the eastern counterpoint to Chelsea, with more light, more space, and less glamor. But glamor does come its way: both The Sopranos and Sex and the City were made at LIC's Silvercup Studios.

appointment; free), the first stop for hundreds of jazz researchers from all over the world.

Flushing and its Little Asia

East of the park, **Flushing** ⑬ is packed with history, and perked up by "Little Asia," with one of the biggest Hindu temples in North America, on **Bowne Street**.

The **Quaker Meeting House**, built in 1696, is the oldest place of worship in New York City. A good place to learn about the area is the **Queens Historical Society** (143–35 37th Avenue, www.queenshistoricalsociety.org, tel: 718-939 0647; Tue, Sat–Sun 2.30–4.30pm). At the back of the building is a weeping beech tree over 150 years old – one of two "living land-

RIGHT: nearly one quarter of Queens is reserved for parkland.
BELOW: geese strut their stuff at Jamaica Bay Wildlife Refuge.

marks" in New York City (the other is a magnolia tree in Brooklyn).

Most people assume the largest stretches of land in Queens belong to **JFK** and **LaGuardia airports**. These sprawling terminals with their long runways *are* huge, but an even more impressive acreage remains undeveloped – nearly a quarter of the borough of Queens is kept as parkland, under preservation orders.

South of the JFK runways, **Jamaica Bay Wildlife Refuge** ⑭ (Cross Bay Boulevard, www.nps.gov/gate, tel: 718-318 4340; free) gives a home to more than 300 species of birds, as well as scores of small creatures like raccoons, chipmunks, and turtles.

Trail maps, available from National Park Rangers at the visitor center, guide hikers and strollers to some beautiful routes through luscious groves of red cedar and Japanese pine trees. Workshops about birds are also available year-round. The birds of Jamaica Bay avoid tangling with passing jet-powered flyers thanks to an innovative program using falcons to encourage them away from the danger areas.

Museum of the Moving Image

The Museum of the Moving Image was the first institute in the US devoted to exploring the art, history, technique, and technology of film, TV, and video. It is part of the Kaufman Astoria Studios complex – Paramount Pictures' East Coast facility in the 1920s. Along with nearby Silvercup Studios, this is the largest and busiest production facility between London and Hollywood, favored by Woody Allen and Martin Scorsese.

The museum has a pleasing feel, with plenty of early film and TV equipment. Modern exhibits include interactive workstations where you can select sound effects for famous movies, or insert your own dialogue into classic scenes.

Film screenings are held most Friday evenings and weekend afternoons in the 200-seat Riklis Theater; other viewing theaters include a 1920s-style living room, complete with shag rug and vinyl furniture, and the knockout Tut's Fever by artist Red Grooms, a delightful homage to the neo-Egyptian picture palaces of the 1920s.

Recommended Restaurants, Bars, & Cafés on page 291

Big beach

Along the southernmost strip of Queens, **The Rockaways** ⓭ form the biggest municipal beach in the country, easy to reach by subway from midtown Manhattan. To the east is **Far Rockaway**; to the west is **Neponsit**, where old mansions echo the bygone splendor of Rockaway days when wealthy New Yorkers vacationed here. Sadly, **Belle Harbor** was the site of the tragic incident on November 13, 2001, when American Airlines Flight 587 crashed shortly after take-off from JFK, killing 260 people, including some residents and rescue workers from 9/11.

Astoria and movieland

On the other side of Queens, facing Manhattan across the East River, **Astoria** ⓮ is a modest section of small apartment buildings and semi-detached homes. Traditionally a Greek enclave, Astoria has lately attracted migrants from across the world. Along main drags like **Steinway Street** and **Broadway** are Greek delis, Italian bakeries, Asian markets, and restaurants. And despite

the movie stars working nearby, the side streets remain pretty quiet.

Astoria has also regained its old status as the center of New York's film industry. The motion-picture business here dates back to the 1920s, when the Marx Brothers and Gloria Swanson were among those working at what was then the Famous Players-Lasky Studios. The **Kaufman Astoria Studios** (KAS) now occupy the old site. Films and commercials are rolling again, here and at **Silvercup Studios** in nearby Long Island City.

Museum of the Moving Image ⓱

✉ 35th Ave (at 36th St), Astoria, www.movingimage.us ☎ 718-784 0077 🕐 Tue–Fri 10am–3pm 💲 charge 🚇 Steinway St

The Museum of the Moving Image is a fun, stylish ride through aspects of modern visual culture.

LEFT: Silvercup Studios.
BELOW: Jacob Riis Park on The Rockaways, the country's biggest municipal beach.

TIP

On Sundays, a special shuttle bus runs to the Isamu Noguchi Garden Museum from the Upper East Side in Manhattan. It picks up at Park Avenue and 70th St (by the Asia Society), and runs at 30 minutes past each hour, 12.30–3.30pm. Buses return from the garden on the hour, 2–5pm.

RIGHT: the garden of Japanese sculptor Isamu Noguchi is easy to reach from Manhattan.
BELOW: innovative P.S.1, affiliated with the Museum of Modern Art, has its premises in an old schoolhouse.

This museum evokes the glory days of early New York filmmaking, when Astoria's studios were known as "Hollywood on the Hudson." It also has fascinating and fun exhibits that demonstrate how movies are made and the possibilities of new technologies, and hosts regular film screenings (Fri–Sun) in some of the city's most enjoyable movie theaters. *See also box on page 280.*

Long Island City ⑱

West of Astoria, Long Island City also has much to offer visitors. An aging industrial section, it was discovered in the 1980s by the arts community. Until recently, MoMA QNS was relocated here, while it awaited the completion of its improved premises in Manhattan. **P.S.1 Contemporary Art Center** (22–25 Jackson Avenue, at 46th Avenue; www.ps1.org, tel: 718-784 2084; closed Tue–Wed; charge), is an exuberant exhibition space attached to the Museum of Modern Art that's dedicated to showing the work of emerging artists, and one of the city's most exciting venues.

Sculpture parks

A lovely, leafy landmark is the **Isamu Noguchi Garden Museum** ⑲ (32–37 Vernon Boulevard at 33rd Road, www. noguchi.org, tel: 718-204 7088; closed Mon–Tue; charge). Almost 250 works by the Japanese sculptor are displayed in 13 galleries created from a converted factory building, while others encircle a garden of the artist's design. The overall effect is one of harmony and serenity, a far cry from Manhattan's screaming streets.

Just up Vernon Boulevard, more outdoor art can be enjoyed in the 4½-acre (2-hectare) **Socrates Sculpture Park** (www.socratessculpturepark.org, tel: 718-956 1819; free). Started by

Recommended Restaurants, Bars, & Cafés on page 291

artists, this grass expanse has been made an official city park. The view across to Manhattan, through giant sculptures, is delightful.

Garden suburb

A neighborhood worth exploring is **Forest Hills ❷**. Best known for the West Side Tennis Club (tel: 718-268 2300), once host to the US Open, this part of Queens was inspired by the English "Garden Suburb" movement. Planning began in 1906 with a low-cost housing endowment, but in 1923, the project only half completed, residents took over management and began vetting newcomers. The mock-Tudor district turned fashionable, and styled itself "lawn-tennis capital of the western hemisphere."

For a change of pace, a day at the races can be fun. Events at **Aqueduct Racetrack** (110–00 Rockaway Boulevard; tel: 718-641 4700), include the Wood Memorial and the Turf Classic.

STATEN ISLAND ❷

Once upon a time in New York, there was an island with roads paved by oyster shells, where yachts swayed by resort hotels, European-style fin-ishing schools were founded, and where Americans first played tennis.

Could this be Staten Island, the least-known borough? To most New Yorkers, this is just the place where the famous ferry goes. As the poet Edna St Vincent Millay wrote: "We were very tired, we were very merry – we had gone back and forth all night on the ferry." Yes, come for the ride, but try to reserve some time for Staten Island itself.

The ferry lands at **St George ❷**, where part of the extensive ferry collection is shown at the **St George Ferry Terminal** (1 Bay Street). Two blocks away is the **Staten Island Institute of Arts & Sciences** (tel: 718-727 1135; charge), in a dignified 1918 building at 75 Stuyvesant Place.

Snug Harbor Cultural Center (1000 Richmond Terrace, tel: 718-448 2500; closed Mon; charge) is a short bus ride from St George. The handsome visitor center first opened in 1831 as a home for retired seamen. Now its 83 acres (34 hectares) of wetlands and woodlands are a Smithsonian affiliate. Within the center's grounds is the **Staten Island**

EAT

The most historic restaurant in New York City is on Staten Island. The Old Bermuda Inn opened in 1716. This landmark Colonial house – said to be haunted – is at 2512 Arthur Kill Road, Rossville, tel: 718-948 7600. The Wedding Cottage on the grounds is a high-end B&B.

LEFT: a day at Aqueduct Racetrack can be fun.
BELOW: Staten Island ferry passengers.

TIP

Don't miss the Jacques Marchais Museum of Tibetan Art. Built in the style of a Himalayan mountain temple and surrounded by tranquil gardens, the museum was the vision of a Victorian-era actress who wanted to bring Tibetan culture to New York. It's open Wed–Sun 1–5pm.

Botanical Garden (tel: 718-448 2500; free), with an orchid collection and Chinese Scholar's Garden (charge). Here, too, is the fun **Staten Island Children's Museum** (tel: 718-273 2060; closed Mon; charge), an interactive experience for kids.

Rosebank ㉓

East of the ferry is Rosebank, home to Staten Island's first Italian-American community. The **Garibaldi-Meucci Museum** (420 Tompkins Avenue, www.garibaldimeuccimuseum.org, tel: 718-442 1608; closed Mon; charge), commemorates Antonio Meucci, who invented a type of telephone years before Alexander Graham Bell. Exhibits focus on this and his other inventions, and his friendship with Italian hero Giuseppe Garibaldi, who stayed here on his 1850 visit to New York. This simple house was Meucci's home until his death in 1889.

A bus or taxi ride away, the **Alice Austen House Museum** (2 Hylan Boulevard, www.aliceausten.org, tel: 718-816 4506; closed Mon–Wed and Jan–Feb; charge) is a 1690s cottage surrounded by a pretty garden that was

RIGHT: Verrazano-Narrows Bridge as seen from the ferry.
BELOW: scenic Alice Austen House Museum.

the home of a pioneering woman photographer from 1866 to 1945.

Verrazano-Narrows Bridge ㉔ features in many of the island's easterly views. When built in 1964, it was the longest suspension bridge in the world. The Verrazano connects Staten Island to Brooklyn and brought great change to the island. The traffic that poured across its magnificent span brought Staten Island's fastest, least controlled construction boom. Now, laws are in place to prevent this from happening again.

Taking to the Staten hills

Because a glacier ridge runs through the middle of the island, Staten's six hills – **Fort**, **Ward**, **Grymes**, **Emerson**, **Todt** and **Lighthouse** – are the highest points in New York City. Handsome mansions with breathtaking views stand on the ridge of Todt Hill, the highest point on the eastern seaboard south of Maine. Take a taxi up **Signal Hill**, a narrow hairpin lane. Along the way, alpine homes peek out of the cliff, half-hidden by rocks and trees. At the top, beyond the wonderful views from the ridge, is the core of the island. Called the **Greenbelt** (www.sigreenbelt.org, tel: 718-667 3450, for information on walking trails), this

Recommended Restaurants, Bars, & Cafés on page 291

enormous expanse of meadows and woodland has been preserved by a civic plan that tightly controls or prohibits development. **High Rock Park** is a 90-acre (36-hectare) open space.

On **Lighthouse Hill** is an idyllic corner imported from the Himalayas, the **Jacques Marchais Museum of Tibetan Art** (338 Lighthouse Avenue, www.tibetanmuseum.org, tel: 718-987 3500; closed Mon–Wed; charge; *see also margin, opposite*).

Historic Richmond Town 🉂

✉ 441 Clarke Ave, www.historic richmondtown.org 📞 718-351 1611
🕓 Wed–Sun 1–5pm 💲 charge
🚌 Bus 74 from Ferry Terminal

Less than a mile from Lighthouse Hill on Richmond Road is a restored 17th-and 18th-century village, showing 300 years of life on Staten Island. On a 100-acre (40-hectare) site, more than 15 buildings have been restored. The former County Clerk's and Surrogate's office, from 1848, was the first part of Richmond to be brought back to life. Staff in period garb conduct tours, and old-fashioned

skills are demonstrated in this local "living museum."

THE BRONX 🉃

In 1641, a Scandinavian, Jonas Bronck, bought 500 acres (200 hectares) of the New World from Native Americans. After building his home on virgin land, he and his family found the area remote and lonely, so they threw parties for friends.

The Indian land was called Keskeskeck (or Rananchqua, the native Siwanou name), but the name was changed, the story goes, by Manhattanites asking their neighbors,

ABOVE: the Bronx is home to the New York Botanical Garden.
BELOW: demonstrating 18th-century skills in Staten Island's Historic Richmond Town.

Monkey madness at the Bronx Zoo, the country's largest urban zoo.

VISIT TIGERS AT THE BRONX ZOO

SEE OUR STARS IN STRIPES!

NEW YORK ZOOS AND AQUARIUM

RIGHT: visit tigers and then go for a camel ride at the Bronx Zoo.
BELOW: New York Botanical Garden.

"Where are you going on Saturday night?" and being answered, "Why, to the Bronck's."

The tale is certainly questionable, but the Bronx *had* been virgin forest, and *did* begin with Jonas's farm. Idyllic woods seem unimaginable in today's Bronx, but a part of its original hemlock forest remains untouched in the 250-acre (100-hectare) New

York Botanical Garden ㉗ (200th Street and Kazimiroff Boulevard, tel: 718-817 8700; closed Mon; charge).

The **Enid A. Haupt Conservatory**, constructed in 1902, is the botanical garden's grandest structure, a veritable crystal palace with a central Palm Court and connecting greenhouses. There are plenty of outdoor gardens to explore, which are particularly wonderful in the springtime, such as the Rose Garden and the Everett Children's Adventure Garden, which has kid-size topiaries and mazes.

Bronx Zoo ㉘

✉ Bronx River Parkway (at Fordham Rd), www.bronxzoo.com 📞 718-220 5100 🕐 daily 10am–4.30pm 💲 charge 🚇 Pelham Parkway/E. 180th St

This 265-acre (107-hectare) park is the country's largest urban zoo – and shares **Bronx Park** with the Botanical Garden. Popular exhibits include the **African Plains**, the **Baboon Reserve**, the **Aquatic Bird House**, and the **Butterfly Garden**. There's a **Children's Zoo**, a monorail ride through **Wild**

Recommended Restaurants, Bars, & Cafés on page 291

Asia, and a 40-acre (16-hectare) complex with moats to keep the big cats away from their prey – that would be you. The **Congo Gorilla Forest** has acres of forest, bamboo thickets, and baby lowland gorillas.

Along the Grand Concourse

The zoo is at the geographic heart of the Bronx, but its architectural and nostalgic heart may be the **Grand Concourse**. This Champs-Elysées-inspired boulevard began as a "speedway" through rural hills. As the borough became more industrialized, it achieved a classy role as the Park Avenue of the Bronx, stretching as it does for more than 4 miles (6km).

On the Grand Concourse, at 165th Street, is the recently expanded

Bronx Museum of the Arts (www.bronxmuseum.org, tel: 718-681 6000; closed Mon–Tue; charge, free Fri), which hosts exhibitions reflecting the multicultural nature of the Bronx.

Edgar Allan Poe Cottage ㉙

✉ 2640 Grand Concourse (at Kingsbridge Rd), www.bronxhistoricalsociety.org ☎ 718-881 8900
⊘ Sat 10am–4pm, Sun 1–5pm
⑤ charge 🚇 Kingsbridge Rd

At the north end of the Grand Concourse, writer Edgar Allan Poe's cottage sits humbly among the high-rise apartment blocks on Kingsbridge Road. Poe moved here in 1846, hoping the then-country air would be good for his consumptive young wife and cousin, Virginia. But she died at an early age, leaving Poe destitute; the haunting poem *Annabel Lee* was a reflection of his distress. The cottage has been a museum since 1917, run by the Bronx Historical Society.

Belmont

The Little Italy of the Bronx is **Belmont**, between the zoo and the

Bronx residents passing by a Grand Concourse mural.

LEFT: Edgar Allan Poe lived in the Bronx for three years before his death in 1849.
BELOW: inspecting what's on offer at Belmont Market.

Having a Ball

New York is very much a baseball town, and from April through October eyes are fixed on two very important diamonds

New York-based baseball-lovers are literally divided into two groups – Yankee fans and Mets fans. It's not the most congenial of competitions, either. The Yankees, regarded by their fans as the primary hometown team, are proud of their recent winning streak; the Mets, who see themselves as the inheritors of the Brooklyn Dodgers mantle, a team that moved to LA in 1958, have a less glowing record but just as much pride. Fans spar often, in offices and bars around the city.

But both had reason to be proud in 2009: at the beginning of the baseball season, both of New York City's major league teams opened new stadiums. In 2008, the old stadiums had been broken down, and seats sold to fans.

It was the first time in America that two teams opened new stadiums in the same town at the same time. Both fields are open-air, and have natural grass; both are right across from the old stadiums, and therefore still reached by most attendants by subway.

Citi Field replaced the Mets' previous stadium, Shea, in Flushing, Queens. The architecture of the new building makes a lot of references to the Dodgers, including a rotunda named for Jackie Robinson, the first modern-day African-American major league baseball player. Much of the talk after the opening was about the name, though, as Citibank went through financial difficulty before the stadium opened, and was one of the American banks that had to be bailed out by the government. (Fans jokingly call the new building "Taxpayer Field.") Another new feature: on the field level, Citi has food concessions including outposts of the popular Manhattan spots Shake Shack (for burgers, hot dogs, and milkshakes) and Blue Smoke (for barbecue food).

Yankee Stadium, which had opened in 1923, was replaced by a new site of the same name at 161st Street in the Bronx. The architects also managed to keep some aspects of the old stadium that fans were sentimental about, such as the view of the elevated subway line from the bleachers.

Much of the discussion after it opened was of the higher cost of tickets, and of the luxury boxes called "Legends Suites," which come with cushioned seats, fancy food concessions, and a through-the-roof price tag. (To fans and critics alike, it felt like a misstep to tout the more expensive choices in the middle of a recession). There was also talk at the beginning of the first season about whether the new stadium was "cursed" – a construction worker's plot to bury a Boston Red Sox jersey in the concrete was foiled; the wind pattern was blamed for blowing balls off their course. But all these discussions were laid to rest when, in the first season on the new field, the Yankees won the World Series. ❑

LEFT: the Mets' Johan Santana pitches.
ABOVE: young Yankee fans.

Recommended Restaurants, Bars, & Cafés on page 291

Grand Concourse. **Arthur Avenue**, near the fork of Crescent Avenue and 3rd Avenue, teems with people who flock here from all over the city to buy cured meats, pasta and freshly baked bread. It's also a great place for restaurants.

The West and North Bronx

Just west of the Grand Concourse is **Bronx Community College**'s most famous landmark, a tile-roofed, bust-lined colonnade, the **Hall of Fame for Great Americans**. It wraps around the **Gould Memorial Library**, designed by Stanford White. No longer used as a library, the building's great copper dome was known to scholars as the Great Green Nipple of Knowledge.

Farther up to the northwest is **Riverdale** ㉚. It's hard to believe this is the Bronx, as the curvy roads wind through hills lined with mansions. A drive down Sycamore Avenue to Independence Avenue leads to **Wave Hill** (www.wavehill.org, tel: 718-549 3200; closed Mon; charge, free Tue). This once-private estate, now a city-owned environmental center, has greenhouses and gardens overlooking the Hudson. It's a pretty spot, and the site of outdoor concerts and dance performances.

East of Riverdale, **Van Cortlandt Park** ㉛ stretches from West 240th to West 263rd streets, and includes stables, tennis courts, and acres of playing fields. The **Van Cortlandt House Museum** (Broadway at W. 246th Street; www.vancortlandthouse.org; tel: 718-543 3344; closed Mon; charge), overlooks the park's lake. Built in 1748 by Frederick Van Cortlandt, a wealthy merchant, it is filled with some of the family's original furnishings and possessions.

On the park's east side, **Woodlawn Cemetery** (Webster Avenue; tel: 718-920 0500) is permanent home to

In 2007, the mayor announced big plans for the South Bronx. When it is completed, the South Bronx Greenway will add over a mile of waterfront greenery, 8 miles (13km) of new green "streets," and 12 acres (5 hectares) of waterfront open space.

LEFT: the Van Cortlandt House Museum.
BELOW: Wave Hill in fall.

City Island is a slice of New Engand tucked away in the Bronx.

about 300,000 New Yorkers. Herman Melville, Duke Ellington, and five former mayors are just a handful of the celebrities at rest in the elaborate mausoleums. Over 400 acres (162 hectares) of trees, hills, and streams have made this a place for strolling since it opened in 1863.

Farther east is **Orchard Beach**, a summer destination with nature trails, riding stables, and a golf course. On the way, the road passes Co-Op City, a sprawling 1960s housing development that looms over the horizon like a massive urban beehive.

The road ends at **City Island** ㉜, a little slice of New England. Accessible by car, bus, or boat, this 230-acre (93-hectare) island off the Bronx coast has remained quietly detached from the rest of the city. The boatyards along **City Island Avenue** yielded masterworks like *Intrepid*, twice winner of the America's Cup race. Today, the street has fishing-gear emporiums and craft shops, along with galleries and seafood restaurants. Be sure to see stately **Grace Church**, and at No. 586, the romantic hideaway **Le Refuge Inn** (tel: 718-885 2478).

The South Bronx

The opposite end of the borough – in location and reputation – is the **South Bronx**. Its best-known landmark is the baseball stadium with the nickname The House That Ruth Built, though actually, this is the house built for Ruth; its shortened right field was originally designed for player Babe Ruth's special home-run record.

More championship flags and American League pennants have flown over **Yankee Stadium** ㉝ (http://newyork.yankees.mlb.com, tel: 718-293 4300) than any other baseball field in the US.

Since Babe Ruth, other stars of the field have included Joe DiMaggio, Lou Gehrig, Mickey Mantle, and the team that in the 1990s won the World Series four years in a row. But, just like Shea Stadium, it too was replaced by a new stadium in 2009 *(see page 288)*. As a result, tickets are more expensive. Fortunately, the team is justifying the extra fees – they won the World Series in 2009, too. ❑

BELOW: City Island feels a world away from the rest of the city.

BEST RESTAURANTS, BARS, AND CAFÉS

Restaurants

Prices for a three-course dinner per person with half a bottle of wine:
$ = under $20
$$ = $20–$45
$$$ = $45–$60
$$$$ = over $60

Blue Ribbon
✉ 280 5th Ave (between 1st and Garfield Pl), Park Slope, Brooklyn ☎ 718-840 0404 ☉ D daily
$$$
No reservations means a wait for this excellent New American menu.

Bohemian Hall and Beer Garden
✉ 29–19 24th Ave, Astoria, Queens ☎ 718-274 4925 ☉ L & D Mon–Fri, L only Sat–Sun $$
Reasonably priced goulash and *kielbasa*, washed down with plenty of beer: something they've been doing here for almost 100 years.

The Good Fork
✉ 391 Van Brunt St (at Coffey and Van Dyke sts), Brooklyn ☎ 718-643 6636 ☉ D only Tue–Sun $$
Hip Red Hook has a waterfront winner here when it comes to good and reasonably priced food. There's also a warm, comforting room.

Grimaldi's
✉ 19 Old Fulton St (at Front and Water sts) ☎ 718-858 4300 ☉ L & D daily $
One of Brooklyn's original pizza spots, Grimaldi's still has lines around the block for their thin-crust, coal-fired pizzas.

The Grocery
✉ 288 Smith St (between Sackett and Union sts), Carroll Gds, Brooklyn ☎ 718-596 3335 ☉ D only Mon–Sat $$$
Local four-star, one-room phenomenon serving New American cuisine.

Noodle Pudding
✉ 38 Henry St (at Middagh and Cranberry sts), Brooklyn ☎ 718-625 3737 ☉ D Tue–Sun $
Come for the warm atmosphere, practically-giving-it-away wine list, and great pasta dishes.

Peter Luger Steakhouse
✉ 178 Broadway (at Driggs Ave), Williamsburg, Brooklyn ☎ 718-387 7400 ☉ L & D daily $$$$
Brooklyn's oldest restaurant still holds the grand title of "King of all Steak Places." No credit cards.

River Café
✉ 1 Water St (at Fulton Ferry), Brooklyn ☎ 718-522 5200 ☉ L & D daily $$$$ The unsurpassed location and views of Manhattan from under the Brooklyn Bridge, plus excellent haute cuisine, make this a magical spot. Bookings can be difficult, so start early.

Sripiphai
✉ 6413 39th Ave (at 64th St), Woodside, Queens ☎ 718-899 9599 ☉ L & D Thur–Tue $
Regarded as the best Thai food in the region.

Stone Park Café
✉ 324 5th Ave (at 3rd St), Brooklyn ☎ 718-369 0082 ☉ D Mon–Fri, Br & D Sat–Sun $$$
Comfortable, casual New American food that is a big hit with the Park Slope crowd.

Water's Edge
✉ 44th Dr and East River (at Vernon Blvd), Queens ☎ 718-482 0033 ☉ L & D Mon–Fri, D Sat $$$$
From a Long Island City location with great views, this romantic spot serves delicious food with an emphasis on fresh fish. A free ferry service is available from Manhattan.

Bars and Cafés

Almondine, 85 Water St, in Brooklyn's trendy DUMBO, is a great place to dip into hot coffee, pastries, or sandwiches while touring galleries.

Athens Café, 32–07 30th Avenue (at 32nd and 33rd sts), Astoria, Queens, is a lively sidewalk café, good for pastry and coffee and people-watching.

Jacques Torres Chocolate, 66 Water St, DUMBO, Brooklyn, is a gourmet chocolate shop serving decadent hot cocoa in winter, and spectacular ice creams in summer.

Juniors, 386 Flatbush Ave, Ext. at De Kalb Ave, Brooklyn, is a dessert spot where the cheesecake is a NYC tradition.

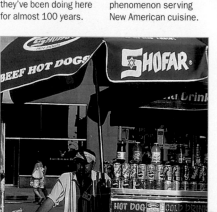

INSIGHT GUIDES

NEW YORK
Travel Tips

RANSPORTATION

GETTING THERE AND GETTING AROUND

From the song *On the Town* comes the saying: "The Bronx is up and the Battery's down – New York's geography makes it easy to get around," which pretty much sums things up. The layout of Manhattan couldn't be simpler, with a grid of numbered streets through most of the island that makes it near impossible to get lost. Compactness also makes most of Manhattan easy – and inviting – to explore on foot. After a while, when the feet get weary, you're never far from a subway station, a bus, or a bright yellow taxi.

GETTING THERE

By Air

New York's two major airports, **John F. Kennedy International** (**JFK**) and **LaGuardia**, are both in Queens, east of Manhattan on Long Island, respectively 15 and 8 miles (24 and 13km) from Midtown. Driving time to/from Kennedy is estimated at 90 minutes, but heavy traffic can often double this, so leave lots of time if you're catching a flight. LaGuardia is only used for shorter US domestic and some Canadian routes, and does not have any intercontinental flights.

New York's third airport, **Newark Liberty International**, is used by a growing number of international flights. It's really in New Jersey but, although a little bit farther from Manhattan than JFK, it's often quicker to reach. It's also newer, cleaner, and less chaotic than Kennedy.

By Sea

Stretching along the Hudson from 46th to 54th streets in Manhattan (at 12th Ave), the **Manhattan Cruise Terminal**, tel: 212-246 5450, has customs facilities and good bus connections to Midtown. Manhattan remains the primary New York City port for passenger ships, but in 2006 the **Brooklyn Cruise Terminal**, tel: 718-246 2794, opened with the arrival of the *Queen Mary 2*.

By Rail

Trains arrive and depart from two railroad terminals in Manhattan: **Grand Central** at Park Ave and 42nd St (lines to the northern suburbs, upstate New York and Connecticut), and **Pennsylvania Station** at Seventh Ave and 33rd St (for Long Island and most other destinations). City buses stop outside each terminal and each has a subway station. Amtrak information, tel: 212-630 6400, or (toll-free) 1-800-872 7245.

By Road

From the south, the **New Jersey Turnpike** leads into lower Manhattan via the Holland or Lincoln tunnels (Midtown) and offers access farther north via the George Washington Bridge. From the northwest, the **New York State Thruway** connects with Henry Hudson Parkway into northern Manhattan. Driving in from the Long Island airports, access is via either the **Midtown Tunnel** or the **Triborough Bridge**, and down Manhattan's FDR (East River) Drive.

The busy **Port Authority Bus Terminal** (Eighth Ave, at 40th and 42nd sts) sits atop two subway lines and is used by long-distance companies (including **Greyhound**, tel: 1-800-231 2222) and local commuter lines. City buses stop outside. A modern terminal with stores and other facilities, nevertheless, it tends to attract more than its share of shady individuals; though well policed, it's not a place to trust strangers or to leave bags unguarded.

GETTING AROUND

On Arrival

Orientation

Generally, avenues in Manhattan run north to south; streets east to west. North of Houston Street, streets are numbered, which makes orientating oneself very easy. Even-numbered streets tend to have one-way eastbound traffic; odd-numbered streets, westbound. There are very few exceptions. Most avenues are one-way, north or south, the major exception being Park Avenue, which is wide enough for two-way traffic north of 44th St.

Buses do not run on Park Avenue but do on most other avenues, as well as on major cross-streets (also two-way): Houston, 14th, 23rd, 34th, 42nd, 57th, 66th, 86th, 116th, 125th, and a few others. Subway trains cross town at 14th and 42nd sts, but there is no north–south line east of Lexington Ave or west of Eighth Ave and Broadway above 59th St.

Airport to City Transportation

AirTrain is an airport rail system that connects **JFK** and **Newark** airports with the subway and rail networks, at Howard Beach (A train) and Sutphin Boulevard (E, J, and Z train) subways and at Jamaica Long Island Railroad station for JFK, and at a special airport rail station in Newark. At each airport AirTrain runs every few minutes and takes about 10 minutes from each terminal.

Traveling between Midtown Manhattan and JFK by AirTrain and subway takes about one hour; traveling from Newark (by AirTrain and then Amtrak or NJ Transit train to Penn Station) can take only 30–45 minutes.
AirTrain JFK information: www.airtrainjfk.com, tel: 877-535 2478.

AirTrain Newark information: www.panynj.gov/airports/ewr-airtrain. html, tel: 888-397 4636.
New York Airport Service (www.nyairportservice.com, tel: 212-875 8200) **buses** run between both JFK and LaGuardia airports and Manhattan. Pick-up and drop-off points include: Port Authority Bus Terminal, Penn Station, and Grand Central Terminal, with a transfer service available to or from Midtown hotels. Buses from JFK run 6.15am–11.10pm.

From LaGuardia, the **M60** bus to upper Manhattan subway stations operates 5am–1am, while **Triboro Coach** bus **Q-33** runs to 74th St subway stop in Jackson Heights, Queens, from which various trains run to Manhattan.
Newark Liberty Airport Express (www.coachusa.com, tel: 877-8NEWARK) operates express buses daily between Newark airport and Manhattan, stopping at the Port Authority Bus Terminal, Grand Central and Fifth Ave, at 42nd St. Buses run 4am–1am.

There are several **minibus** services from all three airports to Manhattan. A big plus is that they take you door-to-door, direct to hotels or private addresses, but this can be slow, with many stops.
Super Shuttle (www.supershuttle.com, tel: 212-258 3826) offers a frequent service. It can be booked online, at airport ground transportation centers, or from courtesy phones at the airports.

The **cheapest routes** from JFK to the city are by AirTrain, or by Green Bus Lines to one of several subway stations in Queens.

Don't forget to leave plenty of time getting to and from the airports if traveling by road; the traffic can be very bad, especially during rush hours on business days, and on holidays.

Public Transportation

Subways and Buses

Subways and buses run 24 hours a day throughout the city, although they are less frequent after midnight. There are many subway routes, identified by letters or numbers; some share the same tracks, so be careful to get the right train. Subway directions are available online at www.hop stop.com.

The standard single fare for a subway journey (no matter how far you travel) is a flat fee, which must be paid in exact change. However, a much better way to travel than buying single tickets is with a **MetroCard**, which you charge up with a minimum amount and swipe through the entry gates each time you use the subway, or in machines on city buses. If you charge it with over $10, you get a discount on each journey. Unlimited-ride cards are also available, valid for seven or 30 days, or a one-day "Fun Pass." MetroCards and passes can be bought at subway

BELOW: subways operate 24 hours a day.

stations and at newsstands and some hotels.

For general **bus and subway** information, check www.mta.info or tel: 718-330 1234; for details about **MetroCard** and other passes, call 212-METROCARD.

PATH (Port Authority Trans-Hudson) trains run under the river between Manhattan and New Jersey. For more information check www.panynj.gov, tel: 800-234 7284.

Taxis

Taxis, all metered, cruise the streets and must be hailed, although there are official taxi stands at places like Grand Central and Penn Station. Be sure to flag down an official, yellow cab, not an unlicensed gypsy cab. Flat fares to and from the airports can usually be negotiated, but bridge and tunnel tolls, and the tip, of course, will be extra.

One fare covers all passengers up to four (five in a few of the larger cabs). Between the hours of 4 and 8pm, there is a small surcharge on all taxi rides. Taxis are now able to accept credit cards.

24-hour hotline: telephone 212-NYC TAXI (692 8294).

Car Services
Allstate, tel: 212-333 3333
Limos and town cars.
Delancey, tel: 212-228 3301
Good for Downtown.
Dial 7, tel: 212-777 7777
Reliable, especially to airports.

Private Transportation

Driving in New York

Driving around Manhattan is not fun. Visitors arriving by car would do well to leave their vehicle parked in a garage and use public transportation, as traffic and scarce parking space make driving in the city a nightmare.

If you must drive, remember certain rules of the city: the speed limit is 30mph (50kmh) unless otherwise indicated; the use of seat belts is mandatory; the speed limit on most highways in New York is 55mph (90kmh) and is strictly enforced – look out for signs, as on some major highways this has now been raised to 65mph (105kmh).

Parking

While street parking is at least possible in some areas outside of Midtown, a garage or parking lot is the safer (though far more expensive) choice. If you happen to find a parking spot on the street, obey posted parking regulations, which may include parking only on one side of the street on alternate days, or call **311** for more information. Never park next to a fire hydrant and don't leave your car over the time limit, or it may be towed away.

Buying Gas

Service stations are few and far between (11th and 12th avenues on the West Side are good hunting grounds). They are often open in the evening and on Sundays.

Breakdowns

Your car rental company should have its own emergency numbers in case of breakdown. Otherwise, the **Automobile Club of New York** (ACNY), a branch of the American Automobile Association (AAA), will help members and foreign visitors affiliated with other recognized automobile associations. In case of a breakdown, or for other problems along the way,

call their Emergency Road Service (tel: 800-222 4357) or wait until a police car comes along.

Car Rental

Since New York City has the highest car rental and parking rates in the US, we don't recommend you rent a car unless you plan to leave the city a few times. If you do need a car, you'll find it's generally cheaper to rent at the airport than in Manhattan, and cheaper still to rent a car outside of New York City, where prices are more competitive. It's a good idea to make car rental reservations before you leave home, online. (A curious twist is that weekend rentals in Manhattan are more expensive than weekday rates, since most New Yorkers do not own cars and rent when they go away for weekends.)

You will need a major credit card to rent a car, plus your driver's license. The minimum age for renting a car is 21, but some companies will not rent to drivers under 25, or when they do will impose a high, additional fee.

CAR RENTAL

Alamo:		
US	1-800-327 9633	
International	1-800-522 9696	
Avis:		
US	1-800-331 1212	
International	1-800-331 1084	
Budget:		
US	1-800-527 0700	
International	1-800-527 0700	
Dollar:		
US	1-800-800 4000	
International	1-800-800 6000	
Enterprise:		
US	1-800-325 8007	
International	1-800-325 8007	
Hertz:		
US	1-800-654 3131	
International	1-800-654 3001	
National:		
US	1-800-227 7368	
International	1-800-227 3876	
Thrifty:		
US	1-800-847 4389	
International	1-918-669 2168	

TRANSPORTATION

ACCOMMODATIONS

SHOPPING

ACTIVITIES

A – Z

ACCOMMODATIONS

TIPS FOR CHOOSING A HOTEL ROOM

The old adage that New York has more of everything is only a slight exaggeration when it comes to hotel accommodations. The following list is hardly exhaustive, but represents a sample of hotels in Manhattan in the budget-to-luxury range, plus a few inexpensive places of distinction, and alternatives. Be aware that, with the exception of "Luxury," these categories are not hard and fast. When making reservations, ask about special weekend or corporate rates and package deals. It's a good idea to book by credit card to secure a guaranteed late arrival; New York City is the last place you want to be stranded late at night without a room. In addition to regular hotels, we've included a few "suite hotels," and bed and breakfast services. The former are basically apartments, available from a few nights up to a month; the latter are modeled on those in the UK and Europe. Make room reservations as far in advance as possible, and remember that the prices listed here are for low season, and rates go up over holidays and peak travel times. In New York, the low season is January–March, as well as July–August.

ACCOMMODATIONS LISTINGS

MIDTOWN

HOTELS

Luxury

Algonquin Hotel
59 West 44th St
Tel: 212-840 6800,
1-888-304 2047
[p337, C2]
www.algonquinhotel.com
Once a haven for New York's literary Round Table set, and still an all-time favorite, the Algonquin retains its low-key, oak-paneled charm. Clubby and Victorian in demeanor, civilized in its treatment of guests, it's near theaters and is less expensive than its rivals. Its website offers a best-rate guarantee.

**Millennium
UN Plaza Hotel**
United Nations Plaza (44th St and First Ave)
Tel: 212-758 1234,
1-866-866 8086
[p337, E3]
www.millennium-hotels.com
The clientele here is as you might expect, and some appreciate the busy atmosphere as UN representatives bustle

through the heroically proportioned lobby. Benefits to non-ambassadorial guests include rooms with views of the East River, a fitness center, a tennis court, and a swimming pool.

Peninsula New York
700 Fifth Ave (at 55th St)
Tel: 212-956 2888
[p335, B4]
www.peninsula.com

One of the city's most lavish hotels, where richly appointed rooms go for about $500 (slightly less with corporate rates). The hotel's health club and spa are truly luxurious. It's also in a prime location on Fifth Avenue and has a wonderful rooftop bar.

The Plaza
Fifth Ave (at 59th St)
Tel: 212-759 3000,
1-800-850 0909
[p334, C4]
www.fairmont.com

Edwardian-style splendor top to toe. The high ceilings are decorated with murals and the service is close to old-world elegance. The Oak Bar and the Oak Room are traditional favorites as pre- and post-theater spots. Sadly, many floors are now condos (the penthouse sold for $56 million – NY's largest condo deal), but there are still

BELOW: New York Palace.

ABOVE: the Palace is a New York experience.

some hotel rooms, and suites, that are open to the public. Fortunately, most of the hotel's iconic rooms, like the ballroom and the Palm Court, have been refurbished and retain their original elegance.

St Regis
2 East 55th St (at 5th Ave)
Tel: 212-753 4500,
1-800-759 7550
[p337, D1]
www.stregis.com

A grand Edwardian wedding cake of a building, filigreed and charmingly muraled (by the likes of Maxfield Parrish). The St Regis is a magnet for somewhat older, moneyed guests who appreciate the ambience of a more regal age. The location doesn't hurt; nor does the Alain Ducasse-helmed restaurant.

The Sherry-Netherland
781 Fifth Ave (at 59th St)
Tel: 212-355 2800,
1-877-743 7710
[p334, C4]
www.sherrynetherland.com

An old-fashioned luxury hotel with such a faithful club of visitors that reservations must be made well in advance. Grandly expansive spaces, both public and in the 40 rooms and suites (the rest of the

building is private apartments), with royal treatment to match.

Expensive

Hotel Iroquois
49 West 44th St
Tel: 212-840 3080,
1-800-332 7220
[p337, C2]
www.iroquoisny.com

Built in the early 1900s, this once-shabby hotel has received a facelift and now offers upscale but good-value accommodations on the same block as more expensive hotels.

InterContinental The Barclay
111 East 48th St
Tel: 212-755 5900,
1-800-782 8021
[p337, D2]
http://new-york-barclay.intercontinental.com

Opened in the 1920s as The Barclay, this hotel blends executive-class efficiency with majestic spaces and a full range of pampering services. Includes two fine restaurants, a clothier, and a gift shop.

New York Palace
455 Madison Ave (at 50th St)
Tel: 212-888 7000,
1-800-804-7035
[p337, D1]
www.newyorkpalace.com

A grandiose monument

to lavish pomp and excess and appointed in a style that can only be called postmodern Rococo, the Palace has a regime of flawlessly detailed service to make the average guest feel like an imperial pasha. The hotel's Gilt restaurant has two Michelin stars.

Omni Berkshire Place
21 East 52nd St
Tel: 212-753 5800,
1-800-THE-OMNI
[p337, D1]
www.omnihotels.com

Although it's been acquired by the Omni chain, the Berkshire retains its old-fashioned grace and attention to personal service. Known by some guests as "a junior Plaza," it's comfortable and comforting, a tastefully appointed oasis of calm in the heart of the Midtown bustle.

Le Parker Meridien
119 West 56th St
Tel: 212-245 5000,
1-800-543 4300
[p337, B4]
www.parkermeridien.com

Part of the internationally known French chain: modern, airy, with an excellent restaurant, Norma's (known for its great breakfast), and health facilities that include a swimming pool.

Renaissance New York
714 Seventh Avenue (at W. 48th St)
Tel: 212-765 7676,
1-800-228 9290
[p337, C1]
www.renaissncehotels.com

One of the stars of Times Square, with 300-plus rooms, most of them featuring large-screen TVs, oversized bathtubs, and other ample comforts. Convenient for theaters, restaurants, Midtown businesses.

The Royalton
44 West 44th St
Tel: 212-869 4400,
1-800-691 1791
[p337, C2]
www. morganshotelgroup.com

Another chic and ultra-modern creation from Ian Schrager of Studio 54 fame. Every line and appointment – from the lobby to the lavatories – is as boldly, coldly futuristic as the set of a sci-fi film, complete with video and stereo gadgetry. Still, the Royalton bends over backwards to provide the scurrying, "can-do" pampering expected by its clientele. Handy for the theater district.

The Westin New York
270 West 43rd St
Tel: 212-201 2700,
1-800-837 4183
[p336, C2]
www.westinny.com

With its multicolored-mirrored exterior, this 45-story hotel near Times Square is one of the more popular hotels in the neighborhood.

Moderate

Dylan Hotel
52 East 41st St
Tel: 1-866-553 9526
[p337, D2]
www.dylanhotel.com

ABOVE: step up to quality.

A small, sleek, upscale boutique hotel at reasonable prices, centrally located blocks away from Grand Central Terminal. Housed in a 1903 Beaux Arts building once home to a chemists' society.

Hilton New York
1335 Avenue of the Americas (at 53rd St)
Tel: 212-586 7000,
1-800-HILTONS
[p334, B4]
www.newyorktowers.hilton.com

A typical Hilton: huge, modern, impersonal, but consistent, and with the service expected.

Hotel Edison
228 West 47th St
Tel: 212-840 5000,
1-800-637-7070
[p337, C1]
www.edisonhotelnyc.com

Hotels in the bottom price ranges hardly ever really stand out here, but the Edison is an exception. Though the Art Deco lobby can be chaotic, the rooms in this huge hotel are quite comfortable, pleasantly if simply decorated, and quiet. May be the best deal in NYC.

Hotel Pennsylvania
401 Seventh Ave (at 33rd St)
Tel: 212-736 5000,
1-800-223 8585
[p336, C3]
www.hotelpenn.com

This vast hotel is across from Madison Square Garden and Penn Station and near the Javits Center. Its range of packages makes it good value for few frills, and nothing can take away its history. Built in 1919 by the Pennsylvania Railroad, the Café Rouge Ballroom played host to many of the Big Band era's greats, including Count Basie, Duke Ellington, and the Glenn Miller Orchestra – who immortalized the hotel and its phone number in the 1938 hit *Pennsylvania 6-5000*. It has had the same phone number ever since.

Hudson Hotel
356 West 58th St
Tel: 212-554 6000,
1-800-697 1791
[p334, A3]
www.morganshotelgroup.com

Another Ian Schrager invention, but a little less expensive than the Royalton, since rooms are smaller. Trendy and stylish, it's a favorite

due to its location (not far from the Time Warner Center). The restaurant, Cafeteria, is a magnet for hot nightlife.

The Mansfield
12 West 44th St
Tel: 212-277 8700,
1-800-255 5167
[p339, D2]
www.mansfieldhotel.com

Less expensive than the Algonquin and the Royalton hotels, which are located on the same street, this intimate, elegant boutique-style hotel mixes old world style (the building dates from 1903) with modern details. Rooms are small, but the quality and the service is high. The Mansfield is one of those places that happy, satisfied guests return to on subsequent visits to New York City.

The Paramount
235 West 46th St (at Broadway and Eighth Ave)
Tel: 212-764 5500
[p336, C1]
www.nycparamount.com

A fashion statement in the heart of Times Square. The rooms and public spaces, designed by Philippe Starck, dazzle and amaze: amenities include beds with

BELOW: parlor of the Royal Suite, the Waldorf.

headboards made of reproductions of famous paintings, a fitness club, and the intimate Library Bar. Rooms are small but well equipped.

W New York
541 Lexington Ave (at 49th St)
Tel: 212-755 1200,
1-877-946 8357
[p337, E2]
www.whotels.com
The flagship of a chain of sybaritic hotels-asspas, W's interior was designed by David Rockwell and features Zen-like rooms where grass grows on the windowsills and quilts are inscribed with New Age-y aphorisms. There's a juice bar, a spa with good fitness facilities, and a trendsetting restaurant called Heartbeat.

The Waldorf-Astoria
50th St and Park Ave
Tel: 212-355 3000,
1-800-925 3673
[p337, D2]
www.waldorfastoria.com
The most famous hotel in the city during its heyday in the 1930s and 1940s, with a pre-war panache that's been restored to something like its early glory. The look of the lobby and public spaces combines H.G. Wells's heroic con-

cept of the future with Cecil B. DeMille's view of Cleopatra's Egypt; the combination never fails to lift the spirits. Rooms have an old-world charm, and the connected Waldorf Towers is luxurious.

Budget

Comfort Inn Javits Center
442 West 36th St
Tel: 212-714 6699,
1-877-424 6423
[p336, B2]
www.comfortinn.com
Very far west, but good access to public transportation. Perfect for conventioneers.

Comfort Inn Manhattan
42 West 35th St
Tel: 212-947 0200,
1-877-424 6423
[p337, C3]
www.comfortinn.com
Near Macy's and other shopping.

Comfort Inn Midtown
129 West 46th St
Tel: 212-221 2600,
1-877-424 6423
[p337, C1]
www.comfortinn.com
Located in the heart of the Theater District and extremely reasonably priced. Rooms are fairly small, but a well-situated location makes up for it.

The Hotel at Times Square
59 West 46th St
Tel: 212-719 2300,
1-800-848 0020
[p337, D2]
www.applecorehotels.com
Reasonably priced lodging geared for the business traveler. Located between Fifth and Sixth avenues, it has a business center, a conference room, and an 80-seat meeting room. Budget to moderate rooms available.

The Pod Hotel
230 East 51st St
Tel: 212-355 0300,
1-800-742 5945
[p337, E2]
www.thepodhotel.com
The former Pickwick Arms hotel has been gutted and re-baptized The Pod. With teeny tiny rooms and hipster decor, it's perfect for budget-conscious young people looking for a modern hotel experience. All rooms have iPod docks, Wi-Fi, and flat-screen TVs.

La Quinta Manhattan
17 West 32nd St
Tel: 212-736 1600,
1-800-551 2303
[p336, C3]
www.applecorehotels.com
Like others in the Apple Core Hotels group, rates at this 182-room hotel, a short walk from Macy's and Madison Square Garden, are extremely reasonable, especially considering that the comfortable rooms come with data ports, Wi-Fi, and voicemail. There's also a lobby café with entertainment, a restaurant with room service, and – rare in this price category – an open-air rooftop bar where music

ABOVE: Midtown central.

and snacks can be enjoyed in summer, along with views of the Empire State Building.

Red Roof Inn
6 West 32nd St (between Broadway and Fifth Ave)
Tel: 212-643 7100,
1-800-755 3194
[p337, C3]
www.applecorehotels.com
Smaller rooms for singles; larger rooms for families, complimentary Continental breakfast; some rooms with microfridges. In a convenient location to all Midtown attractions.

Wellington Hotel
871 Seventh Ave (at 55th St)
Tel: 212-247 3900,
1-800-652 1212
[p334, B4]
www.wellingtonhotel.com
The location is great for Central Park, Lincoln Center, and Carnegie Hall. A reliable standby for reasonable rates. Some rooms have kitchenettes, and there are two restaurants, including Molyvos, as well as valet parking.

BELOW: observe the Empire State from your hotel.

UPPER EAST AND WEST SIDE

HOTELS

Luxury

The Carlyle
35 East 76th St
Tel: 212-744 1600,
1-888-ROSEWOOD
[p335, D2]
www.thecarlyle.com
Posh, reserved, and
serene, The Carlyle
remains one of the city's
most acclaimed luxury
hotels. The appoint-
ments are exquisite, the
furnishings antique, and
the service tends to be
on the formal side.
Home of Café Carlyle
(Woody Allen plays here)
and Bemelmans Bar, two
of the city's most endur-
ing and upscale evening
spots. The Carlyle is a
favorite with royalty.

products are Bulgari,
and the robes are
Frette. Plasma TV
screens, Wi-Fi access,
and in-room movies
from a library of
classics.
Mandarin Oriental
80 Columbus Circle
(at 60th St)
Tel: 212-805-8800,
1-866-801 8880
[p334, B3]
www.mandarinoriental.com/newyork
One of the city's newer
luxury hotels, tucked
into the aerie of the
Time Warner Center at
Columbus Circle. Spec-
tacular views of Central
Park and the city sky-
line, hushed surround-
ings, and the latest of
everything make this a
sought-after spot for
high-end visitors to NY.
Try the Thai yoga
massage in the spa.

those intent on busi-
ness or Midtown shop-
ping; there is a lovely
view of Central Park.
Rooms are large and
elegant, service is top
flight, and dining in the
Café Pierre or having
afternoon tea in the
beautiful Rotunda are
among the city's most
civilized experiences.
The Surrey
20 East 76th Street (between
Madison and Fifth aves)
Tel: 212-288-3700,
1-800-978-7739
[p335, D2]
www.thesurreyhotel.com
This Beaux Arts gem
reopened in November
2009 after a $60 million
renovation. Rooms are
as elegant as any in this
tony neighborhood, and
the hotel is home to an
impressive art collection
as well. Grab a meal at
the Café Boulud restau-
rant, just off the lobby;
in the summer, check
out the rooftop garden
for a rare experience
that is often exclusive to
locals with penthouses.
**Trump International
Hotel and Tower**
1 Central Park West
Tel: 212-299 1000,
1-888-448 7867
[p334, B3]
www.trumpintl.com
Overlooking Central Park
with sweeping views pro-
vided by floor-to-ceiling
windows, the hotel
comes complete with a
spa, fitness center, and
indoor pool. As flashy as
its namesake, the hotel
houses a celebrated
restaurant, Jean-
Georges, and has an
enormous silver globe
sculpture marking its
spot at Columbus Circle.

Moderate

Beacon Hotel
2130 Broadway (at 75th St)
Tel: 212-787 1100,
1-800-572 4969
[p334, B1]
www.beaconhotel.com
This busy and friendly
Upper West Side favorite
is adjacent to the Bea-
con Theater, a good
venue for pop groups.
Deals are to be had for
families who book rooms
with foldaway couches.
The location is a great
launch pad thanks to the
West 72nd St and Broad-
way public transportation
hub, with subway and
bus connections leading
just about anywhere.
Gracie Inn
502 East 81 St
Tel: 212-628 1700,
1-800-404 2252
[p335, E3]
www.gracieinnhotel.com

ABOVE: enjoy the view from a suite at the Carlyle.

The Franklin
164 East 87th St
Tel: 212-369 1000,
800-607 4009
[p335, E1]
www.franklinhotel.com
Once a bargain for the
Upper East Side, this
boutique hotel has been
upgraded and is now
much more expensive,
but be on the lookout
for special rates. The
atmosphere is
charming, the breakfast
delicious, the bath

The Pierre
2 East 61st St
Tel: 212-838 8000
[p334, C4]
www.tajhotels.com
Justly renowned as one
of New York's finest
hotels, with a fabulous
pedigree that goes back
to its opening in the
early 1930s. (It's now
run by the Taj Hotels luxury chain.) The hotel
was renovated in 2009,
and the location on Fifth
Avenue is perfect for

PRICE CATEGORIES

Price categories are for
a double room for one
night in the low
season. Be aware that
rates can almost
double over holidays:
Luxury: over $375
Expensive: $275–$375
Moderate: $175–$275
Budget: under $175

ABOVE: West Side dad.

Located on a quiet side street not far from Gracie Mansion (the NY mayor's residence), this is a cross between a city townhouse and a country inn. From single-room studios to a penthouse, rates depend on the length of stay.

Hotel Wales
1295 Madison Ave (at 92nd St)
Tel: 212-876 6000,
1-866-925 3746
[p335, E1]
www.waleshotel.com
The Wales was once known for its low rates and splendid views of Central Park. Today it costs more, but still

offers a great location in the upmarket Carnegie Hill neighborhood, close to Museum Mile and Central Park. You can feast on the best breakfast in NY next door at Sarabeth's Kitchen, or enjoy the light breakfast offered in the hotel's tea salon, also the setting for afternoon teas and chamber music.

The Lucerne Hotel
201 West 79th St
Tel: 212-875 1000,
1-800-492 8122
[p334, B1]
www.thelucernehotel.com
This landmark hotel is a great place to experience the trendy Upper West Side, where bars and restaurants exist side-by-side with families in brownstones conducting their daily life. The Nice Matin on the corner has become one of the area's better and more popular restaurants.

Budget

**Comfort Inn –
Central Park West**
31 West 71 St

Tel: 212-721 4770,
1-877-424 6423
[p334, B2]
www.comfortinn.com
A boutique hotel at bargain prices on the Upper West Side. It's less than a block from Central Park.

Days Hotel Broadway
215 West 94th St
Tel: 212-866 6400,
1-800-834 2972
[off map]
www.dayshotelnyc.com
Good location by subway; events at Symphony Space are usually interesting.

ABOVE: Gracie Mansion.

Hotel Excelsior
45 West 81st St
Tel: 212-362 9200
[p334, C1]
www.excelsiorhotelny.com
An old-fashioned hotel dating from the 1920s, located on a pleasant block between Central

Park West and Columbus Avenue shopping. It's convenient for museums, shopping, and Central Park.

Marrakech Hotel
2688 Broadway (at West 103rd St)
Tel: 212-222 2954
[off map]
www.marrakechhotelnyc.com
This budget hotel (formerly The Malibu) with a Moroccan-themed decor is a bargain for quality, comfort, and style. It's on the upper end of the Upper West Side, but only a quick subway ride from everywhere.

The Milburn
242 West 76th St
Tel: 212-362 1006,
1-800-833 9622
[p334, B1]
www.milburnhotel.com
The decor is basic and unimaginative, but this hotel is a good deal, with rooms equipped with kitchenettes, televisions, and internet access. There's also a fitness facility downstairs. It's located on a quiet street not far from Lincoln Center.

MURRAY HILL/GRAMERCY PARK/CHELSEA

HOTELS

Luxury

Gramercy Park Hotel
2 Lexington Ave
Tel: 212-920 3300,
1-866-784 1300
[p339, D1]
www.gramercyparkhotel.com
The now very fashionable (thanks to Ian Schrager) Gramercy has an impressive and sumptuous Baroque-inspired decor by New

York artist Julian Schnabel. A drawback: the

BELOW: the Gramercy.

rooms can be dark, and the public bar off the lobby can be very crowded at night. A plus: guests are allowed to use exclusive Gramercy Park across the road. In 2009, Danny Meyer opened trendy restaurant Maialino in the hotel.

Inn at Irving Place
56 Irving Place
Tel: 212-533 4600,
1-800-685 1447
[p339, D2]
www.innatirving.com
A pair of graceful town-

houses transformed into a facsimile of a country inn, with a cozy fireplace-lit tea salon, and 12 elegant rooms and suites featuring four-poster beds. A two-block walk from Gramercy Park and a short distance from Union Square. There's a nice little restaurant on the Inn's lower level that provides guests with room service.

The Roger Williams Hotel

131 Madison Ave (at 31st St)
Tel: 212-448 7000,
1-888-448 7788
[p337, C3]
www.rogerwilliamshotel.com

The Roger Williams has exchanged its sleek, stark style for a warmer approach, using bold colors and natural wood. The lobby has a soaring atrium, while the bedrooms are home-from-home cozy, with lots of space, thick bathrobes, down comforters, and CD players. The penthouses have lovely balconies with views of the Empire State Building.

BELOW: no squares here.

Expensive

W New York Union Square

201 Park Ave South
(at 17th St)
Tel: 212-253 9119,
1-877-946 8357

[p339, C1]
www.whotels.com

Bordering the Flatiron District, this stylish hotel has one foot in Gramercy Park and the other in a Downtown "attitude." Everything here is top-of-the-line, including the under-bar lounge and Olives restaurant.

Moderate

Affinia Shelburne

303 Lexington Ave (at 37th St)
Tel: 212-689 5200,
1-866-246 2203
[p337, D3]
www.affinia.com/nyc-hotel/
Shelburne-Murray-Hill

Affordable prices for large or small suites with kitchen facilities in a pleasant hotel – with the added bonus of a rooftop bar and garden. Good value for families.

Jolly Madison Towers Hotel

22 East 38th St
Tel: 212-802 0600
[p337, D3]
www.jollymadison.com

Renovated with a European flair, this large hotel offers special rates throughout the year, making it an affordable option compared to other hotels of its standing nearby.

Morgans

237 Madison Ave (at 37th St)
Tel: 212-686 0300,
1-800-697 1791
[p337, D3]
www.morganshotel.com

The original brainchild of Ian Schrager and the late Steve Rubell, and, surprisingly for New York, still one of the most fashionable temporary addresses in Manhattan; an ultra-modern enclave for hip movie stars and other

ABOVE: the Jade Bar at the Gramercy Park Hotel.

millionaires. The decor's original stark, dramatic grays have been replaced by warmer tones, but there's still a minimalist ambience. Service is known to be extraordinary.

Budget

The Chelsea Hotel

222 West 23rd St
Tel: 212-243 3700
[p336, B4]
www.hotelchelsea.com

A Victorian landmark of bohemian decadence, home to beatnik poets, Warhol drag queens, Sid Vicious, and "ordinary" guests. For some, a stay at the Chelsea can be part of a ritual pilgrimage to all that is hip Downtown. Accommodations vary from a few inexpensive "student rooms" to much bigger suites. Long-stay discounts may be available; discuss at the desk.

Gershwin Hotel

7 East 27th St
Tel: 212-545 8000
[p336, C4]
www.gershwinhotel.com

An artsy hotel just north of Madison Square Park inspired by Andy Warhol and aimed at the young, fashionable, and cash-

strapped. One floor provides housing for struggling models, many rooms have bunk beds, and there are good packages for families and weekend stays. Temporary art exhibits in the lobby.

Hampton Inn Chelsea

108 West 24th St
Tel: 212-414 1000
[p336, B4]
www.hershahotels.com

Hi-tech decor sets the tone at this Chelsea spot situated at the doorstep of the gallery scene. Great location for shopping on nearby Avenue of the Americas.

Ramada Inn Eastside

161 Lexington Ave at 30th St
Tel: 212-545 1800,
1-800-625 5980
[p337, D4]
www.applecorehotels.com

A friendly, cozy, 1900s hotel. Conveniently located for Downtown and Midtown.

PRICE CATEGORIES

Price categories are for a double room for one night in the low season. Be aware that rates can almost double over holidays:
Luxury: over $375
Expensive: $275–$375
Moderate: $175–$275
Budget: under $175

GREENWICH VILLAGE/EAST VILLAGE/ SOHO & TRIBECA/LOWER MANHATTAN

Luxury

Cooper Square Hotel
25 Cooper Square (on Bowery between East 5th and East 6th sts)
Tel: 212-475 5700,
1-888-251 7979
[p339, C3]
www.thecoopersquarehotel.com
A hot hotel in a trendy part of town, the Cooper Square is a shiny new build. It has 145 rooms and Govind Armstrong's restaurant Table 8.

The Crosby Hotel
79 Crosby St (between Spring and Prince sts)
Tel: 212-226 6400
[p338, B4]
www.firmdale.com
This sleek hotel has a spectacular location in the middle of Soho. While the standard rooms may be small, the ones on upper floors have spectacular views.

Hotel Gansevoort
18 Ninth Ave at 13th St
Tel: 212-206 6700,
1-877-426 7386
[p338, A1]
www.hotelgansevoort.com
The Meatpacking District's first luxury hotel

has a huge rooftop bar and swimming pool, as well as breathtaking views of the Downtown skyline and sunsets. Bedrooms are fashionably appointed.

BELOW: Tribeca Grand.

Mercer Hotel
147 Mercer St
Tel: 212-966 6060,
1-888-918 6060
[p338, B3]
www.mercerhotel.com
In the heart of Soho, a converted 1890s landmark with 75 rooms featuring high loft ceilings, arched windows, and spacious bath facilities. Owner Andre Balazs also has Chateau Marmont in LA, plus hotels in Miami, and the clientele here is

BELOW: lobby of the Soho Grand.

similarly stylish. There is a second-floor roof garden, a library bar with 24-hour food and drink service, and the highly regarded Mercer Kitchen restaurant.

Soho Grand Hotel
310 West Broadway
Tel: 212-965 3000,
1-800-965 3000
[p338, B4]
www.sohogrand.com
A sophisticated yet totally comfortable 18-story hotel, with industrial-chic decor and stunning views. The service is excellent, and the lobby and bar are the rendezvous of choice for media types and music stars. As befits a place owned by the heir to the Hartz Mountain pet empire, pets are welcome. Exercise, grooming, and feeding services are available.

Tribeca Grand
2 Avenue of the Americas
Tel: 212-519 6600,
1-800-519 6600
[p340, B1]
www.tribecagrand.com
Cool, subtle, and modern, the Tribeca is the sister hotel to the Soho Grand, and has similar amenities. The guest rooms are welcoming and calm, while the Church Lounge is a meeting place, a cocktail bar, and a place for brunch. Wi-Fi, iPods, and Bose sound systems are just some of the tech toys in the guest rooms.

Moderate

Abingdon Guest House
21 Eighth Avenue (at West 12th and Jane sts)

Tel: 212-243 5384
[p338, B1]
www.abingdonhouse.com
It's romance on a shoe-string at this nine-room hostelry between the West Village and the Meatpacking District. Accommodation is spread between two townhouses, and each of the tiny rooms is individually decorated: some have four-posters, some fireplaces. The rooms facing Eighth Avenue can be a little noisy, so ask for the Garden Room in the back. No smoking.

Blue Moon Hotel
100 Orchard St
Tel: 212-533-9080
[p341, D1]
www.bluemoon-nyc.com
Once a run-down tenement building, now a modern hotel with a historic feel in a neighborhood famous for housing immigrants. Rooms are named after stars of the Vaudeville era such as Al Jolson and Fanny Brice, and are twice the size of an average New York hotel room.

The Hotel on Rivington
107 Rivington St
Tel: 212-475 2600
[p339, C4]
www.hotelonrivington.com

This high-design, high-end hotel towers above other buildings, making for spectacular views from the floor-to-ceiling windows of the large guest rooms. The hipster neighborhood means the hotel – and its bar and restaurant – draw the young and fashionable rather than business clients.

BELOW: Rivington style.

The Maritime Hotel
363 West 16th St (at Ninth Ave)
Tel: 212-242 4300
[p338, B1]
www.themaritimehotel.com
Located at the north end of the Meatpacking District, the hotel draws in the fashion crowd, and its outdoor cafés are a nightlife destination in warm weather. Its porthole windows and austere 1960s design make this an original – or an eyesore.

The Millennium Hilton
55 Church St
Tel: 212-693 2001,
1-800-445 8667
[p340, B2]
www1.hilton.com
Adjacent to Wall St and its "canyons" of financial movers and shakers, this Hilton hotel affords the opportunity to be near Hudson River

breezes – after being pampered by the large selection of in-house services. Rooms at the front of the hotel overlook the rebuilding on the site of the World Trade Center.

Washington Square Hotel
103 Waverly Place
Tel: 212-777 9515,
1-800-222 0418
[p338, B2]
www.washingtonsquarehotel.com
Once a seedy hotel where musicians and writers penned classics (Papa John of the Mamas and the Papas wrote *California Dreamin'* here in the 1960s), Washington Square has been renovated, but hasn't lost its Greenwich Village charm.

Budget

Best Western Seaport Inn
33 Peck Slip
Tel: 212-766 6600,
1-800-HOTEL-NY
[p340, B3]
www.bestwestern.com/seaportinn
A block from South Street Seaport, this 19th-century warehouse has 72 rooms featuring Federal-era antiques and amenities like DVD players and mini-fridges. Some rooms have Jacuzzis and/or terraces with views of Brooklyn Bridge.

Holiday Inn Downtown
138 Lafayette St
Tel: 212-966 8898,
1-888-HOLIDAY
[p338, B4]
www.holidayinn.com
In a renovated historic building, this hotel right on the edge of Chinatown is much nicer than you might expect from an international chain hotel group.

ABOVE: Downtown deliberations at the Tribeca Grand.

The Jane
113 Jane Street at West St
Tel: 212-929 0060
[p338, A1]
www.thejanenyc.com
This inexpensive far West Village spot looks out over the Hudson River and also has rooms with shared bathrooms, and some with bunk beds.

The Larchmont
27 West 11th Street
(at 5th and 6th aves)
Tel: 212-989-9333
[p338, C2]
www.larchmonthotel.com
Located on a picturesque street of upscale 19th-century townhouses in Greenwich Village, this small, basic hotel is a find – if you don't mind sharing a bathroom.

ALTERNATIVES

A Town House Stay
Tel: 212-717 7500,
1-888-701 7500
www.ancostudios.com
Not a hotel, but sublet studio accommodations for short term on the Upper East Side.

Marmara-Manhattan
301 East 94th St
Tel: 212-427-3100
www.marmara-manhattan.com
Suite stays of 30 days or more are required in

order to stay, but prices are reasonable for a room in the Upper East Side historic district.

New York also has reliable, good-value hostel-style accommodations, like the **New York International Youth Hostel** at 891 Amsterdam Ave, tel: 212-932 2300, www.hinewyork.org. The **YMCA-Vanderbilt** at 224 East 47th St, tel: 212-756 9600, www.hostelnewyork.com, is the best of four Ys in Manhattan, while the **92nd St Y de Hirsch Residence** at 1395 Lexington Ave, tel: 212-415 5650, has a 30-day minimum for furnished rooms. Details on: www.92y.org/content/de_hirsch_residence.asp. The **Brandon Residence for Women**, 340 West 85th St, tel: 212-496 6901, www.thebrandon.org, is located on a beautiful Upper West Side block, providing rooms for women on their own.

PRICE CATEGORIES

Price categories are for a double room for one night in the low season. Be aware that rates can almost double over holidays:
Luxury: over $375
Expensive: $275–$375
Moderate: $175–$275
Budget: under $175

SHOPPING

WHAT TO BUY AND WHERE

New York City is retail heaven – street after numbered street, avenue after avenue are lined with businesses selling goods of all sorts, interspersed with coffee shops, bistros, and restaurants where you can take a break during shop-'til-you-drop marathons. There are the international chain stores of course, but also plenty of independent "mom 'n pop" shops (small family businesses), high-end department stores, designer boutiques, and art galleries. There are exotic paper shops, cutting-edge furniture shops, and establishments selling only light bulbs, religious icons, buttons, or music boxes. Manhattan is the very heart of Western capitalist culture, in one of the wealthiest cities in the world – so if you can't find it in New York, it probably doesn't exist.

WHERE TO BUY

Where you go in the city depends on what you're in the market for. For different New York neighborhoods and the different types of retail items they specialize in, *see pages 60–1.*

Department Stores and Malls

Manhattan is home to many department stores. There's the mid-priced, Midtown **Macy's** running along 34th Street between Seventh Avenue and Broadway, which bills itself as "the world's largest department store," as it's really two huge buildings taking up an entire Manhattan block. Navigating the store takes some patience, but good deals and selections can be found here on clothes, home appliances, and furniture.

Catering to a similar crowd is **Lord & Taylor** farther Uptown at 424 Fifth Avenue between 38th and 39th streets. Famous **Bloomingdale's** at 1003 Third Ave at 60th St carries a more imaginative and upscale choice of clothes and household goods. (Their Soho outpost at 504 Broadway between Spring and Broome streets is smaller, sells only clothes, jewelry and accessories, and is more cutting-edge in its choice of products.)

Saks Fifth Avenue, at 611 Fifth Ave at 51st and 52nd streets, and nearby **Bergdorf Goodman**, at 754 Fifth Ave, are both beautiful upscale department stores selling mostly clothes, jewelry, accessories, and cosmetics. **Barney's** at 660 Madison Ave and 61st St is the *ne plus ultra* of Manhattan department stores, selling carefully selected high-end, high-priced quality and cutting-edge clothes, jewelry, and accessories for the most discerning and sophisticated New York shoppers.

There aren't any real malls in Manhattan, but there are a couple of enclosed areas with high-end shopping boutiques. One is the **Time Warner Center** at Columbus Circle at 57th St where Broadway and Seventh Ave converge. It's home to the cooking goods store Williams and Sonoma, and up-market designers such as Cole Haan and Coach and the jeweler Davidoff of Geneva. **Grand Central Terminal** between Park Ave and Lexington has a concourse of upscale shops (food, wine, books, clothes, and luggage) catering to commuters. Of note here is the good-quality food court in the lower level – a perfect place for a quick snack or to buy something for lunch.

Fashion

Women's Clothes

Agnès b, 1063 Madison Ave, tel: 212-570 9333; 13 East 16th St, tel: 212-741 2585.
Betsey Johnson, 138 Wooster St (and several other locations), tel: 212- 995 5048.
D&G (Dolce & Gabbana), 434 West Broadway, tel: 212-965 8000.
DKNY (Donna Karan), 655 Madison Ave, tel: 212-223 3569.
Eileen Fisher, 1039 Madison Ave, tel: 212-879 7799; 341 Columbus Ave, tel: 212-362 3000; 166 Fifth Ave, tel: 212-924 4777.
Nicole Miller, 780 Madison Ave, tel: 212-288 9779; 79 Greene St, tel: 212-219 1825.
OMO Norma Kamali, 11 West 56th St, tel: 212-957 9797.

Men's Clothes

Alfred Dunhill, 450 Fifth Ave, tel: 212-753 7500.
Brooks Brothers, 346 Madison Ave, tel: 212-682 8800; 666 Fifth Ave, tel: 212-261 9440.
J. Press, 7 East 44th St, tel: 212-687 7642; 380 Madison Ave, tel: 212-687 7642.
Paul Smith, 108 Fifth Ave, tel: 212-627 9770; 142 Greene St, tel: 646-613 3060.
Paul Stuart, 10 East 45th St, tel: 212-682 0320.
Sean, 224 Columbus Ave, tel: 212-769 1489; 132 Thompson St, tel: 212-598 5980.

Men's and Women's Clothes

A/X Armani Exchange, 645 Fifth Ave, tel: 212-980 3037; Time Warner Center at Columbus Circle, tel: 212-823 9321; 568 Broadway, tel: 212-431 6000.
Barneys New York, 660 Madison Ave, tel: 212-826 8900.
Brooks Brothers, 346 Madison Ave, tel: 212-682 8800; 666 Fifth Ave, tel: 212-261 9440.
Burberry, 9 East 57th St, tel: 212-407 7100; 131 Spring St, tel: 212-925 9300.
Calvin Klein, 654 Madison Ave,

tel: 212-292 9000; 104 Prince St, tel: 877-258 7646.
Comme des Garçons, 520 West 22nd St, tel: 212-604 9200.
Club Monaco, 160 Fifth Ave, tel: 212-352 0936; 121 Prince St, tel: 212-533 8930.
Emporio Armani, 601 Madison Ave, tel: 212-317 0800; 410 West Broadway, tel: 646-613 8099.
J. Crew, 91 Fifth Ave, tel: 212-255 4848; 99 Prince St, tel: 212-966 2739; Time Warner Center at Columbus Circle, tel: 212-823 9302.
Polo-Ralph Lauren, 650 Madison Ave, tel: 212-715 0146; 381 West Broadway, tel: 212-625 1660; 381 Bleecker St, tel: 212-645 5513.

For Kids and Teens

American Eagle Outfitters, 575 Broadway, tel: 212-941 9785; 40 West 34th St, tel: 212-947 1677.
Gap, 750 Broadway, tel: 212-674 1877; 11 Fulton St, tel: 212-374 1051, plus other locations.
Old Navy, 150 West 34th St; tel: 212-594 0049; 610 Ave of the Americas, tel: 212-645 0663; 503 Broadway at Broome St, tel: 212-226 0838.
Urban Outfitters, 2081 Broadway, tel: 212-579 3912; 374 Ave of the Americas (Sixth Ave), tel: 212-677 9350; 628 Broadway,

tel: 212-475 0009, plus other locations.

Discounted Goods

There are ways to beat the high prices in New York. Upstairs at the **Burlington Coat Factory** at 707 Sixth Ave are discounted coats. Find a great selection of discounted designer fabrics at **Mood** in the Fashion District at 225 West 37th St, or Downtown on the Lower East Side at **Joe's Fabric Warehouse** at 102 Orchard St. For discounted shoes, try the huge self-serve emporium **DSW** (Designer Shoe Warehouse) upstairs at 40 East 14th St on the south side of Union Square, or **Shoe Mania** a few doors down on at 853 Broadway. And for deals on sunglasses, handbags, and watches, and for the city's best selection of tourist T-shirts and baseball caps, try bustling **Canal Street** between Sixth Ave and the Bowery, as it skirts through Soho and Chinatown.

Other places to find designer discounts include: **Century 21**, 22 Cortlandt St, tel: 212-227 9092.
Daffy's, 125 East 57th St, tel: 212-376 4477; 462 Broadway, tel: 212-334 7444.
Filene's Basement, 620 Ave of the Americas, tel: 212-620 3100; 4 Union Sq South, tel:

WOODBURY COMMON

Woodbury Common outlet mall features 220 stores where savings are 25 to 65 percent off the original retail price. Designers include Diane Von Furstenberg, Balenciaga, Gucci, Max Mara, Burberry, Betsey Johnson, Nike, Polo Ralph Lauren, Brooks Brothers, and Versace. Buses make the one-hour journey several times a day from the Port Authority Terminal, and overnight packages are also available. For details, go to www.chelseapremiumoutlets.com.

212-358 0169; and at 2222 Broadway (79th St), tel: 212-873 8000.

Loehmann's, 101 Seventh Ave at 16th St, tel: 212-352 0856.

Vintage

Resurrection, 217 Mott Street, tel: 212-625 1374.

Tokio7, 64 East 7th Street, tel: 212-353 8443.

What Comes Around Goes Around, 351 West Broadway, tel: 212-343 1225.

Art and Antiques

There are hundreds of art galleries in New York, ranging from the major auction houses **Christie's** and **Sotheby's**, to the of-the-moment commercial galleries in the neighborhood of **Chelsea**, concentrated on 22nd, 24th, and 25th streets between Tenth and Eleventh avenues (for a detailed listing of galleries and exhibits see www.chelseaartgalleries.com). Many established galleries are found Uptown on **57th Street** near Madison and 5th avenues – the beautiful Art Deco Fuller Building at 41 East 57th St in particular is home to many prestigious galleries. Smaller spaces line the side streets of the Upper East Side off Madison Avenue above 70th St. There's still a strong presence of art dealers in **Soho** despite the gravitational pull of the commercial art world to Chelsea and other places during the past decade; the building at 560 Broadway at Prince

St houses more than a dozen small and mid-sized galleries.

There are several neighborhoods in New York where antique shops are clustered. One area is on 10th, 11th, and 12th streets between University Place and Broadway – many of these stores feature high-end Art Deco and neoclassic designs. Other reputable antique shops line this stretch of Broadway, and farther up Broadway you'll find the high-end New York shopping institution **ABC Carpet** (888 Broadway at 19th St), carrying several floors of modern and traditional antiques, along with exotic bedding, imported carpets, and home goods. Antiques can be found along 60th St between Madison and Second avenues, and a wide selection can be found at some of the city's indoor art "malls." These include the **Manhattan Arts & Antiques Center**, 1050 Second Ave at 55th and 56th sts, tel: 212-355-4400, which is full of rug galleries and

tapestry shops as well as antique stores. With the budget in mind, try the **Garage Flea Market** on weekends at 112 West 25th St, or the **Hell's Kitchen Flea Market** on weekends outdoors at 39th Street between Ninth and Tenth avenues.

Books

Barnes & Noble dominates the booksellers' market with its many superstores. **Borders** also has a commanding presence in the city. The stores of both chains tend to have cafés and book-readings. The best place for secondhand and antiquarian titles is the **Strand Book Store** at 828 Broadway at 12th St, which claims to have 2 million volumes in stock.

Some of the best independents are **Three Lives & Co.** at 154 West 10th and Waverly St, and **Biography Bookshop** at 400 Bleecker St at West 11th St, both in the West Village. There's also **Shakespeare and Co.** Uptown at 939 Lexington at 68th St (also Downtown locations), as well as the **Crawford Doyle Bookstore** at 1082 Madison Ave. For mysteries, go to **Partners & Crime** at 44 Greenwich Ave in the Village.

Electronic Goods

One of the best (and without a doubt the most entertaining) places in the city to buy cameras and photographic equipment is **B&H Photo-Video** at 420 Ninth Ave at 34th St. It's a huge, bustling store with good prices that runs like clockwork thanks to a large staff and a system of overhead bins and pulleys. The store closes according to the Hasidic calendar, so be sure to check for opening days and hours. A good bet for electronic goods of all sorts is the series of stores that make up **J&R Music World** at 23 Park Row, across from City Hall. Electronic goods can be found in small stores all over the city, especially in Midtown and near Times Square, but buyers beware: many stores

don't offer warranties and are selling you factory seconds or very slightly damaged goods that you may discover only on the airplane. That explains the prices.

To indulge in the latest iPod, be sure to visit the city's flagship **Apple Store** on 103 Prince St at Mercer in Soho; there are also other locations. Those looking to accessorize their Mac products do best at the authorized Apple dealer **Tekserve** at 119 West 23rd St at Sixth Ave in Chelsea, which sells headphones, cases, and other goodies "for the care and feeding of your iPod."

Music Stores

West 48th Street is particularly good for musical instrument stores: be sure to go to **Sam Ash**, 160 West 48th St, tel: 212-719 2299. There's also:
Guitar Center, 25 West 14th St (at 5th and 6th aves), tel: 212-463 7500.
Matt Uminov Guitars, 273 Bleecker St (at 6th and 7th aves), tel: 212-675 2157.

Other music stops
Bleecker Bob's, 118 West 3rd St, tel: 212- 475 9677. Good for rare recordings.
Colony Records, 1619 Broadway, tel: 212 265 2050. In business since 1948. CDs, DVDs, and sheet music.
House of Oldies, 35 Carmine St, tel: 212- 243 0500. Vintage vinyl in Greenwich Village.
J&R Music World, 23 Park Row, tel: 212-238 9000. Downtown near City Hall; great jazz and classical recordings.
Jazz Record Center, 236 West 26th St (8th Floor), tel: 212-675 4480. Chelsea's best for jazz.
Other Music, 15 East 4th St (between 8th and 9th sts), tel: 212-477 8150.

Sports Stores

Eastern Mountain Sports, 530 Broadway (at Spring St), tel: 212-966 8730.

Modell's (several locations), 51 East 42nd St (at Madison and Vanderbilt), tel: 212-661 4242; 1535 Third Ave at 86th St, tel: 212-996 3800.
NBA Store (National Basketball Association), 666 Fifth Ave at 52nd St, tel: 212-515 6221.
Niketown, 6 East 57th St, tel: 212-891-NIKE (6453).
Paragon Sporting Goods, 867 Broadway, tel: 212-255 8036.
Patagonia, 101 Wooster St, tel: 212-343 1776; 426 Columbus Ave, tel: 917-441 0011.
Super Runners Shop (several locations), Grand Central Terminal, tel: 646-487 1120.
Tent & Trails, 21 Park Pl (between Broadway and Church St), tel: 212-227 1760.

Toys

Babies "R" Us, 24–30 Union Square at East 16th and East 17th sts, tel: 212-798 9905.
FAO Schwarz, 767 Fifth Ave at 58th Street, tel: 212- 644 9400.
Venerable kids' store selling toys you won't find in other shops.
Toy Tokyo, 121 Second Ave at 7th St and St Mark's Pl, tel: 212-673 5424.
Toys "R" Us, 1514 Broadway at 44th St, Times Square, tel: 646-366 8800. Megastore complete with working indoor Ferris wheel.
West Side Kids, 498 Amsterdam Ave at 84th St, tel: 212-496 7282.

CLOTHES CHART

The chart listed below gives a comparison of United States, European, and United Kingdom clothing sizes. It is always a good idea, however, to try on any article before buying it, as sizes between manufacturers can vary enormously.

● **Women's Dresses/Suits**

US	Continental	UK
6	38/34N	8/30
8	40/36N	10/32
10	42/38N	12/34
12	44/40N	14/36
14	46/42N	16/38
16	48/44N	18/40

● **Women's Shoes**

US	Continental	UK
4½	36	3
5½	37	4
6½	38	5
7½	39	6
8½	40	7
9½	41	8
10½	42	9

● **Men's Suits**

US	Continental	UK
34	44	34
—	46	36
38	48	38
—	50	40
42	52	42
—	54	44
46	56	46

● **Men's Shirts**

US	Continental	UK
14	36	14
14½	37	14½
15	38	15
15½	39	15½
16	40	16
16½	41	16½
17	42	17

● **Men's Shoes**

US	Continental	UK
6½	—	6
7½	40	7
8½	41	8
9½	42	9
10½	43	10
11½	44	11

ACTIVITIES

THE ARTS, NIGHTLIFE, EVENTS, SPORTS, AND TOURS

It's just possible there may be somebody somewhere who comes to New York to sleep. But it's certainly the least likely place to choose, because in the Big Apple there's something happening 24 hours a day, 365 days a year. A calendar of events is included in the *Official NYC Guide,* published by NYC & Company Visitor Information Center, 810 Seventh Ave, New York, NY, 10019, or for more week-by-week details, check the local media and freebie listings publications. Information is also available online at www.nycgo.com.

THE ARTS

Theater

Few Broadway theaters are actually on Broadway. The alternative to Broadway is Off-Broadway, where performances scarcely differ in quality from the former category, although they are performed in smaller spaces.

The vast majority of Off-Broadway theaters, and the more experimental Off-Off-Broadway theaters, are Downtown – particularly in the East Village area. Here you'll find the influential **Public Theater**, a complex of several theaters in one building at 425 Lafayette St, tel: 212-539 8500. The **Theater for the New City** at 155 First Ave, tel: 212-254 1109 and **La MaMa**, 74A East 4th St, tel: 212-475 7710, are both nearby in the neighborhood and also show new work by experimental artists.

Interesting Off-Broadway productions can also be found around Union Square at the **Union Square Theatre**, 100 East 17th St, tel: 212-307 4100; in Soho at the **HERE Arts Center**, 145 Sixth Ave, tel: 212-352 3101; and in the West Village, at the **Lucille Lortel Theater**, 121 Christopher St, tel: 212-484 1222, and the **Cherry Lane Theater**, 38 Commerce St, tel: 212-727 3673. Near Times Square, the group of Off-Broadway theaters on West 42nd St between Ninth and Eleventh avenues are known as **Theater Row**, of which the best-known is **Playwrights Horizons**, tel: 212-564 1235. One block north, **The Westside Theatre**, 407 West 43rd St, tel: 212-239 6200, is home to new dramatic comedy. In Midtown East, **59E59**, at 59 East 59th St, tel: 212-753 5959, is a fine venue.

The *New York Times* offers good listings, as do *The New Yorker, Time Out New York,* and *New York* magazines; all are worth checking regularly. A useful source for ticket prices, availability, and/or information about current shows is the non-profit Theatre Development Fund's NYC/On Stage, at www.tdf.org.

Dance

Numerous renowned dance troupes are based in the city, including the Martha Graham Dance Company, Paul Taylor Dance Company, Alvin Ailey American Dance Theater, and the Dance Theatre of Harlem.

Performance venues vary widely but include:
Ailey Citigroup Theater, 405 West 55th St. Tel: 212-405 9000.
Brooklyn Academy of Music (BAM), 30 Lafayette Ave, Fort Greene, Brooklyn. Tel: 718-636 4100.
City Center, 131 West 55th St. Tel: 212-581 1212.
Cunningham Studio, 55 Bethune St. Tel: 212-691 9751.
Dance Theater Workshop, 219 West 19th St. Tel: 212-924 0077.

Danspace Project, St Mark's Church, Second Ave at East 10th St. Tel: 212-674 8112.
The Joyce Theater, 175 Eighth Ave. Tel: 212-691 9740.
New York City Ballet, 20 Lincoln Center. Tel: 212-870 5570.
Wave Hill, 249th St and Independence Ave, Riverdale, the Bronx. Tel: 718-549 3200. Public garden and cultural center that hosts occasional outdoor, site-specific performances.

Magazines with listings, such as the publications mentioned under "Theater", have information about dance performances, as does the Theatre Development Fund, www.tdf.org.

Concert Halls

Lincoln Center for the Performing Arts, on Broadway between 62nd and 66th streets, is the city's pre-eminent cultural center, with a total of 22 venues. It's home to America's oldest orchestra, the New York Philharmonic, which gives 200 concerts annually in **Avery Fisher Hall**, as well as touring worldwide.

Nearby is the **Alice Tully Hall** – renovated extensively in 2008, it reopened in 2009 – which houses the Center's Chamber Music Society. The New York City Opera and New York City Ballet perform at different times in the **New York State Theater**.

Also in this complex are the **Metropolitan Opera House**, home of the Metropolitan Opera Company and, in spring, the American Ballet Theater; **Frederick P. Rose Hall**, home of the prestigious **Jazz at Lincoln Center** series; the excellent **Vivian Beaumont Theater**, the **Mitzi E. Newhouse Theater**, and the **Walter Reade Theater**, where the New York Film Festival is held. Here too are the **Juilliard School**, and the **New York Public Library for the Performing Arts**, an excellent reference source for music and the arts. Tours of Lincoln Center are offered daily between 10am and 5pm; for details, see www.lincoln center.org, tel: 212-875 5000.

New York's oldest joke concerns the tourist who asks how to get to **Carnegie Hall** and is told "practice, practice." It's quicker to take the N or R subway to 57th St and walk to Seventh Ave or catch a crosstown 57th St bus to this century-old hall, where the world's greatest performers have appeared – and still do on a regular basis. For information on how to see them, call 212- 247 7800.

Venues for classical (and other) music also include **Town Hall**, 123 West 43rd St, tel: 212-840 2824; **Merkin Concert Hall**, 129 West 67th St, tel: 212-501 3330; the **Kaye Playhouse**, 695 Park Ave at 68th St, tel: 212-772 4448; **Brooklyn Center for the Performing Arts**, Brooklyn College, tel: 718-951 4600; and the **Brooklyn Academy of Music (BAM)**, 30 Lafayette Ave, Brooklyn, tel: 718-636 4100.

Opera

In addition to the performances of New York City Opera and the Metropolitan Opera at Lincoln Center, opera can be enjoyed at cozier venues, including:
DiCapo Opera Theatre, 184 East 76th St. Tel: 212-288 9438.

Contemporary Music

Apollo Theater, 253 West 125th

St. Tel: 212-531 5300.
Beacon Theatre, Broadway at 74th St. Tel: 212-465 6500.
Madison Square Garden, 4 Penn Plaza, Seventh Ave, between 31st and 33rd sts. Tel: 212-465-6741.
Radio City Music Hall, 126 Ave of the Americas at 50th St. Tel: 212-307 7171.
Symphony Space, 2537 Broadway, between 94th and 95th sts. Tel: 212-864 5400.
Town Hall, 123 West 43rd St. Tel: 212-840 2824.

Art Galleries

There are well over 400 art galleries in the Big Apple – but note that most are closed on Mondays. They're spread around various neighborhoods.

In **Midtown** along 57th St between Sixth Ave and Park Ave; on the **Upper East Side** along upper Madison Ave; in **Chelsea** (particularly around West 22nd and West 24th streets near Tenth Ave); in the **Meatpacking District** around 13th and 14th streets between Tenth Avenue and the West Side Highway; and a few remain in **Soho** (Swiss Institute of Contemporary Art; Deitch Projects; Phyllis Kind; Weinberg).

From the mid-1990s onward, most of Soho's best-known galleries either closed or moved to **Chelsea**, where the big gallery scene is happening these days. Others relocated to the more traditional 57th St or Fifth Ave/Madison Avenue area (Gagosian,

Leo Castelli), while still others fled to Brooklyn's DUMBO, Williamsburg, or Queens.

As with restaurants, stores, and clubs, galleries spring up overnight and disappear just as quickly. Art fans should consult the listings magazines, as well as the art section of the *New York Times* on Friday and Sunday. A free comprehensive monthly, *Gallery Guide*, can be picked up at various arty locations.

It's also worth checking out the following, most of which have some sort of artist participation:
A.I.R. Gallery, 111 Frost St, DUMBO, Brooklyn. A women's art collective.
Artists Space, 38 Greene St. New trends, new artists, visual screenings, and performance art.
New Museum of Contemporary Art, 235 Bowery. Video installations, sculpture, and other works in a stunning new building which is guaranteed to make the entire neighborhood reverberate.
Printed Matter, 195 Tenth Avenue. Books on, by, and for artists.
P.S.1 Contemporary Art Center, 22–25 Jackson Ave, at 46th Ave, Long Island City, Queens. Tel: 718-784 2084. Up-and-coming artists, multimedia installations, and much more. Affiliated with the Museum of Modern Art and always worth checking out.
White Columns, 320 West 13th St (entrance on Horatio St), in the West Village.

Multimedia

Performance art, multimedia presentations, and various uncategorizable events are held at spots around the city, including:
Dixon Place, 258 Bowery. Tel: 212-219 0736.
The Kitchen, 512 West 19th St. Tel: 212-255 5793.
La MaMa, 74A East 4th St. Tel: 212-475 7710.
P.S.122, 150 First Ave. Tel: 212-477 5288.
Symphony Space, 2537 Broadway (at 95th St). Tel: 212-864 5400.

NIGHTLIFE

Clubs appear and disappear in New York even more abruptly than restaurants. While flagship music venues like the Village Vanguard seem eternal, others, especially the ultra-chic dance clubs, are more ephemeral, seeming to rise and fall (or fail) literally overnight. With these clubs, it's even more important to consult up-to-date listings in publications like the *New Yorker*, *New York* magazine, *Time Out New York*, and the *Village Voice*.

The following represent a range of clubs offering various kinds of live and recorded music, and comedy, cabaret acts, and even poetry readings. Because cover charges, reservation policies, and show times vary from club to club and act to act, it's best to call and ask for specific details geared to a specific night.

Jazz

Midtown

Birdland, 315 West 44th St, www.birdlandjazz.com, tel: 212-581 3080. Elegant jazz club and restaurant. Big-name big bands and jazz greats are the norm, along with smaller well-known or up-and-coming groups holding sway from around 8.30pm. There's a second set at 11pm.

Iridium, 1650 Broadway (at 51st St), www.iridiumjazzclub.com, tel: 212-582 2121. Relocated from the Upper West Side, this club/restaurant has presented some of jazz's most gifted denizens. Definitely worth checking out, especially Monday nights, when guitar legend Les Paul is often holding court to admirers.
Swing 46, 349 West 46th St, www.swing46.com, tel: 212-262 9554. An all-swing jazz and supper club with live bands every night, and dance lessons. George Gee and his 15-piece Make Believe Ballroom Orchestra get the joint jumping whenever they appear. There's a cover charge.

Uptown

Jazz at Lincoln Center, Broadway at 60th St, www.jalc.org, tel: 212-258 9500. The Frederick P. Rose Hall must be the most lavish purpose-built jazz space in the world: as well as two concert auditoria it contains **Dizzy's Club Coca-Cola**, named for iconic jazzman John Birks "Dizzy" Gillespie, an intimate club combining breathtaking views, great food, and top jazz performers, seven nights a week – from 6pm dinner seatings to jam-packed after-hours sets. Cover charge, with student discounts at late-night sessions.
Smoke, 2751 Broadway (between 105th and 106th streets), tel: 212-864 6662. Latin jazz, jazz, blues, and soul vocalists at this Uptown haunt; no cover charge most nights.

Downtown

Blue Note, 131 West 3rd St, www.bluenotejazz.com, tel: 212-475 8592. The West Village is home to the most famous jazz clubs in the world, and first and foremost is the Blue Note, packed virtually every night for years. The reason is simple: the club presents the very best of mainstream jazz and blues, from time-honored greats to more contemporary acts. The line-up has featured such luminaries as the Modern Jazz Quartet, Etta James, Joe Williams,

Betty Carter, the Count Basie Orchestra… the list goes on and on. For die-hard fans, there's a late-night session that jams until 4am, after the last set.
The Jazz Standard, 116 East 27th St, www.jazzstandard.net, tel: 212-576 2232. Everything from duos to nine-piece bands and beyond in this basement club. There's a popular restaurant, "Blue Smoke" upstairs, but food downstairs, too. Closed Mondays.
Village Vanguard, 178 Seventh Ave South, www.villagevanguard.com, tel: 212-255 4037. Born over 70 years ago in a Greenwich Village basement, this flagship club cut its teeth helping to launch talents like Miles Davis and John Coltrane. In its adulthood, it hardly keeps up with the "vanguard" anymore, but presents the greats and near-greats of what is now the mainstream. It's also a chance to catch acts that rarely tour. The VV is a terrific evening out, but an extremely popular one – call well in advance or book online to avoid disappointment.

Rock, Dance, Blues

Midtown

B.B. King's Blues Club & Grill 237 West 42nd St, www.bbking blues.com, tel: 212-997 4144. In the heart of Times Square, the legendary bluesman's New York venture (there are others around the country, including Memphis) packs them in for the best of the biggest names in R&B. This can include the King himself, stroking the only thing that's never let him down – his guitar, Lucille.
Rodeo Bar, 375 Third Ave at East 27th St, www.rodeobar.com, tel: 212-683 6500. A kitschy Southern roadhouse theme; a loose and lanky honky-tonk atmosphere, and (sometimes) live performances by "cowboy rock" bands.
Roseland, 239 West 52nd St, www.roselandballroom.com, tel: 212-247 0200. Historically, a venue for traditional ballroom dancing; lately, also for private parties,

special events, and performances by alternative rock bands or DJ-driven dancing to classic R&B. Check the website for schedules.

Downtown

Arlene's Grocery, 95 Stanton St, between Ludlow and Orchard, www.arlenesgrocery.net, tel: 212-995 1652. A low-key, casual Lower East Side bar offering rock, folk, punk, and everything in between.
The Bitter End, 147 Bleecker St, between Thompson and Laguardia, www.bitterend.com, tel: 212-673 7030. A Greenwich Village landmark, the Bitter End books an eclectic mishmash of folk, folk rock, soft rock, blues, some comedy and cabaret… whatever. A classic example of eternal bohemianism, it's popular with young adult tourists and can be mobbed on weekends.
Fillmore New York at Irving Plaza, 17 Irving Pl, www.irvingplaza.com, tel: 212-777 6800. A renovated and relaunched hall near Union Square that's been through more than one incarnation; currently features top indie rock bands.
Joe's Pub, 425 Lafayette St, www.joespub.com, tel: 212-539 8778. Singers, performance artists, musicians: there's a mix here, by Joseph Papp's theater.
Mercury Lounge, 217 East Houston St, www.mercuryloungenyc.com, tel: 212-260 4700. Intimate Lower East Side club with excel-

lent acoustics, catering to a more sophisticated alternative music crowd than usual.
S.O.B.'s, 200 Varick St (at Houston St), www.sobs.com, tel: 212-243-4940. Funky, global jazz, lots of Brazilian beat, but runs the gamut of world and dance music.
The Village Underground, 130 West 3rd St, www.thevillageunder ground.com, tel: 212-777 7745. For night-time revelers who like all different types of music, this candlelit, intimate venue might be for you. No cover most weekdays.
Webster Hall, 125 East 11th St, www.websterhall.com, tel: 212-353 1600. Discount passes can be had by booking online for this large, always-jam-packed East Village club which attracts a young crowd. Open Wednesdays to Saturdays from 10pm, it offers all-night dance sessions for fans of everything from rock, reggae, and R&B to house, techno, and who knows; theme nights range from "runway parties" to 1960s psychedelia.

And just out of Town at:

Izod Center, The Meadowlands, East Rutherford, New Jersey, www.meadowlands.com, tel: 201-935 3900.
Nassau Coliseum, at Veterans Memorial, Uniondale, Long Island, www.nassaucoliseum.com, tel: 516-794 9303.

Comedy and Cabaret

Midtown

Carolines on Broadway, 1626 Broadway (between 49th and 50th sts), www.carolines.com, tel: 212-757 4100. A well-established restaurant and club with a roster of young comic hopefuls along with some of the biggest names in the "biz."

Don't Tell Mama, 343 West 46th St, www.donttellmamanyc.com, tel: 212-757 0788. A merry spot, long favored by a theatrical crowd. In the front there's a piano bar; the back room is non-stop cabaret, with comedians and torch singers. Leave inhibitions behind, and bring cash (no credit cards accepted).

Gotham City Comedy Club, 208 West 23rd St, www.gothamcomedyclub.com, tel: 212-367 9000. A club that runs the stand-up comedy gamut from unknown first-timers to the irrepressible and unmissable all-star acerbic wit, Jackie Mason.

The Metropolitan Room, 34 West 22nd St, www.metropolitanroom.com, tel: 212-206 0440. Sophisticated classic cabaret performers, as well as talented newcomers. An elegant yet surprisingly affordable New York night out that has a reasonable cover charge along with the usual two-drink minimum.

The Oak Room Supper Club, Algonquin Hotel, 59 West 44th St, www.algonquinhotel.com, tel: 212-840 6800. Intimate piano bar with great singers (Harry Connick Jr used to play here). It's also a chance to dress in cocktail finery. Dinner is served here, too.

Uptown

Café Carlyle, 35 East 76th St, www.thecarlyle.com, tel: 212-570 7184. In the elegant Carlyle Hotel, an upper-crusty institution of sorts for the social set. There's a hefty cover charge and a two-drink minimum. When he's in town, Woody Allen sits in with the New Orleans Jazz Band headed by Eddy Davis.

Comic Strip, 1568 Second Ave at 82nd St, www.comicstriplive.com, tel: 212-861 9386. A popular proving ground for young stand-ups, both known and unknown. Open seven days a week, with three shows on Friday and four on Saturday nights.

Feinstein's at Loews Regency, 540 Park Avenue at 61st St, http://feinsteinsattheregency.com, tel: 212-339 4095. Singer Michael Feinstein is so devoted to cabaret that he opened his own high-end club in the Regency Hotel.

Stand-Up NY, 236 West 78th St, at Broadway, www.standupny.com, tel: 212-595 0850. Small Upper West Side club that often takes the inventive approach of searches for "funniest doctor," "funniest banker," with hilarious results.

Downtown

The Comedy Cellar, 117 MacDougal St, www.comedycellar.com, tel: 212-254 3480. A cramped basement where the tables are packed so close that, even if you don't get the jokes, you may make new friends. The show starts at 9pm.

Comedy Corner, 89 MacDougal St, www.comedyvillage.com, tel: 212-777 7532. Remember *Animal House*? That's the atmosphere at this rowdy Downtown joint.

The Duplex, 61 Christopher St, www.theduplex.com, tel: 212-255 5438. A landmark of the gay West Village, attracting a friendly, mixed audience for comedy and cabaret.

Nuyorican Poets Café, 236 East 3rd St (between Aves B and C), tel: 212-780 9386. From poetry slams and hip-hop to multimedia, comedy, and music, at a cutting-edge East Village landmark.

Movies

Movie theaters are scattered all over town, with first-run films often shown at cinemas in Midtown; in the East and West 60s in multiplex film houses; on East 34th St near Third Ave; and in Greenwich Village. The city's newspapers and magazines carry complete listings, as well as, usually, the performance times.

There are at least a score of venues that are devoted to showing revival, cult, experimental, and genre films which never make the mainstream circuit. The theaters often have a neighborhood feel, and the films are subtitled.

Theaters worth checking out include the **French Institute/Alliance Française**, 22 East 60th St, tel: 212-355 6100, and the **Japan Society**, 333 East 47th St, tel: 212-832 1155, which specialize in screenings from their respective countries. Places such as **Anthology Film Archives**, 32 Second Ave, tel: 212-505 5181; **Cinema Village**, 22 East 12th St, tel: 212-924 3363; **Angelika Film Center**, 18 West Houston (at Mercer St), tel: 212-995 2000), the **Sunshine Cinema**, 143 East Houston, tel: 212-330 8182, and the **Film Forum**, 209 West Houston St, tel: 212-727 8110, all show films of an arty nature.

Independent and foreign films are a specialty at the **BAM Rose Cinemas** at the Brooklyn Academy of Music, 30 Lafayette Ave, Brooklyn, tel: 718-636 4100, and at the **Walter Reade Theater** at Lincoln Center, tel: 212-875 5600, where the annual New York Film Festival takes place.

Rarely-seen movies or obscure directors are also featured at the **Museum of the Moving Image** in Queens, tel: 718-784 0077, and at the **Museum of Modern Art**, tel: 212-708 9480.

In summer **Bryant Park**, behind the Public Library at 42nd St, hosts free outdoor film screenings; check www.bryantpark.org or tel: 212-512 5700 for current programs.

EVENTS

January

Martin Luther King Day Parade.
National Boat Show,
Javits Convention Center.
Winter Antiques Show, 7th Regiment Armory, Park Avenue.

February

Black History Month.
Chinese New Year celebrations in Chinatown (sometimes Jan).
Empire State Building Run-Up race.
Westminster Kennel Club Dog Show, Madison Square Garden.

March

The Art Show, 7th Regiment Armory, Park Avenue.
Artexpo New York, Pier 94.
Circus Animal Walk, Ringling Brothers, Barnum & Bailey Circus, Queens Midtown Tunnel.
New York City Opera (through April), Lincoln Center.
The Photography Show, 7th Regiment Armory, Park Avenue.
St Patrick's Day Parade, Fifth Avenue.
Whitney Biennial exhibition, Whitney Museum.

April

Belmont Racetrack opens.
Cherry Blossom Festival at Brooklyn Botanic Garden (sometimes May).
Dachshund Festival in Washington Square Park (also Oct).
Earth Day Celebrations.
Easter Parade on Fifth Avenue.
Greek Independence Day Parade.
Green Apple Music & Arts Festival in Central Park.
Havana New York Film Festival.
Macy's Spring Flower Show.
New York International Auto Show, Javits Convention Center.
New York Mets and **New York Yankees** baseball season begins.

May

American Ballet Theater (through July) at Lincoln Center.

June

Five Boro Bike Tour, the country's largest recreational cycling event.
Fleet Week, ship tours in Manhattan and Staten Island.
New York beaches open.
New York City Ballet (to June) at Lincoln Center.
Ninth Avenue International Food Festival.
Salute to Israel Parade, Fifth Ave.
Taste of Tribeca Food Festival.
Tribeca Film Festival (sometimes earlier).
Ukrainian Festival, 7th St and Second Avenue.
Washington Square Outdoor Art Exhibit.

June

Buskers Fare Festival, Lower Manhattan.
Central Park SummerStage shows (through Aug), Rumsey Playfield, Central Park.
Free Metropolitan Opera performances in parks of all five boroughs (through Aug).
Gay and Lesbian Pride Day Parade, Fifth Avenue.
JVC Jazz Festival throughout the city.
Mermaid Parade,
Coney Island, Brooklyn.
Midsummer Night Swing dancing at Lincoln Center (through July).
Movies Under the Stars, Bryant Park (through Aug).
Museum Mile Festival.
Puerto Rican Day Parade, Fifth Avenue.
River-to-River Festival.

July

Free New York Philharmonic concerts in major parks. Free concerts also at South Street Seaport.
Macy's Fourth of July Fireworks, East River.
Mostly Mozart Festival (to Aug) at Lincoln Center.
Museum of Modern Art Summergarden concerts.
Nathan's Hot Dog Eating Contest, Coney Island, Brooklyn.
Thunderbird American Indian Midsummer Pow Wow, three-day event at the Queens County Farm Museum.
Washington Square Music Festival, Greenwich Village.

August

The Hong Kong Dragon Boat Festival, Flushing, Queens.
New York Giants football season begins.
The New York International Fringe Festival.
Tugboat Challenge on Hudson River, sometimes early Sept.

US Open Tennis Championships, USTA National Tennis Center, Queens (through mid-Sept).

September

Broadway on Broadway, Times Square. Free live concert.
Brooklyn Book Fair, Borough Hall Plaza, Brooklyn.
Feast of San Gennaro Festival, Little Italy.
German-American Steuben Day Parade, from Alphabet City to Williamsburg, Brooklyn.
Metropolitan Opera (to April), Lincoln Center.
New York Film Festival (to Oct), Lincoln Center.
New York Philharmonic (to March), Lincoln Center.
Next Wave Festival (to Dec), Brooklyn Academy of Music (BAM).
Richmond County Fair, Historic Richmond Town, Staten Island.
UN General Assembly opens.
Washington Square Art Show.
West Indian-American Day Carnival (Labor Day), Eastern Parkway, Brooklyn.

October

American Ballet Theatre (to mid-Nov), New York City Center.
Aqueduct Race Track opens, Queens.
Atlantic Antic, Brooklyn.
Big Apple Circus (to Jan), Lincoln Center.
Columbus Day Parade, Fifth Avenue.
Halloween Parade, Greenwich Village.
Hispanic Day Parade, Fifth Avenue.
New York Rangers hockey and **New York Knicks** basketball starts, Madison Square Garden.
Pulaski Day Parade, Fifth Avenue.

November

Christmas Holiday Spectacular (to Jan), Radio City Music Hall.
Macy's Thanksgiving Day Parade.
New York City Ballet (through Feb), Lincoln Center.

New York City Marathon, Staten Island to Central Park.
New York Comedy Festival.
The Nutcracker (running to January), New York City Ballet at the Lincoln Center.
Veterans' Day Parade, Fifth Avenue.

December

Lighting of Christmas Tree, Rockefeller Center.
Lighting of Giant Chanukah Menorah, Fifth Avenue.
New Year's Eve Celebration in Times Square.
New Year's Eve Midnight Run, Central Park.

SPORTS

Participant Sports

New York offers a huge array of recreational facilities. Many are found in the city's **parks** – including Central Park, where roads are closed to traffic on summer weekends for the benefit of bicyclists and in-line skaters. For general information call the Department of Parks and Recreation at 311 (within New York City) or 212-NEW YORK (from elsewhere) – or visit www.nycgovparks.org.

Tennis can be played in Central Park and various other parks. The city's largest public tennis facility is the USTA National Tennis Center in

Queens, home of the US Open, tel: 718-760 6200.

Rowboats can be rented at the Central Park Lake boathouse (and at Prospect Park in Brooklyn, Kissena Park in Queens, and Van Cortlandt Park in the Bronx), as can bicycles.

Ice skating is available in winter at both Wollman (tel: 212-439 6900) and Lasker Rinks in Central Park, and also at Rockefeller Center, tel: 212-332 7654, and year-round at Sky Rink, Pier 61 at the Hudson River, tel: 212-336 6100, part of Chelsea Piers.

Basketball courts and **baseball** and **softball** diamonds are located in city parks, as are miles of **jogging** tracks and trails. (The New York Road Runners Club maintains a running center, tel: 212-860 4455.)

You'll find public **golf courses** at Pelham Bay Park, Van Cortlandt Park (both in the Bronx), and at Latourette Park in Staten Island, among other parks in the Outer Boroughs.

For numerous sports in one place, try the **Chelsea Piers Sports and Entertainment Complex** (www.chelseapiers.com, tel: 212- 336 6666), which stretches along the Hudson River between 17th and 23rd streets. Facilities include a multi-tiered **golf driving range**, **boating, bowling, horseback riding**, and **in-line skating**; day passes are occasionally available at the sports/fitness center, which has an Olympic-size swimming pool, a running track, and a **rock-climbing wall**.

Spectator Sports

The city is very proud of its teams, the **New York Yankees** and the **New York Mets**, who play **baseball** from April to October at Yankee Stadium in the Bronx, tel: 718-293 6000, and Citi Field in Flushing, tel: 718-507 TIXX. Both had new stadiums built in 2009. A pair of new Class-A minor league baseball teams are also attracting enthusiastic local crowds: Mets' affiliate the **Brooklyn Cyclones**, at Key Span Park in Brooklyn (tel: 718-449 8497), and the **Staten Island Yankees**, at Richmond County Ballpark at St George.

The **New York Knicks** (tel: 212-465 6741) play **basketball** between October and May at Madison Square Garden, where the **New York Liberty** (tel: 212-564-9622) women's team can be seen in summer. College team schedules are listed in the daily papers.

The **ice hockey** season runs from October to April, with the **New York Rangers** at Madison Square Garden (tel: 212-465 4459) and the **Islanders** playing at Nassau Coliseum on Long Island (tel: 516-501 6700). Madison Square Garden is also the main site for important events in **boxing** and (indoor) **tennis**, although the US Open is at the **National Tennis Center** in Flushing Meadows Corona Park, Queens (tel: 718-760 6200), in late August.

The **football** season starts in late August and lasts through December or January, with both the **New York Giants** (tel: 201-935 8111) and **New York Jets** (tel: 800-469 JETS) playing at Giants Stadium in The Meadowlands, East Rutherford, NJ, until the Jets' new stadium is ready in late 2010.

Soccer takes place between March and September, with the New York Red Bulls currently playing matches at The Meadowlands (tel: 877-RBSOCCER), where their new stadium – Red Bull Arena – opened in early 2010. **Cricket** matches are held on summer Sundays in Van Cortlandt Park in the Bronx, as well as on Randall's Island in the East River and at various parks in Brooklyn and Staten Island.

The closest thoroughbred **horse racing** is at **Belmont Park** in Elmont, Long Island (Long Island Railroad from Pennsylvania Station), tel: 516-488 6000.

TOURS

Sightseeing Tours

Among the dozens of operators offering sightseeing trips around the city, one of the most popular is **Gray Line New York**, www.grayline.com, tel: 800-669 0051, which features double-decker buses with hop-on, hop-off itineraries.

Manhattan is, of course, an island, so there's a big choice of boat tours, including: **Circle Line**, www.circleline.com, tel: 212-563 3200, which operates boat trips around Manhattan and harbor cruises from South Street Seaport; **NY Waterway**, www.nywaterway.com, tel: 1-800-533 3779, featuring harbor cruises, entertainment cruises, and boat trips to Yankee Stadium in the baseball season; **Shearwater Sailing**, www.shearwatersailing.com, tel: 212-619 0907, which cruises near the Statue of Liberty in a beautiful 1929 double-masted schooner; and **Spirit Cruises**, www.spiritcitycruises.com, tel: 866-483 3866, which offers luxury cruises with dinner and entertainment afloat.

Other interesting or off-the-beaten track options include:
Art Horizons International, www.art-horizons.com, tel: 212-969 9410. Visits to galleries, museums and artists' studio lofts.
Big Onion Walking Tours, www.bigonion.com, tel: 212-439 1090. Historic, ethnic neighborhood tours with zing.
Central Park Bicycle Tours, www.centralparkbiketour.com, tel: 212-541 8759. Guided bike tours, including rentals, through the park.
Central Park Carriage Rides, www.centralparkcarriages.com, tel: 212-736 0680.
Central Park Conservancy, www.centralparknyc.org, tel: 212-310 6600. Free walking tours. Also **Urban Park Rangers Tours**, tel: 311 or 212-NEW YORK.
Elegant Tightwad Shopping Tours, www.theeleganttightwad.com, tel: 631-841 2111. Designer showroom tours, sample sales.
Harlem Heritage Tours, www.harlemheritage.com, tel: 212-280 7888. Walk around the streets with a local resident.
Harlem Spirituals/New York Visions, www.harlemspirituals.com, tel: 212-391 0900. Gospel tours.
Hush Tours, www.hushtours.com, tel: 212-714 3527. Hip-hop tours.
Lower East Side Tenement Museum, www.tenement.org, tel: 212-431 0233, offers walking tours, led by local historians.
Municipal Art Society, www.mas.org, tel: 212-935 3960. Architectural walks.
Museum of Chinese in the Americas, www.mocanyc.org, tel: 212-619 4785; another walking tour of the immigrant experience.
On Location Tours, www.screentours.com, tel: 212-209 3370. See the locations of *Sex and the City*, *The Sopranos*, *Gossip Girl*, and various movies that have been filmed in NY.
Radio City Music Hall, www.radiocity.com, tel: 212-307 7171. Go behind the gold curtain to find out who plays the gigantic Wurlitzers.

TRANSPORTATION

ACCOMMODATIONS

SHOPPING

ACTIVITIES

A–Z

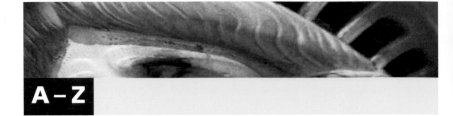

A–Z

AN ALPHABETICAL SUMMARY OF PRACTICAL INFORMATION

A Admission Fees 318
B Budgeting for Your Trip 318
Business Hours 318
C Children 319
Climate & Clothes 319
Consulates & UN Missions 319
Crime & Safety 319
Customs Regulations 320
D Disabled Travelers 320
E Electricity 320

Emergency Telephone Numbers 320
Entry Regulations 320
G Gay & Lesbian Travelers 320
H Health & Medical Care 320
I Internet & Websites 320
City Websites 320
L Lost Property 321
M Maps 321
Media 321
How to See a TV Show 321
Money 322

N Non-Emergency 322
P Postal Services 323
Public Holidays 322
R Religion 323
S Smoking 323
T Telephone & Faxes 323
Time Zone 323
Tipping 323
Tourist Information Offices 323
W Weights & Measures 324
What to Read 324

A dmission Fees

Fees to attractions range from about $10–15. A few museums, like the Met or MoMA, cost more. At some public museums, the entry fee is not strictly obligatory, but a "suggested donation." On Thursdays or Fridays after 4pm, some museums are free.

B udgeting for Your Trip

Your biggest expense will be your hotel room. Expect to pay $199 for a room at a budget hotel in low season; $325 for a moderate establishment; and $525 at a deluxe hotel. It's possible to eat out cheaply in New York, with main

courses ranging from $12 at the lower end to $16 at a moderate place and $28 at an expensive venue. The average cost of a beer is $4 and a glass of wine $8 – and remember to tip $1 per drink. A taxi from JFK Airport to Manhattan costs $45, plus tip and tolls. A single bus or subway ride is $2.25 and a one-day unlimited MetroCard pass will set you back $8.25.

Business Hours

New Yorkers work long and hard in a city where this is generally seen to be an advantage. Normal business hours are 9am–5/6pm, but stores, particularly, tend to stay open much later. They can

get crowded at lunchtime. Some shops also open on Sundays. Banking hours are nominally 9am–5pm but increasingly, banks are opening as early as 8am and staying open until early evening. ATM machines are everywhere. **Port Authority Bus Terminal** (Eighth Ave at 42nd St) stays open 24 hrs: tel: 212-564 8484. **Penn Station** (Seventh Ave at 32nd St) is open 24 hrs. Long

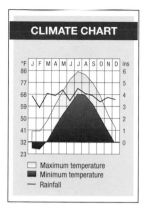

CLIMATE CHART

Maximum temperature
Minimum temperature
— Rainfall

Island Railroad Information: tel: 718-217 5477; New Jersey Transit Info: tel: 973-275-5555.
Grand Central Terminal closes at 1.30am. MetroNorth Information: tel: 212-532 4900.

C hildren

At museums you'll find strollers, kid-friendly exhibits, and discounts galore. Navigating the stairs in the subway system with strollers and small children can be tricky, so splurge on taxis when possible.

Climate & Clothes

New York has four distinct seasons, and is at its best during the spring and fall months. Summer temperatures hover in the mid-70s to mid-80s°F (24–29°C), although heatwaves where the mercury rises to 100°F (37.8°C) may occur, and uncomfortable humidity is often the rule, espe-

cially in July and August.
September and October sometimes usher in a balmy, dry "Indian summer" that fills parks and office plazas with sun worshipers. Winter temperatures can drop below 10 or 15°F (–12 or –9°C), with the average for January closer to 32°F (0°C). The average annual rainfall is 44ins (112cm) and the average snowfall is 29ins (74cm). Raincoats are a good idea year-round.
Except for casual wandering, dress tends to be a little bit more formal compared to other US cities. It's a good idea to ask about proper dress codes for restaurants, clubs, etc.

Crime & Safety

Despite its post 9/11 reputation as "caring, sharing New York," parts of the city are still unsafe, and visitors should not be lulled into any false sense of security. Adopt the typical New Yorker's guise of looking street-smart and aware at all times.
Ostentatious displays of jewelry or wealth invite muggers; excursions into deserted areas at night (such as Central Park or Battery Park) are equally unwise. Lock your hotel door even when you are inside, and travel to places like Harlem in a group. And even though Times Square has thrown off its seedy mantle, the streets around it attract pickpockets.
The subways are much safer than they were, but when traveling alone at night, stay on alert. Once through the turnstile, stay within sight of the ticket booth. **In emer-**

gencies, dial **911** for police, fire, or ambulance.

Police Precincts

Midtown
North, 306 West 54th St.
Tel: 212-760 8300.
South, 357 West 35th St.
Tel: 212-239 9811.
Uptown
19th, 153 East 67th St.
Tel: 212-452 0600.
20th, 120 West 82nd St.
Tel: 212-580 6411.
Central Park, Transverse Road at 86th St. Tel: 212-570 4820.
23rd, 162 East 102nd St.
Tel: 212-860 6411.
24th, 151 West 100th St.
Tel: 212-678 1811.
25th, 120 East 119th St.
Tel: 212-860 6511.
26th, 520 West 126th St.
Tel: 212-678 1311.
28th, 2271–89 Eighth Ave (near 123rd St). Tel: 212-678 1611.
30th, 451 West 151st St.
Tel: 212-690 8811.
32nd, 250 West 135th St.
Tel: 212-690 6311.
33rd, 2207 Amsterdam Ave.
Tel: 212-927 3200.
34th, 4295 Broadway.
Tel: 212-927 9711.

Downtown
1st, 16 Ericsson Place (West Canal St). Tel: 212-334 0611.
5th, 19 Elizabeth St (Chinatown). Tel: 212-334 0711.
6th, 233 West 10th St (Greenwich Village). Tel: 212-741 4811.
7th, 19 Pitt St (Lower East Side). Tel: 212-477 7311.
9th, 321 East 5th St.
Tel: 212-477 7811.
10th, 230 West 20th St.
Tel: 212-741 8211.
13th, 230 East 21st St.
Tel: 212-477 7411.

CONSULATES & UN MISSIONS

Australian Mission to the UN
150 East 42nd Street
Tel: 212-351 6600
British Consulate-General
845 Third Avenue
Tel: 212-745 0200
Consulate-General of Canada
1251 Avenue of the Americas
Tel: 212-596 1650

Consulate General of Ireland
345 Park Avenue
Tel: 212-319 2555
New Zealand Mission to the UN
600 Third Avenue
Tel: 212-826 1960
South African Consulate-General
333 East 38th Street
Tel: 212-213 4880

TRANSPORTATION
ACCOMMODATIONS
SHOPPING
ACTIVITIES
A – Z

17th, 167 East 51st St.
Tel: 212-826 3211.

Customs Regulations

For a breakdown of up-to-date US Customs and Border Protection regulations, visit www.cbp.gov. Tel: 800-BE ALERT.

Disabled Travelers

Disabled travelers can obtain information about rights and special facilities from the **Mayor's Office for People with Disabilities**, 100 Gold St, 2nd Floor, New York, NY 10038. Tel: 212-788 2830.

Electricity

The US uses an 110 volt current. Electrical adapters are available in hardware and appliance stores and some drugstores.

Emergency Telephone Numbers

For all emergencies: police, fire ambulance, dial **911**. For non-emergency assistance, dial **311**.

Entry Regulations

Due to increased security, the precise regulations for entry to the United States change often, and vary for citizens of different countries. It's a good idea to check on the current situation before you travel, on http://travel.state.gov or via a US Embassy or Consulate in your home country. And remember the US has strict rules on liquids in carry-on luggage, so check with your airline before you fly.

Gay & Lesbian Travelers

The Gay, Lesbian, Bisexual, and Transgender National Hotline, tel: 888-843 4564, provides information about all aspects of gay life. Locally, **GMHC** (Gay Men's Health Crisis), 119 West 24th St, offers walk-in counseling and a useful hotline, tel: 212-807

6655, and website: www.gmhc.org. The **Lesbian, Gay, Bisexual, and Transgender Community Center**, 208 West 13th St, tel: 212-620 7310, is another helpful local organization. Their website is www.gaycenter.org.

Health & Medical Care

Medical services are extremely expensive; always travel with comprehensive travel insurance to cover any emergencies. **New York House Call Physicians**, tel: 646-957 5444, make house calls on a non-emergency basis, for $400 and up. Their website is www.doctorinthefamily.com.

To find a local pharmacy, go to www.cvs.com or www.duanereade.com. Both drugstores have many locations throughout the city, with varying hours.

Hospitals with Emergency Rooms

Midtown/Downtown
Bellevue Hospital, First Ave and East 27th St. Tel: 212-562 1000.
Beth Israel Medical Center, First Ave at East 16th St. Tel: 212-420 2000.
NYU Langone Medical Center, 550 First Ave at 33rd St. Tel: 212-263 7300.
St Luke's-Roosevelt Hospital, 59th St at Tenth Ave. Tel: 212-523 4000.
St Vincent's Hospital, 153 West 11th St at Sixth and Seventh aves. Tel: 212-604 7000.
Uptown
New York-Presbyterian Hospital/

Columbia University Medical Center, 630 West 168th St. Tel: 212-305 2500.
Lenox Hill Hospital, 100 East 77th St at Park Ave. Tel: 212-434 2000.
Mount Sinai Hospital, Fifth Ave and East 100th St. Tel: 212-241 6500.
New York-Presbyterian Hospital/Weill Cornell Medical Center, 525 East 68th St. Tel: 212-746 5454.

Internet & Websites

Wi-Fi (wireless internet facility) is available in Union Square and other parts of Manhattan, including at least 10 city parks. More and more hotels provide free Wi-Fi, too. For the latest update check out www.wififreespot.com. Email can be sent from most branches of FedEx-Kinko's copy shops or from branches of the New York Public Library, including the **Science, Industry, and Business Library**, 188 Madison Ave at 34th St, tel: 212-592 7000.

Internet cafés are rarer than in years past, since so many people

CITY WEBSITES

Several boroughs have their own websites, listed here under "Tourist Information." Other websites that provide helpful information include:
www.newyork.citysearch.com for listings and reviews of current arts and entertainment events, and restaurants and shopping. It's excellent for links to every conceivable aspect of New York City.
www.nyc.gov, the official site of the City of New York, contains news items, mayoral updates, city agency information, and parking regulations.
www.nycgo.com, the NYC & Co. Visitor Information site, which also has useful links.
www.nypl.org is where you'll find everything you ever wanted to know about the New York Public Library. There's also an online information service.

TRANSPORTATION ACCOMMODATIONS SHOPPING ACTIVITIES A – Z

use their phones and laptops to access the internet. Still, you can find them if you look. Check out the **Cybercafe**, 250 West 49th St, tel: 212-333 4109. For more locations, go to www.easyinternet cafe.com.

Lost Property

The chances of retrieving lost property are low, but items may have been turned in to the nearest police precinct. To inquire about items left on public transportation (**subway** and **bus**), tel: 212-712 4500, open Mon, Tue, Fri 8am–12pm, Wed, Thur 11am–6.30pm. Or call **311** *(see Non-Emergency Services, page 322).*

Lost or Stolen Credit Cards

All 1-800 calls are free of charge:
American Express, tel: 1-800-528 4800.
Diners Club, tel: 1-800-234 6377.
MasterCard, tel: 1-800-826 2181.
Visa, tel: 1-800-847 2911.

Maps

The official **NYC & Co.** provides good maps at its visitors' center (810 Seventh Avenue between 52nd and 53rd streets) and online through its website: www.nycgo.com. Subway and bus maps are available at subway station booths, or from the New York City Transit Authority booth in Grand Central and the Long Island Rail Road information booth in Penn Station, as well as the MTA booth at the **Times Square Visitors' Center**. Maps may also be obtained by calling 718-330 3322 or online through the Metropolitan Transit Authority website: www.mta.info.

The *Insight Fleximap to New York City* is laminated and immensely durable. The most detailed street map is a book called *Manhattan Block by Block*, published by Tauranac Maps.

Media

Print

The internationally known *New York Times* is the paper of choice

---

HOW TO SEE A TELEVISION SHOW

With advance planning, it's possible to join the audience of a New York-based TV show. For more details, go to the NYC & Co. Information Center or www.nycgo.com. Here's a selection:
● **The Daily Show with Jon Stewart**
This very popular satirical show has been so overwhelmed by ticket requests that the producers occasionally have to stop offering them to the public. Tickets can only be ordered online, at www.thedailyshow.com. Audience members must be 18 or older. Mon–Thur at Comedy Central Studios, 733 11th Ave; doors open at 5.45pm.
● **Late Show with David Letterman**
Tapings of this popular talk show are Mon–Thur at 5.30pm. Audience members must be 18 or older; proper ID required. Tickets can be applied for online, or by visiting the theater. Standby tickets may be available if you're at the box office by 9.30am on the day of broadcasting. Ed Sullivan Theater, 1697 Broadway, New York, NY 10019. Tel: 212-975 5853. www.lateshowaudience.com.
● **Late Night with Jimmy Fallon**
Tapings Tue–Fri at 5.30pm, and audience members must be at least 16. Reserved tickets are only available by calling 212-664 3056, for a maximum of four. Standby tickets are available on the morning of the show – arrive by 9am at NBC Studios on the 49th Street side of 30 Rockefeller Plaza. More info at www.latenightwithjimmyfallon.com.
● **NBC Today Show Through the Window**
Tapings of this show are Mon–Fri from 7–10am. An audience is encouraged to watch from the streets outside, but you must get there by dawn. The best place to stand is the southeastern corner. Go to kiosks at 30 Rockefeller Plaza for information.
● **Saturday Night Live**
Tapings of this venerable comedy show are on Saturday, from 11.30pm–1am. Audience members must be 16 or older. A ticket lottery is held each August. Only one email per person will be accepted, for two tickets each. Standby tickets are given out at 7am on the 49th St entrance for the dress rehearsal and the live show, but do not guarantee admission. Email to: www.snl tickets@nbcuni.com. *NBC Tickets*, tel: 212-664 3056; www.nbc.com.
● **NBC Studio Tour**
At least to see the studios of *Saturday Night Live* and other shows (as long as they're not taping), tag along on the NBC Studio Tour. Attractions include blue-screens to let you "join" presenters on the sets. Tours start at the NBC Experience Store at 30 Rockefeller Plaza, every 15 or 30 minutes, 7 days a week (www.nbc.com/tickets, tel: 212-664 3700; charge).

for most well-informed readers, with its bulky Sunday edition listing virtually everything of consequence. On a daily basis, two tabloids compete for the rest of the audience: the *New York Post*, famed for its garish headlines and downmarket appeal; and the *Daily News*. There are two "commuter" dailies distributed free in the mornings: *AM New York* and *New York Metro*. The best sources of information for what's on in the city are the magazines *New York*, the *New Yorker*, and *Time Out New York*, but there are also two useful free weeklies, the *Village Voice* and the *New York Press*.

Television

The three major networks – all with NY headquarters – are **ABC**, 77 West 66th St, tel: 212-456 7777; **CBS**, 51 West 52nd St, tel: 212-975 4321; and **NBC**, 30 Rockefeller Plaza, tel: 212- 664 4444. **Fox Broadcasting** has national offices at 1211 Ave of the Americas, tel: 212-852 7111, and **CNN** has moved into offices at the Time Warner Center at Columbus Circle, tel: 866-426 6692.

The **Public Broadcasting System** (**PBS**) can be found on channels 13 and 21 on the VHF band (for those without cable). Other local stations are affiliated with the **Fox** (Channel 5), **UPN** (9), and **WB** (11) networks. These channels broadcast nationally aired shows as well as local programming. In addition, there are half a dozen UHF stations

which broadcast in Spanish and other languages.

Cable companies in the city offer 70 or more basic cable and movie channels, although the exact number differs from borough to borough and depending on whether there is a satellite connection, which provides hundreds of channels.

Most hotels offer cable in their guest rooms in addition to – for a fee – up-to-the-minute Hollywood movies.

Money

Most ATMs will charge a fee for withdrawing cash. Credit cards are accepted almost everywhere in the city, although not all cards are accepted at all places.

There are numerous outlets for exchanging currency in New York, but a few banks still charge a fee to cash traveler's checks, and a passport must be produced. Dollar traveler's checks are accepted in many hotels, restaurants, and stores in the US, so long as they are accompanied by proper identification, so it's generally easier just to use them as cash rather than change them at a bank.

Travelex, tel: 1-800-287 7362; 1590 Broadway at 48th St, tel: 212-265 6063; 1271 Broadway at 32nd St, tel: 212-679 4365; and 30 Vesey St, tel: 212-227 8156. All Travelex offices sell and cash traveler's checks as well as exchange money, as do the many

American Express offices around town, such as 374 Park Ave, tel: 212-421 8240.
Citibank offers exchange facilities at most of its 200 or so branches around the five boroughs. Tel: 800-285 3000.

N on-Emergency Services

New York has a three-digit number that can be dialed for information on a range of services, whether the caller is a New York resident or just a visitor. Calls to **311** are answered by a live operator, 24 hours a day, seven days a week, and information is provided in over 170 languages.

The purpose of a call can be as wide-ranging as tourist destination inquiries, making a complaint about noise or a taxi; finding out about the tax-free shopping weeks held several times a year, or locat-

PUBLIC HOLIDAYS

As with many other countries in the world, the United States has gradually shifted most of its public holidays to the Monday closest to the actual dates, thereby creating a number of three-day weekends. Holidays that are celebrated no matter what day they fall are:
New Year's Day (January 1).
Independence Day (July 4).
Veterans' Day (November 11).
Christmas Day (December 25).

Other holidays are:
Martin Luther King Jr Day (third Mon in Jan).
President's Day commemorating Lincoln and Washington (third Mon in Feb).
Memorial Day (last Mon in May).
Labor Day (first Mon in Sept).
Columbus Day (second Mon in Oct).
Election Day (first Tue in Nov, every four years).
Thanksgiving (fourth Thur in Nov).

ing lost and found items on public transportation.

Postal Services

Manhattan's main post office on Eighth Ave between 31st and 33rd streets is open 24 hours a day for stamps, express mail, and certified mail. To find out where post office branches are located throughout the five boroughs, and to inquire about mailing rates and methods, call the Postal Service Consumer Hotline: 1-800-275 8777, or go to www.usps.gov.

Religion

New York is approximately 70 percent Christian, 11 percent Jewish, 1.5 percent Muslim, 7.4 percent agnostic, with Buddhists, Hindus, and others also represented. Around 6,000 churches, temples, and mosques are scattered throughout the five boroughs. Consult the *Yellow Pages* or ask at the desk of your hotel for the nearest place of worship.

Smoking

There is now a no-smoking law in effect in virtually all New York City bars, restaurants, offices, and public buildings. A few hotels still have rooms for smokers; ask when booking.

Telephone & Faxes

Most Manhattan numbers have the **212** area code, which has

Tipping

Most New Yorkers in the service industries (restaurants, hotels, transportation) regard tips as a God-given right, not just a pleasant gratuity. The fact is, many people rely on tips to make up for what are often poor hourly salaries. Therefore, unless service is truly horrendous, you can figure on tipping everyone from bellmen and porters (usually $1 a bag; or $2 if only one bag); to hotel doormen ($1 if they hail you a cab); hotel maids ($1–2 a day, left in your room when you check out), restroom attendants (at least 50¢) and room-service waiters (approximately 15 percent of the bill unless already added on). In restaurants, the best way to figure out the tip is to double the tax (which adds up to a little more than 16 percent; add or subtract a dollar or two depending on how good or bad the service was). In taxis, tip as much as 15 percent of the total fare, with a $1 minimum.

been in existence for decades; newer places might use the **646** or **917** prefix. Brooklyn, Queens, Staten Island, and Bronx numbers are prefixed by **718** (or the newer **347** or **917**). Regardless of the number you are calling *from*, the area code of the number being called must now be used: eg, in a 212 area, calling another 212 number, the 212 prefix must still be used, preceded by **1**.

Toll-free calls are prefixed by **800**, **888**, **866**, or **877**; remember to dial **1** first when calling all these numbers.

Public phones can be found in various centers. **Telephone dialing cards**, available from newsstands and corner stores, are an inexpensive way to make calls, especially international ones.

Cellphones are ubiquitous. Anyone staying here for more

than a few days, or who makes repeated trips to NY, might consider buying a local cellphone: prices are cheap compared to those in many cities.

Most major hotels offer **fax services**. Faxes can also be sent from many copy and printing shops, including all branches of FedEx-Kinko's (see *Yellow Pages* for locations), which also offer Internet and email access.

Useful Numbers

- **International calls**, dial: 011 (the international access code), then the country code, city code, and local number.
- **Directory help**, including toll-free numbers, dial: 555-1212 preceded by the area code you are calling from.
- **Wrong number refunds**, dial: 211.
- **Emergencies**, *see page 320.*

Time Zone

New York is in the Eastern Standard Time zone (EST). This is five hours behind London, one hour ahead of Chicago, and three hours ahead of California.

Tourist Information Offices

NYC & Company Visitor Information Center, 810 Seventh Ave (at 52nd & 53rd sts), New York, NY 10019, www.nycgo.com, tel: 212-484 1222, has an abundance of maps, brochures, and information about special hotel packages and discounts at various attractions.

They also publish the *Official NYC Guide*, a listing of activities, hotels, tours, and restaurants. NYC & Co. are able to provide information online, by mail, over the phone, or you can drop by the information center in person (Mon–Fri 8.30am–6pm, Sat–Sun 9am–5pm).

There are also official information kiosks in Harlem and Chinatown, and a **NYC Heritage Tourism Center** at the southwestern tip of City Hall Park, on

TRANSPORTATION · ACCOMMODATIONS · SHOPPING · ACTIVITIES · A–Z

Broadway between Vesey and Barclay sts. www.nyc.gov is another useful website for information.
Times Square Information Center is at the Embassy Theater, Seventh Ave between 46th and 47th sts, tel: 212-869 1890. It's a source of citywide info, with a ticket counter for shows, email facilities, and ATMs. It's open daily 8am–8pm, with free walking tours.
Greater Harlem Chamber of Commerce, 200A West 136th St, New York, NY 10030, www.harlemdiscover.com, tel: 212-862 7200. Information on tours, events, and landmarks in Harlem. There's also an information kiosk at 163 West 125th St.
Bronx Tourism Council, 851 Grand Concourse, Bronx NY 10451, www.ilovethebronx.com, tel: 718-590-BRONX. Information about art, music, and other events.
Brooklyn Tourism & Visitors Center, 209 Joralemon St, Brooklyn, NY 11201, www.visitbrooklyn.org, tel: 718-802 3846. Information on culture, shopping, history, parks, events, and historic sites.
Queens Tourism Council, 90–15 Queens Blvd, Elmhurst, NY 11424, www.discoverqueens.info, tel: 718-592 2082; provides museum and attraction information and tours.
Council on Arts & Humanities for Staten Island (COAHSI), Snug Harbor Cultural Center, 1000 Richmond Terrace, Staten Island, NY 10301, www.statenislandarts.org, tel: 718-447 3329; lists cultural events and places of interest.

W eights & Measures

The United States uses the Imperial system.

What to Read

City in the Sky: The Rise and Fall of the World Trade Center by James Glanz and Eric Lipton. Times Books/Henry Holt & Company, 2004.
From Abyssinian to Zion, a Guide to Manhattan's Houses of Worship by David W. Dunlop.

Columbia University Press, 2004.
History Preserved: A Guide to New York City Landmarks and Historic Districts by Harmon H. Goldstone and Martha Dalrymple. Schocken Books, 1976.
Lower East Side Memories: A Jewish Place in America by Hasia R. Diner. Princeton, 2002.
Manhattan '45 by Jan Morris. Oxford University Press, 1987.
More Than Petticoats: Remarkable New York Women by Antonia Petrash, Globe Pequot, 2002.
The Movie Lover's Guide to New York by Richard Alleman. Perennial Library/Harper & Row, 1988.
A New Deal for New York by Mike Wallace, Bell & Weiland, Gotham Center Books, 2002.
New York: An Illustrated History by Ric Burns, Knopf, 1999.
New York Streetscapes: Tales of Manhattan's Buildings and Landmarks by Christopher Gray. Harry N. Abrams, Inc., 2003.
On Broadway: A Journey Uptown Over Time by David W. Dunlop. Rizzoli International, 1990.

Twin Towers: The Life of New York City's World Trade Center by Angus Kress Gillespie. Rutgers University Press, 2000.
You Must Remember This. An Oral History of Manhattan from the 1890s to World War II by Jeff Kisseloff. Harcourt Brace Jovanovich, 1988.
Waterfront, A Journey Around New York by Phillip Lopate, Crown, 2004.
The WPA Guide to New York City, Federal Writers Project Guide to 1930s NY. The New Press, 1995.

LIFE IN THE CITY: GOOD BACKGROUND READING

Fifth Avenue: The Best Address by Jerry E. Patterson. Rizzoli International Publications, 1998. Describes the gradual development of the city's most famous boulevard, from rocky dirt path to shanty row to elegant thoroughfare.
Flatbush Odyssey: A Journey Through the Heart of Brooklyn by Alan Abel. McClelland & Stewart, 1997. A fond reminiscence by an expat writer (now a Canadian) who grew up in one of Brooklyn's most picturesque neighborhoods.
Gotham: A History of New York to 1898 by Mike Wallace and Edwin G. Burrows. Oxford University Press, 1998. Pulitzer Prize-winning narrative about the city's early years; in-depth, with an emphasis on some of its characters.
Low Life by Luc Sante. Vintage Books, 1992. Everything you

always wanted to know about the gangs, gangsters, and general riff-raff who thrived at the edge of New York's society in the 19th century.
New York Characters by Gillian Zoe Segal. W.W. Norton & Co., 2001. An exuberant and sympathetic account of 66 New Yorkers, photographed in their distinctive environments.
Still Life in Harlem by Eddy L. Harris. Henry Holt and Company, Inc., 1996. A well-written autobiographical take on this famed neighborhood, with poignant details.
Writing New York: A Literary Anthology edited by Philip Lopate. The Library of America, 1998. Observations about life in New York by such literary greats as Henry David Thoreau, Walt Whitman, Maxim Gorky, and F. Scott Fitzgerald. Required reading for city-philes.

NEW YORK STREET ATLAS

The key map shows the area of New York covered by the
atlas section. An index of street names and places of interest
shown on the maps can be found on the following pages.
For each entry there is a page number and grid reference

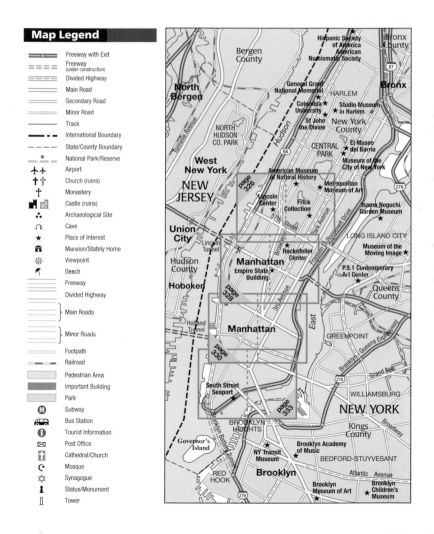

Map Legend

▬▬1▬▬	Freeway with Exit
▬ ▬ ▬	Freeway (under construction)
▬▬▬	Divided Highway
▬▬▬	Main Road
▬▬▬	Secondary Road
▬▬▬	Minor Road
▬▬▬	Track
▬ ▬ ▬	International Boundary
─ ─ ─	State/County Boundary
─ • ─	National Park/Reserve
✈✈	Airport
†✝	Church (ruins)
†	Monastery
🏰🏯	Castle (ruins)
∴	Archaeological Site
∩	Cave
★	Place of Interest
🏛	Mansion/Stately Home
☀	Viewpoint
⚐	Beach
	Freeway
	Divided Highway
}	Main Roads
}	Minor Roads
	Footpath
▬ ▬	Railroad
	Pedestrian Area
	Important Building
	Park
Ⓜ	Subway
🚌	Bus Station
❶	Tourist Information
✉	Post Office
⛪	Cathedral/Church
☪	Mosque
✡	Synagogue
🗽	Statue/Monument
∏	Tower

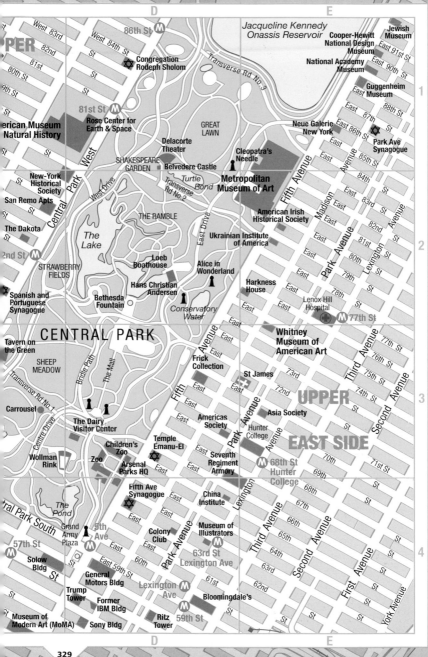

West 83rd
West 84th St
86th St
80th
81st
82nd
St
9th St
St
Congregation
Rodeph Sholom

Jacqueline Kennedy
Onassis Reservoir

Cooper-Hewitt
National Design
Museum
Jewish
Museum
East 91st St
East 90th
National Academy
Museum
Transverse Rd No 3

81st St
Rose Center for
Earth & Space

GREAT
LAWN

Guggenheim
East 89th Museum
88th St
East 87th

Neue Galerie
New York
East 86th St
Park Ave
Synagogue

erican Museum
Natural History

Delacorte
Theater

Cleopatra's
Needle

Fifth Avenue

East
85th
East

Central Park West

SHAKESPEARE
GARDEN
Belvedere Castle
Turtle
Pond

Metropolitan
Museum of Art

84th
East

New-York
Historical
Society
West Drive
Transverse
Rd No 2

Madison
East 83rd
St

San Remo Apts
THE RAMBLE

American Irish
Historical Society

East
82nd
Lexington
Avenue

The Dakota
St

Ukrainian Institute
of America
East
81st
St

2nd St
The
Lake
East Drive
Loeb
Boathouse
Alice in
Wonderland

Park Avenue
East
80th
79th

Spanish and
Portuguese
Synagogue
STRAWBERRY
FIELDS

Hans Christian
Andersen
Bethesda
Fountain

Conservatory
Water

Harkness
House
East
78th
St
Lenox Hill
Hospital

East
77th St

Tavern on
the Green

CENTRAL PARK

Avenue
East
Whitney
Museum of
American Art

Third Avenue
77th
St
76th
St

SHEEP
MEADOW
Transverse Rd No 1
Bridle Path
The Mall

Fifth
Avenue
East
East
Frick
Collection

73rd
East
East
St James
72nd

75th
St
74th
St

Second Avenue

Carrousel
Centre Drive

Park Avenue
East
Americas
Society
Asia Society

UPPER

EAST SIDE
71st St

The Dairy
Visitor Center
Children's
Zoo
Zoo
Temple
Emanu-El

Hunter
College

70th

Wollman
Rink
Arsenal
Parks HQ
Seventh
Regiment
Armory

68th St
Hunter
College
69th

The
Pond
Fifth Ave
Synagogue
China
Institute
Lexington Avenue
68th

67th

ral Park South
Grand Army
Plaza
5th
Ave
East
Colony
Club
Museum of
Illustrators

Third Avenue
Second Avenue
66th
65th

57th St
East
East 59th St
60th
63rd St
Lexington Ave

64th
63rd

First Avenue

Solow
Bldg
St

General
Motors Bldg

61st

62nd

York Avenue

Trump
Tower
Former
IBM Bldg
Lexington
Ave
Bloomingdale's

Museum of
Modern Art (MoMA)
Sony Bldg
Ritz
Tower
59th St

A

B

Pier 83
Circle Line
Boat Tour

West

West

West

West

West

West

West

West

THEATER

81

West

St Clements

48th

47th

46th

45th

DISTRI

Manhattan
Plaza Apts

44th

495

78

West

West

St Raphael

43rd

42nd

Astor P

Lincoln Tunnel (Toll)

Holy
Cross

E-Walk

76

J.K. Javits
Exhibition and
Convention
Center of
New York

West

West

Port Authority
Bus Terminal

42nd St

1 Tim

73

West

West

West

40th

41st

New York
Times

72

West

39th

38th

1411 B'v

Heliport

West

West

West

West

West 32nd St

37th

36th

35th

GARMEN

Navarre
Bldg

DISTRICT

34th

34th St

Penn Station

West

33rd

General
Post Office

1 Penn
Plaza

Nelson
Tower

Macy'

West

31st

Madison
Square
Garden

Penn
Station

34th St

He
Sq

CHELSEA
PARK

30th

29th

High Line

28th

St John

CHELSEA
WATER-SIDE
PARK

West

27th

28th St

Chelsea Art
Museum

26th

25th

FLOWER
DISTRICT

28th St

Chelsea

St

Piers

West

23rd

24th

23rd St

General Theological
Seminary

23rd St

Chelsea
Antiques Bldg

CHELSEA

22nd

23rd St

21st

Joyce
Theater

20th

19th

23rd St

Broadway

Chelsea
Park

18th

23rd St

MADIS
SQUA
PARK

West 14th Street

16th

West 15th St

17th

Flatiron
Bldg

Chelsea
Market

Ave of the Americas

Metropolit
Insurance

Little W. 12th

West 13th

St

Rubin
Museum
of Art

Street

St

14th St
8th Ave

A

B

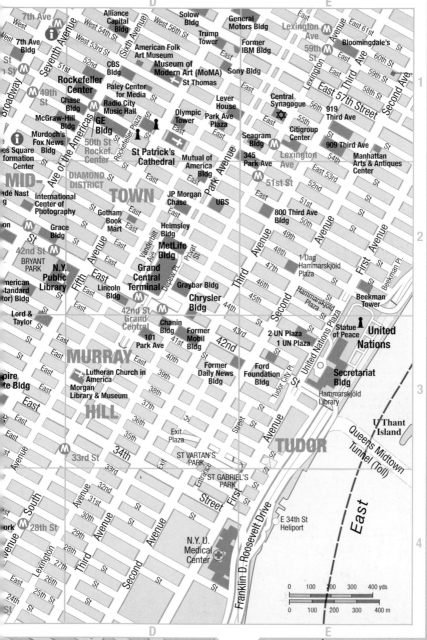

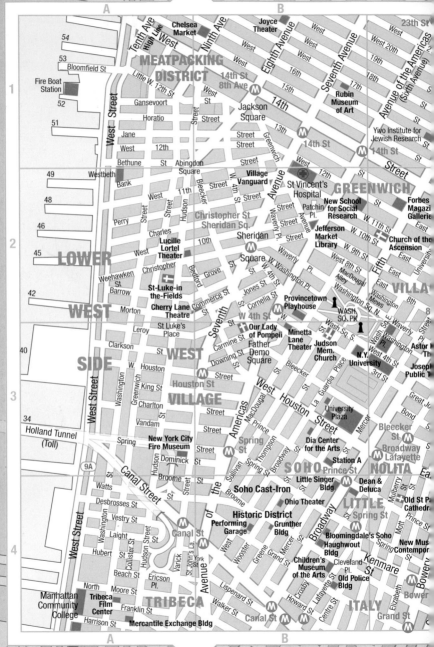

329

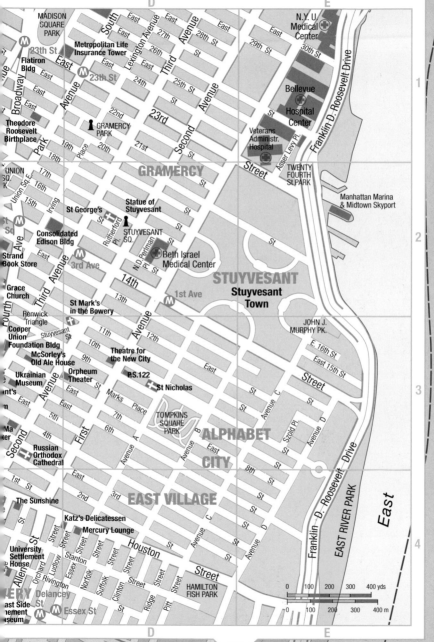

MADISON SQUARE PARK

23rd St

Flatiron Bldg

Metropolitan Life Insurance Tower

23rd St

Theodore Roosevelt Birthplace

GRAMERCY PARK

N.Y.U. Medical Center

Bellevue Hospital Center

Veterans Administr. Hospital

Franklin D. Roosevelt Drive

GRAMERCY

TWENTY FOURTH St PARK

Manhattan Marina & Midtown Skyport

St George's

Statue of Stuyvesant

Consolidated Edison Bldg

STUYVESANT SQ.

Strand Book Store

3rd Ave

Beth Israel Medical Center

STUYVESANT

Stuyvesant Town

Grace Church

14th

St Mark's in the Bowery

1st Ave

JOHN J. MURPHY PK.

Renwick Triangle

Cooper Union Foundation Bldg

E. 16th St

East 15th St

McSorley's Old Ale House

Theatre for the New City

Street

Orpheum Theater

P.S.122

Ukrainian Museum

St Nicholas

Marks Place

TOMPKINS SQUARE PARK

ALPHABET

Russian Orthodox Cathedral

CITY

East

The Sunshine

EAST VILLAGE

East River Park

Katz's Delicatessen

Mercury Lounge

Houston

EAST RIVER PARK

East

University Settlement House

Street

HAMILTON FISH PARK

Delancey St

Essex St

ast Side ement useum

0	100	200	300	400 yds
0	100	200	300	400 m

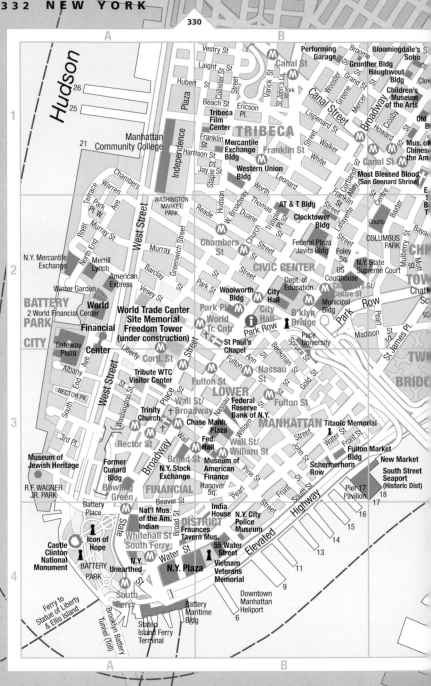

330

A   B

Hudson

Vestry St

Laight St

Canal St

Performing Garage

Broome

Bloomingdale's Soho

Grunther Bldg

Haughwout Bldg

Children's Museum of the Arts

Collister St

Street

Wooster

Greene

Grand St

Mercer

Broadway

Hubert

Varick

York St

Canal Street

St John's La

26

Beach St

Ericson Pl.

Crosby

Howard

25

Plaza

Tribeca Film Center

Lispenard St

Street

Old B

Manhattan Community College

Franklin St

Mercantile Exchange Bldg

Franklin St

Walker

White

Mus. of Chines the Am

21

Independence

Harrison St

TRIBECA

Canal St

Most Blessed Blood (San Gennaro Shrine)

WASHINGTON MARKET PARK

Jay St

Staple St

Western Union Bldg

Leonard

Worth

Franklin

Alley

Centre

E S B T

Chambers

Reade

Hudson

Thomas

Duane

AT & T Bldg

Clocktower Bldg

Street

Courts

Baxta

Warren

Terrace

Park Pl. W.

W. Broadway

Trimble

Lafayette

COLUMBUS PARK

Mulberry St

Mott St

CHI

River

Murray St

West Street

Murray

Greenwich Street

Chambers St

Church Street

Street

Federal Plaza Javits Bldg

Foley Sq.

N.Y. State Supreme Court

US Courthouse

TOW

N.Y. Mercantile Exchange

North End

Merrill Lynch

Barclay

Park

CIVIC CENTER

Dept. of Education

Chambers St/ Centre St

Chat

American Express

Vesey St

St

Park Pl

Woolworth Bldg

City Hall

Municipal Bldg

Park Row

So

Winter Garden

BATTERY PARK CITY

World Financial Center

2 World Financial Center

World Trade Center Site Memorial Freedom Tower (under construction)

Park Pl

World Tr. Cntr

City Hall Park

B'klyn Bridge

Madison

St James Pl.

Pace University

Pearl

TWO BRIDG

Gateway Plaza

Liberty St

Cortl. St

St Paul's Chapel

Ann

Fulton

Beekman St

Spruce St

Gold St

Albany Ave

RECTOR PK

Tribute WTC Visitor Center

Place

Fulton St

Nassau

LOWER

Fulton St

John St

West Street

Washington

Wall St/ Broadway

Federal Reserve Bank of N.Y.

William

MANHATTAN

Gold St

Water St

Titanic Memorial

Front St

3rd Pl.

Rector St

Trinity Church

Chase Manh. Plaza

Wall St/ William St

John St

Fulton Market Bldg

New Market

Museum of Jewish Heritage

Former Cunard Bldg

Broadway

Fed. Hall

Museum of American Finance

Pine St

Schermerhorn Row

South Street Seaport (Historic Dist)

R.F. WAGNER JR. PARK

Bowling Green

N.Y. Stock Exchange

Broad St

Hanover Sq.

Pearl

FINANCIAL

Front

South St

Pier 17 Pavilion

17

18

Battery Place

Beaver St

Nat'l Mus. of the Am. Indian

India House

Highway

16

Icon of Hope

State

Whitehall St

Fraunces Tavern Mus.

Broad St

N.Y. City Police Museum

Elevated

15

Castle Clinton National Monument

BATTERY PARK

South Ferry

N.Y. Unearthed

Water St

DISTRICT

N.Y. Plaza

55 Water Street

Vietnam Veterans Memorial

14

13

11

9

Ferry to Statue of Liberty & Ellis Island

Brooklyn Battery Tunnel (Toll)

Staten Island Ferry Terminal

Battery Maritime Bldg

Downtown Manhattan Heliport

6

A   B

1

2

3

4

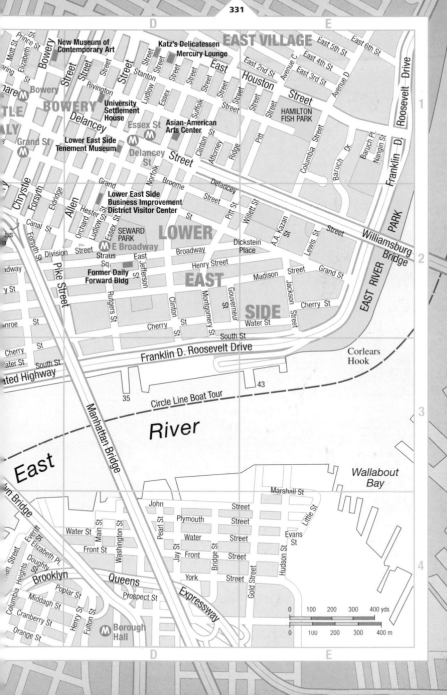

D

E

EAST VILLAGE

Prince St
Mott St
Elizabeth St
Spring St
Bowery

New Museum of
Contemporary Art

Katz's Delicatessen
Mercury Lounge

East 5th St
East 6th St
East 4th St
East 3rd St
East 2nd St

Avenue C
Avenue D

Roosevelt Drive

Street
Stanton
Street
East
Houston
Street

Ludlow
Essex
Street
Street

HAMILTON
FISH PARK

Franklin D.

Bowery

BOWERY

Rivington

University
Settlement
House

Asian-American
Arts Center

Pitt
Columbia Street

Baruch Pl.

Nangin St

1

Delancey

Essex St

Lower East Side
Tenement Museum

Delancey
St

Delancey Street

Suffolk
Clinton St
Attorney
Ridge

Baruch Dr.

Grand St

Christie
Forsyth
Eldridge
Allen

Grand

Lower East Side
Business Improvement
District Visitor Center

Norfolk
Broome

Delancey

Street
St

Willett St

A.A. Kazan St

Street

PARK

Lewis St

Williamsburg
Bridge

Hester St
Orchard
Ludlow
Essex St

Canal St
Forsyth St
Division
Street

LOWER

SEWARD
PARK
E Broadway

Straus
Sq.

Former Daily
Forward Bldg

East
Jefferson

Dickstein
Place

Broadway

Henry Street

Madison

Street

Grand St

EAST RIVER

2

Pike Street

EAST

Rutgers St

Clinton St

Montgomery St

Gouverneur St

Street

Cherry St

Monroe
St

Cherry

Clinton St

SIDE

Jackson Street

Cherry
St

Water St

Cherry
ater St
South St

South St

Corlears
Hook

ted Highway

Franklin D. Roosevelt Drive

43

35

Circle Line Boat Tour

3

River

Manhattan Bridge

East

Wallabout
Bay

Marshall St

Little St

John
Street

Pearl St

Plymouth
Street

Evans
St

wn Bridge

Water St
Main St
Washington St

Front St

Jay St

Water
Front

Street
Street

Bridge St

Hudson St

Brooklyn

Everit St
Elizabeth Pl
Doughty St

Queens

York
Street

Gold Street

4

Columbia Heights

Poplar St

Prospect St

Expressway

0   100   200   300   400 yds

Middagh St
Henry St

Cranberry St

Fulton St

**Borough
Hall**

0   100   200   300   400 m

Orange St

D

E

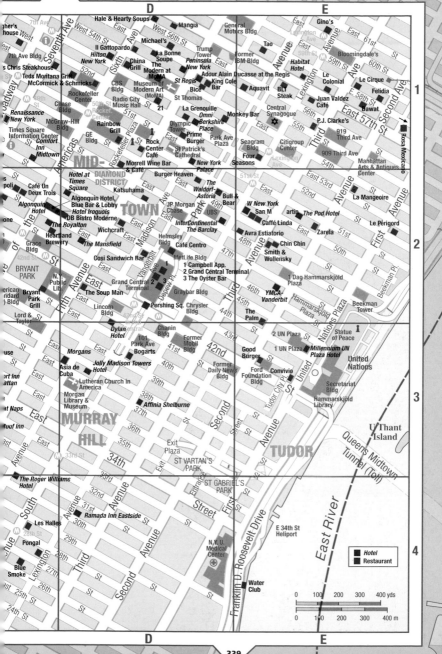

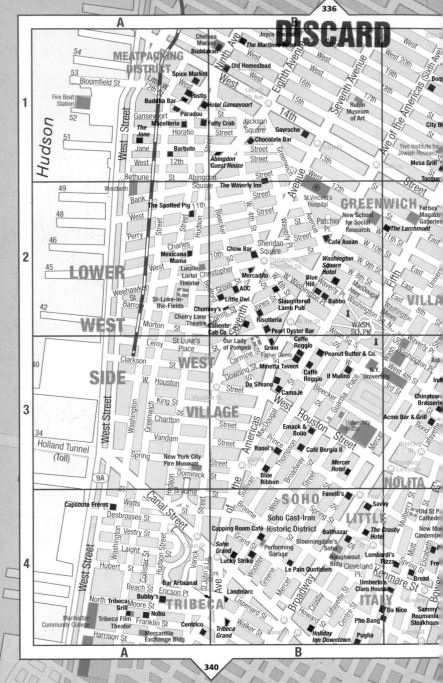

DISCARD

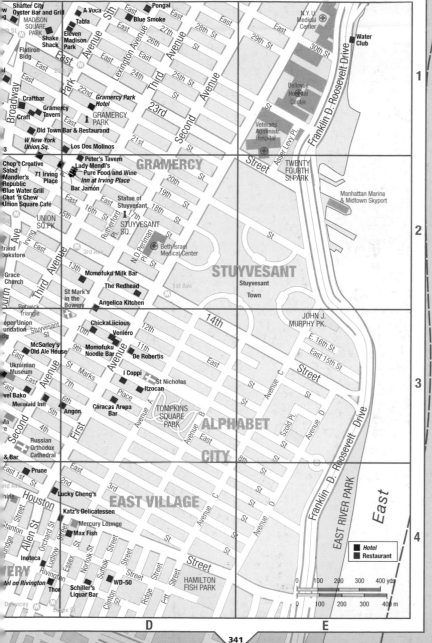

Shafter City Oyster Bar and Grill
MADISON SQUARE PARK
A Voca
Tabla
Pongal
Blue Smoke
Flatiron Bldg
Shake Shack
Eleven Madison Park
N.Y.U Medical Center
Water Club
Craftbar
Craft
Gramercy Tavern
Gramercy Park Hotel
Bellevue Hospital Center
Old Town Bar & Restaurand
GRAMERCY PARK
Veterans Administr. Hospital
W New York Union Sq.
Los Dos Molinos
GRAMERCY
TWENTY FOURTH St Park
Chop't Creative Salad
Mandler's Republic
Blue Water Grill
Chat 'n Chew
Union Square Café
71 Irving Place
Peter's Tavern
Lady Mendl's
Pure Food and Wine
Inn at Irving Place
Bar Jamón
Manhattan Marina & Midtown Skyport
Statue of Stuyvesant
STUYVESANT SQ.
UNION SQ.PK.
Strand Bookstore
Beth Israel Medical Center
STUYVESANT
Grace Church
Momofuku Milk Bar
The Redhead
Stuyvesant Town
St Mark's in the Bowery
Angelica Kitchen
Renwick Triangle
ChickaLiicious
JOHN J. MURPHY PK.
Cooper Union Foundation
Veniero
McSorley's Old Ale House
Momofuku Noodle Bar
De Robertis
Ukrainian Museum
Veselka Bako
I Coppi
St Nicholas
Mermaid Inn
Itzocan
Caracas Arepa Bar
Angon
TOMPKINS SQUARE PARK
ALPHABET
Russian Orthodox Cathedral
& Bar
CITY
Prune
EAST RIVER PARK
East
Lucky Cheng's
EAST VILLAGE
Katz's Delicatessen
Mercury Lounge
Max Fish
Inoteca
Hotel
Restaurant
Schiller's Liquar Bar
WD-50
HAMILTON FISH PARK
Hotel on Rivington
Thor
0   100   200   300   400 yds
0   100   200   300   400 m

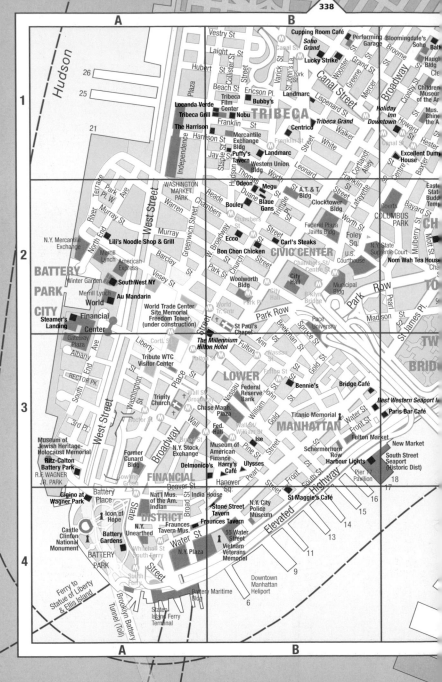

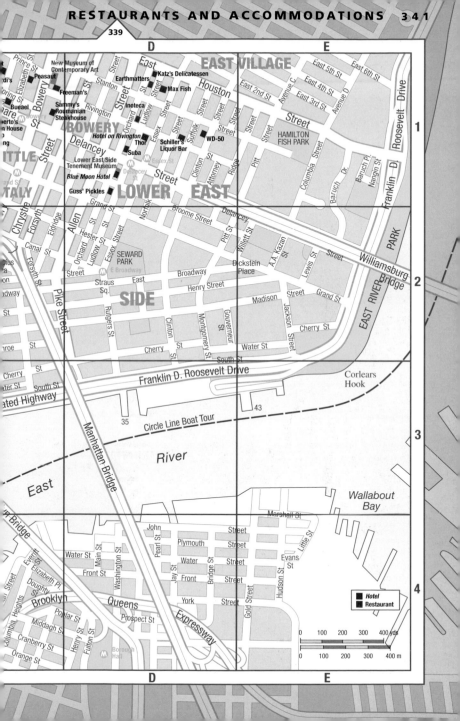

STREET INDEX

1407 Broadway **328** C2
1411 Broadway **328** C2
1700 Broadway Building
 326 C4
1 Dag Hammarskjöld
 Plaza **329** E2
101 Park Avenue **329** D3
345 Park Avenue **329** E1
1 Penn Plaza **328** B2
909 Third Avenue
 329 E1
919 Third Avenue
 329 E1
800 Third Avenue
 Building **329** E2
1 Times Square **328** C2
1 UN Plaza **329** E3
2 UN Plaza **329** E3
55 Water Street **332** B4

A

A.A. Kazan Street
 333 E2
Abingdon Square **330** A1
Albany Street **332** A3
Alice in Wonderland,
 Statue of **327** D2
Allen Street **333** D2
Alliance Capital Building
 326 C4
American Express **332** A2
American Folk Art
 Museum **326** C2,
 329 D1
American Irish Historical
 Society **327** E2
American Museum of
 Natural History **327** C1
American Standard
 (Radiator) Building
 329 C2
Americas Society **327** D3
Amsterdam Avenue
 326 B3–C1
Ann Street **332** B3
Arsenal Parks HQ
 327 D3
Asian-American Arts
 Center **333** D1
Asia Society **327** E3
Asser Levy Place **331** E2
Astor Place Theatre
 330 C3
Astor Place **330** C3
Astor Plaza Building
 328 C1
AT&T Building **332** B2
Attorney Street **333** D1
A. Tully Hall **326** C2
Avenue A **331** D3
Avenue B **331** D3
Avenue C **331** D4–E3
Avenue D **331** E4–E3
Avenue of the Americas
 (Sixth Avenue) **328** B4,
 329 C2, **330** B4–C1
Avery Fisher Hall **326** C3

B

Bank Street **330** A2
Barclay Street **332** A2
Barrow Street **330** A2
Baruch Drive **333** E1
Baruch Place **333** E1
Battery Maritime Building
 332 A4
Battery Place **332** A3
Baxter Street **332** C2
Bayard Street **332** C2
Beach Street **330** A4
Beaver Street **332** A3
Bedford Street **330** A2
Beekman Place **329** E2
Beekman Street **332** B2
Bellevue Hospital Center
 331 E1
Belvedere Castle **327** D1
Beth Israel Medical Center
 331 D2
Bethesda Fountain
 327 D2
Bethune Street **330** A1
Bleecker Street
 330 B2–B3
Bloomfield Street **330** A1
Bloomingdale's **327** D4
Bloomingdale's Soho
 330 B4
Bond Street **330** C3
Bowery **333** C2–C1
Bridge Street **333** D4
Bridle Path **327** D3
Broad Street **332** A4
Broadway **326** B4, C2,
 328 C4, **329** C1
 330 B4, **331** C2–C1,
 332 A3, C1
Brooklyn Battery Tunnel
 (Toll) **332** A4
Brooklyn Bridge **333** C3
Brooklyn Queens
 Expressway **333** C4–D4
Broome Street
 330 A3–B4, **332** B1,
 333 D1

C

Canal Street **330** A3,
 332 B1
Carmine Street **330** B3
Carnegie Hall **326** C4
Carrousel, Central Park
 327 C3
Castle Clinton National
 Monument **332** A4
Catherine Street **333** C2
CBS Building **329** D1
Central Park South
 327 C4
Central Park West **326**
 C3, **327** C2
Central Synagogue
 329 E1
Centre Drive **327** C3
Centre Street **332** C1
Chambers Street **332** A1

Chanin Building **329** D3
Charles Street **330** A2
Charlton Street **330** A3
Chase Building **329** C1
Chase Manhattan Plaza
 332 B3
Chatham Square **332** C2
Chelsea Antiques Building
 328 B4
Chelsea Art Museum
 328 A3
Chelsea Market **328** A4
Chelsea Piers **328** A3
Cherry Lane Theatre
 330 A2
Cherry Street
 333 C3–D2, E2
Children's Museum of the
 Arts **330** B4
Children's Zoo **327** D3
China Institute **327** D4
Christopher Street
 330 A2
Chrysler Building
 329 D2
Chrystie Street **333** C2
Church of the Ascension
 330 C2
Church Street **332** B2
Citigroup Center **329** E1
City Hall **332** B2
Clarkson Street **330** A3
Cleopatra's Needle
 327 D1
Cleveland Place **330** B4
Clinton Street
 333 D2–D1
Clocktower Building
 332 B2
Collister Street **330** A4
Colony Club **327** D4
Columbia Heights
 333 C4
Columbia Street **333** E1
Columbus Avenue **326** B3,
 327 C2
Columbus Circle **326** C3
Commerce Street **330** A2
Condé Nast Building
 329 C2
Con-Edison **326** B2
Confucius Plaza **333** C2
Congregation Rodeph
 Sholom **327** D1
Consolidated Edison
 Building **331** C2
Cooper Square **331** C3
Cooper Union Foundation
 Building **331** C3
Cooper-Hewitt National
 Design Museum **327** E1
Cornelia Street **330** B2
Cortlandt Alley **332** B1
Cranberry Street **333** C4
Crosby Street **330** B4
Cunard Building, Former
 332 A3

D

Daily Forward Building,
 Former **333** D2

Daily News Building,
 Former **329** D3
Dairy Visitor Center, The
 327 D3
Dakota, The **327** C2
Dean & Deluca **330** B4
Delacorte Theater
 327 D1
Delancey Street **333** D1
Depew Place **329** D2
Desbrosses Street **330** A4
Dia Center for the Arts
 330 B3
Dickstein Place **333** D2
Division Street **333** C2
Dominick Street **330** A3
Doughty Street **333** C4
Downing Street **330** B3
Downtown Manhattan
 Heliport **332** B4
Duane Street **332** B2
Duffy Square **329** C1
Duke Mansion **327** E2

E

East 1st Street **331** C3
East 2nd Street **331** D4
East 3rd Street **331** D4
East 4th Street **331** C3
East 5th Street **331** C3
East 6th Street **331** D3
East 7th Street **331** D3
East 8th Street **330** C2,
 331 D3
East 9th Street **331** D3
East 10th Street **331** D3
East 11th Street **331** D3
East 12th Street **331** D3
East 13th Street **331** D2
East 14th Street **331** D2
East 15th Street
 331 C2, E3
East 16th Street
 331 C2, E3
East 17th Street **331** C2
East 18th Street **331** C1
East 19th Street **331** D1
East 20th Street **331** D1
East 21st Street **331** D1
East 22nd Street **331** D1
East 23rd Street **331** D1
East 24th Street **331** D1
East 25th Street **331** D1
East 26th Street **331** D1
East 27th Street **329** C4
East 28th Street **329** D4
East 29th Street **329** D4
East 30th Street **329** D4
East 31st Street **329** D4
East 32nd Street **329** D4
East 33rd Street **329** D3
East 34th Street **329** D3
East 34th Street Heliport
 329 E4
East 35th Street **329** D3
East 36th Street **329** D3
East 37th Street **329** D3
East 38th Street **329** D3
East 39th Street **329** D3
East 40th Street **329** D3
East 41st Street **329** D3
East 42nd Street **329** D3

East 43rd Street **329** D3
East 44th Street **329** D2
East 45th Street **329** E2
East 46th Street **329** E2
East 47th Street **329** E2
East 48th Street **329** E2
East 49th Street **329** E2
East 50th Street **329** E2
East 51st Street **329** E2
East 52nd Street
 329 D1–E2
East 53rd Street **329** E2
East 54th Street **329** E1
East 55th Street **329** E1
East 56th Street **329** E1
East 57th Street **329** E1
East 58th Street **329** E1
East 59th Street **327** D4
East 60th Street **327** D4
East 61st Street **327** D4
East 62nd Street **327** E4
East 63rd Street **327** E4
East 64th Street **327** E4
East 65th Street **327** E4
East 66th Street **327** E4
East 67th Street **327** E4
East 68th Street **327** E4
East 69th Street **327** E3
East 70th Street **327** E3
East 71st Street **327** E3
East 72nd Street **327** E3
East 73rd Street **327** E3
East 74th Street **327** E3
East 75th Street **327** E3
East 76th Street **327** E3
East 77th Street **327** E3
East 78th Street **327** E2
East 79th Street **327** E2
East 80th Street **327** E2
East 81st Street **327** E2
East 82nd Street **327** E2
East 83rd Street **327** E2
East 84th Street **327** E2
East 85th Street **327** E1
East 86th Street **327** E1
East 87th Street **327** E1
East 88th Street **327** E1
East Broadway
 333 C2–D2
East Drive **327** D2
East Houston Street
 331 C4
Eastern States Buddist
 Temple **332** C1
Eighth Avenue **326** B4,
 328 A4–B2
Eldridge Street **331** C4,
 333 C2
Elevated Highway
 332 B4, **333** C3
Eleventh Avenue **326** A4,
 328 A2–B1
Elizabeth Place **333** C4
Elizabeth Street **333** C1
Empire State
 Building **329** C3
Ericson Place **330** A4
Essex Street **333** D2–D1
Evans Street **333** E4
Everitt Street **333** C4
E-Walk **328** C2
Exit Plaza **329** D3

F

Father Demo Square 330 B3
Federal Hall 332 B3
Federal Plaza Javits Building 332 B2
Federal Reserve Bank 332 B3
Fifth Avenue 327 D3–E2, 328 C4, 329 D2, 330 C2
Fifth Avenue Synagogue 327 E1
Fire Boat Station 330 A1
First Avenue 327 E4, 329 D4–E2, 331 D3
Flatiron Building 331 C1
Foley Square 332 B2
Forbes Galleries 330 C2
Ford Center 328 C2
Ford Foundation Building 329 E3
Fordham University 326 B3
Former IBM Building 327 D4
Forsyth Street 331 C4, 333 C2
Forth Avenue 331 C3
Franklin D. Roosevelt Drive 331 E4–E3, E1, 333 D3–E1
Franklin Street 332 B1
Fraunces Tavern Museum 332 A4
Freedom Place 326 B2
Frick Collection 327 D3
Front Street 332 B3, 333 D4
Fulton Market Building 332 B3
Fulton Street 332 B3, 333 D4
Furman Street 333 C4

G

Gansevoort Street 330 A1
Gateway Plaza 332 A2
GE Building 329 D1
General Motors Building 327 D4
General Post Office 328 B2
General Theological Seminary 328 A3
Gold Street 332 B3, 333 E4
Gouverneur Street 333 D2
Grace Building 329 C2
Grace Church 331 C2
Grand Army Plaza 327 D4
Grand Central Terminal 329 D2
Grand Street 330 B4, 332 B1, 333 D1–E2
Graybar Building 329 D2
Great Jones Street 330 C3
Greene Street 330 B4
Greenwich Avenue 330 B1
Greenwich Street 330 A3, 332 A2

Grove Street 330 B2
Guggenheim Museum 327 E1
Gunther Building 330 B4

H

Hammarskjöld Library 329 E3
Hammarskjöld Plaza 329 E2
Hanover Square 332 B3
Hans Christian Andersen, Statue of 327 D2
Harkness House 327 E2
Harrison Street 332 A1
Haughwout Building 330 B4
Hearst Tower 326 B4
Heliport 328 A2
Helmsley Building 329 D2
Henry Street 333 C2–D2, 333 D4
Herald Square 328 C3
Hester Street 332 C1, 333 D2
Holland Tunnel (Toll) 330 A3
Holy Cross 328 B1
Horatio Street 330 A1
Howard Street 332 C1
Hubert Street 330 A4
Hudson Street 330 A4–A2, 332 B2, 333 E4
Hunter College 327 E3

I

Icon of Hope 332 A4
Independence Plaza 332 A1
India House 332 B4
International Center of Photography 329 C2
Intrepid Sea, Air, and Space Museum 326 A4
Irving Place 331 C2

J

Jackson Square 330 B1
Jackson Street 333 E2
Jane Street 330 A1
Jay Street 332 B1, 333 D4
Jefferson Market Library 330 B2
Jefferson Street 333 D2
Jewish Museum 327 E1
J.K. Javits Exhibition and Convention Center of New York 328 A1
John Street 332 B3, 333 D4
Jones Street 330 B2
Joseph Papp Public Theater 330 C3
Joyce Theater 328 A4
JP Morgan Chase 329 D2
Judson Mem. Church 330 B3
Juilliard School 326 C2

K

Kenmare Street 330 C4
King Street 330 A3

L

Lafayette Street 332 B2
La Guardia Place 330 B3
Laight Street 330 A4
La MaMa Theater 331 C3
Lenox Hill Hospital 328 C4
Leonard Street 332 B1
Leroy Street 330 A3
Lever House 329 D1
Lewis Street 333 E2
Lexington Avenue 327 D4–E2, 329 C4, E1
Liberty Street 332 A3
Lincoln Building 329 D2
Lincoln Center 326 B3
Lincoln Square 326 C3
Lincoln Tunnel (Toll) 328 A1
Lispenard Street 332 B1
Little Singer Building 330 B4
Little Street 333 E4
Little West 12th Street 330 A1
Loeb Boathouse 327 D2
Lord & Taylor 329 C2
Lower East Side Business Improvement District Visitor Center 333 D1
Lower East Side Tenement Museum 333 D1
Lucille Lortel Theater 330 A2
Ludlow Street 333 D2–D1
Lutheran Church In America 329 D3

M

MacDougal Alley 330 B2
MacDougal Street 330 B3
Macy's 328 C3
Madison Avenue 327 E2, 328 C4
Madison Square Garden 328 B3
Madison Street 332 B2, 333 E2
Main Street 333 D4
Maine 326 C3
Mall, The 327 D3
Manhattan Arts & Antiques Center 329 E1
Manhattan Bridge 333 D3
Manhattan Community College 332 A1
Manhattan Marina & Midtown Skyport 331 E2
Manhattan Plaza Apartments 328 B1
Marshall Street 333 E3
McGraw-Hill Building 329 C1

McScrley's Old Ale House 331 C3
Mercantile Exchange Building 332 B1
Mercer Street 330 B4–B3
Merchant's House Museum 331 C3
Merrill Lynch 332 A2
MetLife Building 329 D2
Metropolitan Life Insurance Tower 328 C4
Metropolitan Museum of Art 327 E2
Metropolitan Opera 326 B3
Middagh Street 333 C4
Minetta Lane Theater 330 B3
Mobil Building, Former 329 D3
Monroe Street 333 C2
Montgomery Street 333 D2
Morgan Library and Museum 329 D3
Morton Street 330 A2
Most Blessed Blood Church (San Gennaro Shrine) 332 C1
Mott Street 332 C2, 333 C1
Mulberry Street 332 C2, 333 C1
Municipal Building 332 B2
Murdoch's Fox News Building 329 C1
Murray Street 332 A2
Museum of American Finance 332 B3
Museum of Arts & Design 326 C3
Museum of Illustration 327 D4
Museum of Jewish Heritage 332 A3
Museum of Modern Art (MoMA) 329 D1
Museum of Chinese in the Americas 332 C1
Mutual of America Building 329 D1

N

Nangin Street 333 E1
Nassau Street 332 B3
National Academy Museum 327 E1
National Museum of the American Indian 332 A4
Navarre Building 328 B2
N.D. Perlman Place 331 D2
Nelson Tower 328 C2
Neue Galerie New York 327 E1
New Museum of Contemporary Art 330 C4
New School for Social Research 330 B2

New York City Fire Museum 330 A3
New York City Passenger Ship Terminal 326 A3
New York City Police Museum 332 B4
New York Historical Society 327 C2
New York Life 329 C4
New York Mercantile Building 332 A2
New York Plaza 332 A4
New York Public Library 329 C2
New York State Supreme Court 332 B2
New York State Theater 326 B3
New York Stock Exchange 332 A3
New York Times 328 C2
New York Unearthed 332 A4
New York University 330 B3
New York University Institute of Fine Arts 327 E2
New York University Medical Center 329 D4
Newsweek Building 326 C4
Ninth Avenue 326 B4, 328 A4–C1
Norfolk Street 333 D2
North End Avenue 332 A2
North Moore Street 330 A4

O

Ohio Theater 330 B4
Old Police Building 330 B4
Old St Patrick's Cathedral 330 C4
Oliver Street 332 C2
Olympic Tower 329 D1
Orange Street 333 C4
Orchard Street 333 D2–D1
Orpheum Theater 331 D3
Our Lady of Pompeii 330 B3

P, Q

Pace University 332 B2
Paley Center for Media 329 D1
Park Avenue 327 D4–D3–E2, 329 D2
Park Avenue Plaza
Park Avenue South 329 C4, 331 C1
Park Avenue Synagogue 327 E1
Park Place West 332 A2
Park Row 332 B2
Park Street 332 B2
Patchin Place 330 B2
Peace, Statue of 329 E3

Pearl Street **332** B3, C2, **333** D4

Pennsylvania Station **328** B3

Perry Street **330** A2

Pier 17 Pavilion **332** B3

Pier 83 Circle Line Boat Tour **328** A1

Pike Street **333** C2

Pine Street **332** B3

Pitt Street **332** D2–E1

Place Street **332** A3

Plymouth Street **333** D4

Poplar Street **333** C4

Port Authority Bus Terminal **328** B2

Prince Street **330** B3–C4

Privat Street **329** D2

Prospect Street **333** D4

Provincetown Playhouse **330** B2

P.S.122 **331** D3

Queens Midtown Tunnel (Toll) **329** E3

R

Radio City Music Hall **329** D1

Reade Street **332** B2

Renwick Triangle **331** C2

Ridge Street **333** D1

Ritz Tower **327** D4

River Terrace **332** A2–A1

Riverside Drive **326** B1

Rivington Street **331** C4

Rockefeller Center **329** D1

Rockefeller Plaza **329** D1

Roosevelt, Eleanor, Statue of **326** B1

Rose Center for Earth and Space **327** D1

Rubin Museum of Art **328** B4

Russian Orthodox Cathedral **331** C3

Rutgers Street **333** D2

Rutherford Place **331** D2

S

San Remo Apartments **327** C2

Schermerhorn Row **332** B3

Seagram Building **329** E1

Second Avenue **327** E4–E3, **329** D4–E1, **331** C3–C1

Secretariat Building **329** E3

Seventh Avenue **326** C4, **328** B4, **329** C1–B1

Seventh Regiment Armory **327** D3

Shakespeare Garden **327** D1

Sheridan Square **330** B2

Sixth Avenue **329** D1

Soho Cast-Iron Historic District **330** B4

Solow Building **327** C4

Sony Building **327** D4

South End Avenue **332** A3

South Street **332** B3, **333** C3

South Street Seaport (Historic District) **332** B3

Spanish and Portuguese Synagogue **327** C2

Spring Street **330** A3–B3–C4

Spruce Street **332** B2

St Clements **328** B1

St George's **331** D2

St James **327** E3

St James Place **332** C3

St John **328** B3

St John's Lane **332** B1

St Luke-in-the-Fields **330** A2

St Luke's Place **330** A2

St Luke's Roosevelt Hospital **326** B3

St Mark's in the Bowery **331** D3

St Marks Place **331** D2

St Nicholas **331** D3

St Patrick's Cathedral **329** D1

St Paul's Chapel **332** B2

St Raphaël **328** B1

St Thomas **329** D1

St Vincent's Hospital **330** B2

Stanton Street **331** C4

Staple Street **332** B1

State Street **332** A4

Staten Island Ferry Terminal **332** A4

Strand Bookstore **331** C2

Straus Square **333** D2

Strawberry Fields **327** C2

Street John's Lane **330** A4

Stuyvesant, Statue of **331** D2

Stuyvesant Street **331** C3

Stuyvesant Town **331** D2

Suffolk Street **333** D1

Sullivan Street **330** A4

Szold Place **331** E3

T

Tavern on the Green **327** C3

Temple Emanu-El **327** D3

Tenth Avenue **326** B4, **328** A4–A3–B2–B1

Theodore Roosevelt Birthplace **331** C1

Third Avenue **327** E4–E3, **329** D4–E1, **331** C2–D1

Thomas Street **332** B2

Thompson Street **330** B3

Time Warner Center **326** B3

Times Square **328** C2

Times Square Information Center **329** C1

Titanic Memorial **332** B3

Transverse Road No.1 **327** C3

Transverse Road No.2 **327** D2

Transverse Road No.3 **327** D1–E1

Tribeca Film Center **332** B1

Tribute WTC Visitor Center **332** A3

Trimple Place **332** B2

Trinity Church **332** A3

Trump Tower **327** D4

Tudor City Place **329** E3

Twelfth Avenue **326** A4, A3, **328** A2–A1

U

UBS #299 **329** D2

Ukrainian Institute of America **327** E2

Ukrainian Museum **331** C3

Union Square East **331** C2

Union Square West **331** C2

United Nations **329** E3

United Nations Plaza **329** E3

University Place **330** C2

University Plaza **330** B3

University Settlement House **331** C4

US Courthouse **332** B2

V

Vandam Street **330** A3

Vanderbilt Avenue **329** D2

Varick Street **330** A4

Verdi Square **326** C1

Verizon Building **329** C2

Vesey Street **332** A2

Vestry Street **330** A4

Veterans Administr. Hospital **331** E1

Vietnam Veterans Memorial **332** B4

Village Vanguard **330** B2

Vivian Beaumont Theater **326** B2

W

Walker Street **332** B1

Wall Street **332** A3

Warren Street **332** A1

Washington Mews **330** C2

Washington Place **330** C3

Washington Square East **330** C3

Washington Square North **330** B2

Washington Square South **330** B3

Washington Street **330** A4–A2, **332** A3, **333** D4

Water Street **332** A4, B3, **333** C3, E2

Watts Street **330** A4

Waverly Place **330** B2

Weehawken Street **330** A2

West 3rd Street **330** C3

West 4th Street **330** B2–C3

West 8th Street **330** B2

West 9th Street **330** B2

West 10th Street **330** B2

West 11th Street **330** A2

West 12th Street **330** A1–B2

West 13th Street **330** B1

West 14th Street **330** B1

West 15th Street **330** B1

West 16th Street **330** B1

West 17th Street **330** B1

West 18th Street **328** B4

West 19th Street **328** B4

West 20th Street **328** B4

West 21st Street **328** B4

West 22nd Street **328** B4

West 23rd Street **328** A3

West 24th Street **328** B3

West 25th Street **328** B3

West 26th Street **328** B3

West 27th Street **328** B3

West 28th Street **328** B3

West 29th Street **328** B3

West 30th Street **328** B3

West 31st Street **328** B3

West 32nd Street **328** A2, C3

West 33rd Street **328** B2

West 34th Street **328** B2

West 35th Street **328** B2

West 36th Street **328** B2

West 37th Street **328** B2

West 38th Street **328** B2

West 39th Street **328** B2

West 40th Street **328** B2

West 41st Street **328** C2

West 42nd Street **328** B1

West 43rd Street **328** C1

West 44th Street **328** C1

West 45th Street **328** C1

West 46th Street **328** C1

West 47th Street **328** C1

West 48th Street **328** C1

West 49th Street **328** C1

West 50th Street **326** B4

West 51st Street **326** B4

West 52nd Street **326** B4

West 53rd Street **326** B4

West 54th Street **326** B4

West 55th Street **326** B4

West 56th Street **326** B4

West 57th Street **326** B3

West 58th Street **326** B3

West 59th Street **326** B3

West 60th Street **326** B3

West 61st Street **326** C3

West 62nd Street **326** C3

West 63rd Street **326** C3

West 64th Street **326** C3

West 65th Street **326** C3

West 66th Street **326** B2

West 67th Street **326** C2

West 68th Street **326** C2

West 69th Street **326** C2

West 70th Street **326** C2

West 71st Street **326** C2

West 72nd Street **326** C2

West 73rd Street **326** C2

West 74th Street **326** C1

West 75th Street **326** C1

West 76th Street **327** C1

West 77th Street **326** C1

West 78th Street **327** C1

West 79th Street **327** C1

West 80th Street **327** C1

West 81st Street **327** C1

West 82nd Street **327** C1

West 83rd Street **327** C1

West 84th Street **327** D1

Westbeth **330** A2

West Broadway **330** B4–B3, **332** B2

West Drive **326** C3, **327** D2

West End Avenue **326** B3–B1

Western Union Building **332** B1

West Houston Street **330** A3–B3

West Side Highway (Miller Highway) **326** B2–B1

West Street **332** A3–A2, **330** A4–A1

West Washington Place **330** B2

White Street **332** B1

Whitney Museum of American Art **327** E3

Willett Street **333** D2

William Street **332** B3

Williamsburg Bridge **333** E2

Winter Garden **332** A2

Wollman Rink **327** C3

Woolworth Building **332** B2

Wooster Street **330** B4

World Financial Center **332** A2

World Trade Center Site Memorial Freedom Tower (under construction) **332** A2

Worth Street **332** B1–B2

Y, Z

Yivo Institute for Jewish Research **330** C1

York Avenue **327** E4

York Street **332** B1, **333** D4

Zoo, Central Park **327** D3

ART AND PHOTO CREDITS

Photography by **Britta Jaschinski/APA** except for:
akg-images 33
Alamy 97B, 167B
Algonquin Hotel 117
Dave Allocca/Rex Features 150B
Arcaid 39R
Art Archive 41T
Antonio Bonanno 287BR
Brooklyn Museum of Art/Central Photo Archives 274T, 275(all)
Bridgeman Art Library 30L, 31BR
Howard Brier 280BR
Carlyle Hotel 301
Franco Caruzzo 222B
Jennifer Calais Smith/Four Seasons 100
Collections of the New York Historical Society 233T&B
Corbis 27, 28R, 34B, 39TL, 40L, 42BL, 43(all), 48R, 105B, 288B
Design Trust for Public Space 287TR
duluoz cats on flickr 281TL
Fotolia 190R, 213TR
The Frick Collection 127TL&B
Glyn Genin/APA 21B
Getty Images 30/31, 34TL, 35, 38TR&B, 49B, 54, 104B, 144T&B, 167T, 192R, 193BR, 267, 278T&BR
Gramercy Park Hotel 175, 302B, 303T
greyloch on flickr 131TR
Bob Gruen 36TL
Tony Halliday 145T, 255B
Robert Harding Picture Library 86
Sarah Heiman 273TL
Hotel Elysee 101
Hotel Gansevoort 10B
Daniel Huggard 272B
Illustrated London News 26
iStockphoto 37R, 92B, 184B, 243BR, 269BL, 292
Jens Karlsson 234B
Catherine Karnow 181L
Ozan Kilic 286TL
Jason Kuffer 312
Patrick Kwan 223B
Library of Congress 31TR, 287TL
Daniel Lobo 134
Lordcolus on flickr 193C
Paul Lowry 104TR
Maya Lin Studio/MCA 221T
Joe Mazzola 276TL
Ellen McKnight/fotoLibra 286B
Merchant's House Museum 205TL&B
Adrian Miles © 276TR
Anna Mockford & Nick Bonetti/APA 9TR, CL, C, CR,

BL&BR, 93, 95TR, 96TL, 114T, 146T, 166T, 176, 206B, 242, 243T, 250B, 254BR, 257B, 299T, 311B, 317, 324
Momos 207T
Morgan Library 89L&BR, 191T
Mount Vernon Hotel Museum and Garden 132BL
Museum of Contemporary Art 217T
National Museum of the American Indian 249T
National Park Service 178T
New York Botanical Garden 285T
New York City Ballet 148B
New York Mets 39BL
New York Palace Hotel 298T&B
New York Public Library 28L, 29, 32T&B, 40R
Keiko Niwa/LES 214CR, BL&BR
Abe Nowitz/APA 8BL, 9TL, 11CR, 14/15, 20TR, 51BL, 55, 70, 74TL, 78BR, 79B, 91TL&B, 92TR, 96BR, 97TR, 102, 106BL&BR, 107B, 108T&B, 128T, 129BL&BR, 131B, 132T, 142, 146BL, 163, 169B, 170T, 172/173, 174, 177T, 178L&BR, 179L&BR, 180B, 181R, 182TR&B, 183L&R, 186B, 193T, 196T, 197B, 198T, 199R, 200, 202, 213B, 217B, 218T&B, 219TR, 223TR, 226, 228L&BR, 230T&B, 236TL, 241, 243L, 244B, 245T&B, 248(all), 251TR&B, 252T&B, 253L&R, 254T, 256C, 257T, 258B, 283B, 284T, 297, 311T
Oscar's Restaurant 97TL
PA/EPA 38TL
Padraic on flickr 281B
Douglas Palmer 272T
Tony Perrottet 7T&BR, 170B, 189
Photolibrary 162
Andrea Pistolesi 18
David Poe 50T
Radio City Music Hall/Kozlowski 13C, 113T
Mark Read/APA 1, 11CLB, 79TL, 96TR, 106TL, 110B, 125, 194TL&R, 211T, 216T, 225, 240, 303T, 308T&B, 309
Rubin Museum of Art 180T, 184T
Roger Schultz 113BL
Soho Grand Hotel 304T&B
Martin Solli 221B
Sony 99B
SuperStock 11B, 44/45, 48L, 77B, 114, 124, 198B, 199L, 216B, 256B, 264/265, 269R, 274B,

276B, 277BR, 284B, 285B, 289B
TIPS Images 8R, 16/17, 37BL, 64/65, 146BR, 266
Tony the Misfit on flickr 207BR, 277BL
TopFoto 22B, 34TR, 36TR, 40B, 195R
David Trawin 290B
Tribeca Film Festival 13T, 49R, 237B
Tribeca Grand Hotel 234T, 305R
ukanda on flickr 283T
United Nations 95TL
Waldorf-Astoria Hotel 299B
Charlie Walker 209B
Bill Wassman 37TL
Whitney Museum of American Art 131TL
Marcus Wilson-Smith/APA 42BR
Marcin Wichary 280BL
Jay Woodworth 270B, 271TL
Ed Yourdon 12L, 19, 20L, 22TL, 23, 24L&TR, 47, 62/63, 92TL, 151B, 188, 191B, 288T, 315

52/53: All **Ronald Grant Archive**
58/59: Thérèse De Belder/Wafels & Dinges 59BL; **iStockphoto** 58BR; **Gary Li/NYC Cravings** 58TL, 59T; **Abe Nowitz/APA** 58CR; **Rickshaw Dumplings** 59BR; **Ed Yourdon** 58BL, 58/59
60/61: Dan Callister/Rex Features 60/61; **Century 21** 61BR; **Kevin Foy/Rex Features** 61TR; **Mark Read/APA** 60TL, BL&BR, 61C&BL;
82/83: All **Ed Yourdon** except 82BL **Mockford & Bonetti/APA** and 83CR **Jaschinski/APA**
84/85: All **Jaschinski/APA** except 84/85 **LAIF/Camerapress** and 85BR **Ed Yourdon**
118/119: Jaschinski/APA 119C; **Nowitz/APA** 118TL, 118/119C, 119BL; **TopFoto** 118BR, 119BR; **Marcus Wilson-Smith/APA** 119TR
120/123: All **Museum of Modern Art** except 120TL&121BL **Jaschinski/APA**
136/137: Jewish Museum/John Parnell 137BR; **Museum of the City of New York** 136/137, 137CL; **Nowitz/APA** 136TL&BR; **Project for Public Spaces**

137TR; **Mike Yamashita/Woodfin Camp** 137BL
138/141: all **Metropolitan Museum of Art** except 138/139 **Jaschinski/APA** and 138BR, 139CR, 140B **Mockford & Bonetti/APA**
154/157: all **American Natural History Museum** except 155TR, CR&BR, 156T&BL **Jaschinski/APA** and 154TL **Mockford & Bonetti/APA**
158/161: all **Jaschinski/APA** except 158/159 **Alamy**; 158CR, 159CR, 160/161 **Juillard School** and 159CL&BL **Metropolitan Opera**
260/261: all **Jaschinski/APA** except 260L **Library of Congress**
262/263: Corbis 262CR; **iStockphoto** 263BR; **Library of Congress** 263TR; **Mockford & Bonetti/APA** 262L, 263BL; **Nowitz/APA** 262/263

Works of art have been reproduced with the permission of these copyright holders:
● Marilyn Monroe 20 Times, 1962 Andy Warhol Foundation © The Andy Warhol Foundation for the Visual Arts. Inc/ARS, NY and DACS, London 2007
● Les Demoiselles d'Avignon, 1907, Pablo Picasso © Succession Picasso/DACS 2007
● Sleeping Woman, 1929, Man Ray © Man Ray Trust/ADAGP, Paris and DACS, London 2007
● The Wall Street Crash c.1929, Fred Zinnerman © Private Collection/The Stapleton Collection/The Bridgeman Art Library
● Pershing Square Bridge, 1993, Bascove © Bascove Museum Purchase, Museum of the City of York
● Paulo Cornino, First Night Game, Yankee Stadium, 1945, gift of the artist

Map Production: Original cartography Berndtson & Berndtson, updated by James Macdonald and Mike Adams © 2010 Apa Publications GmbH & Co. Verlag KG, Singapore Branch

Book Production:
Linton Donaldson, Rebeka Ellam and Mary Pickles

GENERAL INDEX

9/11 19, 38, 242–4, 253
21 10, 78, 80
22nd Street 183
57th Street 96
79th Street Boat Basin 151
125th Street 165–6
173 East Broadway 216

A

Abingdon Square 195
accommodations 297–305
Actor's Studio 110
Adam Clayton Powell Jr Boulevard 166
admission fees 318
African Burial Ground 255
air travel 294, 295
Algonquin Indians 27
Allen, Woody 22, **53**, 280
Alphabet City 22, **211**
American Academy and Institute of Arts and Letters 170
American Civil War 30
American Revolution 28–9
American-Irish Historical Society 127
Americas Society 127
Anglo-Dutch Wars 28
Aqueduct Racetrack 283
Armstrong, Louis 11, 279–80
art galleries see museums and galleries
Arthur Avenue 289
the arts 21–2, **47–51**, 310–12
Asia Society 132
Astor, John Jacob 29
Astor Place 206
Astoria 281
Atlantic Avenue 271
Audubon Terrace 170

B

Bank Street 196
Bargemusic 270
Barnard College 169
Barnum's Circus 275
bars see restaurants, bars and cafés

Bartholdi, Auguste 263
baseball 288, 290
Battery Maritime Building 257
Battery Park City 36, **244–5**
Battery Park Esplanade 245
Bayside 279
beaches 256, 277–8, 281
Bedford Avenue 276
Bedford Street 196
Beekman Place 95
Belle Harbor 281
Belmont 287–9
Belvedere Castle 85
Berry Street 276
Bickmore, Dr Albert S. 155
"Big Apple" 25
Black Friday 61
Bleeker Street 193, **195**
Bloomberg, Michael 38–9, 144
Blue Note 47, **193**
books on New York 10, 324
Borough Hall, Brooklyn 271
the Bowery 207, 217, 219
Bowne Street 280
Brighton Beach 277–8
Broadway 23, 25, 34, 47, 51, 106, **108**, **147**, 150, 229–30
tickets **50**, 107, 118
The Bronx 267, **285–90**
Bronx Community College 289
Bronx Zoo 12, **286–7**
Brooklyn 22, 29, 267, **269–78**
see also **Coney Island; DUMBO; Red Hook; Williamsburg**
Brooklyn Academy of Music 23, 47, 50, **272**
Brooklyn Bridge 254, **255**
Brooklyn Heights 270–1
Brooklyn Historical Society 271
Brooklyn Navy Yard 270

Broome Street 232–3
Brownsville 277
brunch 57
budgeting 318
Burr, Aaron 29
buses 295–6
business hours 318–19
Butterfly Conservatory 147

C

cafés see **restaurants, bars and cafés**
Canal Street 233–4
Cannon's Walk 256
car rental 296
Carnegie, Andrew 31, 115, 251
Carnegie Hall 31, 47, 48, **115**
Carnegie Hill 130
carousels 12
Castelli, Leo 230
Castle Clinton 247
Cathedral of St John the Divine 169
Central Park 9, 12, 79, **82–5**
Central Park Zoo 84
Chatham Square 219
Chelsea 39, **180–4**, 302–3
Chelsea Historic District 181
Chelsea Piers 11, 184
children 12, 319
Chinatown 219–25
Chinatown Arcade 223
Chinese Community Center 221–2
Christopher Street 194
Chrysler Building 8, 35, **92–3**, 246
Chumley's 196
churches
Abyssinian Baptist 167
Ascension 191
Canaan Baptist 167
Cathedral of St John the Divine 169
Cathedral of the Transfiguration 276
First Chinese Baptist 222

Grace, Bronx 290
Grace, Greenwich Village 190
Incarnation 87
Judson Memorial 192
Mother AME Zion 167
Old St Patrick's Cathedral 217
Plymouth Church of the Pilgrims 270
Quaker Meeting House 280
Riverside 169
St Ann and the Holy Trinity 271
St Bartholomew's 97
St Mark's-in-the-Bowery 207
St Nicholas 208
St Patrick's Cathedral 12, **78–9**
St Paul's Chapel 242, **252–3**
St Peter's 96
St Philip's Episcopal 167
St Vartan's Armenian 90
St-Luke-in-the-Fields 196
Transfiguration 222
Trinity 25, **252–3**
Circle Line tours 11, 12, 111
Citicorp Building 36
CitiField 279, 288
Citigroup Center 95
City Hall 253–4
City Island 290
Civic Center, Brooklyn 271
climate 319
Clinton 110
Clinton, Hilary Rodham 38
Clocktower Building 235
CNN 145
Colonnade Row 205–6
Colony Club 132
Columbia University 169
Columbus Circle 85, **143**
Coney Island 11, 25, **277–8**
Confucius Plaza 219
consulates 319
Cooper Square 207

Cooper Union Foundation
  Building 206–7
Cotton Club 34, 165
credit cards 321
crime 319
Crown Heights 276–7
cruises 111, 184,
  256, 258
customs regulations 320

D

da Verrazano,
  Giovanni 27
Dakota Building 37, 82,
  145–6
dance 50–1, 310–11
Desmond Tutu
  Center 182
Diamond District 113
disabled travelers 320
Doyers Street 222–3
driving 296
Duane Street 235
Duke Mansion 125
DUMBO 22, **269–70**
Dutch West India
  Company 27
Dylan, Bob 22, 47,
  192, 193

E

East Brooklyn 276–7
East Harlem 168–9
East River 93, 94,
  95, 133, 254, 255,
  269, 281
East Village **203–11**,
  224–5, 304–5
Eastern Parkway 273
Eastern States Buddhist
  Temple 222
Edison, Thomas 25
electricity 320
Ellis Island 33, 35, 247,
  258, **260–1**
emergency numbers 320
Empire State Building 9,
  11, 35, **71–4**, 246
Enid A. Haupt
  Conservatory 286
entry regulations 320
ethnic mix 20–1

F

Fashion Institute of
  Technology 12

fast food 58–9
Federal Hall National
  Memorial 251–2
Federal Reserve
  Bank 252
ferries 257–8, 283
festivals and events 13,
  315–16
  Central Park events 82,
    206
  Chinese New Year 223
  Feast of St
    Anthony 218
  Feast of San Gennaro
    13, 218
  Halloween Parade
    189, 193
  Museum Mile
    Festival 137
  New Wave Festival 13
  Ninth Avenue Food
    Festival 13, 110
  St Patrick's Day 13
  Shakespeare
    Festival 206
  Thanksgiving Day
    Parade 13
  Tribeca Film Festival 13,
    49, 50
Fifth Avenue 31, 49,
  71–81, 125
Fillmore at Irving Plaza
  176–7
Flatiron Building 96,
  177–8, 246
Flatiron District 177–8
Flower District 180
Flushing, Queens 280
Foley Square 254
food and drink 55–9
food trucks 59
Ford Center 109
Ford Foundation 94
Fordham University 147
Forest Hills 283
Fort Green 272
Four Seasons 98, 100
Frank Lloyd Wright
  building 48, 129, 136
free attractions 12
Freedom Tower 38, 39,
  71, **242**, 246
Frick, Henry Clay
  127, 251
Fuller Building
  96, 177
Fulton Ferry
  Landing 269
Fulton Street 255

G

galleries see museums
  and galleries
Gansevoort Street 197
Garment District 104–5
gay and lesbian travelers
  194, 320
GE Building 76–7
General Post Office 106
General Theological
  Seminary 182
Giuliani, Rudolph 37–8
Governor's Island
  39, 257
Gracie Mansion 133
Gramercy Park **175–7**,
  302–3
Grand Army Plaza 79
Grand Army Plaza,
  Brooklyn 273, 274–5
Grand Central Terminal
  90–2
Grand Concourse 287
Grant's Tomb 169
Great Depression 34,
  35, 119
Great Fire (1835)
  29, 249
Great Hall, Ellis Island
  260, 261
Greene Street 231–2
Greenwich Street 236
Greenwich Village 9, 22,
  24, 29, 31, 36,
  189–201, 304–5
Greenwich Village
  Historic District 196
Ground Zero 38, **241**
Grove Court 196
Guggenheim Museum
  11, 48, 49, 60,
  128–9, 136
Gunther Building 232

H

Hall of Fame for Great
  Americans 289
Hall, Tammany 31,
  32, 34
Hamilton, Alexander 29,
  251, 252
Hamilton Heights
  165, 169
Hanover Square 249
Harkness House 125
Harlem 22, 34, 36,
  163–71

Harlem Globetrotters 11
Harlem River 133
Harrison Street 237
Harvard Club 112
Haughwout Building 231
Hayden Planetarium
  147, 155
health 320
Hearst Tower 39,
  115, 246
Hell Gate 133
Hell's Kitchen 110
Henry Luce Nature
  Observatory 85
Henry Street
  Settlement 216
Herald Square 103
Hillman, Dr James 24,
  25, 144
Hispanic Society of
  America 171
Historic Richmond
  Town 285
history 27–43
horse-drawn carriages
  84, 115
hotels 297–305
  Algonquin 10, 112
  Ansonia 151
  Blue Moon 215
  Carlyle 10
  Chelsea 10, 180
  Gansevoort 10, 199
  Gramercy Park 175
  Grand Hyatt 93
  Hotel des Artistes 145
  Hotel on Rivington 213
  Mercer 10, 229
  NY Palace 97–8
  Pennsylvania 105–6
  Plaza 79
  Soho Grand 228
  The Standard 198, 199
  Tribeca Grand 234–5
  Trump
    International 143
  Waldorf-Astoria 35, **97**
Hudson, Henry 22, 27
Hudson River 39, 94,
  151, 184, 189, 198,
  244–5
Hudson Street 195
Hughes, Langston 22,
  163, **167**

I

IAC Building 182
IBM Building 36, **99**

ice-skating 11, 82
Illustration Museum 132
immigrants 20–1,
    31, 33, 35–6, 110,
    163, **220**
    Castle Clinton 247
    Ellis Island 33, 35, 247,
        258, **260–1**
    Jewish **32**, 211–12,
        215–16, 248, 276–7
Independence Plaza 237
India House 249
intellectuals 19–20, 23
International Building
    77–8
internet 107, 160, 179,
    320–1
Irving Place 176
Italian Cultural
    Institute 127

J

Jamaica Bay Wildlife
    Refuge 280
Javits Center 110–11
jazz **34**, 47, 145, 147,
    158, 165, 193, 194–5,
    279–80, 312–13
Jefferson Market Library
    193–4
JFK Airport 35, 280
Juilliard School of Music
    147, 158, 159, 161
Jumel Terrace Historic
    District 170

K

Kaufman Astoria Studios
    280, 281
Kim Lau Memorial
    Arch 219
Kips Bay 90
Knitting Factory 47
Koch, Edward 36

L

LaGuardia, Fiorello
    34–5, 133
LaGuardia Airport 280
Lennon, John 37, 146
Liberty Island 263
Libeskind, Daniel
    38, 39
Lighthouse Hill 285
Lincoln, Abraham 30–1,
    207, 227

Lincoln Center 8, 39, 47,
    48, 50, 145, **147–9**,
    158–61
Little Asia 280
Little Britain 196
Little Germany 210
Little India 210
Little Italy **218–19**,
    224–5, 287
Little Odessa 278
Little Singer
    Building 230
Long Island City 267,
    280, **282–3**
lost property 321
Lower East Side 31, **32**,
    211–16, 224–5
Lower Manhattan
    241–59, 304–5

M

MacDougal Alley 191–2
MacDougal Street
    192, **193**
McSorley's Old Ale
    House 36, **209**
Madison Avenue 35, 90,
    130–1
Malcolm X
    Boulevard 166
maps 321
Martin Luther King
    Boulevard 165
Meatpacking District 11,
    39, **197–9**
media 23, 321–2
medical care 320
Mercantile Exchange
    Building 236
Mercury Lounge 212
MetLife Building 97
Metropolitan Club 125
Metropolitan Life
    Insurance Tower
    177, 246
Metropolitan Opera 12,
    47, 48, **148**, 158, **159**
the Mets 279, **288**
Middagh 270
Midtown East **87–101**,
    297–300
Midtown West **103–17**,
    297–300
Millionaire's Row 125
Minuit, Peter 27,
    248, 249
money 322
money-saving tips 13

Morgan, J.P. 31, 89, 125
Morgan Library &
    Museum 89
Morningside Heights
    165, 169
Morris-Jumel
    Mansion 170
Mott Street 31, 219, 221
movies 49–50,
    52–3, 314
MTV 109
Mulberry Street 31, 216,
    218–19, 219
Municipal Building 255
Murray Hill **87**, 90,
    302–3
Museum Mile 39, 49,
    128–9, **136–7**, 168
museums and galleries
    311–12
    African Art Museum
        136, 165, **168**
    Alice Austen House
        Museum 284
    American Finance
        Museum 251
    American Folk Art
        Museum **114**, 149
    American Museum of
        the Moving Image 50
    American Museum of
        Natural History 9, 25,
        146–7, **154–7**
    Arts and Design
        Museum 115, 143
    Asian-American Arts
        Center 223
    Bronx Museum of the
        Arts 287
    Brooklyn Children's
        Museum 12, 277
    Brooklyn Museum of Art
        273–4
    Chelsea Art
        Museum 183
    Children's Museum of
        the Arts 12, **231**
    Children's Museum of
        Manhattan 12, 150
    Chinese in the Americas
        Museum 221
    City of New York
        Museum 129, **169**
    The Cloisters 171
    Cooper-Hewitt National
        Design Museum
        129, 136
    Dahesh Museum of
        Art 99

    Dia Center for the Arts
        182, 232
    Dyckman Farmhouse
        Museum 171
    Edgar Allan Poe
        Cottage 287
    Ellis Island 258, 260
    Forbes Galleries 191
    Fraunces Tavern
        Museum 11, **250**
    Frick Collection 49, **127**
    Garibaldi-Meucci
        Museum 284
    Guggenheim Museum
        11, 48, 49, 60,
        128–9, 136
    Herman Melville
        Gallery 256
    Historic Richmond
        Town 285
    Illustration
        Museum 132
    International Center of
        Photography 112
    Intrepid Sea, Air &
        Space Museum 111
    Isamu Noguchi Garden
        Museum 282
    Jacques Marchais
        Museum of Tibetan Art
        284, **285**
    Jewish Heritage
        Museum 245
    Jewish Museum 49,
        129, 136
    Lefferts Historic
        House 275
    Leo Castelli Gallery 230
    Louis Armstrong House
        279–80
    Lower East Side
        Tenement Museum
        214–15
    Merchant's House
        Museum 205
    Metropolitan Museum of
        Art 9, 48–9, **128**, 136,
        138–41, 171
    Modern Art Museum
        (MoMA) 8, 39, 49, 50,
        114, **120–3**
    Morgan Library &
        Museum 89
    Mount Vernon Hotel
        Museum 132–3
    Moving Image Museum
        280, **281–2**
    El Museo del Barrio
        129, 136, **168**

National Academy
   Museum and School of
   Fine Arts **129**, 136
National Museum of
   the American Indian
   12, **249**
Neue Galerie 136
New Museum of
   Contemporary Art 217
New York City Fire
   Museum 233
New York City Police
   Museum 257
New York Hall of Science
   278–9
New York Transit
   Museum 91
New York
   Transit Museum,
   Brooklyn 271
Pace Wildenstein
   Gallery 183
Paley Center for
   Media 114
P.S.1 Contemporary Art
   Center 282
Queens Museum of
   Art 278
Roosevelt Birthplace
   178–9
Rubin Museum of
   Art 181
Skyscraper
   Museum 247
Socrates Sculpture Park
   282–3
Sony Wonder Technology
   Lab 12, **99**
Staten Island Children's
   Museum 284
Studio Museum in
   Harlem 166
Tony Shafrazi Gallery
   182–3
Trinity Church
   Museum 252
Ukrainian Museum 209
Van Cortlandt House
   Museum 289
Westbeth 196
Whitman Gallery 256
Whitney Museum of
   American Art **130**, 199
music 47–8, 311

N

National Arts Club 176
neighborhoods 267–8

Neponsit 281
Nevelson Plaza 251
New Amsterdam
   27–8, 248
**New School for Social
   Research** 191
New York Aquarium 277
New York City Ballet
   51, 161
New York City Opera 48
**New York Historical
   Society** 146
New York Philharmonic
   47, 48, 148, 158
New York Public Library
   49, **74–5**
New York Skyride 73
**New York State Supreme
   Court** 254
New York State Theater
   50, **148**
**New York Stock
   Exchange** 251–2
New York Times 110,
   118, **119**, 246
New York Unearthed 248
New York University 192
**New York University Med-
   ical Center** 90
New York Yacht Club
   112–13
newspapers 23, 321–2
nightlife 312–14
No. 18 Bowery 219
NoHo 203
NoLita 11, **216–17**,
   224–5
Nom Wah Tea House
   222, **223**
**non-emergency
   services** 322
**Northern
   Dispensary** 194
NoSLIta 217
NY Knicks 11, 105

O

Oak Bar 10, 79
**Old St Patrick's
   Cathedral** 217
Old Slip 257
Olmsted, Frederick Law
   22, 82, 85, 151, 171,
   268, 275
Orange Street 270–1
Orchard Beach 290
Orchard Street 212–14
Outer Boroughs 267–91

P

Park Avenue 35, **131–2**
Park Slope 273
parks and gardens
   22, 47
   Astroland Amusement
      Park 277
   Battery Park 244, **247**
   Bowling Green Park 249
   Brooklyn Botanic Garden
      12, 274
   Brooklyn Bridge
      Park 270
   Bryant Park 75, **112**
   Carl Schurz Park 133
   Central Park 9, 12, 79,
      82–5
   Channel Gardens 76
   Christopher Park 194
   City Hall Park 254
   Columbus Park
      219, 221
   Damrosch Park 149
   Duane Park 235
   Flushing Meadows
      Corona Park 35, 36,
      278–9
   Fort Tryon Park 171
   Greenbelt 284–5
   High Line 39, 182,
      198, 199
   High Rock Park 285
   Hudson River Park 237
   Isamu Noguchi Garden
      Museum 282
   Madison Square
      Park 177
   Manhattan Park 133
   Mount Vernon Hotel
      Garden 132–3
   New York Botanical
      Garden 286
   Paley Park 98–9
   Prospect Park
      269, 275
   Queens Botanical
      Garden 279
   Riverbank State
      Park 170
   Riverside Park 151
   Robert F. Wagner Jr
      Park 245
   Snug Harbor Cultural
      Center 283
   Socrates Sculpture Park
      282–3
   Staten Island Botanical
      Garden 283–4
   Strawberry Fields 146
   Tompkins Square Park
      210–11
   Van Cortlandt Park 289
   Washington Market
      Park 237
   Wave Hill 289
   Winter Garden 244
Patchin Place 194
Payne Whitney House
   125–7
Pell Street 222
Penn Station 91, 105
people 19–25, 144
Peter Minuit Plaza 248
Pier 17 256
Players Club 176
Poe, Edgar Allan 287
police 319
Police Building 217
**Port Authority Bus
   Terminal** 109
postal services 323
Prince Street 228–9
Prohibition 33, 34, 118
Prospect Heights 273–5
public holidays 322
public transportation
   295–6
Pulitzer, Joseph 263

Q

Queens 35, 267, **278–83**
**Queens Historical
   Society** 280

R

Radiator Building 112
Radio City Music Hall 49,
   113–14
Red Hook 22, 269, 270,
   275–6
religion 23, 323
Restaurant Row 110
**restaurants, bars and
   cafés** 55–7
   *see also bars and cafés
   list*; *restaurants list*
   East Village to
      Chinatown 224–5
   Fifth Avenue 80–1
   Gramercy Park to
      Chelsea 185–9
   Greenwich Village
      200–1
   Harlem 171
   Lower Manhattan 259

Midtown East 100–1
Midtown West 116–17
Outer Boroughs 291
Soho and Tribeca 238–9
Upper East Side 134–5
Upper West Side 152–3
Riis, Jacob 32, 33
Riverdale 289
Riverside Drive 151,
169–70
road travel 294
The Rockaways 281
Rockefeller, John D. 31,
76, 251
Rockefeller Center 11,
35, **75–7**, 113
Rockefeller Plaza 76
Rockettes 113
Roosevelt, Franklin D.
34, 35, 94
Roosevelt, Theodore
178–9
Roosevelt Island
132, **133**
**Rose Center for Earth
and Space** 147, 155
Rosebank 284

S

safety 319
St Ann's Warehouse 269
St George 283
St Luke's Place 197
**St Mark's Historic
District** 207
St Mark's Place 208–9
**St Nicholas Historic
District** 167
St Patrick's Cathedral
12, **78–9**
Saks Fifth Avenue 77
sales 61
Salmagundi Club 191
**San Remo
Apartments** 145
Schermerhorn Way
255–6
Schomburg Center
166–7
**Science, Industry and
Business Library** 74
Scorsese, Martin 22, 30,
53, 219, 280
sea travel 294
Seagram Building 98, 246
**Seventh Regiment
Armory** 132
Sheridan Square 194

shopping 60–1, 306–9
Barney's 60, 130,
131, 150
Bergdorf Goodman 79
Bloomingdale's 60,
131, 229
Brooks Brothers 90
Calvin Klein 29
Cartier 79
Chanel 96
Dean & Deluca
61, **230**
Dior 79
E. Rossi and Co 219
Ecko Unlimited 109
Gucci 79
Hammacher &
Schlemmer 96
Henri Bendel 79
Hermèès 96
for kids 151, 307
Kiehl's 61, 149
Ladies' Mile 178, 203
Lord & Taylor 74
Macy's 60, 103, **104**
Manhattan Art and
Antiques Center 95
Manhattan Mall 103
Myers of Keswick 195
Prada 79, 228
Pucci 79
Ralph Lauren 228
Saks Fifth Avenue 77
Scholastic Books 230
Sotheby's 133
Strand Book Store
24–5, **190**
Tiffany & Co 79
Zabar's 150
**Shrine of St Elizabeth
Ann Seton** 248
Shubert Alley 106
Signal Hill 284–5
**Silver Screen
Studios** 184
Silvercup Studios
280, 281
Sixth Avenue 111–13
skyscrapers 246, 247
slavery 30
smoking 183, 323
Sniffen Court 89–90
**Snug Harbor Cultural
Center** 283
**Society of
Illustrators** 132
SoFi 178
Soho 22, 24, **227–34**,
238–9, 304–5

**Soho Cast Iron Historic
District** 227
**Soldiers' and Sailors'
Memorial Arch** 274–5
Sony Building 36, **99**
South Bronx 289, **290**
South Street Seaport 12,
29, 36, **255–6**
Staple Street 235–6
Staten Island 267,
283–5
**Staten Island Ferry
Terminal** 257–8
**Staten Island Institute of
Arts & Sciences** 283
Statue of Liberty 9, 11,
35, 237, 245, **258**,
262–3
Stone Street 247
Stonewall Inn 194
street food 58–9
Striver's Row 167
Stuyvesant, Peter
28, 207
**Stuyvesant-Fish
House** 207
subway 295–6
Surrogate's Court 254
Sutton Place 95
Sylvan Terrace 170
synagogues
Central 96
Eldridge Street 216
Temple Emanu-El 125

T

taxis 24, **296**
telephones 323
television 321, 322
Theater District 106
theaters 48, **51**, **108**,
310–11
American Ballet 148
Apollo 165
Asian-American
Dance 223
Astor Place 206
Avery Fisher Hall 148
BAM Harvey
Lichtenstein 272
Beacon 150
Belasco 51
Broadway **108**
Cherry Lane 51, **197**
Dance Theater of
Harlem 51
Dance Theater
Workshop 181

Embassy 107, 118
Ford Center 109
The Gatehouse 164–5
Joseph Papp 206
Joyce 51, **181**
The Kitchen 182
La MaMa 205
Lincoln Center 39, 47,
48, 50, 145, **147–9**,
158–61
Lucille Lortel 51,
194, 195
Lyceum **107**, 108
Metropolitan Opera 47,
48, **148**, 158, **159**
Minetta Lane 193
National Black 166
New Victory 108
NY State 50, **148**
Ohio 232
Orpheum 208
Palace 51, 108
Performing Garage 232
P.S. 122 208
Public Theater 12, 51,
82, 108
Radio City Music Hall 49
Shubert 51
Symphony Space 150
Theater for the New
City 208
Union Square 180
Vivian Beaumont 148
Winter Garden 108
York 96
Theatre Row 110
tickets
Broadway 13, **50**,
107, 118
sports events 105
transportation 13
Time Warner Center 39,
143–5
time zone 323
Times Square 9, **106–10**,
118–19
tipping 323
**Titanic Memorial
Lighthouse** 255
**Todt Hill, Staten
Island** 284
Top of the Rock 77
tourist information 107,
323–4
tours 13, **317**
Broadway 147
Chelsea cruise 184
Federal Reserve
Bank 252

Lower Manhattan 245
TOAST 234
TV & Movie 177
transportation 294–6
see also **cruises**; **ferries**
Tribeca 49, 50, **234–9**,
304–5
Tribeca Film Center 236
Tribute WTC Visitor
Center 39, **243–4**
Trump, Donald 37,
79, 144
Trump Tower 79, 143
Tudor City 93–4
Turtle Bay 95
Twain, Mark 128, 191
Tweed, William M.
"Boss" 31, 254
Tweed Courthouse 254

U

Ukrainian Institute 127
Union Square
179–80, 190
United Nations 11, 35, **94**
United States
Courthouse 254
University Place 190–1

University Settlement
House 213
Upper East Side 125–41,
301–2
Upper West Side
143–61, 301–2
US Custom House 12,
248–9
USTA Billie Jean
King National Tennis
Center 279

V

Vanderbilt, Cornelius 29
Vaux, Calvert 82, 138,
217, 268, 275
Verrazano-Narrows
Bridge 284
Vietnam Veterans
Memorial 257
Village Vanguard 47,
194–5
Villard Houses 97–8

W

Walker, Jimmy 34, 197
walks 13, 198

Wall Street 25, 29, 37,
250–2
Washington, George 11,
29, 252, 253
Washington Arch 189
Washington
Heights 171
Washington Mews 191
Washington Square
189–93
Water Taxi Beach 256
Wave Hill 289
Waverly Place 194
websites 320
weights and
measures 324
West 14th Street 197
West Broadway 228
West End Avenue 151
West Harlem 169–71
West Village 193–7
Western Union
Building 236
White Horse Tavern
10, 195
Williamsburg, Brooklyn
267, 269, 270, **276**
Williamsburg Savings
Bank 276

Williamsburg Art &
Historical Center 276
Williamsburg Bridge 276
Willow Street 270–1
Woodbury Common
13, 307
Woodlawn Cemetery
289–90
Woolworth Building
246, **253**
Wooster Street 232
World Fairs 36, 278
World Financial
Center 244
World Trade Center 36,
37, **38**, **241–4**, 246
World War II 35
WPS1 Art Radio 235

Y

Yankee Stadium 288, **290**
Yeshiva University 171
Yorkville 132

Z

Zito, Dr Anthony 144
zoos 84, 286–7

RESTAURANTS

Bars and cafés

71 Irving Place Coffee
and Tea Bar 187
Acme Bar and Grill 225
Almondine 291
Athens Café 291
The Bar 259
Bar Artisanal 239
Boathouse in Central
Park 135
Bogarts 101
Brick Oven Pizza
33, 187
Buddha Bar 201
Bull & Bear 101
Café 2 at MoMA 117
Café Borgia II 239
Caffè Reggio 201
Campbell Apartment
at Grand Central
Terminal 101
ChicaLicious 225
Chocolate Bar 201

Chop't Creative Salad
101, 187
City Bakery 187
Le Colonial 101
Cosi Sandwich Bar 81
Cupping Room Café 239
De Robertis 225
Los Dos Molinos 187
Elaine's 135
Emack & Bolio 239
ESPN Zone 117
Fanelli's 239
Fred's at Barneys 135
Grand Central
Terminal 101
Heartland Brewery 117
Jacques Torres
Chocolate 291
Juniors 291
King Cole Bar 81
Lady Mendl's 187
Lucky Cheng's 225
Max Fish 225
Momofuku Milk Bar 225

Monkey Bar 101
Morrell Wine Bar
& Café 81
Oak Bar ar The Plaza 10,
79, **81**
Old Town Bar and
Restaurant 187
Le Pain Quotidien
135, 239
Paris Café 259
Peanut Butter & Co. 201
Pete's Tavern 176, **187**
Puffy's Tavern 239
Rainbow Grill 81
St Ambroeus 135
St Maggie's Café 259
Sardi's 107, **117**
Serendipity 135
Slaughtered Lamb Pub 201
The Soup Man 81
SouthWest NY 259
Stone Street Tavern 259
Ulysses 259
Veniero's Café 225

Restaurants

21 10, **80**
66 Asia de Cuba 100
A Voce 185
L'Absinthe 134
Adour Alain Ducasse at
the St Regis 80
Algonquin Hotel, Blue Bar
& Lobby 116
Amy Ruth's 171
Angelica Kitchen 224
Angon 224
Angus McIndoe 116
AOC 200
Aquavit 80
Artie's Deli 152
Au Mandarin 259
Avra Estiatorio 100
Babbo 200
Balthazar 238
Bar Boulud 152
Bar Jamón 185
Barbetta 116

Barbuto 200
Barney Greengrass 152
Battery Gardens 259
Becco 116
Bennie's 259
Le Bernardin 116
Beyoglu 134
Bice 80
Blaue Gans 238
Blossom 185
BLT Steak 100
Blue Hill 200
Blue Ribbon 238, 291
Blue Smoke 185
Blue Water Grill 185
Boat Basin Café 152
Bohemian Hall and Beer
  Garden 291
Bon Chon Chicken 259
La Bonne Soupe 80
Boquería 185
Bouchon Bakery 152
Bouley 238
Bread 238
Bridge Café 259
Bryant Park Grill 116
Bubby's 238
Buddakan 185
Burger Heaven 80
Café Asean 200
Café Centro 100
Café Frida 152
Café Luxembourg 152
Café Sabarsky 134
Café Un Deux Trois 116
Caffé Linda 100
Caliente Cab
  Company 200
Calle Ocho 152
CamaJe 200
Candle 79 134
Capsouto Freres 238
Caracas Arepa Bar 224
Carl's Steaks 259
Carnegie Deli 116
Centrico 238
Chat 'n Chew 185
Chin Chin 100
China Grill 116
Chinatown Brasserie 224
Chow Bar 200
Le Cirque 100
Co. 185
Convivio 100
Cookshop 185
I Coppi 224
Craft 185
Craftbar 185
Da Nico 224

Da Silvano 200
Daisy May's BBQ USA 116
Daniel 134
Dawat 100
DB Bistro Moderne 80
DBGB Kitchen and
  Bar 224
Del Posto 185
Delmonico's 259
Demarchelier 134
Ecco 238
E.J.'s Luncheonette 134
Eleven Madison Park 186
Eli's Vinegar Factory 134
Excellent Dumpling
  House 224
Fatty Crab West
  Village 200
Felidia 100
Fig & Olive 134
Four Seasons 100
Fraunces Tavern 259
Freeman's 224
Gallagher's
  Steakhouse 116
Il Gattopardo 117
Gavroche 200
Gennaro 152
Gigino at Wagner Park 259
Gino's 134
Girasole 135
Good Burger 100–1
The Good Fork 291
Gramercy Tavern 186
La Grenouille 80
Grimaldi's 291
The Grocery 291
Hale & Hearty Soups 80
Les Halles 186
Harbour Lights 259
The Harrison 238
Harry Cipriani 80
Harry's Café 259
Heidelberg 135
Hourglass Tavern 117
H.S.F. 224
Indochine 224
Isabella's 152
Ise 259
Itzocan 224
Jackson Hole 135
Jean-Georges 152–3
Jewel Bako 225
J.G. Melon 135
Joe Allen 117
John's Pizzeria 117
JoJo 135
Kai 135
Katsuhama 80–1

Katz's Delicatessen 225
Keen's Steakhouse 81
King's Carriage
  House 135
Land 153
Landmarc 239
Lili's Noodle Shop
  & Grill 259
Little Owl 201
Locanda Verde 239
Lombardi's Pizza 225
Londel's Supper Club 171
Lucky Strike 239
Luzia's 153
McCormick
  & Schmick's 117
Macelleria 201
La Mangeoire 101
Mangia 81
Megu 239
Melba's 171
Mercadito 201
Mermaid Inn 225
Mesa Grill 186
Mexicana Mama 201
Michael's 81
Minetta Tavern 201
Miss Maude's
  Spoonbread Too 171
The Modern 117
Momofuku Noodle Bar 225
Morimoto 186
Il Mulino 201
Naka Naka 186
Nica 135
Niko's Mediterranean
  Grill 153
Nobu 239
Noodle Pudding 291
Ocean Grill 153
Odeon 239
Old Homestead 186
The Palm 101
Paradou 201
Pascalou 135
Pastis 201
Pearl Oyster Bar 201
Peasant 225
Peking Duck House 225
Le Perigord 101
Pershing Square 101
Peter Luger
  Steakhouse 291
Pho Bang 225
P.J. Clarke's 10, **101**
Pongal 186
Porter House New
  York 153
Prime Burger 81

Prune 225
Puglia 225
Pure Food and Wine 176,
  186–7
Quality Meats 81
Quest 153
El Quijote 184, **186**
Rack and Soul 153
Rao's 171
Raoul's 239
Red Cat 187
The Redhead 225
Republic 187
Rickshaw Dumpling
  Bar 187
Risotteria 201
River Café 291
Rock Center Café 81
Rosa Mexicano 101
Rub 187
Russian Tea Room 117
Ruth's Chris
  Steakhouse 117
Saigon Grill 153
San Martin 101
Sarabeth's 81
Savoy 239
Schiller's Liquor Bar 225
Sfoglia 135
Shaffer City Oyster Bar
  and Grill 187
Shake Shack 153, 187
Smith & Wollensky 101
Spice Market 199, **201**
The Spotted Pig 201
Sripiphai 291
Steamer's Landing 259
Stone Park Café 291
Sushi of Gari 135
Sylvia's 171
Tabla 187
Tao 101
Ted's Montana Grill 117
Telepan 153
Terrace in the Sky 171
Tocqueville 187
Tony's Di Napoli 117
Trattoria Dell'Arte 117
Tribeca Grill 236, **239**
Union Square Café 187
Il Vagabondo 135
The View 117
Vivolo 135
Water Club 101
Water's Edge 291
The Waverly Inn 201
WD-50 225
Witchcraft 81
Zarela 101